Immaculate Sounds

IMMACULATE SOUNDS: THE MUSICAL LIVES OF NUNS IN NEW SPAIN

Currents in Latin American and Iberian Music

Alejandro L. Madrid, Series Editor
Walter Aaron Clark, Founding Series Editor

Immaculate Sounds

The Musical Lives of Nuns in New Spain

CESAR D. FAVILA

OXFORD
UNIVERSITY PRESS

Oxford University Press is a department of the University of Oxford. It furthers
the University's objective of excellence in research, scholarship, and education
by publishing worldwide. Oxford is a registered trade mark of Oxford University
Press in the UK and certain other countries.

Published in the United States of America by Oxford University Press
198 Madison Avenue, New York, NY 10016, United States of America.

Library of Congress Cataloging-in-Publication Data
Names: Favila, Cesar, author.
Title: Immaculate sounds : the musical lives of nuns in New Spain / Cesar D. Favila.
Description: New York, NY : Oxford University Press 2023. |
Series: Currents in Latin American and Iberian music |
Includes bibliographical references and index.
Identifiers: LCCN 2023024934 (print) | LCCN 2023024935 (ebook) |
ISBN 9780197621899 (hardback) | ISBN 9780197621912 (epub)
Subjects: LCSH: Music in convents—Mexico—History—17th century. |
Music in convents—Mexico—History—18th century. | Music in convents—New
Spain. | Church music—Mexico. | Church music—Catholic Church—17th
century. | Church music—Catholic Church—18th century. | Nuns as
musicians—Mexico—History. | Conceptionists—Mexico—History.
Classification: LCC ML3015.2.F38 2023 (print) | LCC ML3015.2 (ebook) |
DDC 782.32/2200972—dc23/eng/20230606
LC record available at https://lccn.loc.gov/2023024934
LC ebook record available at https://lccn.loc.gov/2023024935

DOI: 10.1093/oso/9780197621899.001.0001

Printed by Integrated Books International, United States of America

For María Elvira, Clemente, and KC, because of their unconditional love and support
And for Asunción Lavrin, an inspiration

Contents

Figures

Examples

Tables

Appendices

Note on Sources

All translations and transcriptions are the author's unless specified otherwise. Standardized Spanish orthography has been used for clarity and ease of reading. Bible quotations are taken from the Knox Bible with occasional modifications by the author. Vulgate numeration was used for the Psalms, consistent with their listing in the early modern New Spanish sources. When I refer to the Encarnación choirbooks, I am referring to the manuscript sources at the Newberry Library called *Mexican choir books*. I do this to foreground their conventual provenance, which is obscured by the generic title of the books in the Newberry's catalog.

Preface, or an *Autohistoria-Teoría**

Ave María Purísima

Late November at Clare's place in the desert, as the sun dips below the San Jacinto peaks, Casey, Clare and I are knee-deep in poetry. Just before dinner, Cesar from the neighborhood arrives. He's writing a book, a history of "the musical lives of nuns in New Spain," and has invited them to join us. Echoes of convent music come wafting in with them, and as we all settle in, we form a new pod, of sorts.

Dinner is *al fresco*, masks at the ready, life lived in the moment, "in this time of COVID"—it's not like it was in Truchas or San Miguel—poets sitting around tables, breathing in, breathing out, suffused in each other's molecules, breathing the mountain or city air, attuned to each other's physical cues, breathing in and out.

Chicken with mushrooms, tiny potatoes, baked eggplant with cheese, the four of us eat every bite. The nuns don't eat a thing. Nothing virtual about chocolate lava cake, vanilla ice cream only melts in real time. I slip into a sugar-based reverie where all I see is that funny screen between the priest and me, the screen in the confessional.

Ave María Purísima, Father says to me in Spanish. *Sin pecado concebida*, I reply. I push back the curtain at the entrance to the confessional. I look out at the church through a huge, life-sized version of that same screen.

It separates the nuns of the Royal Convent of the Most Holy Pure Conception in San Miguel from me. The entire order is there, white habits, blue capes, eyes averted. *Ave María Purísima*, they greet me in unison, our bodies in close proximity. I can feel their pure exhalation through the semi-sheer scrim against my bristled cheek.

Poem by C. W. Emerson

Cloistered convents seem to inspire artists of various sorts. They always have. My friends, poets C. W. (Chris) Emerson and Clare Chu, were in the middle of a poetry marathon one night in November 2020 when Clare hosted a dinner. They had to write one poem every day for a week. It was the first time I had met Chris. Clare lives two doors down and across the street from me. I had only known her for some four months after crossing paths almost daily on dog walks in the pre-vaccine COVID days. During the dinner she hosted, Clare insisted that I tell Chris about my experience visiting the Conceptionist nuns' Mother House in Toledo, Spain, and about the book I was writing, this one. Chris immediately latched on to my story and began jotting down notes on a piece of paper Clare brought to him, developing a poem about the situation at hand for his marathon assignment. What resulted is a mystical weaving together of past and present—now long passed—through the story I told over dinner and his and Clare's recollection of their participation in the San Miguel Poetry Week while lodging at the "Posada de las Monjas" (Lodge of the Nuns), half a block down the street from San Miguel de Allende's eighteenth-century Conceptionist convent church, La Purísima Concepción. They had visited the church multiple times, and throughout the dinner they commented on its beauty and unusual architectural features, the topic of Chapter 2. It is rare to encounter people who have visited these types of old, otherworldly spaces, let alone to be neighbors with one. Thus, I could not think of a better epigraph to open this book than Chris's poem, the product of various fortuitous events. Then again, as Clare often reminds me, "there are no coincidences!"

The convent in Toledo that I visited and told Chris and Clare about was the birthplace of the Order of the Immaculate Conception (the Conceptionists), established in the late fifteenth century. I arrived to it on a sweltering Sunday afternoon in June 2011, seeking to gain access into the nuns' library, which I presumed held primary sources about the order's history. For being cloistered nuns, the Mother House inhabitants were well connected to the outside world. They had internet access, a website, and personal email accounts to confirm my stay in their convent guest quarters.

At the time designated to me by the nuns, I went to the convent's "locutorio" (parlor), where the nuns communicated with guests through an iron grate that kept them physically barricaded from any visitors to the cloister without obstructing the ability to talk to and see one another. I waited some ten minutes in a chair next to the grate, just below a portrait of the order's founder, St. Beatriz de Silva (see Figure P.1). Soon, two women came into the cloistered

Figure P.1 Locutorio with portrait of St. Beatriz de Silva, Inmaculada
Concepción Convent, Toledo, Spain, ca. June 2011

space behind the grate; they were covered from head to toe in white, wearing
black veils on their heads and blue cloaks on their shoulders—walking,
talking likenesses of St. Beatriz. Nearly in sync, the nuns both said out loud,
"Ave María purísima" (Hail purest Mary). Without skipping a beat, I replied,
"sin pecado concebida" (conceived without sin). Sister María Nuria then said,
"You know our salutation!" I said that I was not aware that these words were
used as their salutation, but that I was more than familiar with the phrase
from having grown up in a churchgoing Catholic family.

The "Ave María purísima" dialog initiates the confession ritual for Spanish-
speaking Catholics. When receiving the sacrament of Penance (confession)
one arrives before a priest in a space within a church called a confessional.
The priest says upon one's arrival "Ave María purísima," to which the confessant responds "sin pecado concebida" and proceeds to confess any sins
committed such that God would be convinced by the intercession of the
Virgin Mary, hailed at the opening of the ritual, to forgive the confessant's
sins vocalized to the mediating priest. The opening of the confession ritual
is different in English, in which the confessant begins by arriving to the

confessional and saying, "Bless me father, I have sinned," without the added mediation of the Virgin Mary within Spanish confession. I performed my first confession at the age of seven with the Spanish phrase.

"Ave María purísima, sin pecado concebida" is a short salutatory prayer to the Virgin Mary that acknowledges Mary's Immaculate Conception. Most Spanish-speaking Catholics say this prayer passively without knowing what it implies. Reciting it as a product of my sacramental learning,[1] I gave very little thought to the theology behind "Ave María purísima" prior to engaging in the research for this book. But it is an apropos phrase for confession, a ritual through which practicing Catholics believe their sins are forgiven. The doctrine of the Immaculate Conception instructs that Mary's soul was created by God without original sin—conceived immaculately—from the moment of the Creation, when it was believed that time began. As we will see in the pages that follow, the idea of Mary's immaculacy from sin was bolstered in the early modern period, more so than it is today, especially within the Hispanic Church. The doctrine of the Immaculate Conception of the Virgin Mary was thought to be essential in the Catholic narrative of humanity's salvation.

After making light conversation about my Catholic upbringing and my work as a church organist with Sister María Nuria and the Reverend Mother Julia, who you will recall were locked behind the grates of the Mother House locutorio, I explained to them my interest in exploring the music of nuns who branched out from their order throughout New Spain (as colonial Mexico was called before its independence in 1821). The sisters were delighted with my curiosity about the histories and legacies of cloistered convents outside of Spain. I was then granted access to the convent archive and hosted in their guest quarters located outside the cloister for a week.

The nuns fed me two hearty meals a day in the locutorio during my stay through a small opening on the side wall, where a *torno* (round cabinet) would circle within the wall to deliver food from inside the cloister into the locutorio. I simply had to pull on a rope next to the torno to ring a bell that the nuns could hear inside, and within minutes a voice from behind the wall would say "buenos días/buenas tardes" (good morning/afternoon). It was an acousmatic voice, one whose source always remained unknown, but whose faint echoes I could hear from behind the torno within the wall that separated the interior world of the cloister from me. The torno would then spin around carrying a plate of delicious Spanish fare. My favorite was the paella made with the tiniest and tastiest clams I had ever eaten.

Lunch always came with chilled red wine, which at first seemed peculiar to me, because growing up in Northern California, not too far from the Napa Valley, I was taught that red wine should be consumed at room temperature. But it was summertime and quite hot in Toledo, and so the chilled red was perfect.

The week I was generously hosted by the nuns of the Conceptionist Mother House also coincided with the festivities of Corpus Christi, which filled the streets with tourists for the lavish ceremonies in the city's famous Gothic cathedral. The festivities involved a procession of the cathedral's consecrated communion host (the Blessed Sacrament) through the streets, accompanied by the archbishop, hundreds of priests and clerics, city officials, university faculty, and laywomen dressed in black, crowned with large Spanish *peinetas* (combs) on the back of their heads and draped with long, black-laced *mantillas* (veils). On the Sunday after the town's main procession, the nuns also held their own procession inside their cloister, and they invited me to participate, as they needed assistance holding the canopy that is carried over the Blessed Sacrament during the procession. I was happy to help them out.

The nuns' hospitality was compensated with a promise that I would send them copies of all my published work and the pictures I took, both of their own cloister and sources and of others following my visit. They vouched for me to nuns at other convents, facilitating my entrance into more cloisters as I continued my research in Mexico in a quest for convent music sources.

Through my research travels, I also became an intermediary between nuns in Spain and Mexico, connecting religious communities that will likely never meet in person, through the exchange of digital images of convent lives an ocean apart. All the while, I learned about the musico-religious traditions that tied my own labor as a church organist and my experience in the Mother House during Corpus Christi with convent musicians of the past. As complex and problematic as the Catholic Church has been and continues to be, especially with regard to some of its social and moral teachings, it continues to offer people with varying commitments to its doctrines paths for making a living, making art, and making music, just as it did for the New Spanish cloistered nuns whose lives I reimagine in the subsequent chapters. Along the way, I hope to elucidate some of the Church's early modern complexities—especially surrounding gender, race, sexuality, and mysticism, and their relationship to music and nuns' voices—that might astound contemporary audiences, whether or not they are religious.

Introduction

Veil and Voice

Some two hundred folios of handwritten seven- and eight-syllable rhymed verses make up a conversation between one Sister Clori and a laywoman named Casandra. Through a poeticized dialog, Clori reveals what it is like to be a cloistered nun in New Spain. The lack of reference to a specific convent throughout the whole of the dialog conveys a universalizing anonymity. Clori also mentions other general requirements of living in a nunnery, such as attending Mass and praying the Divine Office. The importance of the Office is highlighted by Clori's allusion to Christ himself coming down from heaven to hear the voices of his spiritual brides resounding with angels in the convent choir:

Y así siempre la primera	And as such always be the first,
sin un grave impedimento	without grave impediment,
te mire el coro, que en el	to let the choir look at you, for in it
te espera tu amante tierno.	your tender lover awaits.
Allí con los serafines	There with the seraphim
se alternan tus acentos;	your cadences alternate;
imítalos, pues dichosa	imitate them, and so blessed,
haces un oficio mismo.	you create one and the same office.[1]

Clori's advice to Casandra is timeless, a reflection of cloistered life in any number of New Spain's convents some one hundred years before the dialog was written (ca. 1728), or even after.

Although the rigors of cloistered life were not for every woman, its prestigious allure was promoted through the New Spanish penchant for sacramental learning. The formal interactions in which sacramental learning took place included participation in, for example, the Church's liturgies, devotions, and seven sacraments, while informal lessons could be imparted from simple

Immaculate Sounds. Cesar D. Favila, Oxford University Press. © Oxford University Press 2023.
DOI: 10.1093/oso/9780197621899.003.0001

conversations between the clergy and its flock or correspondences between nuns and future convent aspirants, like the one between Clori and Casandra.[2]

Sacramental learning would teach Catholics to follow paths leading to their salvation, arrival in God's presence in heaven at the end of life on earth. Conversely, hell was seen as heaven's opposite, the place in which God was absent. A third metaphysical location for the destiny of the souls of the departed, known as purgatory, was an intermediary place. Except for the holiest people and saints who went directly to heaven, most souls were said to be purified in purgatory before going to heaven. Although arrival in purgatory meant that salvation was inevitable, the early modern Catholic Church instilled great fear about purgatory's scorching flames and of the monstrosities and miseries of hell should one not merit salvation.[3] Jesus Christ, whose death and resurrection made it possible for all human souls to go to heaven would be convinced through the prayers and intercessions of cloistered nuns like Clori to reduce the amount of time that souls spent in purgatory.[4] There were of course other types of intercessors and mediators, as we will see shortly, yet nuns' prayers were regarded as being especially effective in soul saving.[5] These types of teachings about heaven, hell, and nuns were culturally engrained in Catholic societies through the formal and informal lay-religious interactions of sacramental learning.

Confessors often sent women like Casandra to converse with nuns to discern if they possessed a potential calling to the soul-saving duties of the cloistered convent. Such generational and recruitment practices were common among New Spanish kin. It would come as no surprise if Sister Clori had been a relative of Casandra or a family friend.[6] And should Casandra, or any woman considering profession, have been a musician, it would be all the better for the nuns to try to integrate her into the community. Music was used as an instrument for convent recruitment. As we saw before with the image of the aspiring novice as part of an angelic chorus, music, or allusions to it, features prominently in Clori's discussion of convent life, not least in her mention of the importance of attending choir. The reference to "cadences" in the second stanza—"with the seraphim your cadences alternate"—imagines a harmonic relationship among the earthly (singing) nuns and heavenly choirs, suggesting various hierarchies of intercession between God and humans, all while attending to Christ's omnipresence. This specific moment in the dialogue underscores the importance of sound, harmony, and music in the liturgical life of the convent necessary for the salvation of humanity.

The performative, visual, and literary aspects of nuns' prayers in the choir are the concerns of this book, insofar as these modes coalesced with music, voice, and sound for the sake of salvation. By singing, listening, keeping silent, and meditating carefully throughout their cloistered lives, nuns could intercede in the service of humanity's peaceful afterlife.[7] The vague, but valuable, cadences that Clori remarked on were expressed in various vocalized forms, including recitation, chant, and polyphony.[8] We learn from Clori of the proper expression of such salvific mediation as an interior (corporeal and mental) and exterior vocal sound:

Reza claro, y no confundas	Pray clearly, and do not mix up
con apresura los ecos,	in haste the echoes,
las clausulas del oficio,	the phrases of the office,
que es cada voz un misterio.	for every voice is a mystery.
Y no salgan las palabras	And words should not come out
solo a hacer ruido en lo externo,	only to make noise on the outside,
cántelas el corazón,	[let] the heart sing them,
y sea el labio el instrumento.	and [let] the lips be the instrument.
Porque si rezas distraída	Because if distracted you pray
se estará mudo lo interno,	the interior will be mute
y Dios que en el alma asiste,	and God who dwells inside your soul
quiere oír allí tus afectos.	wants to hear your affects in there.[9]

These sacred sounds meditated upon and vocalized by nuns were *immaculate sounds*. This phrase derives from the doctrine of the Immaculate Conception of the Virgin Mary. In Catholic societies dominated by the Spanish, devotion to the Immaculate Conception was paramount in the economy of salvation through intercession. Developed by clerics and theologians from the Middle Ages forward, the doctrine of the Immaculate Conception elevated Mary as a type of superhuman by excluding her from the grasp of original sin. She was manufactured worthy of being the mother of the redeemer Jesus Christ, thus becoming a co-redeemer herself. I argue that women who became nuns were elevated to the status of co-redeemer too, and that their voices, veiled behind cloistered walls, were essential for salvation.

Like the doctrine of the Immaculate Conception, the musical and devotional sources with which nuns prayed and learned were frequently authored by clergymen, as were the mediated texts through which we hear nuns' voices. The dialog between Clori and Casandra was not written by a woman, in fact. It is the prescriptive musing of a priest, Martín de Vallarta (1672–1729), known for writing devotional literature for New Spanish nuns.[10] By professing as cloistered nuns and heeding instructions such as Vallarta's, New Spanish women joined and remained in the hierarchy of intercessors for the salvation of humanity.

Examining the words of authors like Vallarta and reflecting on the information they offer up about convent culture and its role in salvation, together with the limited extant convent music sources, enables us to delve into a deeper conversation about nuns' veiled voices, music, and gender. In so doing, this book attends to the rituals and devotions focused on nuns' union with Christ as his spiritual wives and mothers, through the consumption of Christ's body in the Eucharist, through imitation of his suffering and Passion, and by emulating his Immaculate mother.[11] Nuns' voices coalesced in devotional music, art, and literature in the expression of such doctrinal imperatives, shining light on the paths of silence and sound, pleasure and pain, chastity and sex, and prestige and humility navigated by the brides of Christ—as nuns were aptly styled—for the sake of salvation.

Music

Immaculate Sounds attends to the devotional synergy of the performative, visual, and literary arts fostered through the intermediary circumstances of New Spanish nuns. It builds on pioneering work from colonial Latin American music scholarship and early modern Catholic sound studies, continuing the work of the latter to probe the global early modern Post-Tridentine soundscape.[12] To date, only a handful of known music collections remain from eight convents located in central New Spain (see Table I.1).[13] The majority of these manuscripts are from Mexico City, the New Spanish capital built on the ruins of the Mexica capital Tenochtitlan following the 1521 conquest, and from the city of Puebla, established in 1531 from the ground up for Spaniards to inhabit some 80 miles southeast of Mexico City. These cities are the primary geographical focus within this study. They were the largest urban centers in the region, in which thirty-seven convents were established throughout the colonial period—over half of the viceroyalty's fifty-seven total nunneries.[14]

Table I.1 Extant sources of New Spanish convent music

City and Convent	Religious Order	Contents	Collection Format	Compilation Date (est.)	Current Location
Mexico City					
Encarnación	Conceptionist	Polyphony for Mass and Office	6 choirbooks	early 17th cent.–middle 18th cent.	Newberry Library, Chicago
Santa Inés	Conceptionist	Polyphony for Mass and Office	1 choirbook	1627	Museo de El Carmen, Mexico City
San Jerónimo	Hieronymite	Chant for Profession	1 notated ceremonial	17th cent.	Hispanic Society of America, New York
Enseñanza	Company of Mary	Chant for the feast of the Expectation	1 choirbook	1800	Museo Franz Mayer, Mexico City
Puebla					
Concepción	Conceptionist	Chant for Mass and Office; Chant for Profession	1 choirbook (antiphoner); 1 notated ceremonial	1691; early 17th cent.	Biblioteca Palafoxiana, Puebla; Concepción Convent
Santa Inés de Montepulciano	Dominican	Chant for Office	1 choirbook	1705	INAH, Mexico City
Santísima Trinidad	Conceptionist	Chant and Polyphony for Mass and Office; Villancicos	398 works in loose sheets	middle 17th cent.–middle 19th cent.	Sánchez Garza Collection, CENIDIM, Mexico City
Oaxaca					
Regina Coeli	Conceptionist	Organ accompaniment for Matins Psalm tones	1 notebook	late 18th cent.–early 19th cent.	Archivo Histórico de la Arcuidiócesis de Oaxaca

Mexico City and Puebla were not the only cities with music-making nuns, as demonstrated by the existence of an organ manuscript to accompany Psalms in Oaxaca's Regina Coeli convent (bottom of Table I.1). Historical studies have also shown evidence of musical activities in women's convents of Guadalajara, Querétaro, and San Miguel el Grande (now San Miguel de Allende).[15] The devotional and musical practices from convents in these provincial cities reflect what historian Asunción Lavrin calls "inescapable uniformities" guided by convent rules and spirituality that will assist in contextualizing the music sources that do remain from our focal cities.[16]

Some of the extant music manuscripts have already received bibliographic and codicological attention, as well as critical editions of their contents.[17] The sources from the San Jerónimo, Santa Inés de Montepulciano, and Enseñanza convents have essentially remained unstudied (see preliminary overview of the San Jerónimo and Santa Inés de Montepulciano sources in Appendices I.1–I.2). We do not have an entire musical archive preserved from these cloisters, or of any other, to elaborate a detailed account of one institution's full musical practices—to assess how long the manuscripts remained in use to establish historical development, for example—nor do we have extensive documentation such as the chapter minutes (*actas de cabildo*) that have facilitated scholarship on music of the New Spanish cathedrals.[18]

I have been fortunate to gain access to some contemporary active convents (as shown in the preface) to examine their privately held historical sources. These experiences indicate that other collections of convent musical and documentary source materials might still be preserved within active convents and parish churches, or by private collectors.[19] However, when religious institutions serve as archives, challenges can abound. Convents and parishes do not usually have staff available to attend to researchers. Their inhabitants are often suspicious of lay people perusing their materials. This attitude is understandable from the perspective of clerics and especially cloistered nuns, who technically are not allowed to let lay people into their convents but sometimes do so ambivalently depending on the rapport one develops with them. As the preface to this book demonstrates, first impressions count. Both men and women religious whose institutions own primary sources of interest to historians of various sorts often consider their material culture, such as art, music, and ritual books, holy and/or valuable. Historical documents are safeguarded for fear of having them disorganized, damaged, or stolen, violations that have occurred in the distant past, as we will see in Chapter 1, and lamentably within recent memory, according to what I have been told.[20]

Approaching nuns and priests with honesty and a willingness to share knowledge and resources is essential to regain trust from these stewards of such archival material.

Lay people have also preserved colonial documents and manuscripts that formerly belonged to convents—a problematic scenario, since it is difficult to locate such holdings.[21] It is fortunate when owners are willing to part with or share such collectibles and family heirlooms in ways that benefit the public. The music manuscripts of the Encarnación and Santísima Trinidad repertory, for example, having belonged to antiquarian collectors of the previous century, fortuitously made their way into the public archives in which they are now held.[22]

The sources for the topic of New Spanish convent music are scarce, and the archives related to the subject have many gaps in information, but the fraction of music manuscripts that I am aware of so far (listed earlier in Table I.1) serve as templates for what might have been musically possible.[23] They represent the richest remains of notated music sources attesting to women's musical activities in seventeenth- and eighteenth-century New Spain, a period that coincides with the flourishing of convent culture and spirituality across Latin America.[24]

Broadening the time span provides further context for this study. Excursions into the sixteenth century assist with convent-foundational concerns, while nineteenth-century sources demonstrate a continuation of the previous centuries' musico-devotional practices.[25] For example, Fanny Calderón de la Barca's journal from her time living in Mexico City (October 1839 to February 1842), published as *Life in Mexico*, is a worthwhile primary source for context. The wife of the Spanish ambassador to Mexico, Ángel Calderón de la Barca y Belgrano, Fanny imparts a feminine perspective on visiting convents and attending their liturgies from the point of view of an outsider who had not grown up Catholic. Her comment that she "felt transported three centuries back" upon her visit to the Encarnación convent reveals how old-fashioned the convent lifestyle seemed to her and other members of secular society in the first half of the nineteenth century.[26] Other parts of her journal reveal concerns about music and soundscape, such as descriptions of profession ceremonies that can be traced to the previous centuries, discussed further in Chapter 1, and the convent choir structure, the *coro*, examined in Chapter 2.[27]

Thus, guided by the extant sources, I will overlook notions of temporality that restrict the musicological arena to research on a single institution or one collection of repertory and its performance practice consistent within a limited span of time. This book slides among the specificities, assumptions, and generalizations about devotional music that the porous convent archives present, eschewing a fixed date range of performance for the music examples and the devotions discussed. Acknowledging historian Stefan Tanaka's aim to "decenter chronological time," avoiding "a framework that predisposes us toward a progressivist and mechanistic desire," my methodological decision has the advantage of tuning into what Julia Kristeva calls "women's time."[28] An alternate temporal ontology, women's time is less concerned with phenomena across linear chronology, a construct that has often centered men's actions and perspectives. Echoing "women's time," Tanaka validates repetition and cyclicity as characteristics of "diverse times."[29] *Immaculate Sounds* thus attempts to align itself closer to some early modern nuns' experience of history as timeless, cyclical, cosmic, and conducive to mysticism.[30]

In this vein, the sequential ordering of musical development is sidelined to bring out the voices, the liturgical cycles, the mystical revelations, and the doctrinal constructs of the life of the Virgin Mary and Christ that the extant music enhanced for salvation. The mystical experiences most relevant to this narrative include some nuns hearing messages directly from God; nuns having supernatural visions, including visions of themselves being crucified, for example; and nuns experiencing unusual movement, such as bilocation of their own bodies or the miraculous motion of inanimate objects. Such occurrences, sometimes facilitated with liturgical music, as we will see, demonstrate some nuns' abilities to connect directly with the divine.[31] Invoking Tanaka once more, who sought "to broaden the connections of histories to the present," I trust that, in the broadest sense, the context I narrate will intrigue contemporary performers of early modern nuns' repertoires, among others, and arouse current practitioners of Christianity, for whom finding ways to connect with God and seeking salvation through Christ are still paramount.[32]

The availability of more abundant extant primary sources derived from colonial Latin American missionary settings and cathedrals has generated a robust contextual history for European sacred music abroad, with an emphasis on men's musical performance.[33] Yet women's convents had critical ties to their city networks and to these types of male ecclesiastical institutions, especially cathedrals—a remnant of customs that have been well documented in European convents, especially in Italy and, to some extent, Spain.[34] While copies of music from Spanish composers circulated within New

Spanish convents,[35] the music of composers active in New Spain is also well represented in the villancico parts and liturgical music repertory for nuns. These men were often musicians affiliated with local cathedral chapels, and they were considered among the region's most adept composers, vocalists, and instrumentalists.[36]

Musicians affiliated with the Mexico City cathedral chapel in particular experienced upward social mobility and were offered professional advantages not available to other musicians, including performance opportunities in churches around the city for additional pay, which gave them the chance to perform in convents.[37] The Mexico City cathedral music chapel and the Capuchin Franciscan San Felipe de Jesús convent, for example, had close ties, through which the cathedral musicians performed on special occasions, including funerals, professions, convent dedications, or important feasts like Corpus Christi.[38] The 1755 biography of Sister Augustina Nicolasa María de los Dolores, written by Mother Joaquina María de Zavaleta, the San Felipe convent abbess, notes the outstanding music ("más selecta música") composed anew for the vigils and nocturnes associated with Sister Augustina's funeral services. It was performed by the cathedral chapel even though the convent had the tradition of singing its own liturgies.[39]

In addition, nuns and aspiring nuns around New Spain were taught to sing and play instruments by musicians often associated with the cathedral chapels, if not by some of their own musically trained convent sisters.[40] For example, in 1782 the abbess of the Balvanera convent mentioned that the Mexico City cathedral organist Juan Bautista del Águila had spent considerable time giving organ lessons to one of the convent's nuns, and that he had introduced one of his pupils, Antonieta Vaquero from Puebla, into the convent community. Later, the abbess notes that Vaquero had successfully professed as a nun with a dowry waiver.[41] Vaquero's skills thus allowed her to perform for the convent liturgies in exchange for a form of remuneration paid in advance by way of exemption from the entrance dowry otherwise required for all initiates into a convent (Chapter 3). The music auditions for such waivers were also adjudicated by cathedral chapel musicians, whose assessments, often with vague remarks on the candidate's instrumental competence and the sonorousness of the candidate's voice, became a notarized legal record.[42]

The dowry-waiver process was mutually beneficial for all musicians involved.[43] In building his musical career at the cathedral, Águila applied for a promotion to chapel master the same year he brought Vaquero to the Balvanera convent, noting in his application his tenacious dedication "to helping poor girls who want to become nuns as titled musicians."[44] What did he mean by titled musician?

In this context, titled musician was the legal title given to a nun exempted from paying a convent entrance dowry upon profession because her musical skills were proficient for such an exemption. Earning this title required the musician to perform for the convent liturgies. Convent titled musicians could have been the first women of European descent to work as musicians in the Americas, providing an example of how the spiritual and economic components of the New Spanish society could come together through musical networks.[45] Such workaday transactions in Latin American convents are an example of a colonial habit.[46]

The gendered networking among musicians across religious institutions in New Spain imbricated the elevation of women to co-redeemers with social mobility. To summarize that network, early modern nuns' interactions with male musicians often took place when convents purchased or obtained notated music by male composers, when nuns received music instruction, when male musicians acted as guest performers for convent special occasions, and when dowry-exemption auditions were required.[47] These collaborations were in the service of nuns' salvific singing. The opportunity to engage in this resonance, however, was not available to all women in New Spain.

Typically, professing into a convent required proof of "old Christian" Spanish descent, excluding anyone known to have descended from Jewish and Muslim people who had converted to Christianity, known as "new Christians," or *conversos*.[48] In America, this xenophobia fostered *Genealogical Fictions*, according to María Elena Martínez, "the fiction of New Spain's lack of Jewish and Muslim antecedents."[49] To sustain this myth, old Christian purity was archived in baptismal records and bolstered through word of mouth within what Matthew O'Hara calls "audible interactions."[50] Such interactions were the public, agentive vocalizations of difference expressed by individuals and groups, forming the categorical building blocks of colonial societies.[51] In other words, if a woman who wanted to profess in a convent claimed to be Spanish, the procedure typically went as follows: first, her baptismal record was reviewed by a priest; then, witnesses who knew her family for a long time, and who themselves were Spanish, had to declare under oath that the aspirant's family was of Spanish descent; and last, these procedures were documented in a notarized profession record prior to a woman's admittance into a convent (Chapter 3).

In a society as hierarchical as New Spain's, that obsession with blood purity manifested in racialized discourse that called for Spanish people to avoid miscegenation with indigenous locals, enslaved Africans brought to America, and mixed-race people, known as *castas*.[52] The increase in the mixed-race population as the New Spanish viceroyalty matured throughout the seventeenth and eighteenth centuries demonstrates an obvious ineffectiveness in Spanish efforts to promote their prescribed way of life: the practice did not match the philosophy, complicating social mobility for those not deemed Spanish.[53] Local designations of decency and high social standing, or quality of personhood (*calidad*), blended together matters of class and race and developed to give some people access to the services and careers offered by some Spanish institutions, especially the Church, while denying those institutional offerings to non-Spanish citizens.[54] Cloistered convents functioned within these societal tenets, as words like decency, calidad, legitimacy, and virginity were often employed to denote a woman's aptitude for the convent.[55]

Conveniently, convents guarded women from mixture with religious/ethnic male others, while turning them into intercessors of salvation.[56] They became living models of the Virgin Mary's unceasing purity through their notarized "pure" lineage, and even through the apparel of some nuns belonging to Marian orders. The Immaculate Conception's blue cape is worn by Conceptionists, and Our Lady of Mt. Carmel's brown habit is worn by Carmelite nuns. The path leading to the veil and habit was conditioned in some women since childhood through sacramental learning, and it followed a gendered "theology of containment" (*recogimiento*).[57] According to Jessica Delgado, this containment was accomplished through the development of "legal practices, institutions, and resources to contain and quarantine dangerous women, protect virtuous and vulnerable women, redeem repentant women, and maximize the sanctifying power of exceptionally virtuous women."[58] Nuns were not isolated from indigenous or African-descended women, however.

While New Spanish society's pietistic entwinement with racialized elitism generally banned women of indigenous or African descent from professing as nuns, women from these groups were often allowed to live as servants in cloistered convents, earning their salvation by providing the menial labor that gave nuns the time to sing and pray.[59] Only in the eighteenth century were three cloisters founded for noble indigenous women to profess as nuns.[60] These exclusionary practices in convent profession and the establishment of more cloisters throughout the eighteenth century were thought to symbolize successful implementation of Catholic faith among indigenous Americans.[61]

In a region where "pure blooded" Spaniards and elite indigenous women were a minority, nuns found themselves between colonizer and subjugated.[62] In this liminal position, nuns might well constitute part of the carefully calculated pauses and silences of a "colonial counterpoint," David Irving's juxtaposition of European contrapuntal sonority with the social conditions of the Spanish colonial endeavor.[63] Apt here as well is Philip Bohlman's broader assertion that "it is from the power to silence that the power to colonize and to subjugate eventually comes."[64] How did nuns silence other women while at the same time being silenced themselves and at other times being allowed to resound?

On the one hand, the multi-faceted silencing I am referring to is reflected in the nuns' musical agency. It silenced marginalized groups of women, especially indigenous and African women, whose voices and music are hardly documented. On the other hand, the nuns' own literal silencing was a reality. Ritualized discipline that followed rules of obedience designed by male prelates designated when nuns' voices could be heard in prayer and song.[65] There is also the matter of authorial voice in the writings of role-model nuns that inform us about convent musical practices. Because their experiences were often published by men in convent chronicles and nuns' biographies, the words of such nuns have been characterized by literary critic Jean Franco as revealing an "ultimate silence."[66] I hope to show that the discourse about music and the liturgies in the biographies and devotional literature can be seen as valid representations of the convent soundscapes and that being silenced is not equivalent to being silent. Women found alternative ways to communicate even while silenced.[67]

Whether nuns kept silent when they were supposed to, in other words, whether or not nuns followed their rules strictly, is impossible to determine. Descriptions of convent rule-bending and conflicts in convents outside the scope of this book indeed lead to questions about whether women were wholeheartedly committed to living out their orders' restrictions "al pie de la letra" (literally) when they professed.[68] Nonetheless, by focusing on the idealized sonorities governed by the extant sources I have queried, I seek to emphasize the critical role of salvation with which nuns were charged. Even the nun who self-proclaimed as the worst of all—"la peor que ha habido"—was concerned with salvation.[69] I am of course referring to the famous seventeenth-century New Spanish nun-poet Sor Juana Inés de la Cruz, who was known to have said, "I deemed convent life the least unsuitable and the most honorable I could elect if I were to ensure my salvation."[70] We will come back to her later.

Immaculate Sounds demonstrates that the hierarchies constructed by New Spanish citizens on the path to salvation had musical, sonic, and silencing implications that shine light on women's vocal agency within documents often mediated by male clergy—and that the mysteries of faith reverberated through nuns' veiled voices emerge from a motley host of sources in addition to music manuscripts.[71] One more example from Vallarta's constructed dialog between the nun Clori and laywoman Casandra, introduced earlier, will suffice to reiterate how the value of sound and silence in the convent manifested through rhetorical prescription. In a section of the poem that allegorizes various aspects of convent life by anthropomorphizing these qualities as living nuns (Sister Poverty, Sister Mortification, Sister Humility, etc.), Vallarta introduces "Sor Oración" (Sister Prayer) through a gendered binary that prefaces our future discussion of virginity:

Sor Oración tiene aquí	Sister Prayer has here
el lugar más respetable,	the most respectable place,
pues aunque es virgen, de todas	for even though she is a virgin,
estas señoras es madre.	she is mother to all these ladies.
Y a todas las guarda y cuida	And all [the ladies] are guarded and
un varón muy venerable,	cared by a very venerable man,
que es el hermano silencio,	who is brother silence,
muy circunspecto, y muy grave.	very discreet and serious.[72]

Thus, nuns' voices were to be heard only in vocal prayer, silenced at all other times by male authority.[73]

We can discern how gender differences around sound and music manifested across spiritual and practical concerns—the former in Vallarta's excerpt: essentially, "virgin" women's voices should only resound in prayer, otherwise "brother silence" dominates. We have already touched on the latter, in which the gendered soundscape resounded through the practical matter of men validating women's musical skills for dowry-free professions and men composing music for nuns to sing, for example.

Nuns' embodied vocalizations—insofar as they conveyed notions of an idealized, virgin female body, as Vallarta suggests with Sister Prayer—from within the cloister walls are preserved in nuns' rule books, devotional literature, notarial protocols, convent records, and biographies ("vidas de monjas"). These literary sources reveal historic discourses about music.[74] Yet with the added context of Spanish colonialism, some of the sources considered in this book also constitute archives of repertoire, a variation on Diana Taylor's instruction that differentiates the written word as archive from an epistemology of embodied performance she denotes as repertoire.[75]

Notated music sources, too, can be considered archives of repertoire since they are targeted toward performers literate in Western notation.[76] By analyzing the notated music in dialogue with the repertoire archived in print and manuscript discourses, this book begins to piece together the long-fragmented history of women's music making in New Spain's most important urban centers for music and the arts.[77] It reconciles actual events in the lives of early modern nuns with the music of their convents and the perfectionist overtones of devotional literature. In this way, the handwritten records, often missing folios, become more conclusive, while the music and literature, prone to seventeenth- and eighteenth-century rhetorical excess often labeled "Baroque," start to reflect New Spanish life in a more familiar if performative light.[78]

Devotional Literature

To date, an abundance of scholarly spotlighting and popular attention has foregrounded early modern Hispanic nuns who were famous in their own times, such as St. Teresa of Ávila and María de Ágreda, both from Spain, or Sor Juana Inés de la Cruz of Mexico City, mentioned briefly before.[79] Both St. Teresa and Juana Inés have even garnered fictionalized historical dramas on television, including a one-season series by Televisión Española (*Teresa de Jesús*, 1984) and a Netflix miniseries (*Juana*, 2016), attesting to the fascination people have had with these nuns.

Sor Juana Inés de la Cruz (here on out referred to as "Sor Juana" to distinguish her from other nuns with the same name) is a ubiquitous figure in New Spanish convent scholarship. For decades, her face has appeared on various iterations of Mexican currency. She is an icon of erudite femininity in Mexico. And her writings are an essential component of Mexican literary pedagogy.[80] Her literature has been the subject of intersectional analyses and interpretations, as Sor Juana's life and works make their way beyond North American research circles in Hispanic history and literature. Carla Lucero's opera *Juana*, for example, presents an unabashed queering of Sor Juana, climaxing with the nun's love scene with the Countess of Paredes.[81] Sor Juana is often portrayed in scholarship as exceptional for her "refusal to fit within the mold of a good, submissive, and most of all, silent bride of Christ," as Alicia Gaspar de Alba insists.[82] Interpretations of Sor Juana's writings from Gaspar de Alba's Chicana, queer, feminist lens convince us that she was a revolutionary rather than a model of "the epitome of good women: the immaculate Virgin Mary and perfect Mother of God."[83]

There is, however, more to New Spanish convent culture than can be learned from the writings of Sor Juana alone. *Immaculate Sounds* does not intend to re-silence Sor Juana's impressive output—as if that were possible. Rather, I center the musical implications and the lives of seemingly "good women" featured and/or disciplined within other devotional literature to enrich the scholarly discourse with a broader subset of nuns' experiences.[84] Some highlights include the charismatic prescriptions in Bishop Juan de Palafox y Mendoza's rules for nuns in Puebla; the chronicles of the Conceptionist-turned-Carmelite musicians Inés de la Cruz (b. 1567) and Mariana de la Encarnación (b. 1571); the life of the almost-sainted María de Jesús Tomelín (1579–1637); the fire-breathing Isabel de la Encarnación (1594–1633); and the life of Augustina Nicolasa María de los Dolores (d. 1755), written about in a rare biography published by another nun.[85] The subjects in these sources are well known to Hispanists who have probed them for their historical and literary contents, while other sources, such as Fr. Alonso Franco's lives of nuns in the Santa Catalina de Siena convent (1645) and the biography of the widow Bárbara Josefa de San Francisco (1662–1723) of the Santísima Trinidad convent, though not completely obscure, have garnered less attention.[86]

As is well known to historians of colonial Latin America and Spanish literary critics, the devotional literature taken up in this book documents lives within particular convents, and most of the texts were authored by highly educated clergy.[87] Biographies of nuns present the theological expertise of their published authors, who embellished first-hand accounts told by nuns in or out of confession or written by nuns in personal reflections and examinations of conscience.[88] How then might the voices of nuns resonate through the pens of male clerics?

To begin to answer this question, we can build on Taylor's work and consider the biographies as archives of archives.[89] The raw material written by nuns, appropriated by men of the cloth, was often quoted extensively in the final published account, as was the case in Diego de Lemus' 1683 biography of María de Jesús from Puebla's Purísima Concepción convent, whose amanuensis Sister Agustina de Santa Teresa was charged with writing down all of María's divine visions and auditions.[90] Excerpts from nuns' writings made the recontextualized male-authored publication more truthful and even dramatic.[91] The act of writing the preliminary source material for priests, although denying authorship to most nun writers, had certain benefits in some convents, including the promotion of wellness, the inciting of mysticism (if it can be considered a benefit), and the fostering of mutual respect among nuns.[92] In Agustina and María's case, fostering respect among the two seems more plausible, yet, more critically, the anxiety that Agustina experienced in seeking to write as accurately as possible was a concern that María tried to appease by appealing to God's authority.[93] Reading this literature on the lives of nuns out loud was a form of recreation, and informal sacramental learning, for lay and religious alike that was highly endorsed by the Church to reinforce the vow of obedience within cloistered convents and to maintain a faithful citizenry among lay people.[94]

Nuns' biographies circulated widely when published, and because they aimed to sanctify their subjects, they often followed hagiographical models, such as the lives of St. Teresa of Ávila or St. Catherine of Siena, not least in their mystic revelations.[95] The featured nun's exceptionally moral upbringing by devoutly Catholic parents and/or relatives often opens the biography.[96] Upon professing into a convent, the subject leads an exemplary life filled with "humility, mortification, penance, fasting, and poverty," according to Mónica Díaz, following hagiographical precedents.[97] Most nuns with published biographies suffer illnesses and die, while staying true to their vows of obedience, poverty, chastity, and enclosure with the guidance of Christ, the Virgin Mary, and other saints of their personal devotion.[98]

This literary framework in combination with stories of individual nuns' experiences produced published lifelong confessions. As such, the biographies acquired sacramental authority with the power to save those who took their words to heart and confessed their own sins to a priest at least once a year. (Nuns were required to confess at least monthly.)[99] The clergy held the key to salvation through its ability to absolve sins in confession;[100] following that metaphor, the path to the corresponding threshold opened by such a key was illuminated by role-model nuns in the biographies. These women could lead those seeking to imitate their lives to salvation, but all nuns continued to intercede perpetually for the souls of the departed, and every cloistered nun had this responsibility.[101]

Yet, there are no prescriptions for how authors were to include nuns' feelings about workaday concerns or how to bring out a nun's voice in a published biography.[102] Sometimes direct quotations from nuns are highlighted with quotation marks or italics, but sometimes they are not. However, the stories that do develop expose elements of the liturgies that nuns attended round the clock, and they discuss particular convent devotional acts, occasions in which nuns' voices undoubtedly resounded.[103] Thus, *Immaculate Sounds* draws from the biographies a previously unstudied wealth of evidence attesting to music, sound, aurality, and orality within the convents.[104] The history of music I elucidate builds from Helen Myers' affirmation that nuns' biographies supplement the incomplete archival record with "a myriad of details about family and religious life that Latin American historians have difficulty gathering from more traditional sources, such as legal and notarial records."[105] For musicological purposes, the biographies archive musical and sonic colonial habits as well.

Because music was a vital component of the liturgical and devotional life of the convents, music in the biographies could recall the affective quality of music in real life, enlivening the written narrative for readers by jogging their memory about a familiar sacred soundscape and possibly prompting readers to hear it within their own mind's ear. For scholars, music making in the biographies remains as discourse about music.[106] Mentions of liturgical music and the wider convent soundscape enhanced the value of a particular nun's story.[107] This gesture toward worth raises the question as to whom these convent sounds were valuable. They were valuable to the nuns who performed the music; to nuns who sought the intimacy of hearing the voice of God, of his mother, and of the saints directly from their divine source; and to everyone who wished to be saved through nuns' vocalizations. New Spanish citizens were instructed that reading nuns' biographies and heeding their pious lessons—which included listening to music devoutly, as some nuns purportedly did—would help save them.[108]

These volumes also reflect, if only partially, Angel Rama's notion of the colonial Latin American "lettered city." Such an urban center would be governed by a literate upper class that ascribed sacredness to writing even as written words may have "seemed not to spring from social life but rather be imposed upon it and to force it into a mold not at all made to measure," according to Rama.[109] Musicologists have expanded on the lettered city by proposing a sonic parallel that incorporated embodied performance.[110] The resulting "resounding city" relied on music in its written (compositional) and performative aspects, as well as aurality that at times depended on the participation of various ethnic groups living in New Spain, including indigenous people, African and Asian people, Europeans, and mixed-race people.[111]

Music in nuns' biographies springs from social, devotional, and liturgical life. We can observe features of both concepts, lettered and resounding, in nuns' biographies and other sources. Fanny Calderón de la Barca's journal attests to servants pumping the pipe-organ bellows in the Encarnación convent, for example.[112] Rule books refer to church bell ringing, a highlight of early modern soundscape studies,[113] rung by ringers who came from various social classes; bells were essential for the daily function of convents and cities.[114]

The notes written by nuns from Mexico City's Franciscan Corpus Christi convent compared briefly to the resulting published convent chronicle illustrates one example of the lettered and resounding city's molding of actions into illusive writing. This convent was the first of three convents founded for noble indigenous women to profess as nuns in eighteenth-century New Spain. The convent archive retained both the manuscripts written by nuns and the accounts embellished by male clergy, as in the manner of a nuns' published biography. In many other convents where similar writing practices occurred, the manuscripts written by nuns were destroyed after the priests used them to base their publication, but nuns' notes that remain from Corpus Christi are revealing, and they incorporate an instance of music making in that cloister.[115] In the (male) published history of the convent, Sister Antonia de los Santos, one of the indigenous founders of the convent, was said to have sung the hymn to the Immaculate Conception *Tota pulchra es* constantly and to have played the vihuela, the guitar-like stringed instrument ubiquitous in the early modern Spanish world.[116] We will encounter the vihuela and its rich symbolism again in Chapters 4 and 5. In the unpublished notes about Sister Antonia, her convent sisters simply stated that she was a singer and dancer ("cantadora y bailadora"), no more, no less.[117]

At the surface level, the version elaborated by the priest presents Sister Antonia as an exemplary pious musician, while upholding the long-held fact that Franciscans traditionally had been proponents of the Immaculate Conception doctrine (Chapter 1). However, it is also encouraging that musical moments in these types of constructed narratives are plausible enough to be based on the experiences of real nuns, not least musicians like Antonia. A nun known for singing would certainly have sung *Tota pulchra es* at some point, especially in a Franciscan house (say on the feast of the Immaculate Conception, celebrated yearly on December 8). Other writings—such as the convent chronicles of Sisters Mariana de la Encarnación and Inés de la Cruz (remember, not Sor Juana), both of them musicians—indicate that some nuns were as pious as what Antonia's male biographer tried to convey.[118] Such detailed chronicles written by musician nuns are rare. Even though their narratives are not exclusively about music, comments regarding their liturgical duties suggest that music was integral to their daily lives, sometimes overwhelmingly so.[119]

In addition to accompanying the liturgies with their voices and instruments, convent musicians enhanced internal devotional acts, such as processions of patron-saint statues around the cloister. Musicians also accompanied processions of the Blessed Sacrament, the consecrated host in every Catholic Church used for eucharistic devotion, especially for the feast of Corpus Christi (Chapter 4). Nuns performed music to entertain aristocracy, patrons, or high-ranking clergy upon visits to the convents.[120] It is not known what music was heard in New Spanish convents during these visits. In late sixteenth-century Barcelona convents, villancicos and polyphony were performed for visits from royalty.[121] In nineteenth-century Mexico City, Fanny Calderón de la Barca tells of what was performed over dinner during her visit at the Encarnación convent, in which "A young girl . . . brought in a little harp without pedals, and while we discussed cakes and ices, sung different ballads with a good deal of taste."[122] We will see that the performance of villancicos and polyphony, and the ability to accompany oneself on harp, continued in the intervening centuries.

For these visits into the convents, as well as for the convent liturgies, the music would have depended on each convent's financial resources.[123] Generally, one might expect to hear reciting tone and monophonic chant in most convent church liturgies; polyphony and vernacular villancicos would likely be heard in wealthier convents on important feast days. It is no surprise that the Encarnación, having been one of the richest convents in Mexico City, left extant parts to grand polychoral vocal polyphony—an elite Spanish sonority that would enhance important feasts.[124] There is also evidence that villancicos were performed by the Encarnación choir in the 1670s, even if no villancico manuscripts remain from this convent.[125]

Villancicos are popular sacred songs of the early modern Hispanic Church. These polyphonic works were sung with instrumental accompaniment in paraliturgical contexts, such as processions or during the adoration of the Blessed Sacrament. In the liturgies, they were typically performed in groups of eight around the lessons at the Office of Matins through the mideighteenth century,[126] or they were sung at various moments in the Mass, including the offertory and communion.[127] The extant manuscripts from Puebla's Santísima Trinidad convent preserve numerous villancicos whose texts parallel the messages conveyed in sacred paintings, nuns' biographies, and other devotional literature for nuns, including guidebooks for good Catholic practice, order-specific rule books, and printed sermons.[128] The musical, visual, and literary arts thus coexisted in an enclosed aura of devotion that seeped through the crannied wall of the cloisters most conspicuously as the sound of veiled voices.[129]

Veil, Voice, Virginity

There remains much to learn from women's musical lives to flesh out the soundscape of colonial Latin American cities and to amplify women's contributions to Mexican history. As a point of departure, I would like to reflect for a moment on the work of the pioneering scholar of Mexican women's history Julia Tuñon Pablos. I am especially interested in the peculiar translation of her book—so popular in Latin American Studies courses—from the Spanish *Mujeres en México: una historia olvidada* into English as *Women in Mexico: A Past Unveiled*. A more literal translation of the subtitle would be "a forgotten history," as "una historia olvidada" does not mean "a past unveiled." The essential message in both titles is that the book's contents instruct on something not widely known about.

However, the power dynamics change in the translation of "historia" to "past": the ideological bedrock sustaining "historia/history" crumbles into a reference about time lapsing and difference.[130] Indeed, as Zachary Schiffman instructs, "the past is not simply prior to the present but different from it."[131] In addition, the original "olvidada" (forgotten) suggests a more happenstance phenomenon as opposed to the English title's "unveiled," which alludes to having the potential to reveal what is concealed. The less literal translation into English is convenient for the purposes of *Immaculate Sounds*, as the ideology shifts from the Spanish emphasis on a subject ("history") to highlighting an action ("unveiling"), giving the title in English a performative element.

This process of veiling and unveiling in literature is a great entry point for thinking about cloistered nuns, who sang wearing veils on their heads as a marker of distinction. The veil was so cherished by nuns that being deprived of wearing it was used as a form of reprimand across various religious orders.[132] The details of what shortcomings or sins led to such unveiling are scarce, and to recall what I said before, are not the focus of this book, which aims at asserting the co-redemptive capabilities of these women who were doubly veiled. The walls and shrouded grates and screens of convents further concealed already-veiled women and their singing, demarking further their difference from secular society.[133] By emphasizing this double veiling here, we can recall that New Spanish citizens' experience of listening to cloistered nuns' voices was acousmatic, a circumstance in which one hears a voice whose source is unknown, derived from ancient Pythagorean tradition. Pythagoras lectured from behind a curtain—much like the nuns singing from behind the veil and grille and curtain of the choir space (Chapter 2).[134] Reminiscent of the virginal state of the invisible angels in heaven, the bodiliness inherent in the voices of nuns is virgin, as we began to observe with the virgin "Sister Prayer" earlier.[135]

The condition of human sexuality known as virginity was socially constructed.[136] For some women, the label of virginity—attesting to their lack of sexual contact with men—was literal; for others it was rumored; and for some, like widows, it was aspirational and symbolic. Virginity in the case of nuns was more a state of mind, fueled by the vow of chastity, than merely a corporeal attribute that could be concealed physically, though it was often idealized as an allegory for prayerful music and sound (Chapter 1).[137] As such, salvation could be achieved by the songful intercession of any nun, regardless of traditional virginity status.

The salvific power attributed to such vocalizations resided within the unknown dialog with God that existed in the minds of nuns prior to the vocal pre-semantic component of their song.[138] Those internal dialogs between God and nun will never be known to us, however learned they may or may not have been, however manufactured by the influence of male superiors they may or may not have been.[139] There is where a nun's agency resided—within an arena that demanded a singing pure heart (as Vallarta and so many other clerics noted in their directives to nuns), and that required a sonorous embodied voice practical for the convent choir, corroborated by male musicians, often from the cathedral, in dowry-waiver protocols (Chapter 3).

A requisite for nuns, as we observed with Vallarta's dialog between Clori and Casandra at the opening, was that the external sound during the liturgies may as well be mute if the internal did not conform to the divine.[140] For this reason, Sister Isabel de la Encarnación wrote, quoting the Epistle of James (1:26), that the religious fervor of any nun would be in vain if she could not control her tongue ("enfrenar su lengua").[141] Control comes from the interior, which can regulate the muscular organ that assists in articulating the exterior sound.[142] Through the scriptures Sister Isabel adds the tongue to the lips of Clori as a vital instrument of the vocal ensemble, placing it as an embodiment of the discipline and interiority that would be required for divine communication.[143] The messages of the internal voices heard by some nuns and described in their biographies are what gave such role-model women their exemplary valence, revealing that an "intensification . . . of the contemplative process," as Elizabeth Rhodes puts it, was taking place in New Spain.[144]

We can see at play here parallels with contemporary vocal ethics. For Mladen Dolar, the (sounded) voice is quieter than the metaphorical (internal) voice, which, although silent to the outside world, loudly resounds reason, nature, and divinity in the thinker's interiority; it is "the voice of the heart."[145] Adriana Cavarero's problematization of the long-held Western philosophy that "woman sings, man thinks" is apt as well, since there was much for nuns to remember and contemplate—that is, think—while singing.[146] There are examples from Sor Juana's villancicos for the Virgin Mary, in which Sor Juana proposes a (female) counterpoint to God's divine (male) intelligence. That thinker/singer is the Virgin Mary, imitable by her closest imitators—cloistered nuns.[147]

The cultural history of music that follows expands on two themes. The first is acousmatic discipline (Chapters 1, 2, and 3), which carries on as an underlying thread throughout. Building on issues of enclosed and vocalized thinking/singing, this section of the book employs an understanding that the voice of God resounded as the Virgin Mary herself—in other words, that the Virgin Mary was thought to be the voice of God. Such Marian harmonies resound in, for example, sermonized allegories of the Immaculate Conception doctrine preached to nuns and printed and disseminated for posterity.[148] The nuns would be reminded that their own voices could in turn echo back a divine, if veiled, sonority from behind their choir grates. Like the Virgin Mary too, ordinary women became divine resonators—mediums for delivering God's message—when they were initiated as nuns into a life of constant discipline.[149] The convent choir space, where the majority of the sacred music under consideration in this study was performed, was a disciplined space within the disciplined space of the cloister itself.[150] Unity is the book's second theme, which branches out from the ritual components associated with Christic devotion, as Chapters 4 and 5 discuss the earthly joys and sorrows that a disciplined life merited for nuns, a foretaste of union with Christ in heaven—salvation. Such union could be accomplished when nuns participated in the sacrament of the Eucharist, consuming the bread consecrated at Mass, which contained Christ's body. Similarly, mortification rituals and Passion devotion literature helped nuns envision themselves following next to Christ during his Passion step-by-step with some nuns envisioning bodily union, in which their bodies were crucified on top of Christ.

The chapter titles are presented as questions that ask who individual nuns were:

Chapter 1: Immaculate Conflicts: Resounding Mary's Immaculate Conception, or Who Was Sister Flor de Santa Clara?

Chapter 2: Sonic Thresholds: The Grates of the Cloister and the Lips of Nuns, or Who Was Sister Rosa?

Chapter 3: Disciplined Sounds: Dowry Waivers and Race, or Who Was Mariana Josefa de Señor San Ignacio?

Chapter 4: Feasting Sounds: The Eucharistic Honeymoon, or Who Was Sister Paula?

Chapter 5: Redeeming Sounds: Resounding the Passion of Christ and His Spiritual Brides, or Who Was Sister Marina de San Francisco?

In these chapters, I lift the metaphorical veil that posterity has placed on the women named in each title to understand them despite their historical obscurity. Their names were worth writing down in the past because of their voices. These titles are acousmatic questions, recalling from earlier that the nuns discussed in these chapters were invisible to the New Spanish public that attended convent liturgies. The titles are the past-tense iteration of the perpetually repeated, and unanswerable, acousmatic question that listeners articulate when presented with the sound of a voice, "Who is this?" Nina Eidsheim argues that there is no inherent, unique identity in voice, but rather a multiplicity of possibilities raised by the acousmatic question.[151]

Immaculate Sounds presents possibilities for the acousmatic voices of the five New Spanish nuns in the chapter titles. The sources on which their names are found are inconclusive as to the details of these women's lives, but allow us to ponder questions about doctrine, space, discipline, and devotion and their relationship to music and voice. Ruminating on the archival remnants that preserve their names while fleshing them out with other extant historical and musical sources acknowledges the women named in each chapter title as vital components of a collective that was depended on for salvation. Salvation through this apparatus relied on a chain of vocal ideology: the invisible sonorous quality attributed to the Virgin Mary as the voice of God reverberated through the vocal intercessions of invisible cloistered nuns. I want to underscore that this salvific hierarchy was manufactured from audible interactions and archived discourse that elevated the Virgin and nuns to the status of co-redeemers.

Chapter 1 begins with a disagreement over villancicos in the Encarnación convent, setting the tone for the chapter's explanation of the doctrine of the Immaculate Conception and the dramatic founding of the first order of nuns to arrive in New Spain who were dedicated to the Immaculate Conception. For Catholics, the doctrine of the Immaculate Conception was an essential preface to the story of salvation initiated by Christ's birth. Through the doctrine, the Virgin Mary herself, as mother to the Word made flesh, becomes entwined with the Creation narrative. Mary was considered the voice of God at the Creation, a voice for nuns to imitate through their adherence to their profession vows. It was a voice that nuns too could pass on via the concept of auditory imagination, recalling a person's voice when reading the texts that a departed person once created or once vocalized.[152]

Chapter 2 discusses the most important space of the cloister, the church choir, in which nuns like the soloist Sister Rosa sang for all the liturgies, hidden from public view. The grates and screens of the choir were the architectural products of vows of obedience and enclosure that created the acousmatic circumstance of nuns' liturgical music. Rules for behavior within the choir space preserve many gestures to be carried out while singing certain words of the liturgy. The chapter argues that the choir was the quintessential location where agency was negotiated through nuns' efforts to please God, themselves, and their convent patrons with music. The type of written and embodied knowledge transmitted through nuns' biographies and the prescriptive rules for choir behavior reveal a divine epistemology mediated by nuns' musical activities in the choir.

Chapter 3, which builds on the notion that the notarial record is a disciplined space, explores how the sound of discipline manifested in both obvious and ambiguous ways within the music-dowry-waiver process.[153] The racialized restrictions that prevented African, indigenous, and mixed-race women from becoming nuns are examined in the context of the music-dowry audition. We learn that the documentation of such processes preserves a fiction of embodied discipline: that of a nun's family line with the continence to produce a "pure" Spanish daughter, qualified to become a musical bride of Christ. As such, notarial records of the music-dowry-waiver auditions and disbursals are an archive of multiple repertoires of disciplined sounds, from witness testimonies to references to polyphony.

Chapter 4 attends to the various metaphors attributed to the Eucharist in convent villancicos, beginning with a profession villancico for one Sister Paula, the erotic tone of which reminds us how intimate communion was for cloistered nuns. The poetics of eucharistic villancicos and devotional literature were frequently linked to the vow of obedience, to Marian devotion, and to other Christological devotions, such as the Passion. The extensive music and literature dedicated to this most sensual of the sacraments suggests that understanding the doctrine of Christ's resurrected body disguised as communion bread was a formidable task, even as unyielding belief in this mystery was essential for salvation. Nuns were supposed to be advocates of eucharistic faith, as they were the brides of the Body of Christ. The supernatural experiences surrounding the eucharistic devotion of Sister Bárbara and Sister María de Jesús, narrated in their biographies, demonstrate how certain nuns were elevated as role models of eucharistic faith and how nuns could be transformed by and into the Body of Christ for crucifixion.

Chapter 5 brings the salvation narrative to its close by demonstrating how nuns honored Christ's Passion. Following a long tradition of female mysticism, characterized by Jean Franco as a "higher and more immediate form of knowledge than scholastic theology," some nuns experienced ecstatic visions in which they were crucified once they had lived out perfectly the four convent vows of obedience, poverty, chastity, and enclosure.[154] Their biographies were the ideal literature for nuns and novices to learn to love and contemplate Christ's Passion, as required by their orders' rules. Narrative words alone and carnal images of crucified nuns attached to Christ on the cross, however, were not enough to expound on the benefits of the Passion to the most devout cloistered women. This chapter brings to light fascinating musical allegories and hymns buried in Sister Bárbara's biography, as well as an analysis of her convent's villancicos for the Virgin of Sorrows. It argues that singing served both as a channel for Passion devotion and as a prize for achieving monastic perfection, living out the vows in such a manner that would yield immediate union with Christ in heaven upon one's death.

Emphasizing the role of nuns' vocal music in New Spain invites a revised understanding of vocality in religious practice and the sonic qualities of women's personhood.[155] The acousmatic brings attention to nuns' out-of-sight, vocalized prayers as a parallel to Catholic doctrines that required belief without seeing. Notions of discipline and unity were required to promote such beliefs, and the sacrifices made by women who became cloistered nuns brought to life and resounded some of those teachings in a gendered manner.

PART I
ACOUSMATIC DISCIPLINE

1

Immaculate Conflicts

Resounding Mary's Immaculate Conception, or Who Was Sister Flor de Santa Clara?

It was mid-December 1610 in Mexico City. The Church was in its preparatory season of Advent, leading up to the celebration of Christ's birth at Christmas. The nuns of the Encarnación convent had just celebrated the feast of the Immaculate Conception of the Virgin Mary, on December 8. But now, in this time usually filled with joy, some of the nuns were nervous. Their music books were missing. Without them, the nuns would not be able to celebrate the anniversary of Christ's birth adequately.

A musician priest of the metropolitan cathedral, located just three blocks from the convent, had caused the nuns' alarm: Antonio Rodríguez Mata (d. 1643) had all five of the missing books. He had borrowed them from Sister Flor de Santa Clara, the convent "vicaria de coro" (choir vicar), but had failed to return them despite the nuns' repeated requests. The diocesan vicar general and the attorney general were summoned. The nuns of the Encarnación demanded that Mata be imprisoned if he failed to return the books immediately following the denunciation. The threat of jail time was serious, but so too was the alleged offense: Mata was impeding the nuns from performing their liturgical music for Christmas.

According to Sister Flor and some of her convent sisters, the books contained motets and other pieces used for singing the Divine Office ("muchos motetes y otras cosas de música con las cuales se oficiaba y solemnizaba el Oficio Divino").[1] Mata was asked by the vicar general for his testimony to confirm or deny the nuns' claims. He corroborated that he had taken five music books from Sister Flor. Yet, Mata challenged the nuns' report and stated that the missing choirbooks were not books of motets. Instead, Mata asserted that the books in question contained *chanzonetas*—another word for villancicos, essentially—for various liturgical feasts. He also gestured toward the music being the work of his own hand ("puntadas y trabajádaslas [*sic*] más de su mano"), though it is not clear if he meant he

Immaculate Sounds. Cesar D. Favila, Oxford University Press. © Oxford University Press 2023.
DOI: 10.1093/oso/9780197621899.003.0002

had composed, notated, copied, or re-worked the pieces.[2] Villancicos were sung for the liturgies and paraliturgical devotions on important feast days, not least Christmas and various Marian feasts, such as Mary's Immaculate Conception, Nativity, and Assumption. The popularity of villancicos drew citizens into the convent church liturgies, especially Matins. This service of the Divine Office was rich with plainchant and polyphony on major feast days, in which villancicos were often sung in place of or in addition to the responsories.[3] The word *motete* was used liberally in New Spanish music sources for labeling various kinds of sacred songs, especially responsories.[4] How the Encarnación nuns understood musical terminology is not certain, but they did not appear concerned with labels. They just wanted their books back.

Indeed, the nuns' actions reveal that they considered the theft significant, but Mata provided no additional comments about the missing books, as if having composed and/or dealt with the music in some way were enough for him to justify keeping them. Typically for the archive, the historical record ends with no extant written conclusion to the incident, except that Juan de Salamanca, the vicar general, sided with the nuns in a December 24 memorandum ordering Mata to return the books or face imprisonment.

The surviving documentation of this 1610 conflict thus leaves us with more questions than answers: Why did Salamanca side with the nuns? Did Mata give the books back after all? We can assemble some plausible conclusions by applying our knowledge of liturgical concerns, the matter of music ownership and practice, collaboration among musicians in New Spain, and nuns' agency. It is worth speculating over these issues, even if the porous historical record fails to cooperate further, because this account is one of the earliest handwritten historical documents about nuns' music making and their networks in New Spain.[5]

Aside from the conflict, we can appreciate the one-to-one personal collaboration between convent musicians and cathedral musicians and assume that such borrowing—and returning—between people like Sister Flor and Mata was reproduced across many religious institutions for the flourishing of liturgical music programs. The musical networks in New Spain traversed by Mata and the Encarnación nuns reached far beyond the borders of individual cities. Convents in Mexico City, for example, used music composed by chapel masters from nearby Puebla, and Mexico City musicians supplied their music compositions to convents in Puebla. The Encarnación convent was known for recruiting women musicians from outside the region and other cities, and especially from Puebla. This exchange of musicians modeled the networking for the establishment of convents, whereby nuns from one cloister would set off to another cloister in the same city or a different one, either to establish a new community of nuns in the same order or to profess in another order.

The details of the Encarnación convent's singers and ensembles are lost forever, and yet the mention of needing notated music to perform villancicos presupposes that the convent maintained certain performing forces. We can imagine a choir with the skills to sing plainchant for sure, required of all convent choirs, and polyphony as suggested by the presence of books containing multi-voiced villancicos. The convent likely housed competent instrumentalists to accompany the music, as was typical for the execution of both polyphony and plainchant. Moreover, this notarial record also confirms that the Encarnación convent nuns customarily sang villancicos even as no remnants of villancico manuscripts from this convent have come to light. Records of the archbishop of Mexico City's visit to the convent decades later, in 1673, document the nuns' financial investment in musical resources, including notated music and a listing of villancico purchases.[6] The nuns of 1610 ultimately won the legal battle because, most likely, their convent had purchased the books for their liturgies. No other explanation can account for their presumed victory—the vicar general's support—in the documentation.

Given the nature of his defense, Mata clearly considered the music his property. His statement conveys an indifferent assumption that he was not subject to the nuns' demands. Yet, given the events that occurred after the Encarnación nuns' denunciation, we can infer that he returned the books in time for the convent's Christmas liturgies and that the incident did not tarnish his reputation. In 1614, Mata assumed the responsibilities of chapel master of Mexico City cathedral and was promoted with the full title upon the previous chapel master Juan Hernández's retirement in 1618.[7] Mata remained in the post until he died in 1643.

Could Mata's apology to the nuns eventually have come in musical form? More polyphonic music for the Mass and liturgies of Holy Week at the Encarnación survives in six choirbooks at the Newberry Library in Chicago, supporting the convent's ensemble proposed earlier. These choirbooks include some works attributed to Mata, evidence of yet another direct connection between this composer and this convent. Copied within Mata's lifetime in the Encarnación choirbooks are his four-voice St. Luke Passion and an eight-voice setting of the antiphon *Asperges me*.[8] The latter contains no fewer than three utterances of *misericordiam* (mercy), passed back and forth between two choirs (see example in Appendix 1.1). Sung at the start of most Masses throughout the liturgical year, this penitential antiphon speaks of the washing away of sin while the priest, sprinkling water upon the congregants gathered in the church, ritually enacts the text and commemorates everyone's Baptism. Still, in a society so concerned with salvation, such cleansing rituals were not enough to guarantee salvation. The intercession of cloistered nuns was critical for salvation as well.

As such, very little might distress a high-ranking cleric more than knowing that nuns under his jurisdiction were being prevented from performing their liturgical duties, singing for salvation. We will encounter more evidence of the vital need for convent music performance in Chapter 3, where we will look at how nuns sought to recruit musicians for their convents free of dowry waivers. Furthermore, in 1712, another group of Conceptionists in Mexico City, the Jesús María convent nuns, sponsored the publication of a devotional guidebook written by the renowned Jesuit confessor—of Sor Juana, archbishops, and viceroys no less—Antonio Núñez de Miranda, in which he tells the nuns to learn music perfectly ("aprendais perfectamente música") and sing and play as many instruments as possible to praise God and to serve well in the convent liturgies.[9] And around 1815, some two hundred years after the Mata-Encarnación conflict, Archbishop de Fonte y Hernández summarized his visits to the Encarnación convent, in which he encouraged all the nuns to learn to sing the Office well, stating that "no other thing will please their husband [Christ] more than praising him with a song that he likes."[10] These examples are a far cry from supposed bans on convent music imposed by the Council of Trent (1545–1563), a matter we now know was left for local bishops to decide.[11] The Hispanic Church clearly supported, and even encouraged, nuns' musical activities for the liturgies. Liturgical music in women's convents was indispensable for the salvation of humanity.

Thus, Sisters Flor de Santa Clara and Francisca de Jesús at the Encarnación were willing to fight for the return of their music books. They depended on them to sing and could not sit quietly by, allowing themselves to be taken advantage of by a priest-musician who knew the nuns could not simply leave their cloister to chase him down for the books. And notaries were at the ready to aid nuns in their networking with the urban community.[12]

This chapter attends to conflicts around music and sound whose resolutions steered toward the path of salvation, such as the one between the

Encarnación nuns and Mata. The causes of the conflicts can be practical, as we just experienced, but they can also be personal; they can be embodied; and they can be doctrinal, as we will see by diving deeply into the history of the doctrine of the Immaculate Conception. By focusing on conflicts whose resolutions steered toward the ideal path of salvation, through the intercession of cloistered nuns, this chapter argues that nuns' voices, music, and bodies were intimately tied to the doctrine of the Immaculate Conception.

Throughout the early modern period, Church leaders in New Spain had an obsessive desire to confirm the validity of the Virgin Mary's exclusion from original sin, that is, her Immaculate Conception. This doctrine had its own history of conflict, one resolved with politics and propagated in New Spanish convents through notions of aurality and musicality tied to virginity and the virginal Incarnation of Christ. Nuns were required to believe in this doctrine upon professing as full black-veil choir nuns throughout the seventeenth and eighteenth centuries. Some orders required separate oaths defending the doctrine with spoken voice and hands (pen-to-paper signatures), while some nuns even offered their bodies as collateral, wishing to die lest the Virgin Mary be identified as anything other than immaculately conceived.[13]

The Immaculate Conception of the Virgin Mary was a complicated doctrine that defied logic.[14] As we will see, the Immaculate Conception would be bolstered in New Spain by the arrival of the first nuns in the sixteenth century under the title Order of the Immaculate Conception, out of which all other orders of cloistered nuns trickled out to form more convent communities across New Spain. The artistic and devotional creations fostered in and for cloistered convents where women vowed to model the Virgin's purity were especially meaningful given the nuns' gender-normative parallel as spiritual wives and mothers to Christ, female roles that male clerics did not embody.[15] Disclosing the virginity status of male religious was also not of prime concern for the Church the way it was for nuns, a phenomenon that in some orders was expressed musically.[16]

The virginity status and racial status of women wishing to profess in a convent were automatically adjudicated by the Church's doctrinal and liturgical prescriptions. In other words, to the extent that the bodies of indigenous women and non-virgin women (such as widows) wishing to profess as nuns were in conflict with the Church's ideal for the brides of Christ, we will see how that embodied conflict was sublimated to yield more intercessors for salvation. We will observe how musical virginity was echoed in Marian devotion, not least devotion to the Immaculate Conception, sermonized to nuns as music from God's very mouth at the Creation, carrying God's Word made flesh—Christ.

If such messages in printed sermons, which circulated through all New Spanish convents, were taken to heart, we can imagine Sister Flor de Santa Clara urgently needing the convent's missing music books to sing Christ, the savior, to life on Christmas. This song would be consistent with the Virgin Mary's vocal message remaining in humanity's auditory imagination via recitation and singing of her prophetic words in the *Magnificat*, singing words surrounding her miraculous virginity as narrated in scripture, and singing devotional music dedicated to extolling her essence. As we will see, auditory imagination, a component of reading in which lectors imagine an author's voice, precisely because reading is closely tied to hearing,[17] would aptly apply to the veiled voices of New Spain's cloistered co-redeemers.

Conceptions

The founding of the Order of the Immaculate Conception (Conceptionists) at the end of the fifteenth century in Toledo, Spain, was no less political than the doctrine for which this order of cloistered nuns was named (see Table 1.1). Beatriz de Silva (1424–1492) founded the Conceptionists with unwavering support from the Franciscan Archbishop of Toledo Francisco Jiménez de Cisneros and Queen Isabel I of Castile. They both wrote to Pope Innocent VIII pressing him to establish the order.[18] The close relationship among Beatriz, the archbishop, and the queen suggests that favoritism might have been involved in the order's founding. Cisneros was Isabel's confessor, and Beatriz was a good friend to the queen. In 1484, Isabel donated a property in Toledo for the Conceptionist foundational cloister. The property continues to serve as the Mother House grounds for Beatriz's order to this day. Not only did the establishment of this new order serve as a public testament to Isabel of Castile's defense of the doctrine of the Immaculate Conception, but it also fulfilled Beatriz's divinely inspired purpose to establish an order of nuns named after this Marian advocation.

The Conceptionist order's foundation was not without supposed divine intervention. Prior to befriending Isabel of Castile and moving to Toledo, Beatriz was a lady in waiting for Queen Isabel of Portugal. According to legend, Beatriz was locked in a trunk for three days because the Portuguese Isabel was jealous of Beatriz's good looks; she was known to be a very

Table 1.1 Timeline of foundational events for the Order of the Immaculate
Conception

1424	Beatriz de Silva born in Cueta, Portugal
1447	Beatriz becomes a lady in waiting for Queen Isabel of Portugal
1453	Beatriz joins the Royal Santo Domingo Convent in Toledo, Spain, following a vision of the Virgin Mary
1484	Queen Isabel I of Castile gifts property for Beatriz to establish a convent with twelve other women
1489	Conceptionists established under Cistercian rule with Pope Innocent VIII's bull *Inter universa*
1492	Beatriz dies and Felipa de Silva, her niece, continues as abbess of the Toledo Mother House
1494	Conceptionists begin following Franciscan rule ordered by *Ex supernae providentia* bull
1508	Conceptionist breviary developed by Ambrosio Montesino
1511	Conceptionist rule created by Fray Francisco Quiñones and approved by Pope Julius II in *Ad statum prosperum* bull
1516	Conceptionist Ordinances appended to the rule

beautiful young woman, references to her beauty playing into the narrative of sacrifice associated with becoming a nun.[19] Indeed, a beautiful woman of her class would be assumed to have no trouble finding a suitable spouse. And so, the fact that she eventually chose to lock her beautiful body up in a cloistered convent played into the Church's rhetoric of sacrifice.

Blas Fernández de Mesa dramatized Beatriz's conflict in his 1664 comedy *La fundadora de la santa concepción*, which focuses on a vision Beatriz had while trapped in the trunk. This vision was the event that prompted the foundation of the Conceptionists. Within the dark confines of a trunk, Beatriz saw the Virgin Mary, whose presence gave her an assuring message. Beatriz recalls the Virgin dressed in white and blue, informing Beatriz that she would survive her torture and come out of the trunk to become a vigorous defender of the doctrine of the Immaculate Conception as founder of an order of nuns named after this Marian doctrine.[20]

The dramatic version of her story was only partially true. The official history of Beatriz's life, documented in various reprints of the Conceptionist

Order's rule, tells that the Virgin communicated to her without speaking, simply appearing dressed in blue and white. This version in the rule books also narrates another of Beatriz's visions: after she got out of the trunk, she fled Isabel of Portugal's court, and en route to Toledo she heard two men dressed as Franciscan friars call to her in Portuguese, greatly frightening her, as she thought they were the queen's henchmen out to murder her. Instead, they informed her that she would be the mother of many daughters without losing her virginity, a model of the Virgin Mary indeed.[21] She realized that they were actual friars, the two most important Franciscan male saints no less, St. Francis himself and St. Anthony of Padua. Their appearance before her and their message made Beatriz understand that the order of nuns she was to establish should be dedicated to the Immaculate Conception.[22]

Why would the mere presence of Franciscans signal to Beatriz that the order she would found should be dedicated to the Immaculate Conception? The answer lies in the doctrine's origins and history. By the time Beatriz founded the Conceptionists with royal and papal backing, the Marian title "Immaculate Conception" had gained great admiration across Iberian lands since the introduction of the doctrine in 1218. At its fundamental core, the Immaculate Conception centers on the concept of original sin, which stems from Adam and Eve's disobedience and subsequent casting out of the Garden of Eden, as narrated in the Book of Genesis.

In Genesis 2:16–17, Adam and Eve live freely in the Garden, except that they are prohibited from eating the fruit of the tree of knowledge of good and evil. In the following chapter, a snake entices Eve to eat of the forbidden fruit, and Eve convinces Adam to do so as well, which prompts them to notice their nakedness and to hide from God's presence when he calls on them after their sinful consumption. They are subsequently banished from Eden: Adam is destined to toil for his sustenance, and Eve becomes subject to her husband's domination and is told that she will suffer childbirth pains in the future. The snake, as the archetype of sin, is threatened to be crushed under the foot of a "woman," interpreted by Christians as the Virgin Mary, who gave birth to the savior, the conqueror of sin.[23]

Other parallels emerged within patristic texts and beyond. Early Christianity established the Virgin Mary to have birthed Christ without pain.[24] Christ was thought to have been incarnated by the Holy Spirit entering the Virgin Mary through her ear, which can be read against the idea of Eve's sinfulness being initiated when she heard the serpent's message and used her voice to tempt Adam, thus adding an aural and oral component to the downfall.[25] In the biography of Sister María Anna Águeda de San Ignacio (1696–1756), the first prioress of Puebla's Santa Rosa convent, the biographer José Bellido reminds readers in the chapter on María Anna's Marian devotion that just as Adam was assisted in humanity's downfall by Eve, so too was Christ assisted in its redemption by a woman, the Virgin Mary, as a co-redeemer.[26]

Yet as a counternarrative, less so to Mary's elevation than to Eve's downfall, Gloria Anzaldúa interprets Eve psychoanalytically as an inventor of consciousness, "the sense of self in the act of knowing," indeed of realizing "carnal knowledge," as evidenced by the perception of being naked after her consumption of the fruit.[27] Such consciousness did not escape Mary's understanding of the functions of the flesh, as can be ascertained from the Annunciation narrative when she questioned the announcement that she would give birth to the son of God by remarking on her own virginity: "I have no knowledge of man" (Luke 1:34). The critical contrast thus comes in the distinction between the sounds that both virgin women received.[28] The sounds that penetrated Eve's ear, the voice of the snake that caused her to disobey and therefore to lead a life of lost virginity and painful procreation, were simply vibrations carrying uttered words.[29] The sound that entered Mary, by contrast, was the Holy Spirit bringing in God's Word—Jesus, the Word of God made flesh (John 1:1)—that in entering Mary's body through her ear preserved her virginity and yielded an unconsciousness to sexuality.[30]

As we will see, this discursive element, together with Mary's vocal consent to the Incarnation (her vow of obedience), would seem to be the seminal justification for sonifying virginity in some of the convent sources examined later. The Incarnation narrative also supported the sonification of Mary herself as the embodiment of virginity, "revealing," as Leigh Schmidt instructs, "the axial Christian exchange between body and soul, fleshly obedience and divine revelation," in the doctrine of the Immaculate Conception.[31] Christ's Incarnation became inseparable from devotion to the Virgin Mary, as implied by the Marian devotional title Our Lady of the Incarnation—the namesake for the Encarnación convent where Sister Flor de Santa Clara resided and fought for her choir's villancicos. The miraculous Incarnation was especially significant in Franciscan spirituality.[32]

Another central point of Catholic doctrine held that humanity's "first parents," Adam and Eve, had bequeathed their sin upon all people, known as original sin, requiring the sacrament of Baptism for absolution. Therefore, the Virgin Mary's humanity undoubtedly raised questions as to whether she too had inherited Adam and Eve's sin. Two theories arose concerning the Virgin Mary's association with original sin. Maculists believed that Mary was conceived with original sin but was delivered from it—or sanctified—in her mother's womb. The immaculist theory took more time to develop.[33] In the fifteenth century, it was thought that Mary's parents, St. Joachim and St. Anne, conceived Mary chastely through God's miraculous handiwork; artists attempted to capture this moment by painting Mary's parents embracing at the Golden Gate of Jerusalem.[34] Through divine intervention, immaculists came to argue, Mary thus avoided obtaining original sin as inherited by all human offspring conceived through copulation. By the sixteenth century, it was established that Mary's body was conceived through ordinary human intercourse, but that her parents did not experience lust. God kept Mary free from sin altogether at the instant her soul was created in time immemorial at the Creation, preceding Adam and Eve's downfall.[35]

The honoring of and devotion to Mary's Immaculate Conception was not ubiquitously celebrated within the Catholic Church; it had its skeptics. Members of the Dominican and Franciscan orders entered the maculist-immaculist conflict on opposite sides, with Dominican theologians upholding the maculist opinion and Franciscans becoming vehement defenders of the Immaculate Conception, eventually naming the Immaculate Virgin Mary a patron saint of their order and promoting the doctrine in every way publicly. Hence, Beatriz's commitment to establishing the Conceptionists came upon her realization that it was St. Francis and St. Anthony who were talking to her on the way to Toledo. Any kind of Marian devotion suggested by Franciscans would undoubtedly have to be immaculist by custom.

The official proclamation from Rome defining Mary's immaculacy with certainty remained unheard, as even the 1546 session of the Council of Trent avoided specifying how the Virgin Mary had been conceived. By the seventeenth century, impatient immaculist supporters, particularly in Spain, began to pressure the Church for an official definition of the Immaculate Conception.[36] Meanwhile, defense of the Immaculate Conception continued to abound in typical Catholic ways, big and small: from the aforementioned extraordinary royal support for Beatriz de Silva's founding of the Order of the Immaculate Conception to universities requiring oaths from its faculty and students swearing defense of the doctrine; from naming churches and chapels after the doctrine to patronizing artwork dedicated to the Immaculate Conception. Royal support from the Spanish monarchs continued almost as if out of hereditary tradition, with the strongest lobbying to

Rome for papal decree of an immaculist doctrine coming from King Philip IV.[37] As a result, Pope Alexander VII conceded to the immaculists in 1661, officially defining Mary's Immaculate Conception in the apostolic legislation of *Sollicitudo omnium ecclesiarum*:

> The devotion of Christ's faithful toward the Virgin Mary, His most blessed mother, is ancient, according to which they believe that by a special grace and privilege of God her soul was preserved immune from the stain of original sin from the first instant of its creation and infusion into the body in view of the merits of her son Jesus Christ, the Redeemer of the human race, and in this sense honor and celebrate the feast of her conception.[38]

Support for the Immaculate Conception was from its inception contentious and political in Spain and elsewhere in Europe.[39] Not surprisingly, Mesa's play, centered on Beatriz's founding of the Conceptionists, came out in 1664, shortly after Alexander VII's bull solidified the doctrine. That same year, the Church in Spain was granted permission by the pope to celebrate the Immaculate Conception liturgies.

Among the many allegorical pictures honoring Philip's life in Isidro Sariñana's 1665 *Llanto del occidente*, one image shows him singing to the Virgin Mary of the Immaculate Conception (Figure 1.1). The Virgin Mary appears, hair down, hands folded, standing over a globe, cape flowing in the air—key symbols in her Immaculate Conception iconography. The Virgin stands almost dreamlike out of a cloud at the far left, the definition of her Immaculate Conception a dream come to realization for Philip and all immaculist zealots, a fruition worthy of dancing for joy. Below her, a banner displays the solmization syllables *Sol Fax Mi Rex*. The descending tetrachord has a double meaning here: *Sol Fax Mi Rex* stands for "Sun Torch My King" (*Sol hacha Mi Rey*)—a bit of a play on spelling and words on Sariñana's part (*fax* meaning *hacha*/torch in Latin). In this way, he explains that the Virgin would no doubt respond to the king's gestures in song.[40] Her brief song acknowledges that the sovereign is the torchbearer of a light of truth as bright as the sun to illuminate the doctrine of the Immaculate Conception, now clearly defined by the Church, for all to understand.[41]

Because of Philip's insistence that the pope specifically deem immaculate the Virgin Mary's conception, which lead to the bull of 1661, believers were, thereafter, able to sing the Immaculate Conception's praises free of any doubts. The engraving thus shows the king standing in the manner of a

Figure 1.1 Philip IV serenades the Immaculate Conception. Courtesy of the
Getty Research Institute

courtly dance pose with his feet forming a ninety-degree angle, a reverential
sign of respect before and after a dance.[42] The pose harks back to King David
worshiping God in dance before the Ark of the Covenant (2 Samuel 6:14–
15).[43] He gestures with his right hand extended toward the Virgin, as if he
were a chapel master directing the invisible ensemble of Catholic humanity
in singing Mary's immaculacy loudly and unabashedly, notes Sariñana.
But Philip IV also holds his left hand to his lips, giving a hushing signal,
signifying that all naysayers against the Virgin's Immaculate Conception—
such as the Dominicans—would henceforth not be able to contradict immaculacy.[44] Sariñana thus allegorized the king as a fine musician, one who
knew how to manipulate appropriate moments of sound and silence for musical effect, prompting the Virgin to resonate in sympathy and gratitude for
the quieting of the maculists and any other skeptics.[45] This would not be the
last time that music was used as a metaphor in support of the Immaculate
Conception.

Of course, by the time of Philip IV's intervention, Conceptionist nuns had
been swearing oaths to the doctrine and singing the Immaculate Conception's

praises and Office for some 175 years. This devotional gesture was granted to Beatriz de Silva and her new order thanks to her sovereign connections and ties with the ever-immaculist Franciscans.[46] It was Ambrosio Montesino, the famed Franciscan poet of Isabel of Castile's court, who is credited with developing the breviary containing all the texts and hymns for the Office and Mass of the Immaculate Conception in Toledo, circa 1508.[47] Because prior to receiving their own rule in 1511 the Conceptionists followed the Franciscan rule, a proper Conceptionist breviary would have given the order a greater sense of independence, as Beatriz de Silva desired. No copy of this first breviary survives, save for an updated version from 1551, which indicates that the Office was only to be performed on simple days and non-festal Sundays in addition to, and not a substitution for, the regular Divine Office to be performed from the Roman breviary in accordance with the Franciscan tradition.[48]

However, the Franciscan friars retained no administrative control over Conceptionist convents. Since their establishment, the Conceptionists remained under the supervision of a local bishop and not male regulars. In other words, there were no male Conceptionist friars or monks. But even after receiving their own rule in 1511, the Conceptionists held some honorary links to the Franciscan order. The Conceptionist rule itself, after all, had been confirmed by the Franciscan-educated Pope Julius II, and the appended 1516 ordinances were developed by the Franciscan Provincial of Castile.[49] The feast of St. Francis consequently was considered a major feast for Conceptionists. Early modern Franciscan literature on the order's history always considered the Conceptionists a branch of their order in both Spain and its dominions.[50] For example, upon the founding of the first Conceptionist convent in Mexico City, the Purísima Concepción convent, the Franciscan chronicler Augustín de Vetancurt (1620–1700) writes that this cloister was the first of the Order of St. Francis established in New Spain.[51] Similarly, in a 1787 catalogue of Mexico City indulgences, Fray José de Ávila lumps Conceptionist convent churches together with Franciscan churches in a list of places for penitents to visit to gain plenary indulgence on the feast of the Franciscan protomartyrs.[52] Perhaps not so coincidentally, Mexico City's Confraternity of St. Francis was based in the Conceptionist convent of Regina Coeli, where the confraternity celebrated a lavish Mass with a sermon, whose publication was paid for by the Regina Coeli nuns themselves as patrons of the confraternity.[53] And, as has already been alluded to, even the initial arrival of the Conceptionists in the Americas is attributed to the bequest of an influential Franciscan, the first bishop of Mexico City, Fray Juan de Zumárraga.[54]

New Spanish Conceptions, Disseminations, and Soundscapes

The nuns of the Purísima Concepción convent in Mexico City prided themselves on being the first cloistered convent in New Spain, frequently signing their documents with the addendum of "oldest convent in the city."[55] Table 1.2 lists all the convents in New Spain, starting with the cities with the largest number of convents. Other orders of nuns in New Spain branched out from the Conceptionists, such as the Carmelites, Hieronymites, and Franciscans, who themselves founded other convents and more orders, and they expanded into other cities too. For example, the Augustinians were founded from the Hieronymites, and the Dominicans in Oaxaca were established when Franciscans were called to teach the beatas of the Santísimo Rosario how to chant, eventually leading to their full profession as Dominican nuns in 1576.[56] Yet Mexico City's Purísima Concepción convent itself is noted for having fostered the highest number of founding nuns who established other convents.[57]

After the Conceptionists, the Bridgettines and the Company of Mary were the only orders whose founding mothers came from Spain.[58] Sister María Ignacia Azlor y Echevers (1715–1767), founder of New Spain's Company of Mary, was born in New Spain to Spanish aristocrats, then she left for Spain in 1737 to profess in the Company, later bringing this order to Mexico City.[59] In 1752, Sister María Ignacia established the Virgen del Pilar convent in Mexico City, colloquially called the Enseñanza Antigua ("Old Teaching") because of the Company of Mary's emphasis on teaching. This was not her first time in Mexico City, despite having been born in the remote north of New Spain in what is now the state of Coahuila, then part of greater Texas (*Provincia de los Texas* [*sic*]).[60] From 1734, she lived in Mexico City's Purísima Concepción convent after her father died, leaving her orphaned; her mother had passed away the year before that.[61] The nuns of the Enseñanza Antigua convent that she founded published a biography of María Ignacia in 1793, which, among other things, notes that she was a talented musician and assisted the nuns of the Purísima Concepción convent when she lived there by accompanying the choir on violon during the liturgies.[62] Her choice to profess in the Company of Mary in Spain was to satisfy her deceased parents'—especially

Table 1.2 New Spanish convent establishments, drawn from Asunción Lavrin's *Brides of Christ*, 359–361

City and Convent	Religious Order	Foundation Date
Mexico City		
Purísima Concepción	Conceptionist	1540
Regina Coeli	Conceptionist	1573
Santa Clara	Franciscan	1573
Jesús María	Conceptionist	1581
San Jerónimo	Hieronymite	1585
Nuestra Señora de la Encarnación	Conceptionist	1593
Santa Catalina de Siena	Dominican	1593
Santa Inés	Conceptionist	1596
San Juan de la Penitencia	Franciscan	1598
San Lorenzo	Augustinian	1598
Santa Isabel	Franciscan	1601
San José de Gracia	Conceptionist	1610
Santa Teresa la Antigua/San José	Carmelite	1616
Nuestra Señora de la Balvanera	Conceptionist	1634
San Bernardo	Conceptionist	1636
San Felipe de Jesús	Franciscan Capuchin	1666
Santa Teresa la Nueva	Carmelite	1700
Corpus Christi	Franciscan	1724
Santa Brígida	Brigittine	1735
La Enseñanza Antigua (Virgen del Pilar)	Company of Mary	1752
Nuestra Señora de Guadalupe	Franciscan Capuchin	1780
La Enseñanza Nueva (Guadalupe)	Company of Mary	1811
Puebla		
Santa Catalina de Siena	Dominican	1568
Purísima Concepción	Conceptionist	1593
San Jerónimo	Hieronymite	1597
Santa Teresa	Carmelite	1601
Santa Clara	Franciscan	1607
Santísima Trinidad	Conceptionist	1619
Santa Inés de Montepulciano	Dominican	1620
Santa Mónica	Augustinian	1686
Santa Ana	Franciscan Capuchin	1704
Santa Rosa	Dominican	1735
Soledad	Carmelite	1747

(*continued*)

Table 1.2 Continued

City and Convent	Religious Order	Foundation Date
Oaxaca		
Santa Catalina de Siena	Dominican	1576
Regina Coeli	Conceptionist	1576
Santa Mónica	Augustinian	1697
San José	Franciscan	1744
Nuestra Señora de los Ángeles	Franciscan	1768
Guadalajara		
Purísima Concepción	Conceptionist	1578
Santa María de Gracia	Dominican	1588
Santa Teresa	Carmelite	1695
Santa Mónica	Augustinian	1718
Jesús María	Dominican	1719
San Ignacio de Loyola (Concepción)	Franciscan	1761
Querétaro		
Santa Clara de Jesús	Franciscan	1607
San José de Gracia	Franciscan Capuchin	1717
Nuestra Señora del Carmen	Carmelite	1803
Valladolid (Morelia)		
Santa Catalina de Siena	Dominican	1595
Nuestra Señora de Cosamaloapán	Franciscan	1737
San Cristóbal de las Casas		
Nuestra Señora de la Encarnación	Conceptionist	1595
Mérida		
Nuestra Señora de la Consolación	Conceptionist	1596
Villa de Carrión-Atlixco (Atrisco)		
Santa Clara	Franciscan	1618
Pátzcuaro		
María Inmaculada de la Salud	Dominican	1744
San Miguel el Grande (de Allende)		
Purísima Concepción	Conceptionist	1754
Santa María de los Lagos		
San José	Franciscan Capuchin	1756
Salvatierra		
La Purísima y San Francisco	Franciscan Capuchin	1767
Irapuato		
Nuestra Señora de la Soledad	Company of Mary	1804
Aguascalientes		
Nuestra Señora de Guadalupe	Company of Mary	1807

her mother's—wishes,[63] but she selected Mexico City's Purísima Concepción convent before moving to Spain to take her vows primarily because of her personal devotion to the Immaculate Conception.[64] Allegiance to this doctrine was no doubt also the primary reason why the first convents in New Spain had been established under the Order of the Immaculate Conception, almost two hundred years prior to María Ignacia's brief stint in Mexico City's first and oldest convent.[65] All convents and orders that developed from this first convent to cloister women throughout New Spain would likely swear an oath of allegiance to the doctrine of the Immaculate Conception.[66]

Established in 1540 by Mexico City's first bishop, Juan de Zumárraga, the Purísima Concepción convent foundation was preceded by some ten years of unsuccessful attempts to form live-in schools for Spanish laywomen to teach the daughters of Spaniards and to indoctrinate indigenous women.[67] The conflicts resulting in the failed attempts to found the schools were personal and cultural, as would be expected within the gendered power imbalance the Spanish patriarchy sought to instill. Many of the women did not want to live outside their homes.

Moreover, the Spanish curriculum was at odds with the value the indigenous Nahua community placed on women performing hard labor alongside their husbands.[68] The curriculum educated women to become pious household caretakers, and, thus, Nahua men were finding Spanish-educated indigenous women less suitable for marriage.[69] Concerned that the education of indigenous women would negatively impact Christian practices of marriage among indigenous peoples, the Spanish Crown rejected all forms of live-in schooling for indigenous women.

Live-in schooling was allowed to continue for Spanish women following European models. Yet, as cultural historian Pilar Gonzalbo Aizpuru attests, "to talk about women's education in colonial times is to refer to everyday life."[70] Reading, writing, arithmetic, sewing, and cooking skills were learned by seeing and doing and were not taught purposefully with a curriculum. The arrival of the Company of Mary in the eighteenth century with its main purpose as a teaching order has thus been characterized as a revolution in women's education.[71]

As the Spanish community in New Spain grew, the need emerged for the "Old World" tradition of securing women's reputations through belief in the theology of containment, in which women were required to have "a husband or a wall" around them to guard their honor, as Craig Monson puts it bluntly.[72] Cloistered convents served as institutions of basic learning for young women and provided them with the option to become fully professed nuns. The Spanish were not quick to forget the spiritual benefits disbursed by cloistered convents in sixteenth-century Spain, the saving power of cloistered nuns' intercessions.[73] In the absence of a prospective husband in the same or a higher class, or for families who could not afford expensive dowries for their daughters to contract a marriage, becoming a nun maintained a woman's virginity and the social status of her family while providing spiritual prestige, a notion we will come back to later.[74] Some twenty years after the establishment of the Purísima Concepción convent, the Mexico City council wrote to Philip II imploring the Spanish king's financial support to expand the convent church and cloister, which the community had outgrown, meanwhile claiming that the city had some two thousand virgin women unable to secure marriage and who had expressed a desire to become nuns.[75]

The Purísima Concepción convent eventually received the funding for its enlargement through patronage from the Crown, giving it royal designation, a title given to just three other convents in New Spain: the Jesús María in Mexico City, Querétaro's Santa Clara convent, and La Purísima Concepción in San Miguel.[76] The Jesús María convent was famous for supposedly housing Philip II's illegitimate daughter Micaela de los Ángeles, according to Carlos de Sigüenza y Góngora's grand history of that cloister, *Parayso occidental* (1684), in which he speculates over the convent's reception of royal patronage around the time of her arrival.[77] Indeed, Micaela would have been the great aunt of our immaculist zealot Philip IV, and she had previously been cloistered in the Purísima Concepción convent before arriving at Jesús María.

Unlike the other two royal convents, the Purísima Concepción still struggled with overpopulation, with as many as two hundred nuns in 1592. This number does not include their servants—many of them poor Spanish women who could not afford profession, indigenous women, or enslaved African women—or the young women living there under the nuns' tutelage.[78] This might explain the haste with which the number of convents in the city doubled from 1593 to 1598, a relatively short time compared to the thirty-plus years it took to establish the four convents that followed the Purísima Concepción (see Table 1.1).

Evidence of music making in sixteenth-century convents is rare, but so far two sources have been found to exist. A reference to a 1577 Dominican profession ceremony in Oaxaca's Santa Catalina de Siena convent, in which ten novices sang their profession vows ("todas hicieron su profesión cantada"), is cited by Josefina Muriel as evidence of music performance in the early period of New Spanish conventual life.[79] Another source is in an encomiastic poem that singles out the heavenly sonority from Mexico City's Purísima Concepción convent around 1598. In his collection of pastoral poetry *Siglo de oro en las selvas de Erífile* (1608), Bernardo de Balbuena (1568–1627)—the future bishop of San Juan, Puerto Rico, and a capable poet—lauds Mexico City's many monastic institutions within the book's eighth and final chapter. Each convent receives a three-line stanza of eleven syllables in chain verse. On the Purísima Concepción, which begins his almost chronological poetic list of ten convents, he writes,

La Límpia Concepción, cuyas gargantas	The Immaculate Conception [convent], whose throats
Suenan a cielo, y en aqueste fueron	Sound like heaven, and in this were the
De sus vergeles las primeras plantas.	first plants in the gardens of this [city].[80]

Manuel Ramírez Aparicio quotes these verses in his 1861 history of Mexican convents closed as a result of the Reform Laws to suggest that Balbuena enjoyed the music performed by the nuns in the convent church, in which "the daughters of this convent distinguished themselves above all through music."[81] Balbuena's poetry stops with the San Lorenzo convent, founded in 1598. Although *Siglo de oro* was published in 1608, the poetry includes no mention of the Santa Isabel convent, established in 1601. Thus, we can safely assume that his poetry is referring to, at the earliest, a late sixteenth-century musical—vocal—tradition at the Purísima Concepción convent.

Balbuena's use of the word *gargantas* (literally "throats") maintains the rhyme scheme with *plantas*, which *voces*—"voices," his actual meaning—would not do. He could have also used *músicas* but chose not to. His poeticizing of the throat, the human anatomical structure where voice is created, thus re-embodies those heavenly sounding veiled voices—invisible to lay parishioners attending the liturgies in the convent church, as we will see in the next chapter. This relationship between throat and voice follows the Aristotelian model that the throat is the instrument of voice, a notion widely held throughout the early modern period.[82] Thus, Balbuena fulfills the pastoral task he set forth, versifying the body with allusions to garden greenery in the long tradition following from the Song of Songs.[83]

Botanical metaphors for cloistered convents remained in the pen of devotional writers throughout the seventeenth century and beyond. The complete title to Carlos de Sigüenza y Gongora's 1684 *Parayso occidental*, on the history of Mexico City's Jesús María convent, is revealing in this regard and shows Balbuena's influence: "Occidental Paradise: Planted and Cultivated by the Liberal and Beneficent Hand of the Very Catholic and Powerful Sovereigns of Spain, our Lords, within their Magnificent Royal Convent of Jesús María in México."[84] It was common for the archbishop of Mexico City and the vicereine to visit the convent to enjoy the fruits of their administrative labor, especially coming to hear the nuns sing and to take refreshments in the beautiful patios and gardens within the cloister.[85] This was even more symbolically important because the vicereine and her husband represented the convent's most illustrious patrons, the Spanish king and queen.

In 1698, inspired by his friend Sigüenza y Góngora, the Franciscan Agustín de Vetancurt spoke proudly about Mexico City's cloistered convents with similar references to flora and talk of the arts and senses, conflating them with militaristic imagery:

> The prayers of prudent virgins and brides of Jesus are like armies of angels arranged by choirs, [who are] appalling to hell and beautiful to heaven; in nuns' convents God has established His prisons and in them formed armies who suppress the rigors of God with their prayers that soothe and pay homage to the Divine Justice, obliging Him to distribute His mercy; they are an affront to the infernal enemies, dishonor of their deceitfulness, because it is divinity's elegance to conquer with lilies, to triumph with roses, to subject giant demons with women doves! There are no words with which to ponder the majesty celebrated with the Divine Cult, music, fragrances, the greatness of their temples, cleanliness of the altars, and participation in their choirs.[86]

His direct quote from the antiphon for the Common of Virgins, "Prudent virgins" (*Prudentis virginis*),[87] conflates liturgical music with real-life praise for women opting for the salvation-generating conventual life, in which they obliged God to distribute mercy—prudent like the virgins in the parable the antiphon glosses (Matthew 25:1–13). The devotional arts fostered in the convent walls were allegorized as flowers produced by virgin plants. On the one hand, Vetancurt harnesses aesthetic enjoyment to proselytize to female readers or listeners. On the other, together with Balbuena and Góngora, Vetancurt is propagating an agenda *criolla*, in which those born in New Spain of Spanish parents (*criollos*) would self-promote their native land as being as pious as the king's Old Spain and as paradisiacal as the Old

Testament Eden of Adam and Eve.[88] The cloistering of women, presented as essential for the salvation of society, was nothing new, nor was their consistent oversight by male clergy, whether for literary reasons or administrative concerns (as we will see shortly with examples from the archbishop's visits to the convents).

Yet women subscribed to the garden metaphors as well.[89] The 1720 accounting of all the living and deceased nuns at the convent of Santa Clara de Atlixco (now a suburb of Puebla), written by its abbess Sister Leonor de San Antonio, refers to the cloister as a "garden of the Lord."[90] We can also imagine nuns' extant manuscripts as verdant art gardens simulated with doodles and drawings of flora and fauna that the nuns would have admired in their own convent gardens. In Appendix 1.2, several decorated initial letters signal the start of the individual voice parts of the polyphonic works, bringing outdoor life into the more private interior of the nuns' music books. Appropriately, there are snakes depicted around a *Salve Regina* setting, reminiscent of the Virgin Mary's conquering of sin (see Appendix 1.2).

To nuns, their cloistered gardens also had another personal connection to the Virgin Mary, who was allegorically titled *hortus conclusus* (enclosed garden),[91] in reference to her virginal purity, and was often depicted with various other attributes drawn from the Litany of Loretto, the Book of Sirach, the Song of Songs, and Genesis. The attributes, including titles like "tower of David," "sealed fountain," "thornless rose," and "lily of the valley," accompanied images of the Immaculate Conception, encircling the Virgin's floating body, including an example painted by Nicolás de Texada Guzmán for the Jesús María convent profession book of circa 1584 and another anonymous example from circa 1774 (see Appendix 1.3a and 1.3b).[92]

By the nineteenth century, Fanny Calderón writes of a lush garden during her visit to the Encarnación, commenting on its soundscape and pleasantness:

> The fountains sound so cheerfully, and the garden in this climate of perpetual spring affords them such a constant source of enjoyment all the year round, that one pities their secluded state much less here than in any other country. This convent is in fact a palace. The garden, into which they led us first, is kept in good order, with its stone walks, stone benches, and an ever playing and sparkling fountain. The trees were bending with fruit, and they pulled quantities of the most beautiful flowers for us; sweet-peas and roses, with which all gardens here abound, carnations, jasmine, and

heliotrope. It was a pretty picture to see them [the nuns] wandering about, or standing in groups in this high-walled garden, while the sun was setting behind the hills, and the noise of the city was completely excluded, everything breathing repose and contentment.[93]

Perhaps in the seventeenth century the convent gardens were not yet lush enough to provide enough flowers for important feast days. In 1673, the archbishop of Mexico City approved some 110 pesos for the Encarnación convent to spend on flowers and candles for their titular feast on March 25, the Incarnation, which was the same as the feast of the Annunciation.[94] The accounts of Archbishop Payo Enríquez's administrative visits to various convents between 1672 and 1675 are of this practical manner, indicating lists of items owned by convents, lists of feasts and devotions, and costs affiliated with them.[95]

The archbishop's documentation is equally suggestive about musical goings-on in convents and the practices that ensured the nuns' adherence to their vows and to the way of life conducive to salvation.[96] They include mention of singing to the Blessed Sacrament when it was exposed and funding sung memorial Masses for the repose of deceased patrons. Costs for instrument repair and music purchase are enumerated within the bounds of a prohibition on the excessive purchase of music, such as villancicos, as was the case at the Encarnación (see Appendix 1.4). These sources provide a perspective on the management of convents, these milieus where musical activity was both indispensable and monitored to give the impression of a cultivated garden of salvation of which Vetancurt boasted and which nuns presumably tolerated.

Redemption through the song of "prudent virgins," however, assumes that all nuns were virgins, which was not always the case. This matter was certainly not addressed in the archbishop's visits, through which he aimed to produce documentation of the convent way of life that led to salvation. Given that virginity would most closely align nuns with the Virgin Mary's essence, it was, nonetheless, a topic of great concern in other sources that nuns heard, read, and saw.

Virgins and Aspiring Virgins

The portrait of Sister María Manuela Josefa de Zamacona y Pedroza in her profession regalia places before our eyes a blossoming plant of Balbuena's and Vetancurt's flowery language (Figure 1.2). This genre of portraits commemorates the day nuns took their final profession vows.[97] They were commissioned by their families as keepsakes when losing a daughter's presence at home.[98] The crown with flowers symbolized marriage to Christ, who was often held in the sitter's hand in the form of a statue of the Christ Child or a crucifix, while placed in the other hand was a palm frond (symbolizing martyrdom) or a candle.[99] Sometimes the nun is depicted wearing a wedding ring. Art historian James M. Córdova remarks on the affinities that profession portraits had with secular wedding portraiture, not least the rose, a sign of a woman's sexual honor. In the case of María Manuela's portrait, the rose is held in the Christ Child's hand to offer to her, indicating that she was a virgin.[100] Not unrelated, in Marian devotional iconography the rose would symbolize Mary's purity during the birth of Christ, while lilies symbolized her purity post-partum.[101] María Manuela's purity and sexual honor—embodied in her virginity—would also have had musical implications for the profession ceremony, as we will see.

Biographical sketches often accompanied the portraits, either on the bottom of the painting or in a side panel. María Manuela's portrait indicates at the bottom that she took the habit in Puebla's Dominican Santa Inés de Montepulciano convent on June 1, 1795, which means this was the day that she began the novitiate. Her biographical sketch also indicates that she professed fully one year after her trial period as a novice on June 12, 1796.

The 1709 choirbook from María Manuela's very own convent indicates the music she and the choir were to sing when she received all the profession trappings depicted in the portrait: veil, crown, and so on. The music consisted of antiphons and responses from the feast of the virgin martyr St. Agnes:

Posuit signum: He put the sign on my face, that I may receive no other lover.

Amo Christum: I love Christ, into whose nuptial chamber I shall enter, whose mother is a virgin, whose Father does not know woman, whose organ sings to me with melodious notes: when I love him, I am chaste; when I touch him, I am pure; when I receive him, I am a virgin.

Annulo suo: He has pledged to me with his ring and has ornamented me with immense jewels.

Induit me: The Lord has clothed me with a vestment of woven gold and has ornamented me with immense jewels.[102]

Figure 1.2 Anonymous, *Sor María Manuela Josefa de Zamacona y Pedroza*, ca. 1796, Museo Nacional del Virreinato. Used with permission from INAH

The music in the choirbook essentially follows the same plan in a 1789 Puebla Dominican rule book that outlines the profession ceremony.[103] The individualization of the Trinity into Christ (son) and Father (God) in *Amo Christum* is noteworthy and will be salient in distinguishing female spirituality and for making other theological claims, as we will see in later chapters.

The choirbook, however, differs from the rule book regarding the response *Amo Christum* and antiphon *Annulo suo*. In a boastful expression of chastity, purity, and virginity, the response is conspicuously filled with language of musicality, communicating a heavenly performance by the bridegroom

Example 1.1 *Amo Christum*, excerpt, *Libro de Coro del Convento de Santa Inés de Montepulciano*, folio 16r

ac - ce - pe - ro____   vir - - - go__ sum._

Christ's ensemble, and resounded by the convent choir and professing novice. This and all the chants for profession in this choirbook are in mode 7. The most florid among all the chants is the melisma on the word "virgin" in the final phrase of the response *Amo Christum*, "I am a virgin" (virgo sum), expressed in a sine-wave-like melodic gesture whose turns are on the chant final G (Example 1.1). Beneath the chants *Amo Christum* and *Annulo suo* a note indicates, "If [she] is a widow one sings the following in place of this:"

> For widows
> *Ipsi sum*: I am espoused to him, whom the angels serve, whose beauty the sun and the moon admire.
>
> *Annulo suo*: My Lord Jesus Christ has pledged to me with his ring and has adorned me with this crown as his bride.[104]

The message could not be clearer in this localized instance of a music man-uscript, hand copied for the Santa Inés de Montepulciano nuns, departing from their order's prescribed printed, published rules. While we may never know with what frequency widows took the habit and professed into this or other convents, this manuscript confirms that indeed the reality of the circumstances required a slight change in the music, for what an embarrass-ment it would have been to follow the printed rule book precisely in the case of a non-virgin woman, requiring her to chant *Amo Christum* and to sing rhapsodically about unqualified virginity. The 1789 rule book does distin-guish between virgins and non-virgins elsewhere.

The nuns of the Santa Inés de Montepulciano convent were following the already established logic that virgins and non-virgins should be distinguished through music. According to the rule book, at the start of the Dominican profession ceremony the priest, nuns, and choir would sing the antiphon for the Common of Virgins, *Veni sponsa Christi*—"Come, bride of Christ, accept the crown which the Lord has prepared for you forever. Alleluia"—together with a psalm pairing.[105] The instructions for the ritual indicate that the anti-phon was to be sung with Psalm 44 (*Escrutavit cor meum*) if the novice was a virgin, but if she was widowed the choir and novice should instead sing Psalm 84 (*Benedixisti Domine terram tuam*). Like *Amo Christum*, Psalm 44 harnesses music and voice with references to the tongue, lips, and harps to suggest joy and pleasure:

> Joyful the thoughts that well up from my heart, the King's honor for my theme; my tongue flows readily as the pen of a swift writer. Yours is more than mortal beauty, your lips overflow with gracious utterance; the blessings God has granted you can never fail. Gird on your sword at your side, great warrior, gird yourself with all your majesty and all your beauty; ride on triumphant, in the name of faithfulness and justice. . . . God has given you an unction to bring you pride beyond any of your fellows. Your garments are scented with myrrh, and aloes, and cassia; from ivory palaces there are harps sounding in your honor. . . . Listen, my daughter, and consider my words attentively; you are to forget, henceforward, your own nation, and the house of your father; your beauty, now, is all for the king's delight; he is your Lord, and worship belongs to him.

Psalm 84 for widows, non-virgins, is a song of contrition, but it also has an aspect of aurality, referencing what is heard,[106] as the subject seeks to listen for God's forgiving voice:

> What blessings, Lord, you have granted to this land of yours . . . pardoning your people's guilt, burying away the record of their sins, all your anger calmed, your fierce displeasure forgotten! And now, God of our deliverance, do you restore us; no longer let us see your frown. Would you always be indignant with us? . . . Show us your mercy, Lord; grant us your deliverance! Let me listen, now, to the voice of the Lord God; it is a message of peace he sends to his people; to his loyal servants, that come back, now, with all their heart to him.

Hearing both these psalms in relation to virginity suggests a potential never-ending conflict. Psalm 44 touts virginity as the reliable weapon, "your sword at your side," that assists in winning the battles of a skilled warrior, recalling Vetancurt's prudent virgin armies from before. It is also a mark of difference, "an unction to bring you pride beyond any of your fellows." Psalm 84 is only cautiously optimistic that God will forgive those who have lost their virginity.

The Conceptionist and Hieronymite orders shared the same initiation rituals. They also distinguished virgins from non-virgins at the start of the novitiate with *Veni sponsa Christi* and Psalm 83 in mode 8 for virgins. The same psalm in mode 1 would accompany the antiphon *Veni electa mea* for non-virgins, which states, "Come my chosen one and I will place you on my throne, for the king has desired your beauty. With your comeliness and your beauty set out, proceed prosperously, and reign."[107] The distinction here is not just textual but truly musical, as *Veni electa* can be used for both the Common of Virgins and Common of Matrons. And Psalm 83 is considerably neutral:

> How blessed, Lord, are those who dwell in your house! They will be ever praising you. How blessed is the one who finds strength in you! Where there are hearts set on pilgrimage, the parched ravine turns into a water-course at their coming, new-clad by the bounty of returning rain. So, at each stage refreshed, they will reach Sion, and have sight there of the God who is above all gods. Lord of hosts, listen to my prayer; God of Israel, grant me audience! God, ever our protector, do not disregard us now; look favorably upon whom you have anointed! Willingly would I give a thousand of my days for one spent in your courts! Willingly reach but the threshold of my God's house, so I might dwell no more in the abode of sinners! Sun to enlighten, shield to protect us, the Lord God has favor, has honor to bestow.

Singing the same psalm in different modes, even in the closely related modes 8 and 1, which have the same range and set of pitches (D–d), indicates a slight impartiality regarding virginity status, but their differing finals and reciting tones would steer the chant in different directions sonically. It is, of course, the antiphon that governs the selection of the corresponding psalm's mode, and it is not unheard of that *Veni electa mea* could be in mode 8.[108] It is very likely that the mode 1 *Veni electa* was what was commonly circulating in the convents, not least since the Santa Inés de Montepulciano choirbook has such a setting (Example 1.2). This choirbook also has a setting of *Veni sponsa Christi* in mode 8 (Example 1.3).

In the full profession ceremony for Conceptionists and Hieronymites, *Veni sponsa Christi* is sung once more, this time with no indication of mode to correspond with virginity status or with a psalm designation, as was done in the final profession for Dominicans. Curiously, however, two seventeenth-century

Example 1.2 *Veni electa mea, Libro de Coro del Convento de Santa Inés de Montepulciano,* folio 9v

Example 1.3 *Veni sponsa Christi, Libro de Coro del Convento de Santa Inés de Montepulciano,* folio 6v

sources for the ceremony—one extant from the Púrisima Concepción convent in Puebla and the other in *Ceremonial para las religiosas geronimas de México,* a Hieronymite ceremonial book preserved at the Hispanic Society of America in New York—both contain the exact same *Veni sponsa Christi* chant.[109] The setting is not in mode 8, as it would have been sung for virgins entering their novitiate, but rather in mode 7, and with no distinction about virginity at the final profession, as the Dominicans practiced (see Example 1.4). Although the range of the mode 7 chant is higher overall, and both mode 8 and mode 7 versions end on their typical G final, the mode 7 chant is considerably less celebratory, as it is more syllabic and lacks the festive Alleluia at the end. Perhaps this was a concession in the final profession ceremony, using the same chant setting for virgins and non-virgins as a musical symbol that all who professed the vow of chastity would promise to maintain their virginity in perpetuity and that non-virgins would aspire to virginity—hence Vetancurt's aforementioned assumption that all nuns were virgins. Both virgins and non-virgins could become brides of Christ. In so doing, they became intercessors of salvation for all. It would seem, however, that the initiation processes of some orders required the bodies of virgins and non-virgins to be distinguished at some point, and, as we have seen, this distinction could involve music.

Example 1.4 *Veni sponsa Christi, Ceremonial para las religiosas geronimas de México*, The Hispanic Society of America, B2911

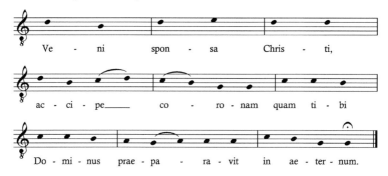

Virginity Continues to Resound

The Carmelites, the Company of Mary, and the Franciscans did not emphasize the virginity status of their initiates, nor did male religious orders.[110] This was unlike the Conceptionists, Hieronymites, and Dominicans. The absence of this distinction in the initiation process did not, however, lower the prestige of virginity in the eyes of some of these orders, as evidenced by attempts to mark virginity with an aesthetically appealing imagined sound in other types of sources.

The Puebla Carmelite Isabel de la Encarnación (1594–1633) once envisioned the whole of heaven opened up as described in the Book of Revelation. She saw a choir of virgins joining Christ with many "dances, feasts and rejoicing, singing a multitude of hymns" (danzas, fiestas, y regocijos, cantándole mil alabanzas).[111] She recognized many nuns from her lifetime who had died and gone to heaven, some singing and others silent because they had been married prior to profession. Isabel remarked,

> O my God, what they are missing out on for not being virgins! O, who could possibly warn the world about the dignity that is lost for those who are not [virgins]. . . . Blessed are the Carmelite nuns if they keep their profession [vows] strictly until they are in the next life; they will never know the great mercy that God has granted them through their vows.[112]

The allusion to nuns keeping their vows strictly would suggest potential loss of virginity post-profession, instances of which were rare in New Spain, but not unheard of.[113] Still, the emphasis in this moment of Isabel's biography is on previously married women, likely widows, entering the convent and living a life that earned them salvation in heaven, but nonetheless resulting in a musical penalty in the afterlife, silence from singing. The Carmelite chronicler José Gómez de la Parra also remarked on Isabel's vision, specifying that it was one Sister María de la Asención that Isabel saw, "not entering in the music of the lamb because she had been married."[114]

Promoting fear of such a post-mortem silence was not unusual for nuns' biographies, which encouraged pious behavior in life and, in this case, virginity.[115] The uncertainty expressed in Psalm 84 for non-virgins in the Dominican ceremonial meets its negative realization in Isabel's vision that attaches sexual morality to music—in opposition to early modern associations of women's public music making with immorality.[116] The lesson for women seems obvious: maintain virginity, become a nun, sing for salvation in this life, and, therefore, sing a more joyful song in heaven.

This lauding of virginity in these texts had its roots in devotion to the Virgin Mary, the virgin of virgins.[117] The "sovereign dignity" of Mary's virgin womb pregnant with Christ, for example, was a topic for profound reflection in one of the chapters of a 1738 Franciscan meditation book for novices.[118] In addition, of course, the Virgin was honored with Marian devotional art and music ubiquitously across the early modern Catholic world.[119]

In some New Spanish convent sources, the Virgin Mary was specifically marked by sound and made to resound—made to echo—to instruct on her Immaculate Conception. This has overtones with the attempts by some orders, not least the Conceptionists, to distinguish virginity sonically. In a sixteenth-century Spanish manuscript of the Conceptionist profession ritual preserved in the Conceptionist Mother House in Toledo, the profession antiphon is not *Veni sponsa Christi* or *Veni electa mea*. Rather, it was the antiphon for the feast of the Immaculate Conception, *Conceptio tua*, which alludes to vocality: "Your conception, Virgin mother of God, announced joy to the whole world: For out of thee arose the sun of justice, Christ our God: Who, by paying for evil, gave blessing; and confounding death, gave life everlasting."[120]

Bringing us closer to an early modern understanding of the Immaculate Conception's sonic implications is the Franciscan profession sermon for one Sister Mariana de San Francisco. She professed in Mexico City's Santa Clara convent in 1686 on the feast of the Immaculate Conception (December 8). The sermon delivered by Juan de Ávila taught on virginity's origins. It is called *Pureza emblemática* (Emblematic purity), and its contents recall the warrior concept alluded to in Vetancurt. In *Discipline and Punish*, Foucault comments at length on the early modern idealization of soldiers whose "docile bodies" were manipulable to the point of creating "small scale models of power."[121] Similarly, the manipulation of early modern female bodies to maintain virginity was leveraged by the Spanish legal system, in which the maternal line was key, because "blood purity and civil legitimacy could only be absolutely established through the maternal line."[122] The most powerful and elite citizens of New Spain tended to be those who maintained their family's pure lineages via female relatives of proven virginity prior to marriage, granting their families high social status and prestige. Elite families whose daughters were not capable of securing a well-to-do husband had their prestige and status secured when their daughters' virginity was guarded in a convent, by becoming a professed nun, rather than being lost to a lower-class suitor. According to Juan de Ávila's sermon, the emblem of virginity is a hieroglyph of an ancient warrior woman with wings, armed and ready to defend herself against the evil of sexual relations, as her sacramental learning would undoubtedly have guided her in doing.[123]

This warrior woman is a direct parallel to the Immaculate Conception doctrine's source in the Book of Revelation (12:1–6), the Woman of the Apocalypse. A favorite topic among New Spanish artists, she is depicted in Miguel Cabrera's famous painting as victorious in the battle over original sin, "exterminator of all things reptilian," symbolized by her winged flight to safeguard the Christ Child from a multi-headed dragon, recalling the snake from Eden (Figure 1.3).[124] Like a warrior, Mariana would take on a battle with concupiscence, arming herself with the vows of chastity and enclosure offered by the cloister.[125]

To vocalize these vows, Mariana would need to rely on virginity's vocal component, as exemplified by the hieroglyph of the pre-historic virgin woman, depicted with her mouth open and with the words "Spirits like yours replenish heaven" (Spiritus eius repleabit Caelos) flowing from it, so as to suggest that virginity yielded salvation.[126] The Virgin Mary too was the model for virginity's vocal component, according to Ávila, because she composed the *Magnificat*:

My soul magnifies the Lord.
And my spirit rejoices in God my Savior.
For he has looked with favor on the humility of his handmaid.

Figure 1.3 Miguel Cabrera, *La Virgen del Apocalipsis*, ca. 1760. Used with permission from Museo Nacional de Arte, INBA, Mexico City

Behold, from henceforth, all generations will call me blessed.
For the mighty one has done great things for me, and holy is his name.
His mercy is for those who fear him from generation to generation.
He has shown strength with his arm,
He has scattered the proud in the thoughts of their hearts.
He has brought down the powerful from their thrones and lifted the lowly.
He has filled the hungry with good things and sent the rich away empty.
He has helped his servant Israel in remembrance of his mercy.
According to the promise he made to our ancestors, to Abraham and
his descendants forever.

The prophetic utterance of the *Magnificat* was the result of human belief in Mary's virgin pregnancy with the savior son of God, which became

musicalized for all religious to sing daily paired with an antiphon at the Office of Vespers. The aurality surrounding the circumstances of the *Magnificat* is closely tied to the virginal Incarnation and has implications for the vow of obedience, hence its inclusion as a topic within a sermon on the profession day of the virgin Mariana de San Francisco—on the feast of the Immaculate Conception. Recalling the salient New Testament narrative confirms that the first human to believe the miracle of the Incarnation was the Virgin Mary herself, impregnated by the Holy Spirit at the Annunciation when she vocalized the words "Behold the handmaid of the Lord" in response to the Angel Gabriel's directive that she would conceive God's offspring (Luke 1:38). As we observed earlier in our discussion of original sin, tradition held that the Holy Spirit entered through her ear. Mary refers to herself as a handmaid both in her words at the Annunciation and within the *Magnificat*, thus differing from the Song of Hannah, long thought to be a model for the *Magnificat* but lacking such humility.[127] Mary's vocalized humility would have been of prime importance to nuns obliged via the vow of obedience to follow Mary's servitude to God.

In the Bible, the Annunciation is immediately followed by the Visitation story: Mary visits her cousin, Elizabeth, also pregnant with John the Baptist. Elizabeth and John represent the second instance of human belief in the Incarnation. Upon Mary's arrival to her cousin's house, John leapt within Elizabeth's womb at the sound of Mary's greeting, and Elizabeth was filled with the Holy Spirit. This interaction with her cousin prompted Elizabeth to exclaim in a loud voice,

> Blessed are you among women and blessed is the fruit of your womb. How have I deserved to be visited by the mother of my Lord? Why, as soon as ever the voice of your greeting sounded in my ears, the child in my womb leaped for joy. Blessed are you for your believing; the message that was brought to you from the Lord shall have fulfilment. (Luke 1:41–42)

These are the words to which Mary responded with the *Magnificat*. And so, the Annunciation and Visitation stories, while making great reflections for the feast of the Immaculate Conception, also add to the devotional weight that accompan ies Ávila's reference to the *Magnificat*. His profession sermon connects the inherent vocality in these stories of the Virgin Mary's life to Mariana's virginity. Vocalizing the profession vows of obedience, poverty, chastity, and enclosure is the definitive step for women to become nuns—perpetual resonators of the *Magnificat* daily, echoing the Virgin Mary's words and meditating upon them. Even the words of Elizabeth's response to Mary became music in antiphon form, *Benedicta tu in mulieribus* ("Blessed are you among women and blessed is the fruit of your womb"); they are the words to the prayer of the rosary as well, an essential component of nuns' vocal Marian devotion.[128]

Benedicta tu in mulieribus was also the verse for the Christmas responsory *Sancta et immaculata virginitas*, a mode 6 setting we have extant from Puebla's Purísima Concepción convent antiphoner, dated 1691 (Example 1.5). The text of the responsory reads, "O holy and immaculate virginity, I know not by what praises I may extol you: for you have born in your womb, whom the heavens could not contain." The chant conveys an overwhelming sentiment: heaven, not capable of containing Christ, sends him to earth, stunning the subject of the chant (humanity) into knowing not how to venerate Mary, whose holy, immaculate, and virginal womb carried the heavenly gift of salvation, God made man. The Franciscan novice meditations elaborate on such an apotheosis, claiming that since for the love of God some mystics were prone to transcendence, "truly the soul faints" at the thought of Mary actually containing God's entirety within her "blessed entrails" ("bienaventuradas entrañas").[129] The chant gives us an alternative to this focus on the Virgin's anatomy. In *Sancta et immaculata virginitas*, the Virgin Mary is rhetorically abridged to the essence of her soul (immaculate) and her body (virgin). These qualities are mysteries of faith that stupefy humanity: Indeed, how could Mary's soul have been conceived immaculately before time at the Creation? How did a virgin body conceive God in the form of a human child? They are theological questions that even music cannot answer.

The chant's melisma on "immaculata," which ends on F, the chant's final, prepares the ear for a long melisma on "virginitas," taking the same pitch (F) from "immaculata" and ascending to the apex of the chant on B-flat. This ascent is echoed in the verse with its opening "Benedicta," Elizabeth's loud exclamation at the Visitation, rising to the same highest point, a musical tribute to humanity's belief in the Incarnation. There was no better praise with which to extol Mary than with the words her cousin Elizabeth taught humanity loudly in the biblical narrative, *Benedicta tu in mulieribus*. The Visitation is thus fused with belief in the Immaculate Conception doctrine via the verse's placement with the responsory *Sancta et immaculata virginitas*, reminding us of the Immaculate Conception's quintessential role

Example 1.5 *Sancta et immaculata virginitas* and *Benedicta tu in mulieribus,* *Proprium de Tempore: Antiphonario General,* 1691, Biblioteca Palafoxiana, folios 45v–46v

in salvation. Redemption commenced with the birth of Christ, with prenatal assertion at the Visitation and Annunciation.

In less than a month after her profession, Mariana de San Francisco would hear and be required to sing these Christmas responsory texts, reminding her of an additional, special vow that Ávila appends in his profession sermon dedicated to her. This fifth vow that Mariana would vocalize, in addition to the four traditional vows of obedience, poverty, chastity, and enclosure, was her defense of the doctrine of the Immaculate Conception.[130] The sound of her voice promising to keep all of these vows would greatly satisfy Christ, her betrothed, as Ávila instructs by quoting the famous passage from the Song of Songs, so pertinent to nuns' vocality, "Show me but your face, let me but hear your voice, that voice sweet as your face is fair" (Songs 2:14).[131]

The Immaculate Conception and the Voice of God

The Virgin Mary too desired to hear her praises vocalized. Because of Jesus' own self-reference as the Light of the World (John 8:12; 9:5), since the mid-sixteenth century Mary has often been allegorized as the one which gives birth to light—or to the sun, as observed in the antiphon *Conceptio tua* quoted earlier. She is the dawn (*aurora/alba*).[132] Quite revealing in this regard is the title of the Augustinian preacher José de Santa Gertrudis' 1699 sermon to the Regina Coeli nuns of Mexico City, *Birth of the Best Dawn, Mary* ("El nacimiento de la mejor aurora, María"), for Mary's nativity celebrated on September 8. But it was in his 1706 sermon for the same feast, delivered to the Balvanera convent nuns, that he explained the aurality surrounding this aurora. "Aurora" is related to *avium oras* (the hour at which the birds sing).[133] Because of this etymological relationship, music was, he argued, the best way to venerate Mary and implore her mediation on behalf of salvation. This belief is exemplified by Santa Gertrudis' sermon titled *Sophisticated Harmonies with which the Musician Nuns of the Convent of our Lady of Balvanera Concluded the Octave of the Birth of Our Lady*.[134] The divinely ordered harmonization of linguistics and the phenomenon of bird song called for Marian music. Santa Gertrudis enjoins the nuns to sing Mary's praises with equal festivity on the octave of the feast as on the day of the feast itself, with the music-theory lesson that the octave in music produces the same sound as the unison, but at a higher pitch.[135]

"Music's purpose is to go up and down [in pitch]," explains Santa Gertrudis further, "because tones are higher or lower than each other, and it makes composition elegant. No good musician descends if not to rise or rises if not to descend."[136] Thus, because of the rise and descent of pitches in music, he claims that Christ and Mary are best modeled in music, since

Christ descended from heaven to be born of a human being and to dwell among mortals, and through this occurrence Mary was elevated—ascended to the state of holy, immaculate, virgin, as we observed before in the responsory *Sancta et immaculata virginitas*.[137] Moreover, "everything sung is about Mary's birth," reminding the Balvanera nuns of what they already knew, that without Mary we do not receive Christ, salvation.[138]

There is no extant music from the Balvanera convent, but a villancico for the feast of Mary's nativity from Puebla's Santísima Trinidad convent, *Con qué gala en el campo* (CSG.285) by the New Spanish musician Francisco Vidales (1632–1702), expresses in music so many of the tropes discussed so far. Vidales started off as an organist in Mexico City cathedral and then moved to Puebla cathedral.[139] His provision of music to convents perhaps came through a connection fostered by his uncle, the Mexico City cathedral chapel master Fabián Pérez Ximeno, whose music is found in the Encarnación choirbooks and in the Santísima Trinidad repertory, and whose three daughters—Vidales' cousins—were Conceptionist nuns.[140] For the Santísima Trinidad nuns' celebration of Mary's birthday, Vidales sets a text about Mary's sinlessness, her association with flowers, and the dawn in typical villancico format with an estribillo and five coplas.

Estribillo

Con qué gala en el campo	With what elegance in the field
nace la rosa,	a rose is born,
desbrochando en candores	with all her splendor
toda su pompa.	blooming in candidness.
Risa es del alba.	She is the dawn's laughter.
Ay, qué graciosa.	Ah, how graceful.
Miren, qué perla.	See, what a pearl.
Noten, qué aurora.	Notice, what a dawn!
Que la gracia en purezas	For grace sews
le hace la costa.	her in purities.

Coplas

1. Rosa, qué agraciada	Rose, gracefully
naces como aurora,	born as dawn,
pues con tu hermosura	your beauty with no
ninguna se roza.	other compares.

2. Señora, que libre	Lady, that freed
de tributos gozas	from tributes you enjoy
el mayor renombre	the highest renown
de reina y señora.	as queen and lady.

3. Hermosa azucena,	Beautiful lily,
entre espinas sola,	alone among thorns,
de quien ya se dijo	of whom it was already said that
toda eres hermosa.	you are all beautiful.

4. Concha peregrina,	Pilgrim shell,
de quien se desbrocha	from whom the clearest pearl
la perla más neta	unfolds without
sin romper la concha.	breaking the shell.

5. Aurora sin llanto,	Dawn without weeping,
mañana sin sombra,	morning without shadow,
luna sin menguante,	moon without waning,
y sin noche aurora.	and dawn without night.

We have already encountered the rose of copla 1 and lily of copla 3 as a reference to Mary's purity; in describing the lily's "all beautiful" isolation among the thorns, Vidales quotes directly from the Song of Songs. The last line in copla 3 is translated from the Latin *Tota pulchra es*, which has been a passage directly associated with the doctrine of the Immaculate Conception since the Middle Ages.[141] To these references, we can add the fourth copla's metaphor of the pearl produced from the pilgrim shell, the icon of the way of St. James (the pilgrimage to Santiago de Compostela). The scallop shell associated with the pilgrimage has traditionally symbolized the female anatomy, here unbroken—virgin—as it produces its pearl.[142]

The piece is set for two tiples (sopranos), alto, tenor, and likely bass accompaniment, though that part is missing. It is in mode 5 (B-flat, F final, C mediation), a suitable mode for the topic because it is joyful, according to Nassarre's 1724 *Escuela música*.[143] The coplas are set homophonically, and both imitative polyphony and homophony texture the estribillo. The most salient moment in the piece comes at mm. 37–38 when "ay" (ah) is sustained with a whole note (darkened semibreve in the manuscript), preceded and followed

Example 1.6 Vidales, *Con qué gala en el campo* (CSG.285), mm. 37–40

by pauses, then repeated for a dotted whole note value before continuing to resound Mary's gracefulness/humorousness—the word "graciosa" means both (Example 1.6). In fact, Mary is full of grace, but in typical villancico popular manner, she is also funny, the dawn's laughter. What else can one do among reflections of her complicated, miraculous attributes that once again stun the subject? Here, the subject does not faint, as with the mystics referred to in the Franciscan novice meditations earlier; this time it gasps—ay, ay—and seeks comic relief in laughter.

"With laughter," notes Brandon LaBelle, "the movements of the mouth exceed so many limits, to occupy and break, as well as reaffirm the edges of the social order."[144] Thus, another aural component is projected onto Mary's attributes that clearly exceed the social order's boundaries and those of the natural order too as suggested in copla 5.

Mary's virginity yielded excess spirituality for women seeking to be more perfect brides of Christ. Puebla's Bishop Juan de Palafox y Mendoza (1600–1659) lauded virginity in his 1640 rule book for Conceptionists as follows:

> O highest condition among the wives of the Lord, justly comparable with the angels in heaven! O highest condition! It is not only comparable with the angels, but rather in some way it exceeds them. Preserving purity in that spiritual nature is easier than preserving it in the human [nature].[145]

The "O" exclamations denote the urgent need for Palafox to find listeners with whom to communicate his valuable point.[146] The bishop emerges as a divine resonator, a medium for delivering a divine message—one that outlasted Palafox.[147] Originally published in 1641, the preface was reprinted verbatim in a 1773 Hieronymite rule book, preserving Palafox in the auditory imagination of nuns with no living memory of him.[148] Charged to lead a life of prayer for their own salvation and that of the secular world they left behind, nuns would best complete their mission by attending to clerical instructions, like those of Palafox and other sermonizers, that reminded them of the virtues they possessed. It was possible for all to be saved, but the status of nuns' virginity yielded different treatment on earth and when they supposedly earned salvation in heaven, as we observed with Sister Isabel's apocalyptic vision.

Their model was the Virgin Mary, Woman of the Apocalypse, defender against sin and defended as immaculately conceived. The words of one convent sermonizer, Marcos Jaramillo, labeled her a well-crafted melody, a fantasia, in a 1712 printed sermon delivered to the Franciscan nuns of the Santa Clara convent in Querétaro:

> Skilled musicians call a tune a song of fantasia when, not pleased with the laws or rules of music, as these would be too mundane, a composer searches for an idea of a different type, using voices, trills, pitches, or instruments without breaking the rules of music, and also not following them strictly; [he] creates a song that delights and even draws admiration from the [other] skilled [musicians]; thus, the rules are not broken, and neither is his art governed by the rules. This is what the Eternal Father did as he sang Mary [into existence] in the high choir of glory.[149]

Aptly titled *Feast of the High Choir* (*Fiesta del coro alto*) for the feast of the Immaculate Conception, this sermon sonified the Virgin Mary with the Trinity, individualized to make a theological point. Since Christ was the Word of God made flesh, then the Virgin Mary—whose soul was conceived without original sin throughout pre-temporal eternity—is the voice of God; the Holy Spirit is God's tongue.[150] Passed on from generation to generation, God's voice, and its message—the Word of God made flesh, Christ—comes to life when nuns vocalize their vows to become perpetual singers of Mary's words in the *Magnificat*:

> In the *coro alto* of this church, it is Mother María de la Trinidad who raises her voice: "a woman in the multitude said aloud" [Luke 11:27]; in

the high choir of glory it is the Virgin Mary, as mother, who is intoned by the Trinity.[151]

We will learn more about the coro alto—the high choir, a structure physically raised off the floor in which nuns sang their liturgies—in the next chapter, but suffice it to say that in this quotation, Jaramillo was speaking directly to the nuns in their place of singing in the back of the church, the inspiration for the sermon's title. The biblical citation embedded in this quote can also be read in line with Marian devotion, appropriate for the feast of the Immaculate Conception. According to chapter 11 in Luke's Gospel, there was a woman in the crowd who responded to Jesus by saying aloud, "Blessed is the womb that carried you and the breasts at which you nursed" (Luke 11:27), so reminiscent of Elizabeth's praise of Mary at the Visitation.[152] Jesus offered a conflicting response to the woman, "Should we not say, blessed are those who hear the word of God, and guard it?" (Luke 11:28), so reminiscent of Mary, the Woman of the Apocalypse, the Immaculate Conception ever the antithesis of sin. What Jaramillo meant was that the nun Mother María in the convent choir is like that woman in the Gospel, who without knowing the Virgin Mary personally still sings her praise and leads the rest of the convent choir in song for the salvation of humanity.[153] It was her duty.

Who, then, was Sister Flor de Santa Clara, who opened this chapter with the conflict arising over the liturgical music books penned by Rodriguez Mata? She was an imitator of the Immaculately Conceived Virgin Mary, or at least she attempted to be. As we have seen, the Immaculate Conception doctrine, which was at first so contentious, resolved into preaching to nuns that Mary was the eternal voice of God. The daily chanting of her *Magnificat* contained the prophecy of salvation, the very Word of God made flesh. Such a vocalization was essential to belief in her virginal status, in constant conflict with the reality of human procreation, and lauded for women in New Spain to imitate, especially if they were to maintain their family honor. Sister Flor's singing of the *Magnificat* and all other liturgical music—since "everything sung is about Mary's birth," as we observed in Santa Gertrudis' published sermon to the Balvanera nuns—would maintain the Virgin Mary, and Christ by association, in humanity's perpetual auditory imagination.[154] Sister Flor too might sing Jesus to life, just in time for Christmas, the birth of humanity's salvation predestined through Mary's Immaculate Conception. Let us now consider the space in which this singing took place.

2

Sonic Thresholds

The Grates of the Cloister and the Lips of Nuns, or Who Was Sister Rosa?

Just under the bass part of the Kyrie to the anonymous *Misa "Bonae voluntatis"* (Mass "of good will") in a New Spanish choirbook, one of the few scripts in prose among the various doodles and drawings within the choirbook's marginalia reads, "This is the *Bonae voluntatis* Mass that Rosa sings" (see Figure 2.1). It perhaps seems meaningless now, centuries removed from the first quarter of the eighteenth century, approximately when it was written.[1] Still, the phrase compels one to wonder about the name Rosa. Is this a first name or a last name? It is likely a first name, given that early modern Spanish societies de-emphasized surnames, especially within informal matters like this.[2] The first scholars to mention this scribble established that the collection of choirbooks in which Rosa's Mass was located belonged to women musicians, noting salient clues such as the lack of text underlay in many low voice parts and the labeling of one of the books as property of Mexico City's Encarnación convent.[3]

The Encarnación's copy of this *Misa* is incomplete, but it corresponds to a nine-voice Mass by Mateo Romero (ca. 1575–1647), a Flemish composer active in Spain.[4] It is polychoral, an impressive sonority, because of its grandeur, popular in New Spain.[5] The choruses are divided into two groups of soprano, alto, tenor, and bass, with a soprano voice making up the third "choir"; the choirs are all meant to be accompanied by organ and string and wind instruments to double the bass.[6] This information solves the composer's identity and slightly clarifies the marginalia's message. Rosa is becoming less anonymous. Did she sing the soprano part? This part is missing,[7] like so many other voice parts in the Encarnación choirbooks' compositions, but yes, perhaps she was the main soloist. Indeed, why else would someone have written such a label on the page?

It was not uncommon for convent musicians to place names on pages of music manuscripts. A roster of close to sixty instrumentalists and singers

Immaculate Sounds. Cesar D. Favila, Oxford University Press. © Oxford University Press 2023.
DOI: 10.1093/oso/9780197621899.003.0003

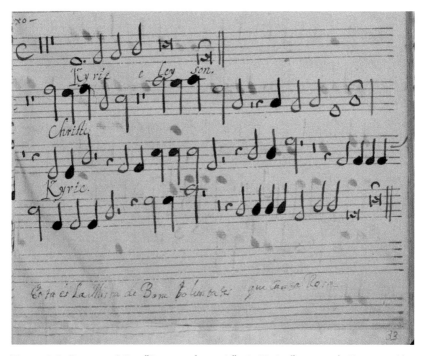

Figure 2.1 Romero, *Misa "Bonae voluntatis"* a 9, Kyrie (bass part), Encarnación Choirbooks, vol. 5, folio 33r

from Puebla's Santísima Trinidad convent (active ca. 1660–1720) has been generated from similar labeling practices in the music manuscripts of that convent.[8] This list includes some eleven nuns named María, and tied for second place are Inés (Agnes, in English) and Rosa with four each. Their names and dozens of others are scattered on loose sheets of music covering all the vocal ranges and instrumental parts of several villancicos. And as with the Encarnación's Rosa, we know little else about these women other than the fact that they were musician nuns.

Like the voices of many nuns, Rosa's was always meant to be anonymous, even as this Mass setting highlighted the soprano voice.[9] A glimpse of the Gloria is instructive as to how Rosa's solo works with the larger ensemble. It demonstrates why the Mass was nicknamed *Bonae voluntatis*. The choirs respond syllabically to Rosa's various iterations of godly worship—"Laudamus te" (We praise you), "benedicimus te" (We bless you), and so on—with antiphonal repetitions of "bonae voluntatis" between each of the solo's iterations (Example 2.1).[10]

Example 2.1 Romero, *Misa "Bonae voluntatis,"* Gloria (mm. 10–32)

Example 2.1 Continued

The contrast between two four-part choirs interjecting the same phrase together in homophonic chunks makes the lone soprano stand out, more so because of the wide distinction in performing force size than through any displays of soloistic virtuosity.[11] Rosa's phrases are hardly melismatic, though slightly less syllabic than the choirs' music. In all the other movements of this

Mass, the soprano solos are typically short and stepwise as they are in the Gloria, here consisting of the same stepwise tetrachord from A to D to highlight a tonal excursion, shifting from the opening tonal center E.

While Rosa's voice joined a one-hundred-plus-year tradition of singing within "the ideal combination of sumptuous sonority and clarity of text setting," as polychorality has been described by Noel O'Regan, her high-stakes singing that would save the world required the utmost decorum.[12] Every detail of when, where, and how convent choirs would sing was prescribed following an ordered monastic tradition. No one was to know that it was Rosa singing *Misa "Bonae voluntatis"*—even those around her in the choir were not to make a fuss about her talent. But whoever wrote her name on the manuscript wanted it known that this *Misa* was Rosa's to sing.

This chapter is a meditation on this attempt to highlight Rosa's identity in the manuscript, offering an exploration on the methods by which nuns' anonymity was established and maintained. To get to know Sister Rosa as well as possible, we must turn to canonical, mystical, acoustical, and architectural circumstances to examine some of the prescriptions around her singing. These sources necessarily invite an examination of the convent grates, especially the grates of the *coro*, the choir space, where Rosa performed her Mass and all other liturgical music within the convent church. The coro grates are thresholds to the outer world the nuns left behind. They are a physical manifestation of the rules of obedience and enclosure, veiling already veiled women's bodies and voices, yet at the same time calling attention to them. They are thresholds that guard the nuns' very own bodily thresholds, their lips.

Drawing on Brandon LaBelle's definition of the lips as entryways into "deeper pleasures, deeper intimacy," and aligning this description onto the lips of nuns singing within their coro, we can appreciate how this space in a convent church building was a privileged place of female spirituality.[13] The early modern notion that speech and song from the open mouths of women would signal their unchastity would be subverted in the coro, whereby unseen, regulated open mouths would still suggest a chaste singer—a nun.[14] The coro was the space where Sister María de Jesús and Sister Bárbara Josefa experienced many of their divine visions and heard divine voices.[15] We will encounter these nuns repeatedly in the chapters to follow, because of the rich narratives about convent culture provided in their published biographies. Their role model lives guided nuns' behavior for the liturgies, nurturing a comportment that might initiate a connection with Christ through song, as both María and Bárbara experienced. Moreover, agency was negotiated in the coro through nuns' efforts to please God, themselves, and their lay convent patrons with their acousmatic voices, which, recall, are voices whose sources—the bodies that generate them—are hidden from sight owing to the coro grates.

This does not imply that the coro was the only place within convents where musical performance took place. The multi-instrumentalist Nicolasa de la Santísima Trinidad, who professed in Puebla's Carmelite convent in 1649, accompanied herself with harp and vihuela, "singing very spiritual words" as a form of weekly devotional recreation in the convent garden.[16] A 1762 ordinal for nuns at the Concepción convent illustrates that the nuns celebrated the feast of St. Sebastian with a procession around the arches of the cloister, singing a litany to the accompaniment of bajón into the open air.[17] These outdoor musical performances have been characterized as open resonances, because they had the potential to be heard by the urban community that surrounded the convent.[18]

Back inside the walls of the convent rooms, the Dominicans at the Santa Rosa convent had the tradition of processing into the refectory for lunch singing a responsorial Kyrie, *De Profundis* (Psalm 129), and *Pater Noster* led by a cantor and answered by the whole community of nuns. And once inside, the cantor intoned the blessing that every practicing Catholic recites before eating to this day: "Bless us, O Lord, and these thy gifts which we are about to receive from thy bounty, through Christ our Lord. Amen."[19] The Hieronymites had a similar ritual before eating.[20] Blessing the food that nourished the community was no small gesture, but as we will see, the sustenance sowed and reaped during the liturgies in the coro satiated a different appetite, one for the senses as the rule for Dominicans nurtured appropriately, "Let the ears hunger for the Word of God."[21]

Structure and Function of the Coro

New Spanish convent churches built in the seventeenth and eighteenth centuries typically had two choir structures, an upper coro alto built on top of a lower coro bajo, as illustrated in Francisco De la Maza's classic diagram from his 1956 architectural overview of convent choirs, *Arquitectura de los coros de monjas en México* (Figure 2.2).[22] These spaces were on the opposite wall of the convent church from the high altar; the nave essentially ended

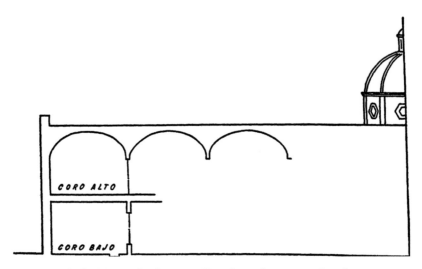

Figure 2.2 De la Maza, side elevation, New Spanish convent church

at the grate of the coro bajo, separating the nuns from the public church space where lay people gathered to attend services, as seen in a modern-day photograph of Puebla's Concepción convent coros (Figure 2.3). Puebla has convent churches with some of the best-preserved coro structures in Mexico; their impracticality for contemporary worship has led many former convent churches in Mexico to demolish the coro to lengthen the church nave.[23]

In Figure 2.3 we can see the nave's central processional aisle, flanked by pews for parishioners, leading to the speaker-like, grilled rectangular threshold of the coro bajo. To the left of it remains a small, square, cabinet-like opening called the *cratícula*, through which priests delivered communion to nuns in the coro bajo. To the right of the coro bajo screen is a door through which women would enter the coro bajo to become initiated into the novitiate during the ceremony for the taking of the habit.[24] Just before the coro on the right side of Figure 2.3, perpendicular to the coro wall, is the wall of the church nave with a large brown portal through which parishioners enter the church from the street. The left side wall of the church nave, as well as the coro wall, guarded nuns' interior claustral spaces.

The coro alto, whose floor makes up the ceiling of the coro bajo, can be seen just above the coro bajo screen in Figure 2.3: three grated, window-like openings demarcated by two central columns. Remnants of this structure

Figure 2.3 Coros, Concepción convent, Puebla, built ca. 1615

in the modified Mexico City Regina Coeli convent church can be seen in Figure 2.4. Both churches still have organs in their coro alto, as can be seen in the pictures, but the grates at the Regina Coeli convent church have been destroyed.[25] The construction of these convent churches along the exterior walls of nuns' claustral compounds, often taking up entire city blocks, resulted in their churches having long facades facing the urban surroundings that ran the whole length of the nave (Figure 2.5).[26]

Lastly, the semicircular gap above the coro alto grate that joins with the barrel-vaulted ceiling would have been covered up by a painting or an ornate fan-like grille called an *abanico* (fan, literally). The only seventeenth-century example of such an ornament is preserved in Puebla's Santísima Trinidad convent (Figure 2.6). Elaborate craftsmanship on features of the coro like the abanico demonstrate "architecture . . . of fabulously advertised distinction," according to Helen Hills. These types of ornamented choir structures have been described by Hills as an inversion of Foucault's panopticon, in which the power of seeing without being seen is given to the cloistered nuns behind the grilles—and behind the lay people in the nave—rather than to the lay people themselves, free to leave the convent church.[27]

Figure 2.4 Coros with modified coro bajo to lengthen nave, Regina Coeli convent, Mexico City, built ca. 1732

Figure 2.5 Long facade, Regina Coeli convent, Mexico City

Figure 2.6   Abanico above coro alto, Santísima Trinidad convent, Puebla, built ca. 1673

Variations on such choir structures and screens for restricting nuns' contact with laity during liturgical services abounded throughout the Catholic world. Enclosure rules date from the late thirteenth century, and they were strictly reinforced by the Council of Trent, not least in Italy with the reforms of Carlo Borromeo in 1577. The application of these rules resulted in "interior churches" for nuns built up and down the walls of European convent churches.[28] The New Spanish double structure opposite the high altar was typical of Spanish convent design, with an example of the same construction located in Zaragoza's Franciscan Santa Catalina convent, as we learn from the biography of Sister Jacinta de Atondo (1645–1716).[29] Another example is in Ávila's Cistercian convent of Santa Ana.[30] In a way, that distance between the high altar and the coro wall created a ceremonial space reminiscent of that found in Spanish and Latin American cathedrals, where the enclosed coros were separated from the altar; in the cathedrals, though, the coros were in a central position within the cathedral nave rather than on the wall of the church building, opposite the altar.[31] Back in nuns' convents, priests attending to special ceremonies for the nuns at the coro grate, which required them to process across the nave, would undoubtedly call attention to the cloistered women to whom the priests were ministering.

But this architecture raises the question about where nuns attended the liturgies—where they sang—within the elaborate space designed for their enclosure: upstairs in the coro alto or downstairs in the coro bajo. One of the earliest references to the split coro alto and coro bajo comes in a 1537 petition to Spain from Bishop Zumárraga and other New Spanish prelates. The bishops of New Spain were still hoping to establish convents for the education of indigenous women, an unsuccessful venture, as we saw in Chapter 1. The bishops requested to build a cloister with a convent church incorporating a coro alto and coro bajo—a structure they must have recalled from living in Spain, since nothing like it existed yet in New Spain. The bishops envisioned the possibility of racial separation, "in which mestizas could be upstairs and the daughters of the *naturales* downstairs."[32] Where the Spanish nuns, who would theoretically educate these women, would sing their liturgies is anybody's guess, but the social hierarchies of the time may provide a clue. In this case, the privileged space in Zumárraga's imagined scenario might be the coro bajo, as indigenous people (implied by naturales, "natives" literally) were seen as pure in comparison to the mestizas, women of mixed indigenous and Spanish blood.[33]

A less likely scenario proposed in a history of the Santa Clara convent in Querétaro suggests that the novices used the coro bajo and the fully professed nuns used the coro alto.[34] This, however, would prevent the novices from learning by seeing and singing the liturgies required of their training. We know that novices who were musicians accompanied fully professed nuns with their instruments and voices. In 1692, the Mexico City cathedral chapel master Antonio Salazar reported that a young woman living in the San Bernardo convent named Ana Javiera de Algora should be allowed to take the habit, in other words to become a novice, to assist the choir by singing and by playing the vihuela and violon.[35] Thus, keeping novices and fully professed nuns in separate coros would not make sense from a pedagogical or liturgical standpoint, unless novices were expected to learn by listening downstairs in the coro bajo.

Other practical uses for the double structure in Spain pertain to less hierarchically charged scenarios, such as the mundane seasonal cycle. During the hot summer in Zaragoza, the nuns of the Santa Catalina convent used the coro bajo, which they colloquially called the "summer Matins coro"; in the winter, they used the coro alto, where the heat would rise to keep them warm.[36] In the Inmaculada Concepción convent of Caracas, polyphony was performed in the coro alto and chant was performed in the coro bajo, suggesting acoustic considerations.[37]

Similarly, a mid-seventeenth-century instruction book from the Franciscan Santa María de Jesús convent in Spain states that singing upstairs was acoustically better than singing in a coro bajo.[38] Could the coro alto have had better acoustics? Perhaps, since a contemporary architectural analysis of several convent coros in Puebla indicates that the coro alto often had a higher ceiling than the coro bajo. Both coros of the Santisima Trinidad Convent measured 63 ft. long x 35 ft. wide—more than half the length of the church nave, which was 105 ft. long. But the coro bajo ceiling at the Santísima Trinidad, built in 1673, was 19 ft. high, while the coro alto had an enormous 44 ft. barrel-vaulted ceiling of grey limestone for reverberating the nuns' voices.[39]

To date, De la Maza's assertion that the coro alto was the space for attending the Office and that the coro bajo was used for attending Mass has remained unquestioned.[40] Plenty of sources indicate subtle nuances that both coincide with and complicate this arrangement, particularly regarding Mass. Perhaps the location of the cratícula for distribution of communion in the coro bajo would indicate that nuns attended Mass downstairs, as communion is typically received during the liturgy of the Eucharist in the Mass. And perhaps the location of the organs, the ideal instruments for liturgical accompaniment, in the coro alto would suggest that liturgical singing took place upstairs, whether for the Office or the Mass.[41]

What the biographies of Sister María de Jesús (active in Puebla's Concepción convent) and Sister Bárbara Josefa de San Francisco (active in the Santísima Trinidad) indicate is that the Office was indeed upstairs and that nuns could attend Mass upstairs as well.[42] Bishop Juan de Palafox's rule for María de Jesús and Bárbara's order also indicates that Mass was attended within the coro alto; its curtain, used to conceal the nuns further, was ordered to be lifted only for the elevation of the Eucharist during Mass so that nuns could partake in spiritual communion (Chapter 4).[43] Most revealing as well is the account in the biography of Sister Sebastiana de la Santísima Trinidad, a Franciscan of the San Juan de la Penitencia convent in Mexico City. Her biographer included many direct quotes from Sebastiana's own writing about her devotional experiences in the coro alto: "After ringing for Prime (which lasted more than a half hour) [I] came down for communion. Upon finishing, I went up to the coro until noon."[44]

In addition to what Sister Sebastiana's quote suggests, we have other clues suggesting that communion for some nuns' orders did not in fact take place during the Mass, but often as a separate devotional activity. Most convent rules comment on the feast days on which communion was to be taken, and these tend to be specified in chapters other than the ones on attending Mass and Office. The Franciscans could take communion during Mass or after confession, though Sister Sebastiana's account would suggest local variants.[45] The Augustinians and Dominicans specify that communion was to be taken after the Office of Terce and not during Mass.[46] The Conceptionists took communion first thing in the morning at 5 a.m. around Prime.[47] The Hieronymite rule also suggests a separate communion session, in which the nuns in the coro bajo received communion, then guarded the communion hosts left at the cratícula while the priest entered the cloister with a handful of hosts to administer communion to the sick nuns within the convent who could not come down to the coro bajo.[48] The San Jerónimo convent conveniently had its confessional in the coro bajo.[49] It would seem that nuns could thus attend Mass wherever they wanted, upstairs or downstairs, though the ones who sang in the choir were likely upstairs if the organ was there; and they were all upstairs for the Office, which they were required to pray together as a community.[50]

Details of Archbishop Payo Enríquez's 1672–1675 administrative visits to various Mexico City convents suggest the coro alto was the most important space: all of his recommendations for the convents were to be read aloud every fifteen days for a year, and his handwritten notice to that effect was affixed to the entrance of the coro alto, presumably because this would be the space where the nuns would see it most often.[51] In addition, specifically for the Encarnación convent, the archbishop insisted that the abbess and vicar not allow the servants to attend Mass upstairs, but rather downstairs in the coro bajo, for no reason other than "as is tradition."[52] Does this mean that the entire convent community—nuns, novices, servants, and so on—all attended Mass downstairs, or are we to assume that this was another attempt at designating liturgical attendance location based on class, nuns upstairs, servants downstairs?[53]

Fanny Calderón de la Barca noted a particularly memorable experience confirming that the coro alto of Mexico City's Encarnación convent was the prime location for singing in the nineteenth century:

> After supper we proceeded upstairs to the choir (where the nuns attend public worship, and which looks down upon the handsome convent church) to try the organ. I was set down to a Sonata of Mozart's, the servants blowing the bellows. It seems to me that I made more noise than music, for the organ is very old, perhaps as old as the convent, which dates three

centuries back. However, the nuns were pleased, and after they had sung a hymn, we returned below.[54]

A priceless glimpse of the musical and liturgical traditions that stem back to the seventeenth century (as we can gather from comparisons to Archbishop Payo Enríquez's visits to this wealthy convent), Calderón de la Barca's journal entry recounts the musical and social dynamics that a musical space like the "upstairs" coro offered, with her mention of "public worship" suggesting the Mass.

Nuns of the Coro

The level of importance of the liturgical feast days determined music selections, from the most elaborate polyphony to chant and reciting tone depending on nuns' musical abilities and convent resources.[55] The times at which nuns gathered into the coro alto for the Divine Office and either coro alto or bajo for Mass varied from order to order, from the strictest observance of Matins at midnight, for ascetic orders like the Capuchins, to a more comfortable afternoon or evening hour for most others (see Table 2.1).[56]

A variety of devotional services and paraliturgical services occurred within and between the basic schedules, depending on particular feast days or convent ceremonies. Many orders, not least those dedicated to the Virgin Mary (such as the Conceptionists), prayed the Office of the Virgin, a shorter Office focused on Marian devotion interspersed with the monastic Office. Matins and Vespers for the Marian Office took place before Matins and Vespers of the monastic Office.[57] The nuns had to pray this Office of the Virgin kneeling.[58]

Administrative and inaugural ceremonies, such as professions and elections of abbesses, took place in the coro bajo because they required male clergy to assist either inside the coro bajo or outside the grate.[59] Nuns' funerals also took place in the coro bajo, as it was the space that contained crypts below the floor to inter the bodies of the deceased sisters. Further emphasizing this area as a space for the dead, the Purísima Concepcion convent nuns in Puebla traditionally used the coro bajo for symbolic reasons as well. A 1762 ceremonial instructs that the nuns would pray Good Friday Vespers in the coro bajo in a quieter volume than usual; this, including the silencing of church bells and shutting the door to the bell tower, was a sonic way to honor Christ's death.[60] Other convents had the daily tradition of

Table 2.1 Sample convent liturgical schedules

Augustinian
6:00 a.m. Prime, Terce, Sext, None
9:00 a.m. Mass, Sext, None
2:00 p.m. Vespers
3:30 p.m. Compline
9:00 p.m. Matins, Lauds (for the following day)

Capuchin
Midnight Matins, Lauds
5 a.m. Prime, Terce, Sext, None
Noon Mass
2:00 p.m. Vespers
5:00 p.m. Compline

Carmelite
4 a.m. Prime, Terce
6 a.m. Mass
8 a.m. Sext, None
2 p.m. Vespers, Compline
9 p.m. Matins, Lauds (for the following day)

Company of Mary
6:00 a.m. Prime, Terce
7:00 a.m. Mass, Sext
Noon None
3:00 p.m. Vespers
5:00 p.m. Compline
7:45 p.m. Matins, Lauds (for the following day)

Conceptionist
5:00 a.m. Prime
6:30 a.m. Mass, Terce, Sext, None
2:00 p.m. Vespers
6:00 p.m. Compline; Matins, Lauds (for the following day)

Dominican
4:00 a.m. Prime, Terce
6:30 a.m. Mass
8:00 a.m. Sext, None
2:30 p.m. Vespers
5:00 p.m. Compline
9:00 p.m. Matins, Lauds (for the following day)

Table 2.1 Continued

Hieronymite

5:00 a.m. Prime, Terce, Sext, None

7:30 a.m. Mass

2:00 p.m. Vespers, Compline

3:30 p.m. Matins, Lauds (for the following day).

Sources: Arenas Frutos, "Mecenazgo femenino," 33; Chowning, *Rebellious Nuns*, 69; *Instituto y constituciones de la orden de la Compañía*, 98–100; Lavrin, *Brides of Christ*, 118–119; Myers, *A Wild Country*, 271–272; Salazar Simarro, "Música y coro," 33–34; *Regla dada por n. padre San Agustin a sus monjas*, 29–30; *Regla y constituciones para las religiosas recoletas dominicas*, 133–144; *Regla, y constituciones que han de guardar las religiosas . . . del glorioso padre San Geronymo*, 81–94.

processing to the coro bajo at noon, reciting Psalm 50, *Miserere Mei*, to pray for the salvation of convent prelates and patrons.[61] It was beneficial to society for nuns to be in their coro interceding for their patrons during special prayer services, the Mass, and the Divine Office, but they could also pray for the repose of their own souls too. The Hieronymites performed twice yearly the Office of the Dead and a Requiem Mass for the departed members of their own order on the day following the Octave of the feast of St. Jerome and the day after the Octave of Epiphany. Those who did not know the Office of the Dead ("las que no supieran")—typically convent servants, as we will see later—had to recite one hundred Our Fathers and Hail Marys with the words *Requiem aeternam* appended at the end of every *Ave María*.[62]

The coro defined hierarchy among convent inhabitants with respect to liturgy and devotion, marking difference of status among women in the convent. The nuns "of the coro," also known as black-veil choir nuns, were elite women who paid an entrance dowry upon profession, or those who were given dowry waivers on account of their musical abilities (Chapter 3). Those who could not afford full profession after the novitiate remained as white-veil nuns who worked as convent servants, known as *legas*, and they were required to do various chores around the cloister, such as cooking and cleaning—and pumping the pipe organ bellows, as Calderón de la Barca pointed out earlier.[63] Indigenous, African, and mixed-race women, denied any type of veil, were tasked with menial labor and were sometimes called *donadas*, literally "donated ones," since it was considered a pious deed when convent benefactors donated a servant or an enslaved woman to the convent or when a nun professed into the convent and brought her own servants who could assist the community.[64]

Convent servants earned their room and board by freeing the choir nuns of hard labor and chores so that the nuns could focus on the liturgical schedule. To show gratitude for the privilege of serving nuns, servants were charged with reciting a certain number of prayers during particular Office liturgies, as in the case of the Hieronymite Office of the Dead mentioned earlier. Daily, they said twenty-four Our Fathers and Hail Marys during Matins, five of each prayer during Lauds, and seven for each other Office. This was dictated by Mexico City Archbishop Francisco Manso y Zúñiga (1587–1655) and became standard practice as later reprints of the rules indicate.[65] The Dominican rule for the Santa Rosa convent nuns in Puebla similarly required twenty-four Our Fathers at Matins, twelve at Vespers, and seven for the rest of the liturgies, but it also justifies their role in the convent eloquently: "The legas, having been welcomed for physical labor, earning their daily bread by the sweat of their brow, are not required at the Office like the choir nuns, as it is sufficient for them only to hear Mass, and in place of the Office they should say the customary Our Fathers and Hail Marys."[66] The Capuchins were only slightly more egalitarian with their legas, calling on them with three bell strikes to join in the choir for quiet reflective prayer at the end of Matins, Prime, and Compline; for each of these three liturgies, the signals for the nuns to have the legas called into the coro were the prayers *Benedictus Dominus Deus Israel*, *In conspectu Domini*, and *Nunc dimittis*, respectively.[67]

The coordination of all the activities that took place in the coro was charged to the vicaria de coro, the leader of musical activities in the convent, third in line to lead in the convent after the abbess and vicar (assistant abbess) in Conceptionist convents.[68] In the absence of the abbess and vicar, for example, the vicaria de coro was considered the highest-ranking nun in the refectory. In any convent, the choir vicar was typically among the most musically experienced nuns there, and it was her duty to ensure that competent musicians were selected to perform and that they rehearsed ahead of time for the liturgies.[69] Bishop Palafox encouraged convent musicians to practice:

> To avoid defects and errors, principally [by] the one who performs the Office, and those who say or sing the lessons, [they should] go over them before entering the coro.[70]

Similarly, Mexico City's Archbishop Manso y Zuñiga notes:

> The Divine Office must always be said in a tone with the appropriate pause that is indicated in the middle of each verse, except on principal feasts, in

which it will be sung, avoiding all vanities and multiplicity of notes in the song. . . . And so that there are no defects in the pronunciation and accents, principally by the one who performs the Office, practice before entering the coro the Antiphons, Chapters, Lections, and prayers to be said or sung. The singers are to do the same.[71]

Clearly, the Office was the most important liturgy for nuns, as evidenced by these prelates' insistence that it be performed as articulately as possible. As we will see in Chapter 3, it is these rules imposed on nuns by their prelates that would seem to justify their (sometimes desperate-sounding) requests to recruit more musicians when their choirs lacked sufficient performers to sing the Divine Office liturgies adequately. The Franciscan Capuchins make it a point in their rule that no one is to be exempted from the Office, regardless of social standing or quality (qualquier calidad); not even the most learned (letrada) could skip the Office.[72] We will see in the next chapter how social standing was enmeshed with convent musical needs for the Divine Office.

Attendance at daily Mass was also critical, as nuns were required to perform in various memorial Masses bequeathed by patrons, but instructions for attending Mass were often looped into convent rules pertaining to the Office. The term "coro" was thus used to enhance convent roles, as observed in the titles of "black-veil choir nuns" and "choir vicars," but it could also denote an equalizing space where all black-veil choir nuns, regardless of class as the Capuchin rule highlights, were required to be present.

More broadly than the previously proposed reverse panopticon, but in the same vein of thought, Foucault's category of "disciplinary space" as it evolved from "mystical calculus of the infinitesimal and the infinite" in early modern monastic models applies well to our consideration of the coro.[73] He suggests that "disciplinary space tends to be divided into as many sections as there are bodies or elements distributed."[74] We could thus consider the coro a disciplinary space within the disciplinary space of the cloister, which altogether would, according to Foucault,

Establish presences and absences, to know where and how to locate individuals, to set up communications, to interrupt others, to be able at each moment to supervise the conduct of each individual, to assess it, to judge it, to calculate its qualities or merits.[75]

The communication "set up" in the coro was an intercession with the divine for salvation as well as a communication in sung prayer between the nuns. In this light, it is no wonder that the coro was also spoken of synonymously with the Divine Office liturgy itself, whose proper execution was analyzed by particular nuns in their leadership roles; by priest and prelate administrators of the convent; and by God, the saints, and the Virgin Mary transmitting their assessments to visionary nuns, as we will see later.

Chapter 3 of the Conceptionist rule ordinances, on praying the Office, is titled "Attending Coro," and it states the care and intimacy with which the nuns should approach their duty:

> With attention [and] great care, the nuns must desire, above all, to observe the spirit of the Lord and his holy work, with purity of heart and with devout prayer, cleansing their consciences of the earthly desires and vanities of this age and becoming one spirit with their husband Jesus Christ through a bond of love, through which the deepest desires of the virtues are reached, and which perpetuates enmity toward the vices that contaminate souls and separate us from the Lord. This prayer is what makes us love our enemies and pray for those who persecute us and slander us, as the Lord says. And through this most excellent task, enclosure, work, and the rigors of the order are turned into great ease. Because this work that is so necessary to save us is best performed in this holy order, [let] those who are of the coro say the Divine Office during solemn feasts, convent feasts, and their octaves, and greater Sundays and minor Sundays and ferial days according to the Roman Breviary.[76]

Archbishop Manso y Zúñiga also emphasized the saving power of nuns' attendance of coro.[77] The liturgies had to be performed with genuine will and piety through the articulation of vocalized prayers and numerous gestures learned by the nuns.

The gestures interspersed throughout various texts of the Office included signs of the cross, head nods, bows, profound bows, genuflecting, kneeling, and full prostrations on the floor. Such outward physical signs of piety are peppered into devotional material from throughout the seventeenth and eighteenth centuries and listed exhaustively in a nineteenth-century manuscript of rules from an unknown Franciscan convent in Mexico City.[78] It draws from the 1703 *Manual summa de las ceremonias de la Provincia de el Santo Evangelio de México* (see Appendix 2.1). Similar instructions for Dominicans are in a 1789 rule book for Puebla's Santa Rosa convent (see Appendix 2.2).

With a few examples of the degree of body contortion indicated for different moments, from the head nod up through the profound bows and prostrations, we can notice seemingly universal instructions as well as order-specific ones. The Franciscans required the nuns to enter the coro alto by passing through the center, facing the high altar, and kissing the floor. Both the Franciscans and Dominicans required a head nod right after the intonation of a psalm and antiphon. Likewise, head nods were required whenever the names of Jesus, Mary, and St. Dominic were invoked in Dominican houses. The Franciscans suggested more specific nods: minimal when St. Francis was invoked, medium for Mary, and a deep nod for Jesus.

A profound bow, described by the Franciscans as one in which the palms of one's loose hands would reach the knees, was performed at the doxology (*Gloria patri*). It also initiated the *Magnificat* during Vespers, as well as the hymn *Tantum ergo*, but only if the Blessed Sacrament at the high altar was not exposed; if it was exposed, *Tantum ergo* was to begin with a full genuflection. The Dominicans defined their profound bow as one requiring the crossing of arms under the habit's scapular, followed by an inward tuck in which the elbows touch the knees; among the various occasions for this gesture were the first doxology of every Office liturgy and the first prayer in both the Mass and Office. For all other instances of the doxology, the Dominicans also had a mid-way bow, *usque ad genua*, that did not require the abdominal tuck, in which the head was to come down parallel to the knees.

These gestures were not supposed to interfere with the singing or reciting of the words—a tension between bodily practice and vocal practice in which the latter was privileged. Indeed, the gestures likely served as mnemonic aides for the prayers, in addition to serving as embodiments of humility and reverence.[79] The genuflections seem to carry the highest risk for mistakes, as indicated by the Franciscans, who specified:

> The genuflections are not performed before the words that require them nor afterwards, but rather at the same time that they are uttered, and all of the community and the cantors must take care not to get out of tune. There is a danger in long clauses for the voice to crack, and as such, if these are being sung only by the cantors, they may genuflect after the words.[80]

Division into groups within the coro functioned to support the overall antiphonal nature of the Office, typically with a group of cantors and then the rest of the community divided into two groups (or choirs) facing each other, plus any number of instrumentalists, all coordinated by the vicaria de coro.

The organ also had its own liturgical voice, often playing instrumentally during odd- or even-numbered verses of psalms and hymns in alternation with the choir, in which case the text was recited quietly by the choir during the organ solo; the organ also accompanied the verses sung by the choir. This was an aesthetic choice, as Gaspar Isidro Martínez de Trillanes, the dean of Puebla Cathedral in the early eighteenth century, commented to the Santa Inés de Montepulciano nuns, as recorded in their choir book's handwritten notes. The nuns inquired whether they needed to sing during the organ solos, to which he responded no—"otherwise, what is the purpose of the organ?"[81]

In addition, the organist could help keep everyone on pitch with brief interludes when the cantors needed to genuflect after their singing. In a 1791 manuscript of hymns for Vespers from the Santísima Trinidad convent, a side note for the hymn *Vexilla Regis* indicates that the organist "can play a bit while the singers kneel," just before the words *O crux ave* (O hail the cross).[82] Both the Franciscan and Dominican choir rules specify this genuflection at these words too, showing how various types of sources across different orders reinforced similar liturgical practices. The Dominicans were slightly more unyielding with regard to mistakes in singing, requiring nuns who faltered in their singing to perform the *venia*, a prostration particular to the Dominicans, which required them to lie on the floor on their right side.[83]

This kind of prescriptive material passed down from bishops, monks, friars, and priests existed together with more rhetorical devotional instructions for the coro, such as the confessor Martín Vallarta's insistence that "among all your [nuns'] duties, let the Divine Office always be the foremost . . . do not pray it outside the coro, I beg you . . . the coro must be your center."[84] The Dominican chronicler Alonso Franco tells of an exemplary nun in Mexico City's Santa Catalina de Siena convent, Juana de Santa Catarina, who was a talented musician but was "of such virginal restraint and modest composure that she never sang alone, but always with her community."[85] Her voice was to be reserved for the coro, only to intercede with Christ for salvation. We will observe in what follows how supernatural occurrences also defined the coro's centrality.

The Mystical Coro

It was no small task for nuns to be mentally and spiritually prepared for the Office several times daily. This was especially the case on important feast days. Antonio Aribol, Sister Jacinta's biographer, describes the coro as a dynamic place on Corpus Christi when the consecrated host was exposed on the church's high altar throughout the day for all the nuns and faithful to adore. He writes, "When the Blessed Sacrament is exposed, the coro is like a celestial beehive, where the ingenious and laborious rational bees enter and exit; and they attend successively all day with fervor."[86] Aribol characterizes the coro as an area where intense work was carried out for the adoration of the Blessed Sacrament, the church's consecrated communion host believed to contain the real Body of Christ, discussed more in Chapter 4. On two separate occasions, Sister Jacinta mentions that working in the coro—that is to say, praying the Divine Office—was refreshing for her. She never let her ailments keep her from her duties in the coro:

> Though poor health had fatigued my body, arriving in the coro to be with my Lord was restful. . . . Matins began, and I persevered to not lose sight of my Lord by removing any impertinent image that attempted to distract me. Once I collected myself, I felt my body being consumed into my heart as my attention focused on my Lord. My ears remained to listen, and my mouth to speak, but even my vision was interiorizing. The affections grew with the sound of the organ as my soul melted in the Divine praises. . . . When I went to the coro, my body felt relieved, with great calm; I could stay for many hours without growing tired. The Lord makes all the expense. When the Divine Office began, I felt a strong desire to love my Lord. And being in this state of mind, I sometimes became so absorbed with the affections I felt for my Lord that I could not hear singing, nor did I realize where I was; I did not even recognize myself; the longing I felt kept me occupied. This did not last long, because I would come back to my normal self and continue singing with the sisters, but, without knowing how, I became absorbed again.[87]

The irony that hard work would be refreshing yields to the spiritual union with Christ experienced by Sister Jacinta and other mystics. Such contradictory effects have been characterized as inversions in hagiographical writing, which is what nuns' biographies aimed to become, the life story of a future saint.[88] Inversions can be traced to St. Teresa of Ávila's experience of the simultaneous pain and pleasure affiliated with her direct contact with God, which she wrote about as if with a "love for oxymora," as described by Cordula van Wyhe, that would set a standard for future biographies detailing mystical experiences.[89] We will observe the commingling of pain and pleasure regarding Christ's Passion in Chapter 5.

Yet, for all that Jacinta de Atondo's transcendence seems to follow mystic precedents, while exceeding the ordinary demeanor required by nuns in the coro, it was the music performed while she was in the right state of mind that heightened her transcendent experience. Instrumental music, and particularly the organ, elevated her affections. "And I would desire to play that instrument," she continued, "to worship my Lord with heart, lips, strength, senses, and with all the limbs of my body."[90] An instrument as technologically sophisticated as an organ would allow her to do so.[91]

Other types of instruments generated different kinds of visions. Sister María de Jesús heard Puebla's Purísima Concepción convent church bell tolling the Office hours as the literal voice of God calling her to the coro, rather than as clanging cast metal.[92] Rumored to have a sixth sense, Sister María once instructed a novice to ring the call for Vespers, claiming that the convent bell ringer had fallen asleep. And when the novice arrived at the bell tower, she was amazed to find that the bell ringer had been sleeping, just as Sister María had foretold; the novice proceeded to fulfill her task.[93] María incorporated the sound of the convent church bell as a vital part of her spiritual and aural experience of the Divine Office. Her biographers further claim that she was never once late to the coro.[94] On the contrary, she always arrived in the coro before the start of the liturgies, because the first bell stroke of the Office brought her a vision of the Virgin Mary surrounded by angels. If María considered the bell toll the voice of God, then the appearance of the Virgin Mary at the sound of the convent bell should come as no surprise given what we learned about the voice of God in Chapter 1. Thus, María de Jesús would arrive at the coro early to welcome her Lady and role model.[95]

Sister María de Jesús received most of her divine revelations specifically within the coro.[96] This location reified the post-Tridentine notion that mysticism, especially that experienced by women, should be carefully controlled (disciplined or analyzed, recalling Foucault), ideally within monastic enclosure as exemplified by the writings of St. Teresa of Ávila.[97] To emphasize Sister María's supernatural virtue, her biography by Diego de Lemus (1683) included a frontispiece with a sketch of María with her eyes partially shut, signifying that she was having a mystical vision (see Figure 2.7).[98] To her left, the cloud shows her being received into heaven by the Virgin Mary and saints.

Figure 2.7 Anonymous frontispiece depicting María de Jesús, Diego de Lemus, *Vida, virtudes, trabajos, favores y milagros*, ca. 1683

The Virgin Mary also visited the convent coro on other occasions, not just at the bell tolls:

The venerable mother [María de Jesús] was attending Vespers on one feast for the Guardian Angel, and as the sisters were singing, seated in their usual spots, she noticed that in between every two nuns, there were angels holding green and beautiful saplings in their hands. She also noticed the Empress of Heaven [the Virgin Mary] presiding over the celestial choir and the monastic choir. Vespers continued as such, and in the time that lapsed, those green saplings . . . had blossomed with attractive and fragrant flowers, and at the end, the angels collected the nuns' zeal and affections, and they offered them to the Lord as sweet aromas. She also noticed that at the time when the nuns intoned the *Gloria Patri et Filio et Spiritui Sancto*, standing and bowing their heads, so too the angels stood to perform the same humble veneration: a worthy correspondence between angelic and human nature.[99]

The angels mimicking the nuns' reverential gestures during the doxology is a moment in which the angels follow the nuns' lead, an inversion of Vallarta's call for nuns to imitate the angels in the choir, as directed through Sister Clori in the introduction. In this vision, the angels had to comply with the nuns, because the Virgin Mary was guiding the nuns in prayer and song. With the Virgin Mary leading, the nuns prayed and sang these Vespers in a state of grace that yielded a sincere offering of praise and intercession for salvation, allegorized as flowers.[100]

That convents were a foretaste of heaven, with angelic voices and all, was a frequent metaphor in convent literature, especially in nuns' biographies. On one occasion during the feast of the Ascension, María de Jesús even demonstrated her abilities in bilocation, her biography setting the scene in both coros to analogize the heavenly hierarchies. María de Jesús and Sister Gerónima went downstairs for communion; Sister Gerónima proceeded first through a staircase that connected both coros and then headed back up the same way, having seen Sister María follow her and take communion after her.[101] The staircase they used was the only way to travel between the coros, but when Sister Gerónima arrived upstairs, she found that Sister María was already there. When she inquired with the nuns about how María de Jesús arrived in the coro before she had, the nuns informed Gerónima that she had been there all day and never left her seat. How could Sister María de Jesús be in both the coro alto and coro bajo at the same time?

The biographer Francisco Pardo explained this as a sign that "this bride of Christ, on account of her merits, went up from the coro bajo, belonging to the angels in heaven, to the coro of the cherubim, who enjoy God's glory with more proximity."[102] Sister María de Jesús was literally ascended on Ascension Day, which commemorated Jesus' ascension into heaven. Her biographies elevated her for the purpose of her beatification.[103] And the convent coro figured prominently in this panegyric because its physical disposition in the church lent itself very well to metaphors with heaven.

We can begin to observe how particular feasts and events within the liturgies were worth mentioning in the biographies as slice-of-life moments. They stirred the mystical thoughts of visionaries in the coro while reinforcing real coro rules and practices, such as the bow at the doxology (*Gloria Patri*). Similarly, the confessor of Sister María Josefa de la Encarnación (1687–1752), active in Mexico City's Encarnación convent, narrated stories from nuns who once witnessed María Josefa go into ecstasy during the singing of the *Magnificat* at Vespers for the feast of St. Lawrence.[104] She became so dazed that she was unreactive to the other nuns slapping her and pulling her hair to try to bring her back to reality.[105] During Matins for the feast of St. Ambrose, she had a vision of Christ in heaven with his five wounds at the same time that she beheld him radiant as the sun, shining from the consecrated host at the high altar—all while kneeling at the *venite adoremus* verse of the invitatory Psalm 94.[106] In return for her exceptionally virtuous meditations and prayers, on the feast of the Assumption in 1735 the Virgin Mary scattered flowers over María Josefa as she took communion at the cratícula.[107] Her confessor described María Josefa's daily prayers as flowers to Christ, his mother the Virgin Mary, and the saints. The Virgin Mary thus returned the favor, assuring María Josefa of her intercession by scattering flowers over her on the day that commemorated Mary's Assumption into heaven.[108] Such visions give us a foretaste of how Christ's Passion and Marian devotion become entwined with eucharistic devotion and music, which we will attend to in Chapter 4.

The liturgical calendar provided points of reference for cloistered nuns to recall their own mystical experiences or those of other sisters in the coro, which they could then retell in their own writing and/or in oral history given to biographers. Indeed, nuns tended to narrate "a process spanning many cycles," incorporating references to convent celebrations, feasts, and liturgies to make sense of mysticism's timelessness, rather than relying on specific dates and linear chronology.[109] The date of the Assumption in the earlier example was almost certainly the Jesuit biographer José María Genovesi's addition to anchor María Josefa's experiences in historical time.[110] Drawing on Julia Kristeva's theory of "women's time," Kathleen Ross examines the juxtaposition of confined space and time, essential to the patriarchy, with the unencumbered, timeless, spaceless ecstasy of mystic experiences in the Jesús María convent, as incorporated into Sigüenza y Góngora's chronicle of that convent.[111] Mystics were free of enclosure within their own bodies and minds. María Josefa's biography likewise incorporates both the nuns' own conception of time and Genovesi's attempt at writing chronological history.

Reflecting on the nuns' cyclical-liturgical thought process in María Josefa's biography allows us to make considerably more sense of her visions occurring on seemingly random feasts: St. Ambrose (December 7), then, some eight months later, St. Lawrence (August 10) and the Assumption (August 15). The phrase *venite adoremus* is sung on all three days. María Josefa's narrative at first alludes to Marian devotion as the stimulation of her transcendence by noting the singing of the *Magnificat* on St. Lawrence Day as the triggering moment. Yet it is also on the feast of St. Lawrence that the words *venite adoremus* (which brought about her vision on St. Ambrose Day mentioned before) feature in the invitatory prescribed at Matins: "Blessed Lawrence, martyr of Christ, is crowned triumphantly in heaven: Come, let us adore the Lord" (Beatus Laurentius Christi martyr triumphat coronatus in caelis: Venite adoremus Dominum).[112] The recollection of María Josefa's mystical experiences closes once more with Marian devotion, as Mary pours flowers over her during the feast of the Assumption, a celebration that calls for a supplemental invitatory antiphon, performed at Matins to enhance the occasion's solemnity. This antiphon quotes directly from the portion of Psalm 94 in which everyone in the coro kneels during the words *venite adoremus*. Within this cyclical-liturgical mindset, then, phrases from liturgical music jogged nuns' memories, while enhancing the mystical experiences of others.

A four-voice polyphonic setting of the invitatory antiphon for the Assumption *Venite adoremus regem regum* was copied in the first half of the eighteenth century for use in María Josefa's convent during her lifetime. The manuscript from the Encarnación choirbooks only includes text underlay for the two highest voices, while the tenor and bass lack full text. The bass includes notes that read "En C Sol Fa Ut" and "En D La Sol Re," referring to the specific pitch according to solmization and thus suggesting that this line would have been performed by a transposing instrument.

The piece is in two sections corresponding with the two halves of the text, the first acknowledging Christ as king of kings and the second the Marian text for the feast:

Venite adoremus	Come let us adore
regem regum,	the king of kings,
cuius hodie aetherium	whose mother, the Virgin, today
Virgo Mater assumpta est caelum.	has been taken up to high heaven.

It begins in a downward imitative cascade across all the voice parts, "ve-nite" drawn out with long note values, as well as "adoremus" with melismas, highlighting this critical moment in the antiphon's psalm source in which the community is supposed to kneel (see Example 2.2). The phrase "regem regum" repeats in the soprano, but not in any other voice, and it is the alto part that takes on a four-measure melismatic emphasis on "regum" (mm. 6–9). The alto once again has a lengthy melismatic role in the second half of the antiphon, embellishing "assumpta" ("taken up," or literally "assumed") in an eight-note flourish across three measures (mm. 18–20).

The start of the antiphon's second half at m. 10 staggers the imitation of its opening phrase "cuius hodie . . . ": the soprano is imitated exactly an octave below by the tenor line, and then the alto's entrance is imitated exactly an oc-tave below by the bass, but only through its opening dotted motive. The gen-eral upward trajectory of these opening lines across each voice fully captures the occasion of Mary's ascent into heaven. The piece then continues in free counterpoint, but the pairing up of voices remains significant. In the second half of m. 18, the soprano pairs up in thirds with the alto's eighth-note figure, followed by the alto pairing in thirds with the tenor at the end of m. 19, then followed by paring between the tenor and bass in m. 20. Finally, the pairing of voices in thirds moves upward again to the tenor and alto parts (m. 22), which proceed into a rhythmic cadence that allows the soprano to take the eighth-note motive in a stepwise ascent leading to the closing of the anti-phon. In this way, the salvific pair, Mary and Jesus, are extolled across every voice part through these third pairings, likely a symbol of Mary's entwine-ment with Christ in the Trinity. The text repetition scheme is also signifi-cant. The second half of the antiphon has more repetitions of the text than the first half. As if to leave no doubt that the piece is for Mary's Assumption, the message "assumpta est caelum" repeats three times in the soprano; "mater" repeats twice in the alto before "assumpta est caelum" repeats twice in this voice, then finally "est caelum" repeats again. Although likely played by instruments and not sung, the tenor part's logical text underlay would repeat "assumpta est caelum."

Polyphony punctuated some of the most salient festivities. It was a con-trapuntal exercise of various repetitions across various voices, which no doubt must have been enhanced—echoed, repeated again—by the walls and ceilings of the coro reverberating the nuns' voices and instrument sounds among themselves and echoing as acousmatic, veiled voices beyond the coro grates. The encounters with sacred texts repeated across the liturgical year,

Example 2.2 Anonymous, *Venite adoremus regem regum*, Encarnación convent choirbook 6, folios 131v–132r

Example 2.2 Continued

whether in polyphony or not, also prompted some to remember particular moments of ecstasy, even if repeated months later, as we saw in María Josefa's biography. Given what we now know about the transcendent effects of repetition,[113] we might also consider Sister Jacinta's ecstasy over the organ's sound and Sister María de Jesús' visions with the convent bell ringing as more than just aesthetically prompted flights of the mind. While their hypnotic effects were potentially owed to their repetitiveness, we know for certain that these sounds, as well as liturgical singing, were closely tied to the space of the coro, with its repetitive rituals and communal intimacy throughout the day and liturgical year.

The joy of music making and listening in the coro documented in the biographies sets an example for proper behavior in the convent, one of the primary purposes of nuns' devotional literature. These examples of liturgical song parallel Caroline Walker Bynum's and Frank Graziano's notion of psychologically inflected mysticism, in which aesthetically induced transcendence through music is the cause for nuns' visions, auditions, and bilocation abilities.[114] These extraordinary events humanize the omnipresence of God. His omniscience is assigned directly to specific nuns without anyone in the convent knowing when their mystic sisters could see, feel, or hear God and the Virgin Mary. Sometimes God communicated messages to particular nuns about the behavior of other nuns in the convent. This added another level of internal surveillance to the so-called reverse panopticon while prescribing agency to certain role-model nuns.[115]

That the voices of nuns had the power to reach God's ears, but that his voice could only be heard by a select few in the coro is also exemplified in the biography of Sister Bárbara Josefa, who lived in Puebla's Santísima Trinidad convent. Once, she was enjoying the villancicos performed in her convent for Corpus Christi, but God intervened with an admonishment:

> Child, that music is not for me; stop enjoying it. Weep over these offenses that your sisters cause me; the secular people come to amuse themselves with the musicians; and your sisters sing to amuse them without any reverence to my blessed body in the Sacrament.[116]

The choir had been singing villancicos requested by lay people throughout the Octave of Corpus Christi.[117] Miguel de Torres, Bárbara's biographer, noted that he would have to write a separate volume to tell of all the occasions in which singers performed such sacrilege.[118] Once more the famous passage from the Song of Songs is used to set an example, as we observed in Chapter 1. "Show me but your face, let me but hear your voice, that voice sweet as your face is fair," is used by Torres to note that the nuns' voices would only resound in the church and never make it to God's ears if their intention was not to sing to him exclusively.[119] Such abuse of sacred music was believed to earn nuns a heavy dose of torment upon their death: Sister Bárbara had a vision of nuns who had repented for their misbehaviors in the coro being cleansed by the fires of purgatory, suggesting eventual salvation was possible after purgation in that liminal space that proceeded death but preceded heaven in Catholic doctrine.[120] Sacred words leaving the lips of nuns could also be sinful if not directed in a certain way, and they could cause listeners to sin without their even knowing it.

Bishop Palafox y Mendoza's rule for nuns in Puebla was specific about what things should be avoided in the coros regarding the performing arts to keep the nuns in a state of righteousness, "comparable to the angels in heaven." Palafox writes:

> In no feast or occasion shall there be dances in either coro, and no plays . . .
> and the villancicos, and all else that is sung, shall not contain profane words,
> unworthy of religious composure and modesty. As such, we prohibit guitars,
> rattles, drums, tambourines, and other instruments that contradict the
> modesty and the seriousness of the divine cult[121] and religious profession.

Such a specific list indicates that these situations must have taken place, revealing some of the convents' possible performative delights and a host of instruments nuns could play, in addition to the suggestion that profane words from secular poetry and the theatrical world could get mixed into sacred songs.[122]

In another moment where Sister Bárbara was listening attentively to villancicos on a different Corpus Christi feast than the previous occasion, she was said to have heard them directly from the angels.[123] Her biographer was inspired by the unspecified villancico of Bárbara's experience to include Thomas Aquinas' "Adoro te devote" in Spanish translation for readers of her biography to contemplate, a hymn that explains the mystery of the Eucharist by recalling that hearing the word of God was enough to believe in his presence within the consecrated host without actually seeing, touching, or tasting.[124] We will come back to this moment in Bárbara's biography in Chapter 4, which treats eucharistic devotional music in more depth, but for now we can consider one villancico that potentially navigates a fine line between sacred and secular poetics in its effort to (de)mystify the Eucharist.

The anonymous villancico *Yo quiero bien* (CSG.122, ca. 1673–1691) from Sister Bárbara's convent is scored for two sopranos, alto, and bass accompaniment.[125] In typical villancico fashion, it consists of a through-composed estribillo notated for the full ensemble and strophic coplas for which the musical texture reduces to two voices.

Estribillo
Yo quiero bien
y es fuerza decir a quién.

I love genuinely,
and I must say whom [I love].

Coplas
1. Yo quiero bien, dice el alma,
cierto galán, y es tan llano,
que le tengo de mi mano
y le miro cara a cara.

I love genuinely, says the soul,
a certain handsome man, so easygoing
that I take him by the hand,
and I watch him face to face.

2. Quiérole como a mi vida,
y es tan grande mi querer,
que quiero que amantes quieran
quererle todos también.

I love him as I love my own life
and my love is so great,
that I want all lovers to desire
to love him as well.

3. Quiero, y no por ser querida,
amo, y no por ser amada,
que quiero estar obligada
sin fin de corresponder.

I desire, but not to be desired,
I love, but not to be loved,
for I want to be committed,
without anything in return.

4. Quiérole, en fin, porque es sólo
digno de querer,
y tanto que de su mano
favor me fuera desdén.

I love him, finally, because only he
is worthy of love,
so much so, that coming from him
any favor would be disdain.

We would expect that the coplas might clarify that this is not a secular love song, that Christ is the object of affection, and therefore the source of redemption, but they do not state this explicitly. We only know that it is a eucharistic song because the title page indicates as much.

Would this piece have broken the bishop's rule against profane poetry? Probably not, as it is reminiscent of the amorous poetry of St. Teresa of Ávila's confessor and spiritual director, St. John of the Cross. Drawing from the Song of Songs, St. John's poetry alludes to God as an un-named lover of a female human soul.[126] "Cast as a woman," as Elizabeth Rhodes notes, the voice of the soul "satisfied the exigencies of hegemonic gender constructs" in the early modern period.[127] Yet the words of the villancico, with references to a "galán/ handsome man" who is "llano/easygoing" in copla 1, allude more to Jesus, the human incarnation of the Trinity, rather than the omnipresent, fatherly God or invisible Holy Spirit.[128] In Chapter 1 we observed how convenient it was for the profession response *Amo Christum* and a sermon for the Immaculate Conception to refer to individual components of the Trinity to convey personal messages and explain doctrinal mysteries to nuns. Thus, in alluding to Jesus, this villancico has a certain vitality when performed by women's voices, musicalizing a physical sensuousness that was just barely avoided in St. John of the Cross' writing.[129] We will attend to more of this direct physical union between Christ and nuns in Chapter 4. The last two coplas of *Yo quiero bien* also suggest a one-directional relationship common in convent devotional material that expounds on self-denial: "desiring without being desired," "loving without anything in return," "favor would be disdain."

While we do not have evidence as to how the words of such vernacular hymns were understood by nuns, Sister Bárbara's biography at least gestures toward appropriate role models for sacred poetry and literature. In addition, Sister María Anna Águeda de San Ignacio of Puebla's Santa Rosa convent wrote a series of meditations for reflecting on various moments of the life of Christ during each part of the Mass, including all parts of the Ordinary and Proper.[130] Sister María de Jesús's biographies also underscore ways of achieving proper contemplation while singing.

Coro Flowers

At Puebla's Purísima Concepción Convent, singers in the perfect state of grace—what Dominicans call virtuous attention ("virtual atención") because of the virtue it requires—could readily generate flowers when singing the Office in the coro.[131] As Sister María de Jesús once claimed to have observed, her assistant Agustina de Santa Teresa was singing during solemn Matins for Christmas and at every cadence an angel removed flowers of various shades and colors from her mouth.[132] Intrigued, Sister María proceeded to ask Sister Agustina what she thought and felt while she was performing, to which she replied:

> I began to sing so that my voice would be heard most sonorously in heaven, in the name of our holy mother church: all my breaths and all the words I pronounced were acts of contrition, of humility, of love and appreciation that I offered from the bottom of my heart to our newborn savior. They were also pleas for abundant grace on behalf of the faithful, for the conversion of sinners, the return of heretics to our holy faith, and other graces, and favors to benefit particular people.[133]

Flowers once more appear as a trope for well-expressed musical sound, symbols of successful intercession for salvation. The Jesuit José Parreño aptly described the flowers of devout prayer and song in his 1794 preface to a novena for the Virgin of Sorrows, sponsored by the Jesús María nuns. Recalling the garden and botanical metaphors we observed in Chapter 1, it is worth observing how Parreño notes that flowers are "a sign of the affects that our lips insinuate and that the heart sprouts,"[134] another rhetorical variation echoing Martín de Vallarta earlier in the century within his dialog between Sister Clori and Casandra we encountered, with hearts singing and lips as instruments to channel salvation. Altogether, the image of the coro is projected as a secret garden within a garden, lush with colorful and fragrant flowers.

If Sister Rosa—"Rose"—who opened this chapter had read Sister Agustina's passage, she might have been inclined to sing her soprano solo in a similarly pious manner. Such rhetoric provides a florid example that outlines church leaders' expectations for prayerful singing, effective in interceding for salvation. Just as the coro grates are a physical manifestation of enclosure rules, the examples in the biographies remain as indications that even thinking about music and its meaning was regulated by vows of obedience and enclosure. The architecture, the prayers, the visions, the metaphors, and the misbehaviors associated with the coros were an integral part of nuns' musical experiences.

Who was Sister Rosa, whose *Misa "Bonae voluntatis"* in the Encarnación convent choirbooks opened our discussion of the coro? She was a singing wallflower whose enclosed resounding took place within an exceptional space, a threshold of female sounds emanating from a world, a garden, veiled from the gaze of New Spanish citizens. The coro was a place for both Rosa's performance and anonymity, a place not only to follow the rules of singing and praying for salvation, but also to express her individual piety and, if she were so inclined, even to experience mystical visions connected to her singing. As we will see in the next chapter, it took a certain type of discipline to arrive in this space, and to be able to remain there.

3

Disciplined Sounds

Dowry Waivers and Race, or Who Was Sister Mariana Josefa de Señor San Ignacio?

We know that on the day of October 13 sometime in the 1790s, Mariana Josefa de Señor San Ignacio professed in Mexico City's San José de Gracia convent. We know this from a profession portrait painted of her and marked with a date, but the portrait itself merits attention before we tackle the mystery of what year it was painted (Figure 3.1).[1] Mariana's white habit and blue cape of the Conceptionist order and the black veil are embellished with embroidery executed in fine gold and white threads. A white pleated scapular drapes down the front of her torso. At the same time, another piece of finely stitched cloth, a stole-like sash called a yoke, frames the strand of rosary beads around Mariana's neck.[2] She wears a circular badge called an *escudo*, here depicting the Immaculate Conception flanked by Saints Joseph and Francis of Assisi, functioning doubly as an artistic device and as an element fundamental to her order's accoutrements. The escudo forms the top of a triangle of devotional art within the portrait, above a Christ Child statue held in Mariana's right hand and a palm frond in her left hand bearing a small oval-shaped picture of Saints Joseph and Clare.[3] The portrait's emphasis on St. Joseph, depicted twice, reminds viewers of Mariana's patron saint and stems from her middle name, Josefa. As shown in a biographical sketch we will discuss momentarily, Joseph (José) was also Mariana's father's name, and thus St. Joseph was likely a family patron saint. The presence of the Franciscans Clare and Francis in the portrait would likewise signify support for the doctrine of the Immaculate Conception, which Mariana swore to defend in her profession ceremony.

We are now familiar with the space within the San José de Gracia convent where Mariana's initiation would have taken place (see Chapter 2). The artist would have peeked through the grates of the coro bajo to see her in her profession regalia, as was sung about in the antiphons discussed in Chapter 1. The convent choir and Mariana herself would have sung antiphons appropriate for a virgin woman. But how do we know that Mariana was a virgin?

Immaculate Sounds. Cesar D. Favila, Oxford University Press. © Oxford University Press 2023.
DOI: 10.1093/oso/9780197621899.003.0004

Figure 3.1 Alcíbar, *Votive Portrait of Sor M. María Anna Josefa de San Ignacio*, 1793. With permission from the Museum of Fine Arts, Budapest

Her relevant family background in the portrait's biographical sketch below her image says nothing about virginity. As we see in the text, it reads,

> Portrait of M. María Anna Josefa de Sr. Sn. Ignacio: Professed nun in the Convent of San José de Gracia: legitimate daughter of Dn. José Francisco Ventemilla and Dña. María Garcia. Professed on 13 October 179[?], 16 years, 13 days of age. Josephus ab Alzibar [*sic*] pinxt. a 179[?].[4]

Diving deep into the fortuitous archival process clarifies both Mariana's virginity status and the portrait's mysterious date. The last numbers on the dates are difficult to read because they appear scratched off at the top. With only the bottom half of the numeral being legible in both instances, it could be either a 3 or a 5—and indeed, art historians have dated the portrait 1795, while the Museum of Fine Arts in Budapest, where the artwork is preserved, has it cataloged as 1793.[5]

My intention was never to solve an art-historical discrepancy, but I found the resolution preserved among the hundreds of convent dowry contracts in Mexico City's Archivo General de la Nación (AGN). On October 2, 1793, the nuns of the San José de Gracia convent requested a dowry waiver from the archdiocese for a sixteen-year-old young woman wishing full profession among the convent's ranks. She had completed her year-long novitiate in the convent, and she sang and played the organ. These skills could qualify her for a dowry exemption as a "titled musician" ("a título de música") in exchange for her performance in the liturgies.[6] The request reads:

> Most excellent and illustrious Lord,
>
> We, the abbess, vicar, and counselors of this convent of our holy father San José de Gracia, affiliated with and in obedience of your excellency, placed at your feet in the most proper fashion, report that one year after having completed her approval and novitiate, Sister Mariana de San Ignacio requests to be admitted into the solemn profession to be a choir and black veil nun as a titled musician, as an organist and singer. For this purpose, we humbly beseech that your excellency approves what is necessary for the usual proceedings. [We sign] in continuous obedience of your illustrious excellency and with the affection of humble and attentive servants who venerate your illustrious lord reverend father.
>
> María Rosa del Niño Jesús, Abbess
> María Micaela del Corazón de Jesús, Vicar
> Ana Ignacia de S. San José, Counselor.
> Juana de la Santísima Trinidad, Counselor.
> Clara de Jesús, Counselor.
> María Dolores de Jesús, Counselor.[7]

The information that follows in the notarial record is decisive in concluding that this Mariana is the sitter of Alcíbar's portrait.

As is typical of dowry contracts, the candidate was asked questions to establish her position as a novice in the convent and her identity within society prior to entering the cloister, as well as her aptitude for the fully professed life. The notary recorded the responses of the young woman in question:

> And being by her name and surname of the religion, calidad, filiation, nature, state, and age, she said: that she is called, as stated, Sister Mariana de San Ignacio; a Spanish virgin, born in Mexico, legitimate daughter of Don José Ventemilla and Doña María Loreto García, [and she is] of the age of sixteen.[8]

The portrait and the AGN record coincide in month and decade; notarizing a dowry waiver ten days prior to profession makes the date range completely logical. The sources are also in agreement on the convent, the candidate's name and age, and both her parents' names. Alcíbar's portrait is the portrait of a singer and organist named Mariana de San Ignacio.[9]

There are some other peculiarities worth unpacking from the AGN document. Calidad is a consequential term that will come up in this chapter regularly. In this instance, the notary was being comprehensive, as calidad encompassed so much of what was already spelled out and understood in the quotation. In these contexts, calidad was what Jesús Ramos-Kittrell calls "an aggregate of attributes (e.g., employment, institutional rank, personal connections) that gave an all-encompassing impression of a person's social reputation and image, and thus defined one's status among Spaniards."[10] More specifically, Ramos-Kittrell argues, "it referred to a number of factors, including economic status, occupation, purity of blood, and birthplace, in short, to 'reputation as a whole.'"[11] Legitimacy, the overlapping word in both the painting and the record, was a designation for blood purity.

Calidad in this case also describes people such that their identity is commensurate with their discipline, their ability to fashion themselves into a particular Spanish social mold. Given that Mariana's notarized dowry record attends to her musical abilities, how might these legal and artistic displays of discipline, both of them visual, correspond to disciplinary or disciplined sound? In other words, does discipline manifest in a musical or sonic equivalent to the visualized disciplinary spaces of the notarial record and the profession portrait? In seeking the answer to this question within the types of sources available, those examined throughout this book so far, this chapter undertakes an "acoustically tuned exploration" to argue that the sound of discipline manifested in both obvious and ambiguous ways.[12]

The painting and notarial record coincide in their capturing of discipline as well. Except for a sitter's biographical sketch and face, the portraits are highly conventional with little change other than minor order-specific details drawn by the artist.[13] "The consistency of pictorial format and bridal iconography effectively lessens differences and emphasizes commonalities," notes James Córdova, "thereby establishing a kind of corporate religious identity among New Spain's nuns."[14] From the notarial side, the formulaic nature of colonial Latin American entrance dowry protocols and dowry-waiver documentations makes them disciplinary spaces.

The disciplined space of the notarial record shapes and molds personal narratives into legal rhetoric believed to be true for the readers and writers of the documents.[15] Like a profession portrait's artist choosing the regalia for his sitter based on her convent order, family devotions, and other such factors, a notary public also had several rubrics of legal phrases with carefully placed blank spaces to fill in personal details, such as dates, personal names, and convent—to discipline an individual into the legally binding social condition at hand. The characterization of notarial writing, in the words of Asunción Lavrin, as "ritual phrases," especially for recording convent admissions, is apt here.[16] Strategic repetition, or redundancy, as with the earlier quote about calidad, is a key characteristic of discipline.[17] The strategy of repeating certain stock phrases in the notarial record would convince Church authorities that the women named in the records were fit for the convent. In other words, the Church carefully vetted every woman before she engaged in spiritual marriage when professing as a nun and becoming a bride of Christ.[18]

Disciplinary sound is central to this book. Thus far, I have posited the resonance of virginal bodies singing from the disciplined, acousmatic space of the coro that hid nuns' identities, but that allowed for their voices to resound into the public's ears in the church naves. This chapter builds on that finding by investigating the disciplinary sounds implied in the music dowry-waiver process itself and exploring how sound became implicated within the disciplined space of the notarial record.[19] The "usual proceedings" the San José de Gracia nuns requested in their letter—which consisted of a music audition and a formal background check of the candidate's calidad—are missing from Mariana's file. Such records, surviving in some cases with more thorough documentation of these proceedings, would provide documentary evidence to Church officials that a woman could initiate into the disciplined life of the convent to intercede for humanity's salvation. That discipline was understood by New Spanish society in a highly racialized manner, as the music auditions woven into testimonies of a candidate's family lineage make evident. As such, this chapter also gives a nuanced sense of how Mariana might have understood herself and how she comprehended the various politics of salvation and its sonic and racialized dimensions.

Profession villancicos document the spiritual ascent of women like Mariana into the salvation economy offered by the Church, a documentation in art that mirrors how the notarial record documented a woman's ascent in society upon profession.[20] The profession portrait seems somewhere in between, at once reproducing biographical material relevant to the notary and using iconography that makes the nun look saintlike. The trope of ascending and descending has been accompanying our narrative in various ways, including Sister María de Jesús' bilocation, ascending to the coro alto (Chapter 2), and the Virgin Mary's elevation to immaculately conceived, allegorized in the rise and fall of musical pitches (Chapter 1). In this chapter, we will dwell momentarily on the phenomenon of rising and falling before arriving at the dowry-waiver process, following a roundabout path that attends to real music and voice first.

Prelude to the Dowry-Waiver Process

Martin de Vallarta's quip that "vows and constitutions are the feathers with which the nun flies to heaven, but even feathers can be heavy" also uses the trope of ascending and descending, with its reference to feathers signaling the wings of either angels or birds that carry the nuns to heaven.[21] It reminds aspiring nuns of the burdensome nature of the disciplined life necessary to thrive in the convent. Delving into the devotional media, such tropes are found in nuns' actual music too, as seen in the anonymous villancico *Tonada sola a lo divino* (CSG.109, ca. 1717), written for Sister Clara Gregoria de la Ascensión of the Santísima Trinidad convent in Puebla. Its title page indicates that she is the dedicatee.

Estribillo

Si el dulce metro de mis ansias	If the sweet rhythm of my longing
vuela por remontarse	soars to climb
en alas del deseo,	by wings of desire,
no se fatigue por subir.	may it not tire from rising.
Pues logro que a mis manos	Because the entire heaven
se venga todo un cielo,	comes into my hands,
ay dulce dueño,	oh sweet master,
ay amor que en ti	oh love that in you
el alma busca su centro.	the soul seeks its center.

Coplas

1. Hoy por buscar al esposo,	1. Today in search for the groom,
se oculta en el casto velo	the one who lovingly solicits,
la que amante solicita	the center of his perfections,
en sus finezas el centro;	hides herself in a chaste veil;
Ay dulce dueño,	oh sweet master,
ay amor que en ti	oh love that in you
el alma busca su centro.	the soul seeks its center.
2. La libertad que consagra,	2. The liberty that she consecrates
es última del deseo	is the last desire,
que dichosamente arde	which happily burns
de puro amor en el fuego;	from pure love in the fire;
Ay dulce dueño,	oh sweet master,
ay amor que en ti	oh love that in you
el alma busca su centro.	the soul seeks its center.
3. Las voces con que se ofrece,	3. The voices with which she offers herself,
son cadenas de su cuello,	are chains around her neck,
dándole a precios el oro,	and the gold of the most loving passion
del mas amoroso incendio;	gives them value;
Ay dulce dueño,	oh sweet master,
ay amor que en ti	oh love that in you
el alma busca su centro.	the soul seeks its center.
4. Por unirse al dulce esposo,	4. To unite herself with the sweet groom,
a el mundo pone en desprecio,	she despises the world,
y llamándole amoroso,	and calling him loving,
repite con dulces ecos;	she repeats with sweet echoes;
Ay dulce dueño,	oh sweet master,
ay amor que en ti	oh love that in you
el alma busca su centro.	the soul seeks its center.

The piece is for solo tiple and bass accompaniment. Its F final, C mediation, and B flat in the key signature place this villancico solidly in mode 5, a joyful mode, appropriate for an initiation ceremony.[22] The text of the first copla suggests profession as the most obvious context for this piece, because it speaks about a one-time occasion, "today," rather than a general yearlong or yearly devotion. Voice is present in copla 3, its localization in the throat reminiscent of Bernardo Balbuena's poetry we read in Chapter 1. This villancico focuses on the external body part—the neck—where a woman would don a (gold necklace) chain of jewelry, conflated in the poetics here with the chains of servitude/slavery. The subject is metaphorically leashed into the professed life when she vocalizes her four vows—united to the unnamed sweet groom of copla 4, which would be Jesus.

The tiple voice and accompaniment interact mostly in intervals of thirds accompanying a text that cheers on the nun—in contrast to Vallarta's cautionary words, "but even feathers can be heavy." The estribillo is prone to word painting: as seen in Example 3.1, the pitches in the tiple gradually ascend over an octave through the words climb ("remontarse") and wings ("alas") in mm. 5–8; the word "wings" is then set to a melisma of fluttering quarter notes (mm. 7–8). Elaborating on the theme of struggle within flight, to which Vallarta referred, the singer finally performs two fatiguing leaps of an octave at the end of the phrase, "may it not tire from rising" ("no se fatigue por subir"). The word rising ("subir") is set to a leap from F4 to F5 in mm. 15–16, then from D4 and D5 in mm. 20–21.

The question remains as to whether Sister Clara Gregoria de la Ascensión, named on the title page of the villancico manuscript, was the singer and/or the woman professing for whom this villancico was composed. In the Santísima Trinidad repertory to which this *Tonada* belongs, Clara's name is not found on any other sheet of music; had her name been written on a particular voice or instrumental part, and not just on the dedication page, that would have indicated with more assurance that she could have been a convent musician, like Rosa in the previous chapter.[23] Her name is also not in the text of the estribillo or the coplas, as in other profession villancicos in the Santísima Trinidad repertory composed specifically for the women named in the poetry.[24] So, if she was not a musician and she is not named in the text, then the most likely possibility is that she was the sponsor of the piece, as it was not uncommon for nuns to give money in support of music, art, and particular devotions within their convents.[25] Or, indeed, she could have been the woman whose profession this was meant to celebrate, except that the text of the profession villancico was more generic and could be sung for all other women professing into the Santísima Trinidad convent and not just for Clara alone.

Listening to these pieces would seem to be similar to listening to a devotional villancico, like those examined in other chapters of this book. It

Example 3.1 Anonymous, *Tonada sola a lo divino* (CSG.109), mm. 5–24

would be like looking at a profession portrait and only experiencing the saintliness of the image without the biographical data about birthdates, family, legitimacy, and calidad.[26] As shown later, calidad was implied for anyone worthy enough to have such a composition written in honor of a bride of Christ.

If Clara had been a musician, she might have even taken part in the singing of this villancico on her profession day.[27] Were she applying for a dowry waiver, she might also play a piece like the *Tonada* to demonstrate her musical skills, as villancicos were reported to have been used for these evaluations.[28] The music dowry-waiver records do not specifically mention villancicos, but indicate "papeles de música" (music papers/parts), as in one Ana Javiera de Algora's 1692 records for her acceptance into the San Bernardo convent as a singer and performer of the violón and vihuela:

> For the purpose of being examined in music and with the assistance of the mother prioress and other nun musicians of said convent who were in the coro bajo, and Antonio de Salazar chapel master of the said holy cathedral church, Br. José de Loaysa Agurto, and José de Espinosa, bajón player from said chapel, whom his mercy appointed for said examination, and after said teachers took out some music parts and the nuns other [parts], [Ana Javiera] sang and accompanied them and also played violón and vihuela for which the nuns were pleased.[29]

Álvaro Torrente explains that in Spain "papeles de música" were manuscripts of "music copied in separate parts and normally implying vocal works with continuo and obbligati instruments." In addition, Torrente adds that such manuscripts consisted of "music in modern style," that is, "music composed by the contemporary cathedral composers" as opposed to *stile antico* polyphony sung at the music stand.[30] There is no reason to believe that this did not include villancicos or that this labeling was any different in Mexico City, as Javier Marín López confirms while also reminding us that the violón was important for "doubling the bass line of the continuo . . . [and it] accompanied and reinforced the low registers."[31] The reductive capacity of the disciplined notarial space thus begins to divulge how its brevity obscures the specificity of what was performed.

The proficiency of a candidate's skills—her usefulness—was completely left to the cathedral chapel masters and musicians to determine. For the notary, a middleman, and the archbishop, who ultimately approved the waivers, the musical selections played at the audition would seem to make no difference so long as the musical skills of the candidate made it worth investing in her profession. Entrance dowries provided by women when they initiated into the convent were expensive and a major source of convent funding that could be invested to gain profitable returns that would sustain the convent.[32] Investing in music would seem to have its own return, principally the benefit of attracting convent patrons who would continue to endow the convents with donations, including sung memorial Masses that maintained the economy of salvation.[33] That specific monetary return was obscured in the dowry-waiver process, however, as it foregrounded the usefulness of the musicians for solemnizing the liturgies instead.

The notarized music dowry-waiver process is preserved in fragments at the AGN in dating from the 1670s through the 1850s. Fanny Calderón de la Barca also witnessed a novice professing with a dowry waiver in the 1840s:

> In the Convent of the Incarnation [Encarnación], I saw another girl sacrificed in a similar manner. She was received there without a dowry, on account of the exceeding fineness of her voice. She little thought what a fatal gift it would prove to her. The most cruel part of all was, that wishing to display her fine voice to the public, they made her sing a hymn alone, on her knees, her arms extended in the form of a cross before all the immense crowd. . . . She was a good-looking girl, fat and comely, who would probably have led a comfortable life in the world, for which she seemed well fitted; most likely without one touch of romance or enthusiasm in her composition; but having the unfortunate honour of being niece to two chanoines [*sic*], she was thus honourably provided for without expense in her nineteenth year. As might be expected, her voice faltered, and instead of singing, she seemed inclined to cry out. Each note came slowly, heavily tremblingly; and at the last she nearly fell forward exhausted, when two of the sisters caught and supported her. I had almost made up my mind to see no more such scenes, which, unlike pulque [agave liquor] and bullfights, I dislike more and more upon trial; when we received an invitation, which it was not easy to refuse, but was the more painful to accept, being acquainted, though slightly, with the victim.[34]

Powerful words from an enlightened woman, at once in awe of Mexico City's religious culture, as already seen in previous chapters with her description of the convent coro and garden, but also taken aback at the sacrifice young women undertook to become co-redeemers along with Christ and the Virgin Mary. She calls this singer a victim and evokes Passion imagery and sacrificial language as did profession sermons of the previous centuries.[35] Moreover, Fanny's writing is clever and picturesque, indirectly citing body size and sex appeal as contributors to the maintenance of cloistered convents and their antiquated lifestyle of uniformity and repetition—discipline.[36] The tone gives her writing verisimilitude.

Once a woman's "exceeding fineness" in performance earned her a dowry waiver, like Fanny Calderón's acquaintance at the Encarnación convent, she was legally bound to perform specifically on the instrument on which she was declared competent, or to sing in the case of vocalists. In 1747, for example, Sister María Rosa de San José was admitted to Mexico City's Purísima Concepción convent as a *bajón* player (bassoonist). She requested archdiocesan permission to stop playing the bajón, which was aggravating an infection on her tongue, provoking much pain and distress.[37] María Rosa assured the vicar that she had already started learning to accompany with the *violón* (viol) since she could no longer play the bajón "to supply the basses with it."[38] She was clearly worried that she could not accompany the choir adequately on the bajón anymore, the stakes of which should be familiar from the discussion in previous chapters about rules calling for music to be well performed in the liturgies. Then María Rosa explains that the choir vicar and musicians she accompanied were satisfied with her progress on the violón, and that therefore her monthly lessons with a teacher were worth the cost.[39]

The nuns at the same convent some fifty years prior described the commitment to a music dowry-waiver's requirements as an obligation too. It was work in the most righteous service of salvation. In 1691, they put forth a candidate named Juana Dominga de Bereo for a reduced dowry at 1,500 pesos raised charitably, which was half the price of a full dowry.[40] She was sixteen years old and had been raised in the convent since the age of two; knowing music—as it was obviously taught to her in the convent—she already assisted in the choir as a singer, the nuns said, "offering herself with many affections that sometimes she edifies us and it touches us to see the punctuality with which she attends to everything even without having the obligation."[41] Fulfilling obligations indeed seems inherent to discipline.[42]

Deep in the Dowry Waiver Process

The "Proceedings performed about the blessing of the habit for Mariana de San José y Machuca, so that she can be received as a choir and black veil nun in the Convent of the Concepción with the Title of Musician" (henceforth "Proceedings") contain the complete notarized dowry-waiver documentation of one Sister Mariana.[43] The first document in the proceedings is her proof of Baptism, which took place on October 3, 1677, as confirmed by a priest who consulted a book of Spanish baptismal records held at the cathedral.[44] Mariana's initial qualification for the convent was confirmed through record of her Baptism, which indicated that she was the legitimate daughter of Agustín Fernández Machuca and Isabel de Salazar, confirming she was the offspring of Spanish parents who had received the sacrament of Matrimony through the Church and that she was not a bastard child ("hija natural").[45] This record documents the Church's reproduction of itself through sacramental process, requiring Mariana's family to have engaged in prior sacraments in order for her to qualify for profession.

After the documentation of Baptism, a letter from the nuns of the convent offers a plea to the archdiocese on the musician's behalf:

> Inasmuch as we are extremely short of singers, due to the death of some who were the entirety of the choir and promoters of divine worship, due to their great skill and dedication, we need to receive others in their place because there are few who have remained for this ministry, and at present we have been introduced with a musician who is very skilled, and she sings with a good voice with much training, which is an advantage because she can start singing without being taught. . . . She is the legitimate daughter of the accountant Agustin Fernández Machuca, deceased, and Doña Isabel de Salazar, his legitimate wife, who is so poor that she is sustained through alms. And to become a nun, to which her virtue inclines her, she has taught [Mariana] music.[46]

This information duplicates what the priest would have confirmed from the baptismal record regarding Mariana's lineage while also supplying a few more details about the convent's seemingly dire need for competent musicians to lead the choir, the presence of a trained musician "with a good voice" capable of filling the vacancy, and the financial affairs of Mariana's family that necessitated a dowry waiver. The class, socioeconomic, and gender power imbalances typical in the "disciplining of sound" on paper begin to reveal themselves from the initial records confirming that Mariana is poor but Spanish, and that musical ability—which had to be certified by men, as shown later—could take a woman out of destituteness.[47] Within the Spanish colonial world view that, according to Andrew Fisher and Matthew O'Hara, "reflected a sliding scale of inferiority among subsets of the Crown's vassals," Mariana found herself in a situation in which both parties, the Concepción convent and the Machuca family, benefited from her musicianship.[48]

The petition was signed by the notary José Rubio on November 9, 1694, and taken to the cathedral canon and Vicar General Antonio de Anunzibay y Anaya, who had it reviewed by Archbishop Francisco Aguiar y Seixas. On November 10, the archbishop granted permission for Antonio de Salazar (ca. 1650–1715) and José de Loaysa Augusto (ca. 1625–1695), cathedral chapel masters, to evaluate Mariana's musical skills. The examination took place on November 15 in the convent parlor. In some records, the assessment took place in the coro bajo. The main concern was that a grate should separate the men and nuns, except under special circumstances. In 1731, for example, the nuns of the Encarnación convent were given permission for the chapel masters to enter the cloister because the audition "could not be done across the grates."[49] The chapel masters would bring sheets of music to the convent for these types of auditions, and the nuns also provided samples of music for the aspirant to perform. Again, the specifics of the pieces of music are unknown, but presumed to have been villancicos and/or polyphony.

After the exam, Salazar and Loaysa's evaluations were summarized by the vicar general in a statement dated the day after the exam, November 15, which makes a point of specifying Mariana's Spanish appearance:

> There appeared a Spanish woman who called herself Mariana de San José, the subject of these accounts, and the said chapel masters took out different sheets of music and the nun-musicians of the said convent took out others, which she sang and accompanied with said musicians. Similarly, she sang another song on her own while playing the harp with much skill, and her voice is very sonorous.[50]

Anunzibay adds another layer of certainty about Mariana's "person, judgment, and circumstances" by confirming her Spanish lineage, idealized as commensurate with the life of a future bride of Christ.[51] The notarial record disciplined Mariana's personhood, in which her calidad and voice became legally fused into the mold of a titled musician nun—"a título de música."[52] For those who were instrumentalists, it was the same molding process. The quality of their instrumental performance was judged on how well it accompanied song or played out vocal lines and organ versets (an important substitute for the voice, as we saw in Chapter 2). In any case, the fact that Mariana looked Spanish in appearance continued to build on the convent nuns' declaration that Mariana was of legitimate birth and on the priest's baptismal verification. The documents reveal a gradual unfolding of witnesses to Mariana's Spanish identity confirmed through vocalized testimonies about her family lineage. All these reiterations were important since merely appearing Spanish was not enough evidence of the calidad necessary to be a bride of Christ.[53]

The vicar general's statement about Mariana's musical skills draws upon a legal rubric repeated many times across the various dowry-waiver protocols to describe generic musicianship competence reported by the cathedral musicians. Loaysa and Salazar stated that her voice was clear, high, and sonorous, making it "very useful and necessary for the celebration of the Divine Office in the said convent, and [she] also plays the harp, with which she can support the rest of the members who remain in the choir."[54] Implied in this prioritizing of usefulness and necessity is the weight of the convent's salvific calidad stemming from the daily vocalized prayers within the nuns' liturgies, which relied on competent musicians to sustain adequate communal singing.

The records, including Mariana's, never explicitly mention what musical skills the cathedral musicians tested, though other documents show that rhythm, multi-instrumentality, and contributions to polyphony were important. For instance, in a later period at the Encarnación convent, the then cathedral organist, Manuel Martínez, who served circa 1784–1809,[55] suggested that Anna Manuela Herrera, who aspired to become a nun with the dowry waiver for organ playing, required more time under the tutelage of her male teacher (maestro) to help her with rhythm. But it was only a small defect ("defectillo"), which would not hinder her from obtaining the dowry waiver. Martinez builds on the formal rubrics of the past cathedral musicians, saying, for example, that Anna Manuela plays with some knowledge ("algún conocimiento") and that she does not lack liveliness in her playing ("viveza parece no la falta"). Furthermore, usefulness is presented in terms of service, as "it appears that she will serve very well if she does not allow herself to forget what she knows, and if she takes the precaution to prepare herself ahead of time and learn what she has to play."[56] In this example the disciplinary space of the notarial record expands to include the traditional disciplinary components required to be a successful musician, alluding to the muscle memory necessary for instrumental competence, developed by repetitive practice.

In 1691, Salazar and his colleagues auditioned the multi-instrumentalist Felipa Rodriguez de Aguilar, who sought a music dowry waiver to become a nun in Mexico City's San José de Gracia convent. She was competent in four instruments: the bajón, *tenor* (tenor bajón), *faraute* (literally "herald," and thus probably a type of trumpet), and *tenor de chirimía* (tenor shawm).[57] These types of instruments could replace a singing voice, although Felipa also sang contralto.[58] With these musical abilities, she could fill a vacancy in the choir after one of its members had died. Indeed, the abbess of San José de Gracia wrote in terms of necessity, stating that "the choir is in much need for the Divine Office, and the one who can actually perform is unavailable because the physicians have warned me that it is a threat to her life."[59] In his evaluation of Felipa, the cathedral bajón player José de Espinosa praised her skills, commenting that her contralto voice alone should earn her a dowry, as there were already many tiples in the nuns' choir.[60] "It will assuredly be a service to God, our Lord, for her to receive the habit," remarked Espinosa, "because this witness knows that the choir of said convent lacks voices and instruments like hers."[61] Though Espinosa specified that low voices were a particular need in the San José de Gracia convent, Felipa's low voice must still have been rare, given the excitement in the tone of the cathedral musicians' account: "even better was the discovery of her contralto voice with which she sang with much skill."[62]

The specification of tiple and contralto voice types suggests polyphonic singing at this convent, despite the lack of extant music sources from San José de Gracia. Around 1728, almost forty years after Felipa's audition, the nuns at the Purísima Concepción convent also requested permission for a music dowry for a harpist and contralto singer named María Rita de San Miguel, identified by the nuns as one "skilled in chant and polyphony."[63] They reflect on why it is so important to have trained singers, exhibiting a concern for aesthetic taste in some unknown degree of musical skill: it is not because other nuns cannot sing—as all are required to sing—but because they "sing by ear without knowing music."[64] They list an organist, two bajón players, and a tenor bajón player among their modest cohort of instrumentalists, but state that one is "blind with cataracts" and "the organist is almost blind."[65] They mention that even though everyone is at least supposed to know how to chant, these women only performed on instruments, because they "lacked voices."[66] Whatever that meant, lacking voices must have been the complete opposite of the equally vague "sonorous" characteristic that earned trained vocalists a dowry waiver, with everyone else in the convent communities falling somewhere in a middle range of amateur singing ability. The mention of the instrumentalists' disabilities would be for the purpose of hastening the matter of María Rita's recruitment, as if at any moment the organist and bajonera could cease accompanying on account of their visual impairments.

The convent choir vicar Sister Gertrudis Angela de Jesús Nazareno also shared her concern for the lack of musicians in the choir. She self-described as being in "charge of caring for music and chant in the choir and [making sure] that the divine worship and regular observance does not decline."[67] Remarkably, hers is the only record that separates chant and music, again suggesting polyphonic practice, and she said that the few choir members that remained were

> overwhelmed with sung chaplaincy Masses and other obligations from our patrons, in addition to the necessary religious functions of funerals, Matins, and other [services] that your illustriousness would agree are indispensable.[68]

The indispensability of liturgical singing in convents, articulated by Sister Gertrudis here, is at once more indicative of why over one hundred years earlier the vicar general of Mexico City sided with the nuns of the Encarnación convent when they demanded that their liturgical music books be returned, which we observed at the opening of Chapter 1. Gertrudis' outline of the responsibilities placed upon her choir suggests that Mexico City's Purísima Concepción convent was a musical hub well into the eighteenth century, carrying on a tradition dating back to the sixteenth century, also explored in Chapter 1. The chaplaincy Masses were those memorial Masses paid for by patron mortgages to be sung in perpetuity, depending on the specifications of their donation, for the repose of patrons' souls after their death.[69]

We do not have evidence as to the number of chaplaincy Masses at the Purísima Concepción, but records from other Mexico City convents, such as for the San José de Gracia Convent around 1673, inform us what was possible for just a few patrons. At San José de Gracia, it was traditional to perform fourteen sung Masses yearly for the repose of the soul of the convent patron Fernando de Villegas and thirteen for the patron Juan Navarro and his wife.[70] The convent choir also sang ten Masses every time one of its nuns died.[71] The number of chaplaincy Masses for the prestigious Purísima Concepción—recall, it was the oldest nuns' cloister in New Spain—would likely be higher than this. In honor of Christ's age of thirty-three when he died, some convents in Spain sang as many as thirty-three chaplaincy Masses for each deceased person.[72] Sister Gertrudis Angela, likely desperate for help to ease the load of so many services, had nothing but positive things to say about María Rita:

> The archbishop has been informed of this necessity and about the availability of a noble and virtuous girl, and skilled in the art and the practice

of music, who has a contralto voice very apropos for the choir and for the necessities of our own [choir]. [She is] equally elegant in accompanying with harp, a legitimate daughter and with all the circumstances necessary for the convent as evidenced by her proof of Baptism.[73]

She does not neglect to reiterate the most important part, of course: María Rita's legitimacy and family lineage, an assurance, as in the preceding baptismal record, of pure Spanish descent.

By the time of María Rita's audition, Manuel Sumaya had taken over the role of cathedral chapel master from Salazar, who retired in 1714. Sumaya was called in to adjudicate, and he noted:

> I made her play various works and other items necessary for the service of the choir on the harp instrument; and she immediately played and solfeged parts and works of polyphonic pieces in diverse tones, as many as I placed in front of her, with skill, accuracy, effortlessness, and intelligence.[74]

This would indicate that sight-reading with solfege was part of the audition. He also auditioned her in voice, which he found "sweet and very apropos for all of those pieces in which she does not play the harp."[75] This hints at a performance practice, indicating that some pieces were accompanied by harp and others were not. Her skills would be "honed and perfected" because of the choir's great need.[76] Sumaya's account is one of the most elaborate in terms of musical detail, and, even so, it reveals very little else other than the involvement of sight-reading and self-accompaniment for instrumentalists. Still, this and the preceding examples show some of the ways in which music commentary, considerably less redundant than the family background check, was embedded into the dowry waiver process.

The handwritten autobiographical notes of María Casilda del Pozo y Calderón (1682–1730), who wanted to become a nun in Mexico City, also reveal the relevance of solfege and routine practice, while indicating her religious fervor and willingness to discipline her life with music and the veil:

> I would say to the Lord that I would first take my own life [rather] than offend him, because my intention was only to love him and never offend him. And since the demon occasioned many situations to offend the Lord, I restrained myself, and as such I desired to come to this city, and to join a convent. And being that I did not have a dowry to become a nun I began

to learn music and soon learned it because I started with the principles of plainchant and I knew how to play the harp, and I learned solfege within two years, well enough that I could accompany any sheet of music on the violón and harp. And with the desire to become a nun, I worked very hard to learn, day and night, and it served as a good distraction.[77]

It is not clear whether she eventually became a nun. She and her sister were under the care of a priest in Mexico City when she penned her autobiography. They were orphaned and essentially lived as the priest's servants. Her words supplement the notarial process for dowry waivers and inform us, however vaguely, of her gradual process of learning solfege by building on her knowledge of plainchant, and even suggesting that learning music was enjoyable, if only "a good distraction."

Returning to the proceedings of our previous harp player and vocalist, Mariana de San José y Machuca: after she passed her music audition, more discussion of her lineage ensued, which was part of the process for all candidates. On November 18, 1694, a day after Mariana's music exam, Anunzibay informed the archbishop that she had passed the test, and the prelate gave permission to investigate her lineage and Spanish identity more thoroughly, requiring two witnesses. A priest, Ambrozio Fernández de Leon, and a longtime family acquaintance named Juan de Arvo stood in, and the latter testified:

> [Her parents] procreated the aforementioned as a legitimate daughter, and, as such, they raised her, fed her, always called her daughter, and she has always called them mother and father in their house and in public and [I know] that [her parents] are Spanish old Christians, pure from all bad lineage of the Moors, Jews, and those punished by the inquisition or other tribunals.... Mariana de San José is a virtuous person of good life and customs, and she has no impediments that will hinder her receipt of the blessed habit which she seeks.[78]

Arvo's testament would assure the church leaders that Mariana was free of the perceived marks of undesirable ancestors. Any variants on these statements for proving Spanish blood purity would have to include the phrase about being Spanish and old Christian, which would suggest no mixture with Muslim or Jewish converts (new Christians). For instance, in the 1667 testimony of Nicolás Neira Barboza in support of Juana Tellez de la Banda, who aspired to enter the Encarnación convent, Barboza swore that Juana's parents were "Spanish without any mixture, nobles of all the calidad of old Christians, pure of all bad race."[79] The term race ("raza") thus had religious overtones, though Covarrubias' 1674 edition of *Tesoro de la lengua castellana o española* adds *Indio* (Indian) to the mix.[80] In addition, the Spanish associated blackness with slavery and infidelity, lumping those of African descent as a type of impure "bad race," the implication of which for convent admissions we will discuss later.[81] The term *casta* (caste) applied for those of mixed Spanish and non-Spanish lineage, whether indigenous, African, or their mixed descendants.[82]

The Spanish thought that the qualities necessary to become a bride of Christ in New Spain were substantiated with these lineage testimonies.[83] At the center of this racialized rubric was the aspirant's bloodline, which was supposed to be indicative of moral, disciplined Spanish parents, who did not miscegenate with religious and ethnic others, and the aspirant's own decent calidad.[84] These features were believed to be passed from one true Spanish Christian to another when they maintained pure Spanish lineage, confirmed through word of mouth.

The final step in a candidate's evaluation involved a scrutiny of her personality, and for Mariana this stage arrived on November 19, a day after confirmation of her Spanish lineage. She was asked for her name, the name of her parents, her age (seventeen), and her assurance that she desired to become a nun by her own free will without being coerced. Her responses were satisfactory enough for the nuns to be granted permission to take a vote on Mariana's acceptance as a musician novice.

Pious Deeds and Racialized Scandals

The Colegio de San Miguel de Belem became a feeder school for this convent dowry-waiver process to receive competent musicians.[85] It was founded in October 1746 by the Archbishop of Mexico City Juan Antonio de Vizarrón y Eguiarreta as a music school where women could learn music before becoming nuns. It was not the first time this prelate centered women in one of his pious deeds (*obras pias*).[86] Three years prior to founding the school, he left a prestigious 4,000-peso lottery dowry for poor women who wanted to profess free of expense. Concerned for his salvation, he believed that the dowry, along with several memorial Masses he funded, would help ensure his soul "a most clement compassion in the divine justice."[87] These charitable dowries were quite common for wealthy citizens to establish, especially for the benefit of orphans. The minimum requirement for reception of a charitable dowry was once again the calidad inherent in Spanish lineage, "strictly excluding all other casta, race, or mixture," a limiting factor imposed on the Colegio de San Miguel as well.[88] As casta denoted people of mixed lineage, the archbishop's redundancy makes this racialized restriction even more emphatic.

When convents knew of a young woman in their midst who wished to profess but was unable to do so because she lacked a dowry, the nuns would enter her name into a general lottery ("sorteo"), which took place on the feast of the archbishop's name day, the feast of St. John the Baptist on June 24.[89] The names of all the candidates from all participating convents were written on slips of paper and placed in an urn for selection. In a symbolic gesture to Matthew's Gospel ("So shall the last be first and the first last," Matthew 20:16), the final name drawn out received the dowry. The woman selected in this way would then participate in a public procession and Mass at the cathedral on the feast of St. Peter on June 29, a major feast in the cathedral liturgical calendar.[90]

These lottery dowries were competitive and a potential source of scandal. As one investigation from 1738 to 1739 preserved at the AGN attests, Spanish physical appearance and proximity to non-Spaniards could be deceiving, and word of mouth was the standard evidence for lineage. The title of the notarized documents discloses the type of rumor that might disqualify a potential candidate: "Inquiry orders regarding the calidad of María Ana de la Cámara, who won the raffle for orphans from the church of the San José de Gracia convent, on suspicion of her calidad as a mulatta woman."[91] It was the sacristan of the San José de Gracia convent, Nicolás de Mujica, who accused María Ana "of being the daughter of the sister of a *negra* [black woman] who is the errand girl of the same convent."[92] He claimed that it was not just suspicion, but that her calidad was "public and known in the entire neighborhood of San José de Gracia."[93] And this was corroborated by a second witness, a priest by the name of Manuel de Estrada, who "considers her [María Ana] a mulatta," the term for a mixed-race person of African descent, because of her mother's relationship to the convent servant.[94] Because of these allegations, on December 24, 1738, Vicar General Francisco Dávila Gómez de Cervantes prevented María Ana from participating in the lottery procession, this one to have taken place on that same Christmas Eve day.

The calidad necessary for María Ana to become a nun was considerably diminished because of her mother's supposed association with blackness. Since 1599 the calidad of black people in New Spain had become appended to the impure calidad of religious "bad race" associated with the Jews, Muslims, and new Christians.[95] The racialization of caste was well underway by the time of María Ana de la Cámara's situation. The documents used both "negra" and "mulata" to describe the convent errand girl, depending on the argument. Those who accused María Ana of being unqualified because of her mother's relationship with the errand girl labeled the errand girl "negra," and those who testified that this girl was not related to María Ana's family used the word "mulata."

María Ana contested, "I am a poor Spanish virgin without protection, circumstances recommended by law for the protection of your holiness."[96] What did she mean by "protection"? Becoming a nun at the San José de Gracia convent, under the administrative jurisdiction of the archbishop, would offer her the archbishop's—the Church's—indirect protection from the secular world.[97] Poor, but Spanish, she was deserving of her family lineage to be safeguarded with her virginity safely preserved in the convent, as discussed in Chapter 1. María Ana requested that the archdiocese send its prosecutor to receive an alternate witness account of her lineage, asking that "the witnesses be especially queried as to the calidad of my mother, and of her parents my grandparents," because it was her maternal grandparents' lineage whose purity was in question.[98]

A slew of (male) witnesses were called upon: one José Rodríguez, married with Clara González, residents of the same neighborhood; one Mario de Valeriano de Arse, married to Juana Tomasa Navarro; a tailor named Juan Ortuñez; and one Juan Sánchez. All were Spanish, citizens of Mexico City who had known María Ana's family for as long as thirty to more than forty years.[99] They all coincided in knowing María Ana since she was born, and they agreed that she was a Spanish virgin, daughter of Juan de la Cámara and María Teresa Quiñones Aguianes, and that "they are Spanish and have not heard anything to the contrary," insofar as they also knew the maternal grandparents José Quiñones and Petra de Salazar to be Spanish.[100] They also confirmed that the grandparents raised a mulatta orphan named Juana who was the convent errand girl, and that they "have no knowledge that she is related."[101]

It was word of mouth, as documented in these notarized protocols and baptismal records, that prevailed in both scandalizing and legitimizing a person's calidad based on the racialized categories of the time.[102] And with the information provided by María Ana's witnesses, on January 9, 1739, Archbishop Antonio Vizarrón y Eguiarreta had her exonerated of "the supposed defect of her mother being the sister of a mulatta."[103] She was to be granted her dowry for the convent. Moreover, she was allowed to join in the public display of her charitably established award by being incorporated into the cathedral's procession for the next available liturgical feast that called for such festivity, which in María Ana's case would be, ironically, the feast of the Purification of the Virgin Mary ("La Candelaria"/ "Candlemas") on February 2, a grand celebration that was solemnized with much music and the performance of villancicos.[104]

Racialized Discourse and the Virgin Mary

Among such high-stakes, legally consequential genealogical oversight for convent admissions, the notarized music dowry-waiver process would seem like obscure pieces of a musical soundscape attesting to the unspecified musicianship skill level of those who wished to become convent musicians. The candidates' suitable Spanish lineage repeats (or resounds) more often— literally a writing down of an oral and aural knowledge—as María Ana's witnesses attest when saying they "have not heard anything" that would deny her adequate calidad for becoming a bride of Christ. There is a gendered component as well, given that the witnesses for these testaments are always men, though the nuns confirm as much about legitimacy in their petitions too.

The rhetoric of hearing and lineage comes together in a particular villancico for the Santísima Trinidad nuns composed by Nicolás Ximénez de Cisneros, who was the Puebla cathedral chapel master from 1726 to 1747.[105] Dedicated to the Nativity of Mary, *Sacratísima Virgen* is set for solo tiple and bass accompaniment. Given the emphasis on self-accompaniment for some of the dowry-waiver candidates, this villancico could have been used as an audition piece. The estribillo's subject comments on a circumstance that was probably more common than not in convents. Not knowing solfege—that is, not knowing how to read music—does not necessarily mean that one cannot sing. The Virgin Mary is implored to hear the devotional offering in song as if she were a chapel master ready to hear an audition. This estribillo reminds us that Mary has been compared to a chapel master before as observed in Chapter 2, when she appeared to Sister María de Jesús conducting the Puebla Purísima Concepción choir.

Estribillo

Sacratísima virgen,	Most sacred virgin,
oíd mi cantar,	listen to my song,
que, aunque no entiendo solfa,	that, without knowing solfege,
muy bien sé entonar.	I can intone well.
Oíd, escuchad mi letrilla,	Hear, listen to my lyric,
y sin jurar	and, without swearing
por la Virgen María,	in the name of the Virgin Mary,
la he de cantar.	I shall sing it.
Escuchad, atended,	Listen, pay attention,
que ya va el sonsonetillo	that the little sound
del tin ti rin tin	of the tin ti rin tin
y del tan ta ran tan,	and the tan ta ran tan
que en un tamborilico	that on a little drum
hace un zagal.	plays the shepherd.
Oíd, escuchad,	Listen, hear,
el tin ti rin tin,	the tin ti rin tin,
con el tan ta ran tan.	with the tan ta ran tan.

The onomatopoetic simulation of drum accompaniment mentioned in the latter part of the estribillo is typical in villancicos that refer to music of percussion instruments.[106] But to convince the Virgin to listen to this drum song, the notation presents the subject's skill in the most basic way. To demonstrate some semblance of musical competence, the singer is given a chance to show her ability to match pitch in the two central instances when the text calls the Virgin to listen. When the bass presents the briefest instrumental interlude in mm. 6 and 14 of Example 3.2, the pitches of that interlude are matched by the voice an octave above in the measures that follow, setting the words "oíd, escuchad / listen, hear" and "escuchad, atended / listen, pay attention" from lines 5 and 9 in the estribillo poetry. Clearly redundancies are necessary when imploring the Virgin, as is also evident if we consider the popularity of reciting the rosary in Marian devotion, for example.

As exemplified in Chapter 1 with Vidales' villancico *Con qué gala en el campo*, also to celebrate Mary's birth, a litany of sorts presented in the coplas of *Sacratísima Virgen* demonstrates fundamental knowledge of the Virgin's attributes essential to teach and/or reiterate her purity, virginity, and immaculacy.

Example 3.2 Ximénez de Cisneros, *Sacratísima Virgen* (CSG.297), estribillo, mm. 4–18

Coplas

1. Que sois nube hermosa	That you are a beautiful cloud,
oí predicar,	I heard being preached,
sí, por mi vida,	Yes, for my life,
de tal calidad,	of such a calidad
que no tenéis sombras,	that you have no shadows, which is
que es más que asombrar.	something more than to amaze.
Sí, por mi alma,	Yes, for my soul,
toca zagal,	keep playing, young shepherd,
el tin ti rin tin,	the tin ti rin tin,
con el tan ta ran tan.	with the tan ta ran tan.
Que esta nube es la Virgen María	That this cloud is the Virgin Mary
y voto a tal,	and I vouch for that,

que no ha habido
señora más linda
en el linaje de Adán.
Toca zagal,
el tin ti rin tin,
con el tan ta ran tan.

that there has never been a more beautiful
lady
in the lineage of Adam.
Keep playing, young shepherd,
the tin ti rin tin,
with the tan ta ran tan.

2. Muy llena de gracia,
sé, Virgen, estáis.
Sí, por mi vida,
y nunca menguáis,
pues dándonos siempre
os queda quedar.
Sí, por mi alma,
toca zagal,
el tin ti rin tin,
con el tan ta ran tan.
Que Dios hizo de vuestra pureza
tan bello cristal,
que en él nunca
se vio la culpa
por más que quiso mirar.
Toca zagal,
el tin ti rin tin,
con el tan ta ran tan.

Most full of grace,
I know, Virgin, you are.
Yes, for my life,
and you never deplete,
for, by always giving to us,
you remain beyond full.
Yes, for my soul,
keep playing, young shepherd,
the tin ti rin tin,
with the tan ta ran tan.
For God made
such a beautiful crystal
out of your purity
that, in it, no guilt has ever been seen,
however much one
wanted to look at it.
Keep playing, young shepherd,
the tin ti rin tin,
with the tan ta ran tan.

3. De Dios sois, Señora,
madre sin igual.
Sí, por mi vida,
pues no hay que ser más,
sois palma, oliva,
y estrella del mar.
Sí, por mi alma,
toca zagal,
el tin ti rin tin,
con el tan ta ran tan.

Of God you are, Lady,
a mother unequalled.
Yes, for my life,
for there is no need to be more,
you are palm, olive,
and star of the sea.
Yes, for my soul,
keep playing, young shepherd,
the tin ti rin tin,
with the tan ta ran tan.

Que María es ciprés,	That Mary is a cypress,
azucena y manantial,	lily, and wellspring,
por espejo, sol,	for mirror, sun,
luna y aurora,	moon, and dawn,
y todo con propiedad.	and all that is fitting.
Toca zagal,	Keep playing, young shepherd,
el tin ti rin tin,	the tin ti rin tin,
con el tan ta ran tan.	with the tan ta ran tan.

4. También sois escala,	You are also a ladder,
no para bajar.	not for descending.
Sí, por mi vida,	Yes, for my life,
que, a los que enseñáis,	that, the ones you teach,
no queréis que sepan	you do not want them to ever know of
nunca declinar.	declining.
Sí, por mi alma,	Yes, for my life,
toca zagal,	keep playing, young shepherd,
el tin ti rin tin,	the tin ti rin tin,
con el tan ta ran tan.	with the tan ta ran tan.
Y con esto, sagrada María,	And, at that, sacred Mary,
lo quiero dejar,	I want to leave it,
que, aunque nadie	for, even though no one
de vos decir puede,	is worthy to speak of you,
no obstante	notwithstanding,
hay mucho que hablar.	there is much to be said.
Toca zagal,	Keep playing, young shepherd,
el tin ti rin tin,	the tin ti rin tin,
con el tan ta ran tan.	with the tan ta ran tan.

Additionally, consistent with the argument that calidad in New Spain is performative, "expressed through behavior as well as appearance," the coplas reveal a performance of the Virgin's calidad.[107] Behavior in the piece is represented by proper singing abilities already established in the estribillo, a musician demonstrating proper singing to the expert musician/chapel master Mary. Appearance is reflected in the Virgin's attributes that associate her with fineness and crystal (copla 2), and with the palm, olive, and cypress trees (copla 3), the arboreal majesties of the Old Testament so prevalent in her Immaculate Conception iconography (recall Appendix 1.3).

Copla 1 sets the tone for the performative list that follows, referencing Mary's beauty stemming from her calidad, stemming from her lack of darkness ("sombra/shadow"), stemming from her lineage. It seems uncannily familiar to much of the rhetoric attended to so far in the dowry-waiver process. Referring to shade as sin is of course not novel in this villancico's poetics, as we saw in Vidales (Chapter 1), and as is common in other Marian villancicos and Christmas villancicos with Marian overtones.[108] All the while, copla 1 also introduces the interspersing of the onomatopoetic drumbeats from the estribillo, reminding listeners of the performance within the performance.

Because the coplas are set strophically, one cannot associate word painting with each one individually. The stepwise ascents and descents that prevail in this melody appear most scintillating if we skip down to copla 4, revealing a text that sets a musical driving force over these ascents and descents, thus tone-painting that individual copla's words. Copla 4 speaks of Mary's attribute as the ladder to heaven—a conduit of salvation—taken from the Book of Genesis, in which Jacob dreamed of a ladder reaching from the ground all the way to heaven, "a stairway for the angels of God to go up and come down" (Genesis 28:12). The music for the tiple in mm. 33–34 is set to a stepwise ascent beginning on "escala/ladder" and a descent of pitches for "no para bajar/not for descending" (Example 3.3). This basic compositional strategy

Example 3.3 Ximénez de Cisneros, *Sacratísima Virgen* (CSG.297), coplas, mm. 32–36

to elucidate the text accompanies all of the previous coplas as well, a performative gesture underlying the topic at hand: Mary's calidad and lineage, as explained in copla 1. As such, copla 1 establishes the topic of the poetic narrative to follow, and copla 4 provides the musical rhetoric based on the tone painting of some of this final copla's key words, recalling that everything associated with the Virgin Mary is about ascending to heaven—salvation—and not descending.

In setting the poetic tone about her calidad, copla 1 presents a superior status, "[the most] beautiful lady in the lineage of Adam," sidestepping her Hebrew (Jewish) lineage from the House of David, of which there is no mention. "In the lineage of Adam" could be a catchall phrase for humanity at large, but when paired with calidad, it is undoubtedly an early modern Spanish code for race.[109] We will see more of this eliding of Mary's Jewish heritage in Chapter 5. Thus, texts about lofty things, cloud without shade (copla 1) and the top of a ladder (copla 4), flank coplas 2 and 3 with their focus on Mary's fine attributes, and all the coplas are accompanied with the tone painting affiliated with copla 4's text. In addition, copla 4 resonates with the word-of-mouth validations in the dowry process that transmitted notions of individuals' and families' calidad among society. Indeed, as line 16 of copla 4 suggests, there is so much to say about the Virgin Mary's calidad, but no one is worthy to speak, because she is the most beautiful human.

Beauty, Blackness, Baptism

Mary's beauty resounds musically when calling to mind the sermon by José de Santa Gertrudis to the Balvanera convent nuns, also for the Nativity of Mary (see Chapter 1). Santa Gertrudis described the most basic function of music being the ascent and descent of pitches. That pitch relationship was best modeled in Christ's descent to earth and Mary's ascent by means of being Christ's mother, as the sermon outlined. The general trajectory of this dialectic is nonetheless upward, toward heaven, toward salvation. But this message begins to resound differently when considering the notarized initiation protocols required for the nuns who would sing and listen to these Marian songs. The gendered power dynamic is flipped in the villancico *Sacratísima Virgen*, as the Virgin Mary herself supersedes any testimonies—even male testimonies like those necessary to confirm calidad in the dowry process that helped certain women become nuns.

As women ascended in society through their initiation into the convent, they had Mary's ascent as a model. The Virgin Mary rises on the metaphorical ladder that she herself represents, according to the Church and the villancico *Sacratísima Virgen*. She is the physical conduit through which the message of salvation, the Word of God made flesh, traverses. And Mary is now the chapel master in *Sacratísima Virgen*, judging whether the subject can indeed intone well—reproduce what the Virgin can do better than anyone else, re-sound salvation.[110]

Like *Sacratísima Virgen*, which documents in musical notation a singer subject's desire to demonstrate singing ability and the Virgin Mary's—superlative—calidad, a baptismal record documented a sacramental ritual and family calidad, but it was ongoing word-of-mouth that kept validating that document within people's lifetime. Likewise, the only way to demon-strate that one can sing is simply to open one's mouth and sing. When María Ana de la Cámara's witnesses reported hearing nothing to the contrary about her pure Spanish lineage, the problem raised by those claiming a defective calidad was settled. A silencing on the one hand of a supposed impurity, in this case María Ana's relationship to blackness, allowed for a resounding of another sort. Like King Philip IV's hushing gesture in his image before the Immaculate Conception in Chapter 1 (Figure 1.1), María Ana's naysayers were quieted. Proof of María Ana's purity, as evidenced by her admittance into the convent, would be echoed when she sang for the salvation of the world in the convent choir.

The testaments of experienced cathedral musicians—the very ones who composed villancicos—remarking on not having heard anything to contra-dict the skill and sonorousness of aspiring musician nuns has some parallels to the attestations of witnesses hearing nothing that would contradict a woman's claim to calidad. Hearing must be disciplined into the notarial archive to triumph over a visual contradiction: seeing the mulatta Juana growing up in María Ana's maternal family house resulted in some people assuming that María Ana's mother was related to Juana, but hearing nothing to contradict pure Spanish lineage after further scrutiny, according to more male witnesses, resolved the issue. The nuns, hearing a musically competent woman, and wishing to have her initiated into their convent free of dowry expenses on account of her potential service in the choir, also required male intervention to audition the skills of the musician and to make an assessment—however vague—that would be credible to Church leaders after it was notarized, disciplined to a legal standard that the nuns' testament alone could not validate.

Blood purity also became the standard for women to initiate into cloisters founded specifically for indigenous women. Their proceedings echo similar language expressed by witnesses for the Spanish validation of legitimacy, such as referring to nobles "known by blood" ("conosidos así por sangre"). To demonstrate something equivalent to old Christians, they include phrases attesting to women's devout Catholicism according to what has been heard or not heard ("ni ha oído decir").[111]

African and African-descended women remained ineligible to become brides of Christ in New Spain, save for one rare case. Juana Esperanza de San Alberto was allowed to profess on her deathbed after a life of enslaved servitude in Puebla's Carmelite San José convent.[112] Her exceptional inclusion in the Carmelite house presents an example of the "episteme whereby Africans assess their colonial Mexican world with a situated knowledge that informs their personhood as black and Catholic."[113] Prior to her profession at death's door, the nuns admired Juana Esperanza's humility, piety, mortification, and—notably—silence.[114] Her attributes leading to her worthiness for profession were justified by Juana Esperanza's proximity to the Spanish nuns, her enslavement having "saved Esperanza from paganism and enabled her to be baptized as a Christian."[115]

Baptism would seem to be the minimum qualification for the salvation of a Christian soul. Yet, in the Church's economy of salvation in New Spain that relied on the continuous sung prayers of nuns, Baptism became the minimum qualification for women to enter the racialized convent entrance proceedings. It was a sacrament of initiation into the Church that at once also initiated people into a particular lineage—disciplined, molded by the notaries to suit the Church's needs by documenting word of mouth with pen and paper. If fictitious naysaying challenged a person's place in that mold, as with María Ana de la Cámara, more word of mouth was sought to prove otherwise to male clergy. As we have seen, the music dowry-waiver process was inserted into that disciplined space, and perhaps the adjudication of musical skills was more objective than proof of blood purity. No records of anyone contesting a woman's musical abilities have come to light.

Who was Sister Mariana Josefa de Señor San Ignacio, whose portrait we reflected on at the beginning of this chapter and adorns the cover of this book? She was a disciplined musician, talented and rehearsed enough to seek out a music dowry waiver to profess in the convent of San José de Gracia. Her family lineage, disciplined by the notarial record, allowed her to join the disciplined convent life, to play the organ and sing in perpetuity for her own salvation, that of her family, that of the convent patrons, and for the salvation of the world she left behind.

PART II
UNITY

4

Feasting Sounds

The Eucharistic Honeymoon, or Who Was Sister Paula?

The spiritual marriage between a nun named Paula and Jesus Christ was celebrated with the composition of an anonymous villancico that commemorates Paula's profession at the Santísima Trinidad convent in Puebla with a very personal take on eucharistic devotion. Most of the music for the villancico is missing from the manuscript, and its date of composition has only been estimated to somewhere in the seventeenth or eighteenth century.[1] What remains of the villancico are fragments with salient indications about the piece. It was polychoral for eleven voices, divided up among three choirs. The first choir's bass part and tenor part survive, but without text, as these parts were performed by instrumentalists.[2] The only part that remains with text is the tiple from the second choir, underlaid with poetry for an estribillo, a solo arioso part, and one copla. Both the estribillo and arioso texts contain gaps as well (indicated by the ellipses), as these lines would have been sung by the other choir parts that are now missing.

Estribillo

Albricias, zagalas,	Good news, maidens,
que Jesús se ha desposado,	for Jesus has married,
[. . .]	[. . .]
y fue cierto, por amor,	and it was true, for love,
que, dando a Paula la mano,	that, by giving his hand to Paula,
ella suba y baje Dios.	[he] let her rise and let God descend.
Que, siendo desiguales,	That, while being unequal,
están conformes,	they are in accordance,
[. . .]	[. . .]

Immaculate Sounds. Cesar D. Favila, Oxford University Press. © Oxford University Press 2023.
DOI: 10.1093/oso/9780197621899.003.0005

es caso de mucho acierto,	it is a very correct case,
nombre singular	singular name
y concierta con el verbo,	and it agrees with the word,
el nombre Paula se ha puesto	the name Paula she has taken
[…]	[…]
y, declinando al ser nuestro,	and, declining to our being,
[…]	[…]
todos le están aprendiendo.	everyone is understanding it.

Arioso	
Pues amor, con casos y tiempos	For love made this word
hizo este verbo	with cases and tenses
[…]	[…]
va de festejo, vaya, vaya,	let it be a celebration, let it be,
pues, ya le declinamos	for we have declined
casos y verbos,	cases and words for her,
[…]	[…]
va de festejo.	let it be a celebration.

Even though this text remains incomplete, the phenomenon of rising and descending, a prominent feature in the devotions discussed in prior chapters, makes its way into this estribillo, modeling the notion of the heavenly divine joining the earthly human. The text that follows elaborates on Christ's union with his new bride Paula as an allegorical grammar lesson, with double entendres that an English translation cannot capture. Critically, "nombre singular/singular name" also means "singular noun," and "verbo/word" is the Spanish term for the Word of God made flesh, Christ (John 1:1). In this allegorical Latin grammar lesson, cases, tenses, and declensions work lovingly, according to this estribillo, to create a cohesive unit of communication with the Word of God. Marrying Christ reconfigures Paula for her proper role—as a bride of Christ—just as words are reconfigured (declined) in Latin to fit their syntactical meaning.[3]

The presentation of Paula's spiritual marriage to Christ as a grammar lesson in the villancico *Albricias, zagalas* would seem to indicate that she and her family were of a well-educated background and might have understood some of these basic rules of Latin grammar for the text to be meaningful. We can also make another assumption about class. A villancico composed in three-choir polychoral style indicates Paula must have come from a well-off family, as it was not uncommon for the rich to honor their daughters' professions with grand-scale polyphony.[4] The exact moment at which profession villancicos were sung is unclear and not prescribed in any ceremonial, but here, the copla that follows the estribillo suggests a practice of singing villancicos after the ceremony. The first line of the copla would not make sense if the villancico were performed before Paula took her vows.

Copla

Esposo de Paula es ya,	Now Jesus is the husband of Paula,
Jesús en el sacramento.	in the sacrament.
Durará el pan de la boda	The wedding bread shall last
si mete al novio en el pecho.	if she inserts the groom in her chest.

Sister Mariana de la Encarnación, who in 1616 left the Jesús María convent together with the musician Sister Inés de la Cruz to establish the first Carmelite convent in Mexico City, recalled villancicos performed at the end of the profession ceremony:

> In the hands of the Lord Archbishop, we made our profession, reiterating the vows and promising to keep the first rule of Our Lady of Mt. Carmel. Then he placed on us the black veils and gave us communion, which concluded the ritual together with the ceremonies of our holy order and with many villancicos.[5]

Mariana de la Encarnación confirms what the text of *Albricias, zagalas* suggests, that profession villancicos were performed after the profession ceremony and that communion was offered to newly professed nuns following their convent initiation, another detail missing from profession ritual books.

Moreover, the copla elaborates on Paula and Christ's mystical marriage and the role of the Eucharist in it, revealing that nuns might approach their relationship with the Eucharist intimately. The Eucharist is the sacrament of the Body of Christ. Catholics believe that the communion bread and wine are converted—transubstantiated—into the Body and Blood of Christ by priests during the consecration at the liturgy of the Mass. The transformed bread and wine, visible as such, contain the invisible resurrected Christ. In this villancico, "wedding bread," or wedding feast, of course refers to the banquet served at a wedding party as analogous to the sacramental feast, the eucharistic bread (host) distributed to Paula at communion. But it is also an idiom that means "honeymoon."[6] Paula's honeymoon—that is, the consummation of her spiritual marriage—would be relived every time she consumes the sacrament, the host containing the Body of Christ Jesus. Unlike the copla in Sister Clara Gregoria de la Ascensión's profession villancico from the previous chapter, the union with Jesus celebrated at the profession ritual is made explicit in *Albricias, zagalas*: this union is facilitated by the Eucharist. Thus, Paula's villancico implores further investigation into how New Spanish nuns engaged in the complex rite of the Eucharist through their music and their own devotion to the Body of Christ, which is the central topic of this chapter.

The late medieval and early modern Catholic Church fostered eucharistic devotion universally. The Eucharist became a sign of Catholic victory over heresy and paganism; a source for drama, music, and art centered on teaching the mystery of transubstantiation; a ritual incentive for the faithful to take part in the Church's sacrament of confession to receive the Eucharist; and the central item of worship at the annual feast of the Body of Christ—Corpus Christi, honored by both Church and city with a major procession on the city streets.[7] Corpus Christi was celebrated in women's convents by processing the Blessed Sacrament inside the cloister while nuns sang eucharistic songs, such as the villancicos we will see later.[8]

Yet, among all believers in the core essence of the Eucharist, nuns stand out as special advocates in the heteronormative Church's eucharistic agenda.[9] Because of their gender, nuns had a more direct union with Christ that did not rely on additional heterosexual allegorizing, such as the feminizing of the soul that was essential for male mystics like St. John of the Cross and others known to employ amorous language in their writing.[10] St. Teresa of Ávila knew this special relationship that nuns had with Christ, reflecting on communion's foretaste of the final union of the brides and groom in heaven in her *Interior Castle*.[11] No other faithful believer could become what they received through communion in the erotic manner described by Paula's villancico. It is so physical in its deployment of the female monastic body as the receptacle of the Body of Christ's divine love, freely given to those who lead a life of sacrifice and obedience, as exemplified in St. Bernard of Clairvaux's interpretation of the Song of Songs.[12] There is a tension between mystic-carnal desire and divine love in St. Bernard's protagonists of the Song of Songs: "Christ is the lover of the Canticle, his bride sometimes the Church, sometimes the individual soul, sometimes the monks of Clairvaux, his audience and sometimes the Virgin [Mary]," as Marina Warner suggests.[13] Among these possibilities, however, we do not often hear of monks and the Virgin Mary *inserting* within themselves Christ the groom, or honeymooning with communion hosts, as is the case with nuns and heard in Paula's profession villancico.

To elaborate on how this carnal banquet of sounds complements the wider trajectory of salvation traversed so far, this chapter will first review some familiar biblical narratives with respect to the Eucharist and address the two ways in which nuns received the Eucharist: sacramental communion (physically receiving the consecrated host and ingesting it) and spiritual communion (not receiving the consecrated host but imagining its consumption vividly). We will observe how villancicos from the Santísima Trinidad convent for eucharistic devotion expressed Church teachings about Christ's humanity dwelling in the consecrated communion host. These types of villancicos enhanced the reception of communion for nuns. Together with devotional literature, they helped to elevate nuns as models of eucharistic piety and contrition. Because the Eucharist is the Body of Christ, some attention must also be given to the saint who gestated Jesus, the co-redeemer who undoubtedly makes her way into eucharistic devotion, the Virgin Mary.

By placing eucharistic villancicos sung by nuns in dialogue with the eucharistic devotional literature nuns read, I argue for a more sonically inclined understanding of spiritual communion for nuns. Indeed, the Body of Christ itself was comparable to music in a sense. Like music, the Body of Christ is invisible. It is conveyed through the communion host just as the tune of a melody is conveyed through an instrument's sound or a resounding voice. When nuns engaged in listening and singing music for the Eucharist, it constituted a form of spiritual communion.

Communion of the Eucharist incorporated all senses. Being the most sensual of the sacraments, it involved seeing, tasting, and even smelling the bread that constituted the communion host. The nuns could see and smell the hand of the priest conveying the host. They could also hear the priest's voice through the cratícula when he announced, "Corpus Christi," the signal to the nuns that they should open their mouths and receive the Body of Christ. Out of the view of the priest, a very bodily experience of Christ could ensue. As the host contacted mouths, tongues, teeth, throats, and various other insides, the Eucharist, an instrument of salvation, touched the nuns' vocal instrument during communion. And as Paula's villancico expressed, it reached the heart, as alluded to in inserting Christ in her breast/chest.[14] Despite this deep penetration—and the symbolism that communion deployed among nuns—the sacrament of the Eucharist never involved seeing the actual resurrected Body of Christ within the communion host, just as sounds and melodies are incapable of being seen.

Sound in the early modern period was increasingly understood in terms of physical vibration.[15] As such, claims within eucharistic villancicos that God himself is in the music notes, and that Jesus is a string instrument, resonate in the ears. This resonance spontaneously provided the deep penetration of Christ's body without sacramental communion (ingesting the host). Communion through hearing music would thus constitute a spiritual communion. It was a quasi-physical reception absent in the ocular-centric devotional literature that often called upon nuns to envision Christ's presence inside them despite not having received the host physically.

So far, we have encountered how the incarnation of Christ, one in the same with God the Creator and the Holy Spirit in the Trinity, elevated the Virgin Mary as timeless, immaculately conceived—the voice of God. Turning now to eucharistic devotion and its importance in nuns' convents through the notion of invisibility brings veiled nuns intimately closer to the common description for the Body and Blood of Christ as veiled by wine and bread for communion. The phenomenon of foodstuffs containing Christ, perceived by the sense of taste, is called "accident," and we will see this word referenced in the relevant devotional literature. The grounding of the Eucharist's metaphysical aspects in the common act of ingesting physical bread (a wafer, actually) during sacramental communion conveys a sensory incongruity that the brides of Christ dispelled when they consumed, prayed to, and sang about the Eucharist. Multiple levels of veiling occur: Christ's body is veiled in bread, and nuns' bodies are doubly veiled by vestments (habits) and grates. Mysteries of faith are thus presented as veiled beings. As we will see in the teachings of Bishop Palafox y Mendoza to Puebla nuns, because both Christ and nuns sacrifice their bodies—the former in death on a cross and the latter in metaphorical death to the world via enclosure—for the salvation of others, their mystical union at communion is synergistic. In other words, the sacrifice that so shocked Fanny Calderón de la Barca at the profession ceremony, as we observed in Chapter 3, is precisely what New Spanish society admired about nuns.

Charged with maintaining and modeling belief in the Eucharist's essence, nuns are once more elevated through their faithfulness manifested in their own experience of receiving communion. Reception of communion was concomitant with their ideal penitence—enjoining nuns to vocalize weeping to cleanse their consciences—and their adherence to rules of obedience. Obedience to a superior, such as an abbess or confessor, prescribed the manner in which a nun could partake in the reception of communion on any given day: sacramentally or spiritually, with the latter achieved through imaginative help from the senses—seeing the host and imagining consumption of it, or listening to the Body of Christ through convent music, as I argue.

However, some of the most privileged nuns, like Sister María de Jesús and Sister Bárbara, from Puebla, superseded vows of obedience. As I will show in this chapter, the divine love that they modeled for other nuns allowed them to receive communion either daily or in extraordinary ways that circumvented their prelates' orders. Just as we observed music enhancing mysticism in Chapter 2, so too did receiving communion yield mystical ecstasies.[16] And why would it not? Indeed, as we observed in Chapter 1, the Body of Christ, the Word of God, and all that is divinely prescribed, such as the Immaculate Conception and virginity, have also been described as musical.

The constructed narratives in nuns' biographies, as well as order-specific rules and other devotional literature, echo the messages in villancicos that nuns sang for the Body of Christ: words of contrition, consumption, contemplation, and belief in the eucharistic mystery. Resonances between eucharistic devotional items, both read and heard, convey nuns' lived experiences and idealized prescriptions to reach divine transformation through communion.

The examples of María de Jesús, Bárbara, and other nuns who had mystical experiences, together with the villancicos, would instruct nuns—like Paula, named in her profession villancico—in how to repent, to feast on, and listen to the Body of Christ. Their example would instruct nuns to become one with their spiritual groom on earth. Nuns would be encouraged to enjoy their "wedding bread," their honeymoon, and as such, they would anticipate a life of imitating Jesus' Passion.

The Virgin Mary Houses the Eucharist

The Virgin Mary was considered the second Eve, a doctrine symbolized by the fact that *Eva* (Eve in both Latin and Spanish) spelled backward becomes the *Ave* (Hail) from Gabriel's salutation to Mary at the Annunciation in the Gospel of Luke: *Ave gratia plena*.[17] So too was Christ considered a second Adam. The sin of disobedience committed by the early ancestors of humanity was acquired by listening to the snake, as we observed in Chapter 1, and reacting with the most mundane of actions: consuming a piece of fruit from the tree of knowledge of good and evil. Therefore, in the Christian New Testament parallel, disobedience would be subverted through a more elaborate feast prepared through obedience, consumption of the Body of Christ.[18]

Adam and Eve's disobedience was reversed by Christ and the Virgin Mary, whose obedience to God's will through her consent to the motherhood of Christ the savior was predestined in her Immaculate Conception.[19] Jesus accepted his Passion to redeem the world, becoming "obedient to death, even death on a cross" (Philippians 2:8). Through Mary, the world received Christ, and through his death and resurrection, God's order was restored. Subsequently, the Church was founded with its seven orders, or sacraments: Baptism, Eucharist, Penance, Confirmation, Matrimony, Extreme Unction, and Holy Orders.[20] The most complicated of these is the Eucharist, in which, to reiterate what was said earlier, the eating of Christ's body, disguised as transubstantiated bread, is partaken as sustenance and healing, a reversal of the sin and destruction caused by Adam and Eve's sampling of forbidden fruit.[21]

In the eleventh century, the Church began to rely on the Virgin Mary to emphasize Christ's actual presence in the Eucharist.[22] "Mary herself was augmented in the eucharistic context. She became . . . the person who had intimately constituted the sacred," according to Miri Rubin.[23] From this intersection of Marian and Christic devotion arose allegorical references to Mary as a type of baker or the oven that cooked the bread for the Mass, didactic allegories that related the divine mother and child with ordinary tradespeople and tools.[24]

Mary's body was also used to represent sacred items that churches used to reserve the consecrated host, such as a tabernacle and a monstrance.[25] The former is a metal box located on the high altar, which houses consecrated wafers (hosts) for communion. Each church usually has a large host referred to as the Blessed Sacrament. The Blessed Sacrament is used for eucharistic adoration, displayed publicly, or processed during feasts. It is placed in a circular viewing glass (*viril*) within an ornate metal display case called a monstrance. Spanish cathedrals commissioned some of the largest monstrances in Christendom for displaying the Blessed Sacrament. Some monstrances could reach up to eight feet high, resembling multilevel houses of palatial grandeur with columns containing niches for inlaid statues of saints, covered in precious metals and jewels.[26] It should come as no surprise that Puebla cathedral, dedicated to the Immaculate Conception, had a statue of the Immaculate Conception built into one of its large monstrances.[27]

The 1738 New Spanish Franciscan novice meditations, discussed in Chapter 1, provide examples of the types of Marian-eucharistic discourses that made their way to New Spain as images to be conjured up for devotional purposes. In emphasizing the astonishing reality of Mary's virginal pregnancy with the entire Trinity, Franciscans were instructed to imagine the Virgin pregnant in her home in Nazareth, surrounded by angels who had moved into Mary's house to adore her womb constantly in song:

There they [the angels] sang sweet hymns taken from the sacred scriptures to the Blessed Virgin and to the Word made human in her purest womb. Your womb, they would sing, is like a pile of wheat surrounded by lilies, because it has within it the bread of heaven surrounded by virginal purities. Lord, you are more beautiful than any other son of man; grace has spilled from your lips and also from the lips of your Blessed mother, especially after using them to consent to the incarnation, saying: "Behold the handmaid of the Lord." O, what immense joys these angelic songs would cause in the soul of the pregnant sovereign![28]

Steeped in vocality in its recollection of the Annunciation dialog, this meditation reprises the metaphor of Mary's womb as the enclosed garden. In contrast with the sin committed in the Garden of Eden, the enclosed garden of Mary was sinless for the sake of producing a salvific crop, as symbolized by lilies guarding wheat. Unpacking the allegory, wheat is the whole grain that becomes processed into the bread of the hosts consecrated at Mass, which contain the veiled Body of Christ.

Villancicos also employed the wheat metaphor, as in the two extant verses of *Trinidad de Dios, señores* (CSG.114) from the Santísima Trinidad convent:

Trinidad de Dios, señores,	Trinity of God, Lords,
que el cielo abajo se viene	that heaven comes down
y, en vez de dorado rocío,	and, instead of a golden dew,
doradas espigas llueve.	it rains spears [of wheat].
A la tierra debe	Heaven owes
tal cosecha el cielo,	such a harvest to the earth,
pues trigo coge	for it harvests wheat
cuando siembra nieve.	when it sows snow.[29]

Only two voice parts remain, a tenor and a tiple part, but a note on the tenor part indicates, "To play with six fingers, to harmonize with three/ Para tañer por seis dedos, para templar por tres."[30] The verb *tañer* suggests accompaniment on a plucked string instrument; the *Diccionario de autoridades* provides the example that Orpheus played (*tañía*) the citole, or vihuela. The three voice parts suggested in the note would allude to the three persons of the Trinity, a combination of eucharistic and Trinitarian devotion, convenient since the feast of Corpus Christi, the Church's major annual celebration dedicated to honoring the Eucharist, fell on the Thursday after Trinity Sunday. Harvesting wheat when snow comes down would be a metaphor for transubstantiation, the conversion of bread by the priest's blessing at the Mass into the consecrated host containing the Body of Christ. Mary's body would thus be the fertile ground, or garden, that yields the fruitful harvest of the Trinity—the indivisible union of God the Father, Christ the Son, and the Holy Spirit. But as we will see, emphasis on the second person of the Trinity, Christ Jesus, was often associated with the eucharistic devotion of nuns, as already implied in Sister Paula's profession villancico *Albricias, zagalas*.

The multi-layered trope of Mary's house in the Franciscan meditation, referring both to her womb and to her physical house, was also employed fruitfully in nuns' profession sermons. In Juan Rojo de Costa's 1668 sermon for María de San Simón's profession in Mexico City's San Jerónimo convent, Rojo adds another meaningful layer by speaking of the purity exemplified by lilies thriving in the warm virginal garden ("las azucenas de sus virginales candores"), representing the convent and hinting once more at the enclosed garden associated with Mary.[31] Rojo's sermon draws a parallel with the literal enclosure of the convent cloister meant to guard María de San Simón's perpetual virginity but also filled with patios and gardens for the nuns to grow plants and flowers, as we observed in Chapter 1.

Given the central role of communion of the Eucharist in the mystical marriage of nuns consecrated at the profession ritual, as well as Mary's role in incarnating God's humanity, Jesus, contained in the communion host, the biographies of nuns also convey Marian-eucharistic rhetoric. For example, Mary was envisioned as the gate to Sister María Anna Águeda de San Ignacio's heart containing the Body of Christ.[32] Puebla's Santa Rosa convent, where María Anna was cloistered, observed a forty-hour prayer service to the Blessed Sacrament. This devotion, popularized by the Jesuits and Capuchins in New Spain, required the nuns to pray before the exposed Blessed Sacrament in the Church's monstrance for forty hours, and eucharistic villancicos could be sung during this service.[33] While María Anna venerated the consecrated host during the forty-hour devotion, God showed María Anna her heart as if it were a tabernacle. María Anna saw herself inside it alongside the Body of Christ and with Mary at the gate, attending to who may enter and join Christ.[34] This gives us a more descriptive account of the intense interiorization that Sister Jacinta de Atondo experienced—"my body being consumed into my heart . . . my vision was interiorizing"—at the sound of the organ (Chapter 2).

The Virgin Mary's role as a chief attendant between her son Christ and his union with his spiritual brides also plays out in Sister Isabel de la Encarnación's eucharistic ecstasy at the Santa Teresa convent in Puebla. In song, Sister Isabel describes Mary as a *madrina*, godmother, though sometimes translated as matron of honor, for Isabel's mystical marriage to Christ, relived on an occasion on which she took communion.[35] These examples all underscore Mary's role as a medium, a go-between, an intercessor for salvation that nuns could imitate. Isabel de la Encarnación meditated upon Mary's Immaculate Conception by referring to sin's representation in the dragon from the Apocalypses (Chapter 1), while honoring Christ in the Eucharist as the sacrificial Lamb of God that takes away the sin of the world and grants peace, as sung in the *Agnus Dei* at Mass before the priest takes communion. Isabel sang:

Ya no más corderito de oro, ya no más.	No longer, little lamb of gold, no longer.
Ya no más corderito de paz, ya no más.	No longer, little lamb of peace, no longer.
Ya está vencido el dragón.	The dragon is slain.
Su obstinación, y porfía	Its determination and stubbornness
Con el Nombre de María	With Mary's name
Ya está vencido el dragón,	The dragon is slain,
Jesucristo lo venció,	Jesus Christ defeated him,
Con los méritos de su Pasión.	With the merits of his Passion.
Ya no más corderito de mi corazón.	No longer, little lamb of my heart.
Ya no más corderito de oro, ya no más.	No longer, little lamb of gold, no longer.
A las bodas del cielo llaman aprisa:	The weddings of heaven call with haste:
Ay, Dios, ¿y quien será esta?	Oh God, and whose will it be?
Cristo es el esposo, y la Virgen la madrina:	Christ will be the groom, and the Virgin the god mother:
Dichosa el alma que fuere digna.	Blessed is the soul that is worthy.
Ay, Jesús mío, ¿y quien será digna?	Oh, my Jesus, and who will be worthy?

The nuns who observed Isabel singing these coplas, as her biographer called them, were amazed at the flames of fire coming out of Isabel's mouth while singing, especially because she was not known to be a musician.[36] In a reversal of what we observed previously in Chapter 2, in which music led to and enhanced mystical encounters, now the Eucharist is exciting a nun to sing in ecstasy, the fire of divine love unable to be contained in Isabel's heart.[37] Just as the Eucharist acted on nuns' bodies, assisted by the Virgin Mary who birthed Christ, so too could the Eucharist act on the Virgin Mary's body to further dispel doubts about Christ's body in the host.

The Assumption of the Virgin Mary has been celebrated on August 15 since the seventh century.[38] While no word of this phenomenon exists in the Bible, tradition in non-canonical texts held that when Mary died, her body and soul were taken up to heaven by Jesus and the angels, who came down to earth and escorted her up.[39] It was a major feast in New Spain for which polyphonic music was considered most appropriate, not least because Mexico City cathedral was dedicated to the Assumption.[40] The Assumption villancico *Al aire que se llena de luces* (CSG.283) by Francisco Vidales from the Santísima Trinidad convent draws on many of the common themes typical of Assumption villancicos. Natural elements—such as earth, wind, and fire, as in the estribillo—are a metaphor for totalizing praise.[41] Mentions of royalty allude to her crowning upon her arrival in heaven, as copla 2 indicates, reminding us that she is Princess/Queen/Empress of Heaven, the latter a title we observed in María de Jesús' mystical vision in Chapter 2 when the Virgin was seen conducting the choir of angels and the convent choir in the coro.[42] The final copla attends to Mary's mediation of the earthly and heavenly as she transitions upward, and all of the coplas allude to the musicality of the angel choirs that would have accompanied and festooned her rise to heaven, the same angels with whom nuns' voices would echo, recalling Vallarta's instructions (Sister Clori's dialogue) to nuns long ago in the introduction.[43] From the perspective of nuns' professions, copla 5 resonates with the vow of poverty and the fire of the estribillo suggests the burning prevalent in divine love. Yet what sets this villancico apart is that the estribillo and copla 3 do not mention Jesus coming down to escort the Virgin up, but rather describe Jesus in eucharistic terms: the bread of heaven, bread and flesh, nourishment to be consumed.

Estribillo
Al aire, que se llena
de luces y claridades.
Al fuego, que en amor
los arpones están ardiendo.
A tierra, que, de pan
de los cielos, toda está llena.

To the air, that fills
with lights and clarities.
To the fire, in which the harpoons
are burning with love.
To the earth, all of which is full
with the bread of heaven.

Coplas
1. Entonen los nueve coros
de las sacras jerarquías
glorias de reyes supremos,
gracias, festejos,
gustos y caricias.

Let the nine choirs
of the sacred hierarchies intone
the glories of the supreme kings,
the graces, celebrations,
pleasures, and caresses.

2. Canten, que a su mismo trono
sube su princesa misma,
cuyo soberano asiento
honra, avasalla,
adora y amplifica.

Sing, for their princess herself
ascends to their same throne,
she honors her sovereign seat,
overwhelms,
adores, and magnifies.

3. Canten, que, si ella se sube,	Sing, for, if she ascends,
baja en ese mismo día	in that same day
aquel fruto de su vientre	that fruit of her womb descends
en pan y en carne,	in bread and flesh,
en manjar y en vida.	in banquet and life.
4. Canten, que mil sacramentos	Sing, that a thousand sacraments
se han hecho por su huida,	have been made because of her flight,
pues piensan que ha de faltarles	for they think that they will lack
gracias, amores,	graces, loves,
prendas y alegrías.	garments, and joys.
5. Canten, que como en sus dones	Sing, for, as the richest thing
faltó la cosa más rica,	was lacking among her gifts,
anda en precio su belleza	the price of her beauty is
alta, estimable,	high, admirable,
cara y muy subida.	costly, and very elevated.
6. Canten, que cielos y tierra,	Sing, for heaven and earth,
cómo deben en justicia,	as they justly owe,
atan su vida hermosura,	bind beauty to her life,
canten, alaben,	may they sing, praise,
y llamen y bendigan.	and call and bless.

The extant music parts present a two-choir polychoral work for eight voices, of which the tiple of the first choir and the alto and tenor of the second choir survive. Like so many of the manuscripts from the Santísima Trinidad repertory, these contain the names of two nuns who presumably performed the parts: Sister María de San Juan on the tenor part and Sister María Teresa de San Francisco on the alto. Remarkably, the latter name is decorated with the same vine-like figures we observed in the decorated initials of the Encarnación choirbooks in Chapter 1, recalling the claustral gardens (see Appendix 4.1).

The disappearance of at least five music parts notwithstanding, we can observe in the estribillo how rhythm conveys the weight of transformation imparted on humanity with Christ's return to earth in the transubstantiated bread that yields the thousand sacraments—infinite, in reality—alluded to in copla 4. Example 4.1 is the estribillo's transition from a sprightly duple

Example 4.1 Vidales, *Al aire que se llena de luces* (CSG.283), mm. 20–30

meter to a long-note triple meter upon the bread of life's arrival to earth, "a tierra." A reprise of the estribillo's previous stanzas about wind and fire continues in triple meter after this weighty arrival to earth. The coplas maintain that rhythm in accompanying the Marian text. Changes between meters are common in villancicos, but when accompanying such thematic gravitas, a compositional decision of this sort raises rhetorical the question as to its technical purpose.

The co-mingling of Marian and Christic reverence was up to each nun's imagination, though the devotional material they engaged with and the liturgical cycle would guide their meditations and prayers. The villancico *Al aire que se llena de luces* would be appropriate for the feasts of both Corpus Christi and the Assumption. Corpus Christi is typically no more than three months away from the feast of the Assumption, and so the villancico would bridge Mary's and Christ's humanity through a seasonal reflection on the Eucharist and support the liturgical mindset of cycling from one feast to another.[44]

Additional examples of Marian (Assumption) and eucharistic devotion in nuns' biographies reflect on the physical concern of coming down from and going up to heaven. Recall that in Chapter 2 Sister Mariana de la Encarnación was showered with flowers from the Virgin Mary as she took communion through the coro bajo wall at the cratícula on the feast of the Assumption. Similarly, the very thought of the Virgin Mary's transition from earth to heaven animated the eucharistic devotion of Sister María Anna Águeda de San Ignacio at the Santa Rosa convent in Puebla as the feast of the Assumption was approaching. In anticipation of the feast, before receiving communion on August 13, Sister María Anna "considered what would be the disposition of the grand queen for her final communion."[45] (There is that signal to Mary's sovereignty once more.) Upon receiving communion, María Anna was taken up next to the Virgin Mary, "having received the divine son and remaining submerged in very close union with the most loving mother."[46]

Because of the Eucharist's power to unite between the earthly and the heavenly, María Anna was elevated to the Virgin Mary's proximity when she took communion, a reciprocity between two mediating sources, the Eucharist and the Virgin Mary. Mary brings Christ to humanity, and Christ's resurrected body in the communion host brings humanity close to Mary. The

Eucharist thus enacts a post-resurrection echo of Jesus' entrustment of Mary to John at the crucifixion that we will examine more closely in Chapter 5, thus yielding a never-ending cycle of dual devotion owed to Mary and Jesus' "incomparable closeness," as Miri Rubin described.[47] Such closeness was also captured with musical allegory. In the chapter on Sister María Anna Águeda's Marian devotion, her Jesuit biographer José Bellido described the relationship between Mary and Christ as being like two citharas that vibrate in sympathy with each other when one is plucked.[48] Thus, Bellido hints at Mary's co-passion with Christ, which we will begin to attend to later and discuss more fully in Chapter 5 as well.

Frequency of Eucharistic Feasting

Given the harmonious effects that were possible when consuming the Eucharist, such as uniting nuns with their husband, Christ, and their quintessential role model, the Virgin Mary, one might expect that nuns would want to receive communion as often as possible. In fact, many of the exemplary nuns with published biographies were known to have received communion daily. But to convey their model obedience as well, limits were imposed on the frequency of communion, which also yielded extraordinary moments involving spiritual communion.

A nun was to take communion as many times as her confessor or convent abbess allowed her, and there were minimum requirements stipulated in each order's rules based on feasts of the liturgical calendar. As discussed earlier, there were two forms of receiving communion: spiritual communion and sacramental communion. The former took the form of personal prayer and penance underscored with a spirit of longing for redemption and for the Body of Christ, deeply imagining reception of the communion host.[49] Sacramental communion involved physically eating the communion host delivered by the hand of a priest into the mouth. We observed in Chapter 2 that nuns received sacramental communion on a schedule around the Divine Office and Mass.

To give a few examples of the feasts on which sacramental communion was required for nuns, the Conceptionists were to receive communion on the feasts of the Immaculate Conception, Christmas, Visitation, Annunciation,

Purification, Assumption, on the first week of Lent, throughout Holy Week, on Easter, Pentecost, Corpus Christi, the feast of St. Francis, and on All Saints Day.[50] The Dominicans were required to take communion every Thursday and Sunday as well as on Christmas, feast of the Circumcision, Epiphany, Maundy Thursday, Easter, Ascension, Pentecost, Corpus Christi, all feasts of the Virgin, the feast of St. Dominic, St. Peter, St. Paul, and All Saints.[51] The Hieronymites took communion on the first Sunday of Advent, on Christmas, Purification, first, fourth, and sixth Sunday of Lent, Maundy Thursday, Ascension, Corpus Christi, Assumption and nativity of Mary, St. Jerome day, and All Saints.[52] The Bridgettines were less specific about feasts, merely mentioning that communion was required twice a week and on every major feast, along with confession twice weekly, or more if the mother superior required it.[53]

Some of the most personal messages about nuns' obedience, the Eucharist, and its meaning within the Mass were left behind by local New Spanish bishops. The liturgy of the Mass requires attendance of all practicing Catholics on a weekly basis, usually on Sunday, and daily attendance by all religious (nuns, monks, priests, etc.). The Mass re-creates the sacrifice of Christ's Passion, relived as communion bread that is transubstantiated into Jesus' resurrected body by priests. This is the liturgy that commemorates Christ's last supper prior to his Passion, in which Jesus instituted the Eucharist: "on the night when he was being betrayed, [he] took bread, and gave thanks, and broke it, and said, take, eat; this is my body, given up for you. Do this for a commemoration of me" (1 Corinthians 11:23–24). The archbishop of Mexico City José Pérez de Lanciego y Eguilaz also had much to say to nuns about the recurrence of Mass in a pastoral letter:

> Consider that the love of Christ was not satisfied with having redeemed us through his Passion, and death, expending all of his being for our love, but rather, he wanted that this benefit be repeated frequently in the sacrifice of the altar [the Mass], because even though he redeemed us, we would still continue to be sinners, and he knew that we would once more offend [him].[54]

Similarly, in a published farewell address by Bishop Juan de Palafox y Mendoza given as he departed back to Spain under political duress in 1649,[55] he instructs nuns on the importance of the Mass and recommends that they take communion as often as possible, "to receive their husband with purity and frequency."[56] Palafox articulates how important communion is for all Catholics, as he also instructed male religious to take part in the sacraments often and to remember to say the daily Mass.[57]

Yet despite the necessity for male clerics to celebrate the Mass and consecrate the Body of Christ for all to partake of it as frequently as possible, Palafox's message to male religious lacks the amorous synergy he appended in his farewell to the nuns. For nuns, then, the distinction between human love and divine love facilitated through communion thus gets muddled, as in the profession villancico *Albricias, zagalas* and as we will see in other examples later.

Moreover, Palafox reminds nuns how important their union with Christ was for the salvation of humanity. He says that when nuns receive communion, "the fire of love enters that consumes our faults"—divine love's burning sensation is characterized by Palafox as capable of incinerating sin.[58] Palafox also reveals the transformation that each nun could experience when taking communion: "[she] converts into [her] God."[59] He concludes with a typically Palafoxian allegorical summation, as we observed in Chapter 1 when he praised virginity, now rhapsodizing on the eucharistic feast:

> O celestial and eternal union, in which heaven and earth unite to make the earth heaven! O celestial and eternal union, in which the divine touches with the human and makes the human divine.[60]

Suggestive of audible speech, we may recall that through these "O" exclamations Palafox beckons listeners.[61] Moreover, I reiterate that Palafox's enthusiastic proclamation of unity with Christ through communion is only within his message to nuns and not to male clerics, whom he addresses in the same document.

For those nuns who, for whatever reason given to them by their confessors and abbesses, could not take communion with the frequency that Palafox alludes to, spiritual communion would suffice.[62] The essence of spiritual communion is that it would yield the same satisfaction that sacramental communion provided for nuns, placing them in "a state of charity" that would lead to salvation.[63] Attending Mass and seeing the host raised up by the priest after quoting Christ's words, "take, eat," was the key moment for spiritual communion.[64] This ritual is referred to as the elevation. For this reason, as we saw in Chapter 2, the coro's curtain was raised so that nuns could see the host during the elevation and imagine taking it and eating it.

Sometimes, spiritual communion was more practical, as when nuns were too sick to come downstairs for sacramental communion. Again, depending on the confessor's advice, sometimes the priest did enter the cloister to administer sacramental communion to sick nuns. But sometimes they did not, and nuns' biographies provide us with useful examples of what nuns could do to make a spiritual communion without being able to see the host elevated at Mass. When Sister Bárbara Josefa was ill and could not attend Mass or receive sacramental communion in person, she was said to attend Mass spiritually, by silently reciting all of the prayers and imagining all of the rituals taking place at the high altar.[65] Bárbara also heard Christ's voice calling her from the tabernacle and inviting her to receive communion.[66] He said to her, "If all the sick raised their wings of the spirit with vehement desire to fly to their sacramental spouse, I guarantee that as a prize for their devotion, you would be healed."[67]

The anonymous villancico *Pide el alma el sacramento* a 4 (CSG.097) from Bárbara's Santísima Trinidad convent augments the Eucharist's healing power, suggesting that it was a lifesaving remedy. The piece takes its title from the first line of the first copla, and it maintains an atmosphere of urgency throughout, because the death of a sickly soul is imminent. Such urgency is conveyed through rhythm. The coplas are in a quick-moving duple meter with a syllabic text on short note values. The poetics of divine bread coming down from heaven in the estribillo are set to notes of longer duration and triple meter, the music alluding to the Eucharist's power to calm through satiation and through its pleasant, sweet taste as the last line suggests. Since the late Middle Ages, mystics had associated the Eucharist with sweetness,[68] and this characteristic is what the estribillo emphasizes with multiple repetitions "dulce sabor" as it moves toward its final cadence (Example 4.2).

Example 4.2 Anonymous, *Pide el alma el Sacramento* a 4 (CSG.097), mm. 70–80

The villancico suggests that tasting sacramental communion's sweet medicine is the only remedy to heal the soul, sick from love for the Eucharist. Naturally, the active ingredient in the communion remedy is the Body of Christ that it contains. Yet copla 4 emphasizes that the soul would nonetheless die eventually without ever seeing Christ in the bread. The true and final remedy is death and reunion with Christ in heaven. The subject in its earthly life must therefore, if convinced by the enticing estribillo sung by the nuns, rely on faith to trust that Christ's body is truly present in the Eucharist and consume it as often as possible.

Estribillo

Pan divino del cielo,	Divine bread from heaven,
que el amor me dio,	that love gave me,
todo es gloria,	everything is glory,
comerle,	eat from it,
que dulce sabor.	what sweet flavor.

Coplas

1. Pide el alma el sacramento,	The soul asks for the sacrament,
dénselo por Dios,	provide it for God's sake,
que se muere de un achaque,	for the soul will die from infirmity,
y es el achaque de amor.	and it is the illness of love.
2. Tiene su vida en la hostia,	Its life is in the host,
dénsela porque es rigor	provide it because it is cruel
que se muera sin remedio,	to die without remedy,
a prisa Cuerpo de Dios.	make haste, Body of God.
3. No te nieguen la comida,	May you not be deprived of food,
déjenle ver el sabor,	allow for its flavor to be seen,
que es milagro de los cielos,	which is a miracle from the heavens,
que coma a quien le crio.	eat the one who has created you.
4. En el pan está el remedio,	The remedy is in the bread,
muérase viendo que no llegue,	die without seeing him arrive,
quien le da la vida,	the giver of life
en el remedio mejor.	in that perfect remedy.

The death of the subject / the soul / the nun without seeing the Body of Christ in the host was also captured through the musicality of birds, a phenomenon encountered in Chapter 1 in affiliation with Marian devotion. The villancico *Cisne, no halagues* (CSG.245) by Miguel de Riva (d.

1711) expounds on the ancient myth that swans sing most beautifully before they die.[69]

Estribillo
Cisnes, no halagues,	Swan, do not flatter
a tu muerte, rigores	rigors with melodiousness
con suavidades.	when you die.

The estribillo's and coplas' text compel the subject to weep over sins committed rather than to sing beautifully in solipsistic neglect of the Eucharist's
great mystery. In these circumstances, copla 5 instructs that "crying is the
sweetest harmony," as is silence, according to copla 6 (see full text and translation in Appendix 4.2).

The harmony that accompanies the estribillo sets the mood for the
whole piece, which consists entirely of homophonic texture performed by
an alto voice, two tenors, and bass accompaniment. The estribillo cadences
back and forth between A minor and A major harmony, a characteristic
taken up as well in the coplas, which carry on the estribillo's homophony
and triple meter. The coplas cadence in A major, but the estribillo finally
cadences in A minor. Example 4.3, taken from the estribillo, shows that
from mm. 7 to 20 several dissonances in the form of tritones are heard,
formed by B natural and F natural sung together by two voice parts. Each
tritone precedes a sighing gesture in a single voice part, moving down a half
step from F natural to E natural. At m. 8 the tritone is formed by the bass
and tenor 1, followed by the sigh in tenor 1. In m. 11, the tritone is created
by the alto and tenor I; the sigh is in the alto, repeated in that voice at mm.
12–13. At m. 16, tritone harmony is once more created by the alto's F natural and tenor I's B natural, putting the sigh in the alto again. At mm. 19–
20, the tritone is in the harmony of the two tenors on the first beat of m. 20,
and the sigh is carried by tenor II across both measures. The minor seconds
between F natural and E prepare the ear for a middle cadence on the sixth
scale degree, F major, in mm. 22, accompanying "rigores/rigors."

The piece is in mode 7 (no key signature, A final, D mediation), whose
affective description from Nassarre's Escuela música places the harmony
in direct service to the poetics. Music in this mode can make listeners
sad, it can move them to tears, or it can deceive the ears.[70] It aligns with
the message of a swan merely singing a pleasant song for its own sake,

Example 4.3 Riva, *Cisne, no halagues* a 3 (CSG.245), mm. 7–22

Example 4.3 Continued

Example 4.4 Cáseda, *Pajarito que en el aire elevado* (CSG.151), mm. 96–99

and yet the tritones would suggest that the swan's final song was not beautiful at all.

Pajarito que en el aire elevado (CSG.151) by Diego de Cáseda (d. 1694) is similarly firm in its message on the need for contrition, with its calls to weeping, to approach sacramental communion (see full text and translation in Appendix 4.3). It is an accompanied duo with only the music for the accompaniment and one tiple voice remaining, and thus missing a second voice. The extant vocal part in the coplas employs a sixteenth-note to eighth-note melisma to simulate birdsong, part of a sequence over fifths in the bass leading to the coplas' final cadence (Example 4.4). The melisma tone paints words that suggest both music and voice (copla 1 "gorjeos/chirps," copla 3 "destemplanza/tunelessness," copla 4 "llanto/weeping," copla 5 "puntos/

notes," and copla 6 "pausas/rests"). The message in copla 2, "firmness of faith in the heart is greater than the flux of the voice," is reminiscent of Sister Clori's words of advice to Casandra from confessor Martín de Vallarta's *Luz que guia el camino*, encountered long ago in the introduction: "let the heart sing them, and let the lips be the instrument." Furthermore, copla 5 reminds nuns to align their singing with God's music because "God is in the notes," a gesture toward the same divine vocality we observed in Chapter 1 with Jesus being the Word and the Virgin Mary being the voice of God. Riva's villancico *Que enigma tan bello* (CSG.249) carries a similar message in its fourth copla, "wholly bread to the eyes and wholly God to the ears" (full text and translation in Appendix 4.4), recalling the advice in the Dominican rule we observed in Chapter 2, "Let the ears hunger for the Word of God."

If God is in the notes and is music to the ears, then singing and listening to eucharistic music would constitute spiritual communion, since through the act of listening to those notes the listener is being penetrated with God. Moreover, singing penitent birds would seem to allude to the never-ending state of contrition and examination of consciences that nuns were implored to engage in so that they could have their minds constantly focused on their spiritual perfection—the better to receive Christ sacramentally on a regular basis and to be prepared for their final union with Christ when they died.

What behavior would cause nuns to be assigned spiritual communion over sacramental communion was not discussed in the published biographies. It was left to the confidential confines of the confessional or within the chapter of faults, in which nuns revealed their misgivings to one another in community.[71] At times, however, confessors and abbesses simply assigned spiritual communion to test a nun's obedience and/or to confirm eucharistic miracles. Such was the case once when Sister María de Jesús' abbess asked her to refrain from sacramental communion. The spiritual communion that she experienced combines much of the amorous rhetoric of union between bride and Christ we have attended to so far together with a reflection on the sweetness of communion and the allegory of the penitent bird singing in the eucharistic villancicos. María de Jesús envisioned the consecrated host traveling directly up into her mouth while she prayed in the coro:

> The same God in the sacrament arrived in Mother María de Jesús' mouth, her husband entering through her lips, then sweeter, for being more communicable, since he came to introduce himself into her chest with sacramental accidents, and flights of tenderness. Through this stronghold of love

that excels in wonder and appears miraculous, the heavenly husband gave
his virgin wife on this occasion the delight of the wedding bread [honey-
moon], the tokens of eternal life, and the communion of his sacramental
body, without the abbess's prohibition interfering, the greater taste of all the
hidden glory, and all the charity revealed in the host, communicated to this
peaceful dove, who thus tasted the purest grain of the most glorious laurel,
in the innocent circle of the sacrament.[72]

There is that word "accidents," referring to the bread of the communion hosts
perceived by taste, now allegorized as the wedding bread, and thus displaying
the erotic undercurrents of nuns' relationship with Christ. The passage
uses the same phrase, "pan de la boda/honeymoon," as Paula's profession
villancico. Here, Sister María takes on the same image of a bird as in the
estribillo of *Pajarito*, but in this case she is a dove, feeding on the sacrament
in the form of laurel seed, a sign of sure salvation as prefaced by the promise
of eternal life previously describing the benefits of consuming the "wedding bread."[73] We can observe in this example how authority was assigned
to certain women in the convent: on the one hand, the reverend mother had
the authority to prevent other nuns from receiving communion; and on the
other hand, exceptional women like Sister María could receive communion
directly from God, bypassing the priest's hand altogether.[74]

Similarly, Sister Bárbara's agency took the form of extreme self-awareness.
She consistently performed her own confessions mentally by examining her
conscience four times daily. Weeping for forgiveness over any imperfec-
tion, she also sought out the sacrament of confession with a priest as often
as possible.[75] According to her biographer, Torres, the copious tears she shed
were pleasing to Christ, as also suggested in the two villancicos *Pajarito que
en el aire elevado* and *Cisne, no halagues*.[76] Convent rules often specify that
confessors "know the core of consciences," but it would seem that Bárbara
was intimately knowledgeable of her own conscience.[77] She took sacramental
communion on a daily basis at the Santísima Trinidad convent. When she
received communion, she described it as an "intimate feast." Informing her
biographer of her experience immediately prior to and after receiving communion, she used now-familiar matrimonial language:

She believed she was like a wife ready for the spiritual nuptials that she
would celebrate with the supreme majesty; and finally, she found herself
as if wedded in the glorious possession, and immanent reciprocation, with

which she enjoyed Christ, her soul completely transformed, and the Lord completely united and transformed in his wife.[78]

Here Bárbara's reception of communion enlivens both the spiritual wedding and the honeymoon. Her body and the body of Christ become one flesh, one sacrifice.

The absorption and assimilation of the Body of Christ in the host, whether through sacramental communion or imagined in spiritual communion, transformed nuns into the same substance of the sacrificial lamb, Christ, whose Passion was re-created at Mass. That sacrifice too, which nuns accepted by taking on the four vows, was one that clergy remarked upon heavily as well. "We are overjoyed," announced Bishop Palafox in his 1641 rule for Conceptionist nuns, "to see the example and spirit with which for divine mercy the virgins of our diocese follow the Lamb of God, their husband."[79] A similar message, over one hundred years later, in a 1760 profession sermon for Sister Josefa María de San Antonio in Mexico City's Purísima Concepción convent, came in the form of Franciscan Diego Ossorio asking a rhetorical question: "who is Josefa's groom?" He answers that it is a lamb.[80] The reason for this, he says, is that Jesus Christ "is known to us as a redeemer and in the holy Passion he humbled himself, surrendering to the torments like a most docile lamb without opening its lips to complain."[81] That obedient silence, taken up by sacrificing himself to the will of God, is inverted in the vocalization of nuns' profession vows, a careful use of sound, silence, and vocality on the sermonizer's part. Josefa modeled the sacrifice of the Lamb of God by solemnizing her profession, vocalizing her vows of obedience, poverty, chastity, and enclosure, and consummating her mystical marriage through communion.[82] As we will see, this consistent message that music and voice is inherent in Christ, the Lamb of God (*Agnus Dei*)—and that understanding his mysterious nature in the Eucharist calls for singing, weeping, chirping, and silence—will also employ instruments in resounding the Eucharist's mysterious tune.

Eucharistic Passion Devotion

On one feast of Corpus Christi, Sister Bárbara was in the coro listening to and meditating upon the words of a eucharistic song, a unique situation of attentive listening among New Spanish convent sources. The pieces she was listening to had to have been in Spanish, since she did not under-stand Latin.[83] In narrating Bárbara's experience, Torres reveals some of the musical practices through which the Santísima Trinidad convent cel-ebrated Corpus Christi. He used whatever details Bárbara told him about the piece she heard as the impetus for a digression on the nature of the Eucharist:

> For these solemn octaves, the nun muses compose some sacred poems that they sing to the sound of well-tuned and sonorous instruments in harmonious music; and, at the same time that these were being sung in the choir, Sister Bárbara meditated on the meaning of the words, which she heard [as if] directly from the sovereign intelligences [the angels]; and in order that, among the many songs that are sung, the good musicians (for the devout souls are that) may have the song composed by the angelic doctor St. Thomas to pay his homage to the Blessed Sacrament, which the highest seraphim celebrate with their singing, I decided to translate into Spanish the same poem that St. Thomas wrote in Latin, both because it is very devotional and because none less than a St. Thomas occupied himself with it. And it was also the occupation of such a sovereign king as David not only to sing, but also to dance in the sight of all his people and be-fore the Ark of the Covenant, which contained the manna, which is a pre-figuration of the sacrament of the Eucharist. And, in fact, the Eucharist [Eucharistia] is the true anagram of the Cithara of Jesus [Cithara Iesu]. And, since it is the sweet and most divine Jesus that plays it while we eat at the table, it will not be an offense to religious seriousness, but rather a praise of our tender devotion, to sing to his majesty the following poem, which contains the heroic virtues and lofty thoughts that those who sing it devoutly will find in it.[84]

Following this passage, Torres then provides readers with a Spanish translation of St. Thomas Aquinas' well-known *Adoro te devote*. In this hymn, the mystery of the Eucharist is explained by recalling that hearing the Word of God was enough to believe in Christ's presence within the consecrated host. "If sight, taste, touch, if they effect you, in as much as they perceive they are deceived," elaborates Torres. He continues, "And only the ear can surely proclaim you because it is a faithful witness of your Word."[85] St. Thomas' words, and Torres' analysis of them, support the no-tion of spiritual communion through listening as well.

The aurality of St. Thomas Aquinas' hymn pairs well with the anagram that Torres presents, Eucharistia / Cithara Iesu, which has concordances in the 1640 Jesuit book of emblems *Imago primi saeculi Societatis Iesu* and in Pedro Calderón de la Barca's sacramental play *El divino Orfeo* (1663).[86] Both sources reflect on Christ as the new Orpheus, with the power to save with musical performance, except that Christ's music, as Torres alludes through the anagram, resounds from Christ's presence in the Eucharist.

Yet the cithara had a long tradition in female spirituality as well, not least in women's Passion devotion,[87] and specifically in the Passion devotion of Sister Bárbara. As we will see in the next chapter, she envisioned and felt herself crucified and performed upon by Christ, indeed, as if Christ were playing her in the manner of strumming a cithara. Given such a vivid encounter with the Body of Christ, the villancico to which Sister Bárbara must have been listening attentively and which she must have described to Torres—leading to his exegetic digression on the Eucharist, its historical worship in song from King David forward, the anagram, and the translation of *Adoro te devote*—was José de Cáseda's *Qué música divina a 4* (CSG.153). Its approximate date range of 1673–1720 coincides with Bárbara's lifetime in the Santísima Trinidad convent.[88] Moreover, the villancico expounds on the Eucharist allegorized as a cithara and/or vihuela.

Estribillo

Qué música divina,	What a divine music,
acorde y soberana.	consonant and sovereign.
Afrenta de las aves	More beautiful than birdsong,
con tiernas, armoniosas consonancias.	with delicate and harmonious consonances.
En quiebros suaves,	With soft, resounding
sonoros y graves,	and profound pauses,
acordes y acentos	it offers chords
ofrece a los vientos.	and stresses to the winds.
Y en cláusulas varias	And it lifts the senses
sentidos eleva,	with various clauses,
potencias desmaya.	weakens the capabilities.

Coplas

1. Suenen las dulces cuerdas	Resound, sweet strings
de esa divina cítara y humana,	of that divine and human cithara,
que a un son que es de los cielos	for it unites high with the low,
forma unida la alta con la baja.	sounding as if from heaven.

2. De la fe es instrumento	It is an instrument of faith
y al oído su música regala,	and it gives its music as a gift to the ear,
donde hay por gran misterio,	where there is, mysteriously,
en cada punto, entera consonancia.	only consonance in each note.

3. Del lazo a este instrumento	The rosette of this instrument
sirve la unión que sus extremos ata,	unites its ends,
tres clavos son clavijas	three nails are [tuning] pegs and
y puente de madera fue una tabla.	a cross is the soundboard.

4. Misteriosa vihuela,	Mysterious vihuela,
al herirle sus cuerdas una lanza,	as its strings were stricken with a lance,
su sagrada armonía	sacred harmony was seen
se vio allí de siete órdenes formada.	formed out of seven orders [strings].

5. No son a los sentidos	Not for the senses,
lo que suenan sus voces soberanas	what your sovereign voices resound,
porque de este instrumento	because from this instrument
cuantos ellos perciban serán falsas.	what the senses perceive will be falsehoods.

6. Su primor misterioso,	Its mysterious delicacy,
que a los cielos eleva al que lo alcanza,	which raises to heaven whomever reaches it,
no le come el sentido	is not consumed by sense
porque es pasto su música del alma.	because its music is sustenance of the soul.

The poetic theme of this villancico can be traced to Origen, who characterized Christ's divinity as a psalterium and Christ's suffering humanity as a cithara.[89] The very image of Christ stretched on a cross like strings across a soundboard was one that convent prelates encouraged nuns to imagine as a lesson in patience.[90] The metaphor lived long and well beyond Origen's time, even taking on new, regional instruments, such as the Spanish vihuela.

The vihuela's *lazo* (rosette) was purely decorative, and the word is used here in copla 3 merely to describe the opening of the soundboard.[91] The opening amplifies the sound of the plucked strings by allowing their vibrations to resonate within the body of the vihuela. The soundboard and strings are essentially less resonant on their own, but when these features are combined on one instrument, they produce a more resonant music. Similarly, Christ's body coming together with the cross redeemed the world; a wooden cross by itself would have been useless.

In copla 4, the performance of the vihuela is compared to the piercing of Christ's side with a lance (*lanza*) while on the cross—an action yielding an outpouring of blood and water (John 19:33–34). The confluence of these two substances in the text invokes Christ's dual human and divine natures alluded to in copla 1. Christ's death on the cross, which was historically confirmed when a Roman soldier pierced his side with a lance (John 19:34), resulted in the redemption of humanity. The vihuela's sonority is redemption; its sound is salvation for listeners immersed in its resonance, supporting once more the notion that singing and listening to eucharistic music would constitute spiritual communion—"God is in the notes." Christ's death was the foundation of the Church and its seven sacraments, also known as orders (*ordenes*). Copla 4 expounds on this definition derived from the fact that each sacrament was "ordered" to have a specific ritual, connecting the seven sacraments to the vihuela's seven ordered strings.[92] The most important sacrament was Holy Orders. Only through this sacrament could the other six take place.[93] The sacrament of the Eucharist, moreover, renewed the nuns' redemption. This same message was extended in symbolic fashion in *Que música divina*, making the piece a most satiating selection for spiritual communion—"sustenance for the soul," as copla 6 describes.

The estribillo's imagery overlaps with the eucharistic allegories suggested in *Pajarito que en el aire elvado* and *Cisne, no halagues*, suggesting that Christ's music is indeed more beautiful than that of birdsong. The silencing and weeping of the birds allow for Christ's song to resound and take over the body's "potencias/capabilities," as the estribillo concludes. Silencing allows for Christ's song to be heard; weeping as a form of contrition qualifies one for reception of communion. Those capabilities, "potencias," frequently referred to in villancicos, are the capabilities of knowledge, love, remembrance, understanding, will, and memory.[94] As Sister Bárbara contemplated the specific meaning of these poetics, she would humbly let the Body of Christ steer her memory toward her exemplary Passion devotion, while reliving her honeymoon with Christ. Because the profession villancico *Albricias, zagalas* also dates from around the time that Bárbara lived in the Santísima Trinidad convent, she may well have known Sister Paula, that villancico's subject.

Who was Sister Paula? She was the Body of Christ, metaphorically transubstantiated in her profession villancico *Albricias, zagalas*, which elevated her up in song, honored through music as Mary and Christ were with devotional villancicos dedicated to their mysterious attributes. We observed in Chapter 3 how profession portraits depicted nuns as saintly. Profession villancicos were a sonic equivalent, resounding to the ears what the profession portrait revealed to the eyes. As such, Paula, like Bárbara and other devout nuns, would be called to walk the way of the cross when feasting on the Body of Christ to imitate him in body, soul, and song.

5

Redeeming Sounds

Resounding the Passion of Christ and His Spiritual Brides, or Who Was Sister Marina de San Francisco?

A mid-eighteenth-century document (ca. 1770) of two folios in length, preserved at the Archivo General de la Nación, reports a request from one Sister Marina de San Francisco, abbess of the Purísima Concepción convent—recall, the oldest—in Mexico City. The document, signed by Marina along with five assistant convent administrators (see Appendix 5.1),[1] explains that they sought to install an indulgence devotion. Such a devotion required people to attend particular liturgies or prayer services, and, in return, they would receive an indulgence, a remission of the temporary consequences for sin.[2] The indulgence devotion that Marina proposed invited people to come to the Purísima Concepción convent to participate in a new feast honoring one of the scenes from the Passion of Christ. In no small number of words, Marina called it the "feast of" Christ, dressed in white, mocked as a lunatic by Herod." Presumably, there would be a statue of Christ dressed in white for devotees to venerate inside the convent church.

Marina's letter was addressed to the Prefect of the Sacred Congregation of Rites in Rome—at that time, Cardinal Flavio Chigi (1711–1771).[3] His prefecture (1759–1771) overlapped with his tenure as the Protector of the Franciscan Order (1765–1771), in which he was charged with promoting worldwide Franciscan interests among the Church's governing body in Rome. Showing keen initiative and an entrepreneurial spirit, Marina made use of her order's very loose ties to the Franciscans. She claimed to be a member of the Order of St. Francis, perhaps intending to curry favor with Chigi. Marina's proposed feast would take place on a Friday in Lent and would consist of Office liturgies and a Mass that the nuns' own convent chaplain, Joaquín Niño de Córdova, had composed. The petition emphasizes that this was already a feast celebrated heartily in Mexico City's Jesús María convent on the Wednesday of Holy Week, a most solemn week in the liturgical calendar that commemorates Christ's Passion leading to Easter Sunday.

Marina also wanted the indulgence to apply retroactively to the souls of those who died prior to the feast's inauguration, that it be designated a privileged

Immaculate Sounds. Cesar D. Favila, Oxford University Press. © Oxford University Press 2023.
DOI: 10.1093/oso/9780197621899.003.0006

indulgence.[4] In this way, Marina's devotion would save as many souls as possible, and not only benefit those who participated in the live festivities. She requested that the feast include exposition of the Blessed Sacrament, so that the surrounding indigenous community ("pobrecitos indios," literally, "poor little Indians," she wrote), who lacked frequent viewings of the Blessed Sacrament, the church's consecrated host, could be inspired by the Eucharist.

In this petition, Marina's concern for representing Christ's humility at the Passion melds the visual and the linguistic. Multiple times, Marina recalls Christ's whiteness, referring to the white tunic that the statue for veneration in the church would be wearing—which would reflect the white habit of her order, but it also had an association with lunacy.[5] Christ's humility is implied in the petition's reference to him as a lunatic for accepting his Passion, another iteration of the silent lamb metaphor we observed in the previous chapter. In addition, the word *loco*, meaning crazy or lunatic, appears frequently in the text and underlined for emphasis.

Whether or not the feast came to fruition remains a mystery. There is no mention of this feast in any other known archival document, its absence implying that even if the feast did occur, it fell far short of the proposed level of grandeur, even locally.[6] Marina de San Francisco's request has the ring of desperation: the Conceptionists hardly referred to themselves as Franciscans, nor did they customarily engage in the purposeful indoctrination of indigenous people, which was the concern of male mendicant friars. If the nuns' devotional offerings within their convent churches brought in the participation of indigenous communities, this would be a welcomed bonus for the Church at large rather than the expectation.[7]

The image of Christ that would be venerated at this feast is somewhat unusual too, because it comes from a singular account found only in Luke's Gospel. Still, reflections on Christ mocked before Herod might have been familiar to Marina and a broader subset of nuns, considering Juan Sebastian de la Parra's Passion meditation hymn assigned to the Office of Prime:

Salve hora sacra,	Hail blessed Hour,
In qua Domine Iesu Christe,	in which the Lord Jesus Christ
Mane ad Pilatum, & Herodem	was led before Pilate and Herod in the
ductus es	morning,
Reductus veste alba illusus,	dressed in a white vestment, mocked,
Fortiter accusatus tacuisti,	accused, keeping silent.
Domine iesu Christe,	Lord Jesus Christ,
Has omnes affictiones tibi offero,	I offer you these affections.
Pro illis gratias ago,	For them I give thanks,
Pro illis miserere mei & Ecclesiae	Because of them, have mercy upon me
totius.	and the entire Church.[8]

These words come from the *Salva hora sacra* meditations, a series of prayers on themes of the Passion to be recited during each Office liturgy. In his explanation, Parra noted that, "just as all the mysteries of the Mass are a living representation of the Passion of Christ our Lord, so too were the canonical hours [the Divine Office] instituted in its memory."[9] Parra's message about the Office was relevant to nuns seeking to imitate Christ's Passion throughout their daily lives. Here, imitation is said to be achieved by constant recollection of Christ's steps on his way to the cross.

Parra's book was recommended by the famous confessor Antonio Núñez de Miranda in his *Distribución de las obras ordinarias* (1712), another guide for nuns like Marina to meditate on the Passion at each liturgy of the Office.[10] The sisters of the Jesús María convent sponsored the publication of *Distribución*. As mentioned before, their convent had already inaugurated the feast of Christ mocked and dressed in white. In the 1755 biography of Sister Augustina Nicolasa María de los Dolores, we learn that Sister Augustina's meditations for the Office at Mexico City's Capuchin San Felipe convent were in line with instructions like Núñez's, as she envisioned particular points of the Passion for each Office hour: Christ's imprisonment at Prime, the coronation with the crown of thorns at Terce, the scourging at Sext, the crucifixion at None, the piercing of the side at Vespers, and back to Christ tied to the column for Matins to begin the cycle anew.[11] Whether in a published devotional book or in an exemplary nun's biography, such examples were intended for nuns' spiritual enrichment and modeling, aids for imitating Christ, achieving perfection, salvation, and union with Christ in the afterlife. As we saw in the last chapter, a foretaste of this union was experienced through communion. However, what did imitating Christ's Passion mean for nuns, beyond constant recollection of the stations of the cross, and what role did music play in achieving successful imitation?

This chapter attends to this question and to some of the year-round Passion devotions in which nuns engaged. Christ's visible presence throughout various steps of his Passion, particularly his crucifixion, takes precedence, a contrast to the invisibility of his resurrected body in the Eucharist that we observed in the last chapter. But just as nuns were charged with contemplating and imitating the bravery and suffering of their spiritual spouse at the Passion, they could also be moved to sadness through sermons, music, and poetry that enjoined them to lament Christ's suffering and death along with his mother in the popular devotion to the Virgin of Sorrows. A Marian title that highlights her anguish over Christ's torture and death, the Virgin of Sorrows stirred conflicting emotions, as we also learn of the joy the Virgin Mary contained in her heart for the salvation narrative of Christ's life to come to fruition with his death. We will observe how music rewarded nuns' perfection when imitating Christ and following the Virgin's example.

St. Francis and the Cross

Marina's love for the Passion of Christ undoubtedly follows a long tradition in Christianity, ingrained in New Spain through Franciscan penitential piety that emphasized humility, bodily suffering, reverence to the cross, and imitation of Christ.[12] In addition to being the founder of the Franciscans and one of the patron saints of various orders of religious and confraternities since the Middle Ages, St. Francis of Assisi was also said to model the imitation of Christ's suffering, not least because of his stigmata, in which he miraculously bled at his extremities, wounded in the same manner as Christ at the crucifixion.[13] Francis was even invoked in convent rules on the role of novice teachers, because of their responsibility for establishing Passion devotion among their pupils at the start of the conventual life:

> She should give them time to read books of the holy doctrine and great devotion, so that they learn to feel the Passion of our Lord and love it and imitate it, since it is the basis on which our father St. Francis and all the saints learned and initiated [their missions]; it is in one's best interest to know how to feel the Passion of our redeemer and to motivate oneself to imitate it because of the tenderness of his love communicated to those who truly focus on his cross and Passion.[14]

Christ's suffering was the very foundation of a saint's saintliness, as described in this excerpt from a Conceptionist rule. Nuns too could become saint-like if they had profound spiritual formations based on imitating the Passion. Here, the rule also emphasizes that the Passion, Christ's physical pain, suffering, and death, might also convey Christ's tenderness and love. How did such a seemingly extreme dichotomy—love and pain—coalesce within convent spirituality?

Sister María de Jesús' convent Lenten devotions emphasized this connection between love and bodily pain, helping to prepare her convent sisters, as well as all who read her biographies, for the Passion recollections of Holy Week. She and her sisters at the Purísima Concepción convent in Puebla would recite thirty-three Credos—one for each year of Christ's life—daily throughout Lent.[15] The prayer took place in the coro, and the nuns who completed all the recitations received a special vision:

> In order to be in a better mindset to celebrate Holy Week, which required daily meditation on the labor, distress, sorrow, and wounds of their crucified spouse and deceased loved one: the convened virgins continued to say the Credo this number of times [thirty-three] every day until the so-called Lazarus Friday (the one before Good Friday), and on the said penultimate Friday of Lent, that squadron of virgin souls (led and commanded by Sister María de Jesús) took a sacred crucifix—which is now venerated in the coro, placed in the middle of one of its niches—and put it on an altar surrounded by reverent decorations and affections. At that time the mute image, or dead image on the crucifix, having always had its eyelids shut, opened its eyes miraculously, and that Lord, nailed on the cross, nailed them [fixed his eyes] or placed them sweetly on all the nuns that had fulfilled the said devotion, and he remained staring at his very wives who had served him well. . . . Sister María de Jesús asked her sovereign and dead-on-the-cross husband himself to deign to give a blessing to all the nuns of that cloister.[16]

The language about the nuns' dead husband is intriguing, because it indicates an ontology of Christ that is omnipresent and vivified to nuns at their pious request. He has always been dead and resurrected to early modern believers, but here a conjuring of his divine infinity, overlooking chronological time, is captured within specific moments of his (after)life signaled through particular devotional images.[17]

Such an affective description within a miraculous event would elevate the nuns as worthy of Jesus' visual attention from the cross. The only other time Christ communicated non-verbally from the cross with a stare was documented exclusively in Luke's Gospel accentuated through another avian-aural phenomenon. At the crucifixion, when the rooster crowed to confirm the Apostle Peter's denial of Christ, Peter wept as Jesus looked directly into Peter's eyes from the cross at that moment (Luke 22:59–62).[18] The nuns' engagement with the crucified Christ would also inspire the communal prayers of anyone who heard or read the biography such that their own prayers before a crucifix or any other work of art depicting Christ's Passion, such as Christ mocked by Herod as described before, might yield a similar blessing.[19]

For religious communities, these types of prayers before Passion artwork could also include mortification, in which nuns physically deprived themselves of food and bodily comfort, which could include wearing uncomfortable hairshirts (cilice) or beating themselves while praying. During these penitential sessions, some orders required the recitation of the psalm *Miserere mei* and the antiphons *Christus factus est* and *In Conceptione tua* along with a verse and prayers.[20] An association of mortification and suffering with music is thus suggested here, given the musicality of psalms and antiphons—familiar from frequent performance during the Office throughout the year—and the daily recitation of the Credo at Mass.[21]

Attempting to experience Christ's physical pain throughout the Passion was a supplementary benefit of mortification, which was primarily intended to prevent the impure thoughts inimical to the vow of chastity and therefore good singing.[22] Maintaining their chastity was a sacrifice compared to martyrdom.[23] Passion devotion connected very well to nuns' vow of chastity, and likewise to their vow of enclosure, which was also meant to guard chastity physically and symbolically. Even convent inhabitants recognized as the most devout, such as Sister Bárbara and Sister María de Jesús, mortified themselves; the self-regulatory tone in their biographies did not preclude the acknowledgment of impure thoughts, which were inevitable but tamable.

For Sister Bárbara, the practice of mortification at the Santísima Trinidad convent in Puebla was essential for overcoming thoughts that contradicted her vow of chastity—whatever they were; her biographer Torres does not provide explicit details.[24] Still, nuns' biographers purposefully compared their subjects' steadfast faith to manly strength, "a characterization that ran contrary to the weakness of character attributed to most lay women," according to Asunción Lavrin.[25] Torres described Bárbara's efforts in gendered terms: the word "masculine" (varonil) animates the force with which Bárbara would beat her body, both in communal discipline and in private flagellation after her meals.[26] Sister Bárbara indeed fasted as a form of mortification, but as an exemplary nun she was known for fasting more than eating; the resulting weakness supposedly empowered her to fight off sins against chastity.[27] In these moments of mortification, Torres calls on the example of the Dominican St. Catherine of Siena as Bárbara's role model, although he could just as easily have invoked her patron saint, Francis, as he too experienced bodily suffering in imitation of Christ. In order to emphasize that even the most renowned saints struggled against yet overcame thoughts of the flesh, Torres notes that Catherine was the saint who fought the strongest battles to repel sins against chastity.[28] Imitating Catherine's mortification practices, "invigorated by her [Bárbara's] masculine force," Torres reports, helped her to triumph over visions of obscene character.[29]

Women from the Old Testament also served as models for mortification rituals, if obliquely through clever association. In his novena for the Virgin of Sorrows statue venerated at the Jesús María convent in Mexico City, the Jesuit priest José Parreño intended for nuns to think of mortification when considering the tambourine with which Miriam accompanied herself and the Israelite women in their song of joy after God had drowned the Egyptian army.[30]

> Miriam the prophetess, Aaron's sister, went out with a tambourine in her hand, and all the women followed her, with tambourine and with dances, and took up from her the refrain, a psalm for the Lord, so great he is and so glorious; horse and rider hurled into the sea. (Exodus 15:20–21)

An instrument made of dead animal skin, the tambourine must be beaten to resound, just as every nun living the chaste life of the convent must mortify herself to be a good singer ("buena cantora"), Parreño instructed.[31] What resonance would a good singer—a mortified, "masculine," nun—resound?

For starters, the most masculine attribute a nun could take on was Christ's very own crucifixion. The 1792 funeral sermon of Sister María Ignacia, abbess of the Capuchin San José de Gracia convent in Querétaro, includes such an image. The print of María Ignacia depicts her crucified on top of Christ while wearing the crown of thorns (see Figure 5.1). An example of what art historian Cristina González calls "eccentric iconography," it depicts violence that is nevertheless peaceful in aspect, because of the tranquility in the nun's and Christ's dead faces.[32] Above the image appears an appropriate citation from Galatians 2:19, "With Christ I am nailed to the cross." Below the image, there is a four-line poem that quotes from Venatius' *Crux fidelis*: "Sweet nails, my love you hold crucified; I see myself on the cross with him, because with him I am to die."[33]

The image has precedents in fifteenth- and sixteenth-century European Passion artwork. It is in accordance with Capuchin piety, demonstrating the order's interest in asceticism and mystical union enhanced with erotic overtones.[34] These crucifixion images are an ascetic alternative to the famed crowned-nun profession portraits we observed in Chapters 1 and 3. Capuchins depicted crucified nuns to assert their order's austere lifestyle amid the late eighteenth-century reform-driven Church and Bourbon monarchy. The Bourbons were at odds with the supposed excesses of monastic

Figure 5.1 *Christo confixus sum cruci*, from Francisco Frías y Olvera, "Cristo Señor Nuestro retratado en la vida, virtudes, y muerte de la Venerable Madre Sor María Ignacia," 1792

life, including the ostentation of individual nuns' piety demonstrated in such paintings.[35]

Perhaps meaningful to New Spanish nuns for political reasons in the eighteenth century, the rhetoric displayed in convent portraiture is legible in nuns' biographies from throughout the seventeenth and eighteenth centuries, and it was not just a product of the Capuchin order's asceticism. The image of María Ignacia resonates with Sister María de Jesús' Passion prayer, taught at the Purísima Concepción convent during her tenure as abbess:

> May my hands be nailed with yours, my heart pierced by the lance that penetrated yours, my feet penetrated like yours with nails: I die, Jesus, with you on your cross, and may I die from your divine love.[36]

Similarly, as a reward for her strict adherence to her vows, Sister Bárbara was granted a transcendent vision, in which God spoke to her as she was nailed to a cross:

> "Child, this is the cross of the religious life: all nuns that take up the cross, and embrace it with joy, are consoled by it. Take it with great love, and tell your sisters to resign themselves to it, and they will live a joyous life, and they will be rewarded when they die." With such divine instruction, Bárbara remained crucified joyfully on her cross.[37]

Here we have another example of a seemingly illogical cause-and-effect, typical of hagiographic inversions, "in part because death was inverted into life's highest achievement: salvation and birth into eternity," according to Frank Graziano.[38] This type of mystical imagery in convent literature also had a sonic component, the resonance of José Parreño's "good singer" signaled earlier, but in the form of a string instrument. What followed Bárbara's crucifixion was her biographer Torres' explicit association of music-making with the nun's perfect adherence to her four vows and devotion to the Passion. The cithara and its affiliation with the Passion sacrifice re-created at Mass through the Eucharist that we observed in Chapter 4 now makes its forecasted return. Recalling that the divine cithara is not just a wooden cross, but the conjunction of Christ's body crucified on the cross that constructs the allegorical instrument, it is implied that Bárbara is crucified on top of Christ, like María Ignacia and María de Jesús discussed earlier:

> And since through the heavenly cross the true Apollo gave his beloved [Bárbara] the best cithara, after having plucked her with the spirit, he filled her with the inspiration that allowed her to sing these verses, congratulating herself because of her crucifixion.[39]

1. A la sombra de la cruz,
vuela ya mi corazón;
porque de la religión
halló en su sombra la luz.

To the shade of the cross,
my heart soars;
because through the religious life,
it has found light in its shade.

2. En la cruz Jesús exalta
su obediencia; y si se funda
en humildad más profunda,
será obediencia más alta.

On the cross Jesus exalts
his obedience; and if it is founded
upon profound humility,
it will be the highest obedience.

3. Vid es con racimos de oro
la cruz; pero esta riqueza,
se disfraza en la pobreza,
porque es oculto tesoro.

A grapevine with clusters of gold
is the cross; but this richness
disguises itself in poverty,
because it is a hidden treasure.

4. Claro espejo es mi Jesús
en la cruz de la limpieza,
si el trono de su pureza
estuvo al pie de la cruz.

A clear mirror of cleanliness
is my Jesus on the cross
since the throne of purity
was at the foot of the cross.

5. En la cruz fijo mi amado,
aquel claustro me labró,
en donde mi alma se entró
por la puerta del costado.

Attached to the cross, my beloved
built me that cloister,
in which my soul entered
through the door on the side.

6. Así la cruz me figura
en su extremada grandeza
la obediencia, y la pobreza,
la castidad, y clausura.

In this way, the cross
in its enormous greatness,
represents to me obedience and poverty,
chastity and enclosure.

The strophes here are in *redondilla* form, common to many villancicos. The form consists primarily of octosyllabic lines, within quatrains following an ABBA rhyme scheme.[40] This will not be the last time that Torres incorporates a Passion hymn without including musical notation. The absence of music suggests that such hymns might have been sung to a familiar tune or an improvised melody by nuns who encountered them in reading about Sister Bárbara's life.

The first strophe functions as an introduction to the poem, with the sixth and final one serving as the conclusion. The first inverts the darkness produced by the shade of the cross into a more optimistic space filled with light, the light of salvation. The foot of the cross becomes a place for comfort by way of the convent life and the four vows—the promised road to salvation in the cross for nuns and for the benefactors invoked in their daily prayers. Each of the next four strophes treats one of the vows individually, and the final verse summarizes all four vows. This sixth strophe also foreshadows a vision attributed to Bárbara later in her biography, an episode in which she witnesses Christ on the cross as a judge on Judgment Day, and she is reminded that the four wounds on Christ's extremities are a symbol of her own four vows and those of every professed nun.[41]

The fourth strophe is somewhat more elusive than the others, expounding on the vow of chastity without explicitly stating it in the way that strophes 2, 3, and 5 recall the other three vows: obedience, poverty, and enclosure, respectively. While the summary in strophe 6 lists chastity among the four vows, strophe 4 replaces the word "chastity" with "pureza/purity" in order to maintain the redondilla form, rhyming "pureza" in the third line with "limpieza/cleanliness" in the second.

But there is more to the word choice than just rules of poetics: strophe 4 also salutes the Immaculate Conception. Because each strophe expounds on the ways in which individual vows derive from Christ's death on the cross, this strophe indicates that Christ was indeed a mirror of purity because the "throne of purity"—the Virgin Mary—accompanied him on his Passion and was at the foot of the cross, in its shade. Furthermore, any reference to Mary as the throne of Christ's purity points directly to Immaculate Conception devotion: Mary's Immaculate Conception was said to enable her pure gestation of the Son of God who redeemed the world by his death on the cross.[42] We have also observed a similar combination of Passion and Marian devotion in Isabel de la Encarnación's spontaneous and fiery eucharistic hymn within her biography, which we attended to in the last chapter.[43]

The Virgin Mary too would be a model of joy, suffering, and love as expressed in these examples and even more explicitly in Diego de Oviedo's Franciscan Passion reflections, *Manual de exercicios para los desagravios de Christo* (Manual of exercises for the reparations of Christ). Originally published in Mexico City in 1705 and reprinted in 1736, the meditations each intersperse a series of miniature hymns, denoted as "música," to be sung to an improvised tune; they gloss the topic of the meditations, meant to be

used for Passion reflection throughout the liturgical year.[44] The final hymn
is a Spanish translation of the entire *Salve Regina*, troped with texts that per-
sonalize the well-known hymn (see Appendix 5.2). Universal Marian devotional hymns aside, there also existed reflections dedicated specifically to the
Virgin Mary's moments at the foot of the cross.[45]

The Sorrowing Mother Weeps

The devotion to the Virgin Mary in anguish over her son's Passion developed its own cult in the twelfth century with strong Franciscan promotion.
It spread across the Catholic world as devotion to the Virgin of Sorrows.[46]
The iconography of the Virgin of Sorrows often depicts the Virgin dressed in
dark mournful drapery with hands clasped, a distressed face with tears, and
between one and seven daggers piercing her heart, the latter representing
the seven sorrows she experienced in her lifetime.[47] The engraving in Figure
5.2, found in Parreño's novena mentioned earlier, is representative of the sorrowful Virgin's iconography. It depicts the statue of the Virgin of Sorrows
venerated at the Jesús María convent in Mexico City with the seven sorrows
combined into one large dagger piercing her heart. At the bottom half of
the engraving, one notices a carefully designed fold in her dress mimicking
the shape of the crescent moon, which, although not a common feature in
Sorrows iconography, is reminiscent of Immaculate Conception iconography, in which Mary stands on the crescent moon.[48]

Because this particular statue was reported to have saved Mexico City from
a flood in 1714, it was given the local title of "Nuestra Señora de las Aguas"
(Our Lady of the Waters).[49] Water, as we will see, was an important element
in the Passion narrative, and not just because of its association with tears.
Although the white color of the paper on which the engraving was made
makes it difficult to see the tears, very recent restoration work on the statue,
still held and venerated by nuns living in the contemporary Jesús María convent, indicates that the original eighteenth-century piece did in fact have tears
carved into the face, appearing as if secreted from the Virgin's eyes naturally.[50]

While the Passion Gospels do not mention the Virgin Mary's crying,
the presumption that she would have reacted in such a way, inspired by
her depiction in the apocryphal Gospel of Nicodemus, captivated and
moved believers.[51] Indeed, devotees could understand the Virgin Mary's
devastation at the Passion, "the anguish of a mother enduring the horrors

Figure 5.2 Nuestra Señora de los Dolores / de las Aguas, Jesús María Convent, Mexico City, 1794

inflicted on a beloved child."[52] In her psychoanalytic discussion of the life of the Virgin Mary and its role in motherhood and femininity throughout Christian history, Julia Kristeva comments on the semiotic role of Mary's tears at the foot of the cross.[53] "The *Mater dolorosa*," she notes, "knows no male body except that of her dead son, and her only pathos . . . comes from the tears she sheds over a corpse."[54] She focuses on a passage from Pergolesi's rendition of the *Stabat Mater* sequence, "Hail, mother, source of love" (Eia mater, fons amoris).[55] Then Kristeva posits that maternal love is expressed at the foot of the cross and resounded in Pergolesi's music, and that this type of love is different from and superior to the divine love through which Bernard of Clairvaux had entwined the Virgin with the Song of Songs in 1135.[56] Divine love, as we saw in the previous chapter, is more universal than maternal love, yet both were carefully prescribed upon nuns to deploy in their devotions.

In addition, Kristeva evades discussing the inherent vocality of the Virgin's weeping, concomitant with tears, which was often represented symbolically in music, especially in the early modern period, including in Pergolesi's *Stabat Mater*, her essay's namesake.[57] She notes that the Virgin Mary effects non-linguistic communication through her tears at the foot of the cross.[58] As we will see later, it is nuns who, moved by the Virgin Mary's sorrow, claimed divine love as they wept, or sang of weeping, communicating their sadness over their divine spouse's death. Their own role-model sisters and clerical leaders would explain the meaning of such crying through other affective metaphors.

In his printed sermon for the feast of Our Lady of Sorrows that took place at Puebla's Santa Inés de Montepulciano convent on March 29, 1697 (the Friday before Palm Sunday), José Sarmiento allegorized Mary's weeping at the foot of the cross with music. He called it a counterpoint with the plainchant of a divine cithara, an allegory for Christ nailed to the cross, as we observed in Chapter 4.[59] Sarmiento's interpretation was approved by high-ranking clerics. Their supportive letters form the pretext of the printed sermon and were included in the publication. The pretexts made sense of Sarmiento's sermon with musical allegories too. The Mercedarian Juan Antonio Lobato's pretext drew on Mary's association with the voice of God to describe her counterpoint as an improvisatory fantasia, for "singing a fantasia, 'the musicians say,' is veering away from the rules of art without detaching from the sonorous tempo."[60] Improvised music thus begins and concludes the cycle of Christ's humanity: Mary now improvises a fantasia that accompanies his spirit—"Jesus cried out again with a loud voice and gave up his spirit" (Matthew 27:50)—in song upon completion of his earthly life. Similarly, the Immaculate Conception of Mary was God's fantasia at the Creation that pre-destined Christ's humanity (Chapter 1).

At pains to move his listeners' and readers' affections, Sarmiento also relied on anti-Semitic rhetoric. Just as the Egyptians in the Old Testament were the enemies of the Jews—and God—so now in the New Testament the Jews were portrayed as hostile to Christians, even as they were essential for the salvation narrative to come to fruition via Christ's death.[61] And whereas Adam and Eve were acknowledged, despite their sin, for making way for a new redeemer and co-redeemer in Christ and Mary, respectively, Christians took the hypocritical stance of blaming Christ's death not just on the specific Jews who were present at his crucifixion, but on all Jewish people, at the time of the crucifixion and thereafter, to justify their ongoing hatred of them.[62]

The Jewish collective in the sermon is encapsulated in the image of a string instrument tuner who prepares the cithara to accompany the Virgin's song. Sarmiento switches to the imperative mood to inflict a diatribe on his audience that cheers on the necessary tuning process:

> And shall this instrument be tuned so that the cithara's sound harmonizes? Yes. And who ought to tune it? The Jew: he is the one that torments Christ, crucifying him with three nails, winding up his blessed nerves, stretched by three pegs. May the Hebrew tremble, for only he knows how to crucify, so that Mary will sing, for only she can feel. Take that cithara, Jew, use its strings for cruel torture. Pull, twist the pegs. O blasphemy, how he tightens! Strong torment! And with all of the trembling tyrants tightening, the tone of that cithara is still low, and that innocent one that you torment desires to suffer more. Pull more, Jew. That nerve is well stretched.[63]

Already, we can perceive the dehumanizing of the Jewish community unfolding while Mary is elevated beyond her own Jewish heritage as one with feeling, empathy. Anti-Semitism of this sort is also at the center of the Spanish obsession with blood purity whose consequences for convent professions we observed in Chapter 3, and it was not unusual in Passion devotion from before and beyond the early modern period. The Jews in the Passion Gospels are often described as extremely violent, as in this sermon, or noisy, particularly in Passion dramas with music.[64] Yet, for all the various artistic responses to the Passion of Christ and the Spanish penchant for mapping his crucifixion onto the cithara, no other source symbolizes Jesus' execution with the process of tuning, the implication being that the metaphorical song that resounds is death itself. Sarmiento continues:

> Let us now pluck that string, hear how it sounds. O my God, it sounds so well! Now Hebrew, torment that cithara some more, don't remove your hand from the strings, so that your cruelty raises the harmony of that divine cithara, its sweet voice. Pull. Tighten, turn the nerves. Hear how the torment raises the pitch! Let us now play this string, to see if its tone is good. O my God, what sweetness! Proceed, Israelite, tighten more, pull those strings

more, tune. Hear how sharp is that pull! Let us pluck that string now to see if its tone is stable. O my God, what delicacy! Now stop, Hebrew, enough, do not tighten anymore; that cithara is tuned now, as there is no more tor-ment to give those strings, the sorrow is complete, these sacred outstretched nerves are dead from three pegs: "It is finished." . . . You have heard how well they sound. How nicely the sweet and the bitter, the torture and the joy, the groan and the song go hand-in-hand in the cross, joined in a wondrous har-mony. And then, who will harmonize with this well-tempered plectrum? Who is to join the sweet song of this cithara? Mary, who is at the foot of that instrument. . . . O Mary co-redeemer of us all![65]

These words would seem enough to intimidate any ancestors of Spanish Jews converted to Christianity by reminding them of their unwelcomed presence in New Spain because of their legacy with the Passion of Christ. Even as Miri Rubin reminds us that the Virgin Mary had been recognized for centuries as "the figure through which Jews may be converted," with "her profound wisdom and understanding of the divine plan [making] her the best teacher of Christian truth," concern that conversos dwelled among the New Spanish population nonetheless lasted well into the mid-nineteenth century, indicating that even conversion was not enough to make Jewish blood toler-able.[66] As "proven" old Christians, or their descendants, nuns were deemed worthy to echo the co-redeeming resonance of Mary's song and avoid any affiliation with the torturous tuner.

Like Christ, nuns too were considered sacrificial lambs, metaphorically martyred by way of their death to the secular world, enclosed in a convent for the salvation of the world they left behind. Sarmiento alludes to this subject in acknowledging the sermon's sponsors: the nuns of the Santa Inés (St. Agnes) de Montepulciano convent, one of Puebla's three Dominican nunneries.[67] He says, "It is a choir of virgins, daughters of the great Dominic . . . who follow the lamb of heaven Agnes . . . applauding in their cadences the glorious sorrows of Jesus, singing in the death of Christ, the joyful sorrows of Mary. . . . Indeed, what appropriate music!"[68] Here, Sarmiento drew on the relationship be-tween Agnes and the Latin root of her name, "agna/lamb"; he promoted the presumption that all nuns are virgins (recall Chapter 1); and all the while, he reminds us of Mary's mixed emotions, at once sad but also joyous because her son's death achieved the salvation that commenced with the Immaculate Conception of Mary's soul at the beginning of time.

The confluence of extreme pain and joy contained in Mary's heart, so rem-iniscent of St. Teresa's oxymora discussed in Chapter 2, prompts Sarmiento to compare her emotions to raging water trapped in the depths of the ocean: she would want nothing more than to have her heart pierced with a lance— as was done to Christ's side at the Passion—to relieve her heart overfilled with emotion, but, instead, her body entraps those emotions, mediating the bitterness of death and the joy of salvation through weeping and tears imagined to have escaped her body.[69] Lastly, in Sarmiento's allegorical music representing the death of Christ, the lance is the clef: just as the piercing of Christ's side with the lance was a sign that he was dead, the clef is the sign that confirms the pitches of the notes.[70] He claims that without the clef there is no music; at worst an exaggeration, perhaps, but at best a signal of a musically literate audience of nuns. Indeed, the extant choirbook from the Santa Inés de Montepulciano convent suggests a musically vibrant cloister (recall Appendix I.2).

Because Mary's heart is not pierced by the lance in the sermon, her counterpoint to Christ's plainchant is inaudible to humans, Sarmiento concludes. Her improvised fantasia is silent, trapped in her heart. Mary's heart thus plays a very different cognitive role in the Virgin's iconography than in the sermonized metaphorical music. The iconography suggests a physical pain because it depicts a pierced heart, Mary's co-passion with Christ.[71] One of the seven sorrows that explicitly comes to mind seeing the dagger-impaled heart on the Jesús María convent statue of Our Lady of Sorrow (las Aguas) is the prophesy of Simeon at the presentation of the Christ Child in the temple, in which Simeon reveals to the Virgin that the pain of losing her son through the salvation narrative would be like the piercing of her heart with a sword (Luke 2:34–36). This prophesy too became musicalized as the canticle for the Office of Compline, *Nunc Dimittis*. The sermon, on the other hand, would suggest a psychological pain. The Virgin Mary's heart in the sermon maintains an audible silence, unable to burst into its mysterious song within its chambers, since in the sermon the lance does not pierce the heart. That song in Mary's heart is her belief in the salvation attributed to her son's death. With Mary so choked up with emotions that her body becomes an archive of silence, Sarmiento suggests that it is up to the brides of Christ to envoice the Virgin.

Music for Widowed Virgins

The metaphorical music of Sarmiento's sermon—to be contemplated when actual music was performed—was closely associated with villancicos for the Virgin of Sorrows, as we will observe in two extant examples from the Santísima Trinidad convent in Puebla, in which nuns join in the counterpoint of Mary and the divine cithara. As both spiritual mothers and brides of Christ, nuns took on the all-encompassing role of widow, martyr, and sorrowing mother in response to the Passion. This multifaceted task for nuns intertwines them with Christ's true mourning mother at the cross in the villancicos, which, typical of Virgin of Sorrows villancicos, also interpolate the poetics of the *Stabat Mater*.[72] The first and penultimate verses of the lengthy *Stabat Mater* sequence suffice to demonstrate how its text begins with third-person references to the Virgin, then moves to a conclusion that is a personal reflection on death and salvation through the intercession of Mary:

Stabat mater dolorosa	The sorrowful mother was standing
Juxta crucem lacrimosa	in tears beside the cross on which
Dum pendebat filius.	her son was hanging.
Christe, cum sit hinc exire,	When it is time, Lord Christ, for
Da per Matrem me venire	me to leave this world, give me
Ad palmam victorae.	through your mother's prayers the palm of victory.

We can observe a similar scheme in the coplas to the anonymous 1718 villancico *Corazón de dolor traspasado* (CSG.024) for two sopranos and accompaniment.[73] The coplas also reveal two possible characters,[74] the Virgin Mary clearly in the odd verses and a bride of Christ represented in the even verses by the multi-charactered dove of the Song of Songs.

Estribillo	
Corazón de dolor traspasado,	The heart pierced in sorrow,
en tiernos motetes	in tender motets
festeja el dolor.	celebrates the sorrow.
A llorar con gran primor,	Weep fervently
a este dolor inflamado	over this swelling pain,
llega a tenerlo.	come to accept it.
No temas, que a su dueño	Do not fear,
inmaculado gima	that it groans and cries
y llore el corazón,	to its immaculate master,
que ya contrito llorando,	crying now contrite,
corazón de dolor traspasado.	the heart pierced in sorrow.

Coplas

1. Virgen, la más dolorosa	Virgin, most sorrowful
que entre los hombres se vio,	ever seen among humans,
pues es tu dolor medido,	for your pain is as great
alta mano de tu amor.	as your bountiful love.
2. Blanca paloma, que lloras	White dove, you weep
de tu esposo la pasión,	the Passion of your husband,
cuya severísima muerte,	whose most severe death
es tu tormento mayor.	is your main torment.
3. Dolorosa madre y pura,	Sorrowful and pure mother,
cuyo triste corazón	whose sad heart,
en medio de un mar de penas	surrounded by a sea of pity,
se alimenta del dolor.	nourishes on sorrow.
4. Tórtola más solitaria,	Most lonely turtledove,
cuyo sagrado candor,	whose sacred nature
te elevas aún con las penas,	elevates you despite the grief,
viendo padecer a un Dios.	seeing a God suffering.
5. Sagrada madre, que gimes	Sacred mother, who groans
la dolorosa pasión	the sorrowful Passion
del hijo de tus entrañas	of the son of your womb,
que en una cruz padeció.	who suffered on a cross.
6. Si tus tormentos alivian	If a human compassion
una humana compasión,	alleviates your torments,
admite por compañero	accept my pain
de tus penas mi dolor.	as a companion to your sorrows.

While the dove has sometimes symbolized Mary in popular devotion, calling on the rhetoric of the Song of Songs,[75] and while Bishop Juan de Palafox y Mendoza even taught of the commingling of Trinitarian and Marian devotion with Mary being the daughter of God, mother of Christ, and wife of the Holy Spirit,[76] we must remember that Palafox also instructed that it was only Christ's body—incarnated in Mary's womb—that expired on the cross.[77] The Holy Spirit did not die at the crucifixion. As such, in the context of this convent villancico, the phrase "the Passion of your husband" in copla 2 suggests that nuns are the more likely protagonist of the even verses, while "son of your womb" in copla 5 would suggest Mary for the odd numbers. The sixth (final) copla provides the personal reflection.

Neither one of the two soprano voices stands out soloistically or floridly in the coplas, set strophically to G minor harmony in homophonic texture (Example 5.1). A dialog of alternating verses between the sopranos would have proven more conclusively that there are two women characters reflected in the poetics, but the estribillo also alludes to the possibility of two hearts pierced in sorrow. In the last third of the estribillo, the poetry speaks of the heart's fear and contrition, characteristics of even some of the most exemplary nuns, as we have observed, but unbecoming of the pure and sinless Virgin Mary who knew and rejoiced within her sorrowful heart that salvation was imminent through the death of her son.

The estribillo also contains much of the tone painting characteristic of villancicos, not least the longest melisma on the word "motete/motet."

Example 5.1 Anonymous, *Corazón de dolor*, 1718 (CSG.024), mm. 5–9

Example 5.2 Anonymous, *Corazón de dolor*, 1718 (CSG.024), mm. 58–63

Highlighting the musicality suggested by the words, the first soprano cascades upward in stepwise motion to F natural, the piece's highest pitch, as the second soprano accompanies it mostly in thirds over G minor harmony, moving to B-flat major to "festeja el dolor /celebrate the sorrow" (Example 5.1).[78] At times one voice will begin half a bar ahead of the other, prompting brief moments of imitation and free counterpoint, as on the arrival of the most repeated phrase in the piece, "gima y llore/groans and cries." Inflections of G major to suggest tears of joy for salvation resolve to C minor (Example 5.2).

A modal affective description from Nassarre's *Escuela música* solidifies the appropriateness of the composition of *Corazón de dolor* in hypodorian mode, or mode 2, for expressing the Virgin's grief. This mode is governed by the moon, whose coldness and dampness provoke tears of sadness, a mood Nassarre notes is well represented by women.[79] Early modern medical treatises reiterated the same adjectives of "cold" and "wet" as conducive to fertility.[80] Beyond these gendered biases, which recall the Virgin Mary's fecundity and miraculous domination of the moon in her immaculacy, Nassarre continues, "All texts dealing with sad things, or painful judgment, or of horrifying things, would certainly best be composed in this mode."[81] As we have observed in the villancico and in the Virgin of Sorrows' attributes, such descriptions only capture her affect partially, since knowledge of the resurrection also implied joy.

Similar characteristics can be found in the poetics, texture, and harmony of *Ay, afligida madre* (CSG.125) by Pedro de Ardanaz Valencia (ca. 1638–1706).[82]

Estribillo

Ay, afligida madre,	Ah, grief-stricken mother,
que así te quejas.	thus you groan.
Ay, tortolica amante,	Ah, loving little turtledove,
que así lamentas	thus you lament
las duras ansías,	the severe longings,
las crueles penas	the cruel punishments
que en ti se encierran	that are enclosed in you
con los puros dolores	with the pure sorrows
que a ti te cercan.	that surround you.

Coplas

1. Afligida tortolica,	Afflicted little turtledove,
que al pie de la cruz demuestras	at the foot of the cross you demonstrate
que en las lágrimas que lloras	that tender voices can be heard in the
se escuchan tus voces tiernas.	tears you shed.
Si es mi Dios la causa,	If my God is the cause,
que bien te quejas.	how appropriate your groan.

2. Ay, dueño del alma mía,	Ah, master of my soul,
que en esas duras afrentas	in those severe affronts,
os contempla como madre	observing you as a mother
entre angustias y tristezas.	between anguishes and sadness.
Viuda y sola he quedado,	I have been widowed and left alone,
que dura pena.	what a harsh punishment.

Another duo for two sopranos, this piece is missing its accompaniment but resides in A durus, a modal area that had significant affiliation with Passion devotion.[83] With its A final and D mediation final, the piece is in the seventh mode,[84] another one apt for the poetic subject of sorrow. Nassarre associates it with melancholy, solitude, and weeping, among other things; it causes sadness

Example 5.3 Ardanaz, *Ay, afligida madre*, ca. 1658–1706 (CSG.125), mm. 37–45

in its listeners: "The composers who compose music in this tone should use it to set words that speak of sad, weepy, and deceitful things."[85] The most dramatic feature in *Ay, afligida madre* is the long sustain of the interjection "ah" (ay) in all of its reiterations. It is reminiscent of Vidales' treatment of *Con qué gala en el campo* for Mary's nativity that we observed in Chapter 1, in which "ah" was also sustained. But that time, this device was used to convey the awe of Mary's miraculous, divine attributes in humorous fashion, while in *Ay, afligida madre*, it calls to mind the musical characteristic of the Spanish lament air.[86] In this way, it draws attention to the opposite affect caused by the gravity of the grief-stricken mother, even if at moments the underlying harmony veers between A minor and major (Example 5.3).

The phrase "widowed and left alone" in copla 2 would more aptly refer to nuns than to Mary, for the Virgin in fact was not left alone, but rather committed to the care of Christ's disciple John. At the crucifixion, Jesus told Mary to behold her son John, and told John to behold his mother Mary (John 19:26–27), an instruction that Palafox incorporated into the preface to his rule for Conceptionist (1641) and Hieronymite (1773) nuns as a way of lauding perpetual virginity, since John was thought to be a virgin. In her Passion meditations, Sister María Anna Águeda de San Ignacio of Puebla's Santa Rosa convent reflects on Jesus' entrustment of Mary to John as a New Testament inversion of the now-familiar downfall of Adam and Eve:

> Just as Adam gave the excuse that his partner helped him and facilitated sin, so too his [Christ's] mother, as a co-redeemer, accompanied him [Christ] to redeem the world, and through her mediation as [a] mother she was

enjoined to facilitate the good merit of redemption; and we oblige her with our love, and we are encouraged by her powerful intercession.[87]

However, upon the death of Christ, nuns were not assigned a new spouse. Once more, reality yields to spirituality, recalling that Christ has always been dead for these nuns. Yet the cyclical commemoration of his death enlivened Christ only for him to be wounded and tortured over and over, sometimes even by the nuns themselves, as shown later. Thus, nuns voiced the Virgin of Sorrows' joyous sorrows with sweet motets, but in their humble humanity they were capable of having deficiencies—perhaps uncertainty in the mysteriousness of the resurrection, prompting feelings similar to those experienced in widowhood. Such expressions of loneliness, a feeling that, however minor, must have at times plagued cloistered women,[88] also required contrition. This would be particularly true on Fridays, often dedicated to Passion devotion throughout the liturgical year, recalling that Good Friday is the day in Holy Week when Christ was considered truly dead.

Good Friday Reflections

In the biography of Sister Bárbara (1662–1723), in whose lifetime these Virgin of Sorrows villancicos were possibly performed within her convent, we also perceive the commingling of pain and sorrow between the Virgin and Bárbara. They lament Christ's crucifixion as an expression of motherly and divine love, respectively. Because the feast of the Virgin of Sorrows took place on the Friday in Lent before Good Friday, devotion to the Virgin prepared people to grieve on the Friday to come. The Virgin of Sorrows appeared to Bárbara on one Good Friday to show her a thorn that had pierced her heart, saying, "My daughter, look at this thorn, one of the hundreds that my son had around his head. You must always have it in mind for relief of your tribulations."[89] Bárbara then felt a piercing in her heart.[90] Similarly, every Friday throughout the year, Sister María de Jesús was said to have felt the prick from the crown of thorns, thus instructing believers in how the events of Good Friday should be contemplated year-round. These women shared the physical pain that Christ endured at the Passion. The Virgin in Bárbara's vision instructed subtly that tribulations are relieved through the pain of the Passion that has earned humanity's salvation.

The interior piety fostered by the devotional literature and music considered up to this point, placing nuns by the Virgin's side at the foot of the cross, reaches its most introspective climax with a final hymn in the Passion devotion chapter of Sister Bárbara's biography. The hymn unites the topics of humility and eucharistic, Trinitarian, and Marian devotion for other nuns to sing. In prayer before a crucifix, Bárbara focused her attention on Christ's wounded feet, "asking them to guide her through the path of humility."[91] She was instantly rewarded for this by being lifted up by St. Michael the Archangel to drink of the blood and water from Christ's side wound.[92] Bárbara's faith in the Trinity was said to have been reassured after drinking from this wound caused by the lance's piercing at the crucifixion.[93]

Bárbara commemorated the crucifixion weekly by meditating on the stations of the cross, always imagining herself watching the Passion in person.[94] At last, seeing Christ's dead body in the Virgin's arms after being taken down from the cross, Bárbara once asked Mary to hand her son over.[95] A "religiosa musa/ nun muse," probably a poet, in the Santísima Trinidad convent later set the words that Bárbara recited to her dead spouse into the Spanish lament meter known as *endechas*.[96] According to her biographer Torres, he included the poem in Sister Bárbara's biography so that it might be sung by devotees:

Endechas	Laments
1. Divino Jesús mío	My divine Jesus,
acerico de mirra entre mis pechos:	pincushion of myrrh between my breasts:
tanto el rigor impío	so much ungodly rigor
Tu beldad ha deshecho, con sus hechos,	has dissolved your beauty with its deeds,
que en toda figura	that in this entire figure
ni especie me dejó de tu hermosura.	not a trace of your loveliness remains for me.
2. Quién (bellísimo esposo)	Who (beautiful husband),
siendo tú de los cielos embelesó	dared decompose so extremely
ese compuesto hermoso	your beautiful composure, [being that]
osó descomponer con tanto exceso?	you are an astonishment from heaven?
Que sola tu paciencia	Your patience alone
excede a la crueldad de su inclemencia.	exceeds the cruelty of its severity.
3. Quién majestad divina	Who, divine majesty,
esa piedra angular, esa cabeza	dared to bash sharply
de oro, preciosa mina	that cornerstone, that head of gold,
presumió penetrar con agudeza?	that precious mine?
Yo fui, que aunque tan ruda	It was I, who, though smooth,
solo para picarte me hice aguda.	became sharp only to stab you.

4. Tus ojos eclipsados!
¿Quién se atrevió mi luz, a hacerles sombra?
Mis azotes pecados;
que en mi maldad, aun tu bondad se asombra,
luego que abrí los ojos
fue para darte mi Jesús enojos.

Your eyes closed!
Who dared darken them, my light?
It was my lashing sins;
your goodness is amazing, despite my evil,
for when I opened my eyes,
it was, my Jesus, only to aggravate you.

5. Tus sagradas mejillas
ya azucenas, ya rosas, y granadas;
como son maravillas
en la mano de un necio están ajadas.
Por no verlas me postro,
que fui yo ingrata la que te di en rostro.

Your sacred cheeks,
now lilies, now roses, now pomegranates;
as they are marvelous,
they wilt in the hands of a fool.
I fall to the ground so as not to see them, for I
was the ungracious one who hit your face.

6. La nariz afilada
para partir los duros corazones;
a mí me huele a espada,
que ha de vengar, aun mis respiraciones;
porque muerto me adviertes,
que en las ventanas te cause mil muertes.

Your nose is sharp
for slicing hearts of stone;
to me it seems like a sword,
that will take revenge even on my breath;
because you, dead, show me through your
nostrils that I caused you a million deaths.

7. La sangre de los labios
se retira a su centro acibarada
de mis muchos resabios;
pero otra puerta miro ensangrentada,
que a beber desafía
sangre, que vierte dulce, y agua fría.

The blood of your lips
fades to its center, embittered
because of my many vices;
but I see another bloody opening
pouring out sweetness and cool water,
and drinking from it, the blood is obscured.

8. De este mar de dulzuras
tu cuello ebúrneo (mi Jesús) venero es,
porque mis venturas
las derrama por el tu amor sincero:
más fue mi maldad tanta,
que oprimí con mis lazos tu garganta.

Your ivory neck is a compass (my Jesus)
in this sea of sweetness,
because I am fortunate
to spill it [the sweetness] for your love:
but it was my great wickedness
that strangled your throat with my cords.

9. Como esposa tus manos
pretendo dulce dueño, y horadadas
de hierros inhumanos

As a wife, I seek your hands,
sweet master, which are pierced by
inhumane iron,

rotas las miro, y aun apedazadas;	I see them broken and torn apart;
pero más dolorosa	but this misguided wife went to your hands
te fue a las manos esta errada esposa.	most sorrowfully.

10. A tus plantas divinas	To your divine feet, my soul aspires
como a más alto trono aspira mi alma;	as if they were the highest throne;
porque son sin espinas	only through your sinless body
plantas, en que se logra eterna palma:	can one obtain the eternal palm:
o, los claveles rojos	oh, those red nails of your feet,
de tus dos pies se rieguen con mis ojos.	may they be washed with my tears.[97]

This type of lament to the dead Christ resonates with and follows a rhetorical scheme similar to Heinrich Schütz's Passion motets from *Cantiones sacrae* (1625), based on the Pseudo-Augustine *Meditations*. The motets include an interrogation of Christ (*Quid commisisti, O dulcissime puer*); the sinner's self-blame (*Ego sum tui plaga doloris* and *Ego enim inique egi*); and repentance, forgiveness, and salvation through the Eucharist (*Ego enim inique egi* and *Calicem salutaris accipiam*). Consistent with his Protestant tradition, the text set by Schütz lacks the explicit carnal nature of the Eucharist in Bárbara's lament and does not include the Marian devotion prefaced by Torres or the sensuality of the Song of Songs. The latter continues to be a relevant source in Bárbara's song, with the start of the hymn recalling Bernard of Clairvaux's meditation on the passage "myrrh between my breasts" (Song of Songs 1:12), in which he associated myrrh's bitterness with the Passion's rigor.[98] A closer precedent is Angelo Grillo's 1607 *Dell'essequie di Christo co'l pianto di Maria Vergine*, whose poetics reflect on Mary's lament and the expired Christ's anatomy, according to Robert Kendrick, "with special emphasis on contemplating the blood, eyes, and ears of the dead Christ."[99] This type of lyric poetry, despite "the static and repetitive character of the texts," common in early modern laments, was among the source texts for Holy Week entombment semi-operas in seventeenth-century Italy known as *sepolcri*.[100]

Such stasis and repetition in Torres' lament are offset by the conflation of the Virgin of Sorrows with the brides of Christ while maintaining a tone of humility. Six stanzas of self-deprecatory language precede a change in the lament's mood to one of forgiveness. The seventh stanza alludes to drinking from Christ's side—the other "bloody opening." After receiving the cool, sweet waters of redemption from Christ's side wound, his spiritual bride turns to one final self-reproach in the eighth stanza, then continues to sing of reaching out to touch Christ's extremities. The singer extends her hand toward his hand penitently in the ninth stanza, concluding with the dispersal of her tears at Christ's feet, the humblest of gestures that would later obtain for her a palm of victory in heaven, the symbol of martyrdom.[101]

What an extraordinary privilege it was for these women to be able to obtain forgiveness for taking on the act of metaphorically torturing Christ because of their shortcomings. Any minor sin could be counteracted by their humble self-deprecation, as narrated by biographers, confessors, and sermonizers. The tone, significantly different from that of Sarmiento's narration of the Jewish cithara tuner, reminds us of the elevated place that nuns could arrive at, singing Christ's death to the inverted tune of joyous sorrow and humbly drawing those outside the cloister walls to come follow the way of the cross. The Virgin Mary was the model, her sorrow and co-passion approximating martyrdom; her joy at the Passion was prefaced by her deep knowledge of salvation—through Christ's death and resurrection, the teleological reasoning for Mary's miraculous Immaculate Conception.[102]

Who was Sister Marina de San Francisco, who so desired a devotional service dedicated to Christ's humility at the first station of the Passion, dressed in white and mocked as a lunatic by Herod? She was a humble imitator of Christ, well on her way to her own co-passion like the Virgin Mary's and to her own crucifixion like Sister Bárbara's. This instance of the Passion narrative in which Christ stood before Herod was but an initial point on a long and arduous road to Calvary that would lead to his death. This path required humility and careful expression of the joy and sorrow of the Passion to assist devotees in treading closer to the foot of the cross, where salvation awaited in its shadow.

Epilogue

On a daily basis, Sister María de Jesús wanted to die, "with a burning longing of love," because in death she would be reunited with Christ.[1] Descriptions of her final hours and passing suggest unceasing Passion devotion and provide a glimpse of the seventeenth-century soundscape of Puebla's Purísima Concepción convent. María de Jesús had an affliction that rendered her incapable of attending the Office.[2] Some of her sister nuns, in charge of taking care of her, reported that she was despondent when the convent bell rang for the liturgies. When she heard echoes of the nuns singing the Office reverberating all the way to her bedroom, she wept inconsolably because she could not be in the coro singing along with them. Her weeping enacted a spiritual Office in the same way that contrite weeping could effect spiritual communion and enact the Virgin Mary's co-passion, as discussed in the two previous chapters. On June 11, 1637, at the start of Vespers for Corpus Christi, she expired after having received the Eucharist. At that same moment, some most unusual festivities were taking place in the convent church, with the entrance of what appears to have been a celebration separated from the main Corpus Christi procession:

> Ultimately, the hour of Vespers arrived . . . the convent bells resounding in festive peals, the entering of a concerted dance through the church doors to celebrate the day with festivity, the piercing of the air with loud shawms and trumpets, and the nuns singing the divine praises in the coro, with delicate canticles.[3]

Meanwhile, the nuns who attended to María de Jesús' postmortem care sang the Credo. They tried shutting her eyes with candlewax, but she opened them for a time amounting to some three Credos, and her eyes focused on a nearby image hung on a wall. That image was of St. Veronica's sudarium, the sweat cloth imprinted with Christ's face from the blood and sweat of his Passion and reproduced in devotional artwork.[4]

Almost one hundred years later, a few blocks away at the Santísima Trinidad convent, Sister Bárbara Josefa de San Francisco also died on a day associated with the Body of Christ: in her case, Passion Sunday. Ailing and bedridden on March 14, 1723, the third day of the Novena for the Virgin of Sorrows, she experienced a "burning desire to see and enjoy her husband eternally."[5] She called for her spiritual director and confessor. After confessing, she asked him to be the spiritual father of the children she was leaving behind. She was a widow with children when she professed at the Santísima Trinidad convent. Her daughter was also a nun in the same cloister, and her son Pedro was a local priest in Puebla.[6] Bárbara entrusted them to the confessor in a manner like Christ on the cross entrusting the Virgin Mary to the Apostle John. Torres, her biographer, elaborated on the similarities between Christ and Bárbara, who imitated Jesus' familial directive: "For Christ our Lord gave on the cross the example of this pious recommendation to all parents."[7] After Bárbara's confession, the Santísima Trinidad nuns came into her room to sing the Credo. The longest chant of the Mass liturgy, the Credo marked the central part of the Mass, preparing believers to reflect on the mystery of Christ's body in the Eucharist and to receive him through communion. It also professed belief in salvation, preparing nuns to be received by Christ in heaven. Bárbara fixed her eyes on the crucifix held by her confessor. Before dying, she beat her breast three times, invoking Jesus, Mary, and Joseph.[8] She died peacefully hearing her sisters sing.[9]

Singing was essential to nuns' daily lives, particularly as it was used to vocalize salvation. Indeed, "the goal for all [nuns] is salvation, and self-perfection, and of that of their neighbor, following this directive in imitation of the glorious Virgin Mary," according to the Order of the Company of Mary's rule book.[10] I hope that after reading the preceding chapters this instruction seems apropos for all cloistered convents, and that I have convinced you that imitation of Mary also drew forth imitation of Christ. The Virgin Mary's virginity, grace, obedience, and suffering have been observed in detail in the chapters of this book to provide an interpretation of the centuries-silent voices of Sisters Flor de Santa Clara, Rosa, Mariana Josefa de San Ignacio, Paula, and Marina de San Francisco referred to in archival fragments. I have suggested possibilities as to the identities of their musical lives, pieced together from a necessarily interdisciplinary host of sources: extant music manuscripts; religious literature, such as the biographies of nuns like María de Jesús and Bárbara; printed sermons; other devotional literature, including order-specific guidebooks and rule books for nuns; and sacred art.

The arts, whether literary, visual, or musical, never existed isolated from one another in convents, but worked together to create an atmosphere of devotion that continues to cause wonder. This is especially true when we think about the words, doctrines, and devotions that were set to the ephemeral sound of live music. What it would have sounded like to New Spanish nuns originally, we will never be able to hear. Their music and voices were idealized—often, as we have seen, through the pen of male clerics who elevated nuns to the status of co-redeemers like the immaculately conceived Virgin Mary. Despite the gendered inequities inherent in early modern musical and writing practices, I have shown that the idealization of the convents' sacred sounds locates certain women's agency within a hierarchy that silenced some women and required others to sing. As we observed in Chapter 3, Mariana de San José y Machuca's mother took advantage of that practice, providing music lessons to Mariana in order for her to profess as a musician at the Concepción convent, because her Spanish lineage—her calidad—qualified her for a role as a bride of Christ.

The musical lives considered in this book have been framed as "good women," models of the Virgin Mary—co-redeemers.[11] Should the archival record prove more generous in the years to come, I hope that scholars attempt to unframe them. (Though, I predict that they will probably not turn out to be as revolutionary as the "bad woman" Sor Juana Inés de la Cruz.[12]) In so doing, scholars will need to contend with the peace of mind New Spanish citizens experienced in knowing that their souls would be saved through pious deeds, endowed memorial Masses, and the voices that resonated from daily convent liturgies and devotional services. The sacredness of the extant music that we know cloistered nuns performed and the purpose for which that music was notated and resounded cannot be neglected. Even at the moment of their own deaths, nuns consoled one another in song, with the Credo in particular, whose length served as a way to track time, as observed with the nuns who experienced the miracle of María de Jesús' eyes opening after having died.

As sources held in private collections and in some contemporary nuns' convents, such as María de Jesús' still active Purísima Concepción convent in Puebla, pass into the hands of future generations of conservators, I hope that new collaborations develop to continue fleshing out the history of women's musical contributions to the New Spanish soundscape.[13] A robust tradition of writing and publishing biographies of nuns, along with other devotional literature read by nuns, can also be traced in early modern Spain, Italy, France, and New France.[14] Here too, we may find iterations of veiled voices by other groups of Christ's brides that helped to save humanity in song.

Acknowledgments

I want to thank numerous individuals and institutions who have supported me and the research that has gone into bringing this book to completion. I would like to start by thanking the sisters of the Conceptionist Mother House in Toledo, Spain, and the sisters of the Jesús María convent in Mexico City for granting me access to some of the rare sources that they preserve in their cloisters.

I want to thank Alejandro Madrid and Norm Hirschy for including this book in Oxford University Press's Currents in Latin American and Iberian Music series. It is a dream come true and a privilege to be able to publish in a series whose authors I consider some of the most important thinkers in my field. I am also grateful to the press staff involved in the book's publication process, especially Rachel Ruisard and Hemalatha Arumugam.

The quality of this book was enriched eminently with critical input from the anonymous peer reviewers selected by the Academy of American Franciscan History and by Oxford University Press. I also want to thank the following colleagues who read parts, if not all, of the manuscript and/or who provided valuable advice in various stages of my thinking for this project. Thank you to Rachel Adelstein, Ana Alonso Minutti, Michael Anderson, Jacky Avila, Ireri Chávez Bárcenas, Charlene Villaseñor Black, Philip Bohlman, Melvin Butler, Mary Channen Caldwell, Andrew Cashner, Herman Chavez, Margaret Chowning, Clare Chu, Walter Clark, James Córdoba, Suzanne Cusick, Andrew Dell'Antonio, Nina Eidsheim, Cathy Elias, Chris Emmerson, Savannah Esquivel, Martha Feldman, Paul Feller, Mike Figueroa, Bob Fink, Sarah Finley, David Garcia, Alicia Gaspar de Alba, Ramona Gonzalez, Bernard Gordillo, Kevin Gosner, John Griffiths, Kali Handelman, Ruth Hellier Tinoco, Eduardo Herrera, Jessica Holmes, Erika Honisch, Jake Johnson, Nick Jones, Ryan Kashanipour, Peter Kazaras, Robert Kendrick, Mark Kligman, Raymond Knapp, Faith Lanam, Melinda Latour, Asunción Lavrin, Elisabeth Le Guin, Javier León, Javier Patiño Loira, Mark Lomanno, Rosalva Loreto López, Erin Maher, Andrew Mall, Adrian Masters, Ruthie Meadows, Suzanne Ryan Melamed, Craig Monson, Mitchell Morris, Ignacio Navarrete, Elizabeth O'Brien, María Luisa Vilar Payá, Jess Peritz, Marysol Quevedo, Jesús Ramos-Kitrell, Colleen Reardon, Ana Sánchez Rojo,

Teofilo Ruiz, Silvia Salgado, Jordan Hugh Sam, Mike Silvers, Jessica Schwartz, Gabriel Solis, Martha Sprigge, Neal Stulberg, Makoto Harris Takao, Stefanie Tcharos, Susan Thomas, Zeb Tortorici, Eizabeth Upton, Lisa Cooper Vest, and Matthew Vest.

I would like to thank the faculty and students who gave me feedback on the book's contents presented during invited talks at the University of Illinois at Urbana-Champagne, UC Irvine, UC Santa Barbara, UC Riverside, McGill, Case Western Reserve, the University of Washington, the University of North Carolina at Chapel Hill, the University of Pennsylvania, and the Universidad Nacional Autónoma de México.

Joining the musicology faculty at UCLA in 2018 greatly enhanced my intellectual perspectives and yielded generous financial support for this project. In particular, I would like to thank the following UCLA offices for the grants, fellowships, and research funds I received: the Herb Alpert School of Music Dean's Office; the Equity, Diversity, and Inclusion Office; the Center for the Study of Women; the Hellman Fellows Program; the Mellon Mays Program; the Humanities Division; the Academic Senate; and the Academic Personnel Office. The UCLA Library's collaboration with the Toward an Open Monograph Ecosystem (TOME) program made it possible for this book to be open access, and I thank Sharon Farb for her assistance with this matter. I am also thankful for receiving grants and fellowships from the University of California Institute for Mexico and the United States and the University of California Humanities Research Institute. The financial support of these UC system affiliates no doubt helped make me a competitive applicant to various grants and fellowships that I received from the Society for American Music, Project Spectrum, the LLILAS Benson Latin American Studies and Collections at UT Austin, the American Philosophical Society, the Institute for Citizens & Scholars, and the American Council of Learned Societies, to whom I am very grateful.

I would also like to thank some of the musicians who have assisted in bringing some of the music discussed in this book back to life through recent performances, especially Sarah Cranor, Adan Fernandez, Ellen Hargis, Lyndsay Johnson, Angèle Trudeau, and Marylin Winkle.

I dedicate this book to my parents, María Elvira and Clemente Favila, and to my partner, KC Vavra, whose love and support have no limits. I also dedicate it to Asunción Lavrin, whose pioneering work on women's convents in New Spain inspired my research for this book. She has been one of the most generous interlocutors in my early career.

Appendices

Profession Chant, *Ceremonial para las religiosas geronimas de México*, San Jerónimo convent, Mexico City, ca. seventeenth century, Hispanic Society of America, New York, Call number B2911

Chant	Genre	Feast	Mode	Page
Prudentes virgines aptate	Antiphon	Common of several Virgins	4	f.5r
Veni filia	Antiphon		7	f.5v
Et nunc sequor in toto corpore			7	f.6r
Veni sponsa Christi	Antiphon	Common of one Virgin	8	f.9r
Mecum enim habeo custodem	Antiphon	Saint Agnes, Virgin Martyr	7	f.9r
Regnum mundi et omnem	Responsory	Common of several Virgins	5	f.9v
Ancilla Christi sum	Antiphon	Saint Agatha, Virgin Martyr	2	f.10r
Posuit signum	Antiphon	Saint Agnes, Virgin Martyr	7	f.11r
Ipsi sum desponsata	Antiphon	Saint Agnes, Virgin Martyr	7	f.11v
Annulo meo subarravit me	Antiphon	Saint Agnes, Virgin Martyr	7	f.12r
Induit me Dominus	Antiphon	Saint Agnes, Virgin Martyr	7	f.13r
Ecce quod concupivi	Antiphon	Saint Agnes, Virgin Martyr	1	f.13r

Chant, *Libro de Coro del Convento de Santa Inés de Montepulciano*, Puebla, ca. 1709, Instituto Nacional de Antropología e Historia, Mexico City, Colección Antigua Vol. 968

Chant	Genre	Feast	Mode	Page
Salve Regina	Antiphon	Various feast days for Virgin Mary	1	f.3r
O lumen ecclesiae doctor	Antiphon	St. Dominic	6	f.3v
Maria ergo unxit pedes Jesu	Antiphon	Mary Magdalene	6	f.4r
O Petre martir inclite	Antiphon	Peter the Martyr	6	f.4r
Iste sanctus digne in memoriam	Antiphon	Common of one Confessor (Pope)	1	f.4v
O Thoma laus et gloria	Antiphon	Thomas Aquinas, Priest and Doctor of the Church	1	f.4v
Adsit nobis propitius	Responsory Verse	John the Baptist	8	f.5r
Ista est virgo sapiens quam	Antiphon	Common of one Virgin	8	f.5r
Veni sponsa Christi	Antiphon	Common of one Virgin	8	f.5v
Stella caeli	Antiphon	Five feasts of Virgin Mary	1	f.5v
Dixit Dominus		Common of one Confessor	1	f.6r
Confitebor tibi Domine			2	f.6r

Beatus vir/Latetatus sum		Gregory the Great, Pope and Doctor	3	f.6v
Laudate Pueri/Nisi Dominus			4	f.6v
Laudate Dominum/ Lauda Jerusalem			5	f.6v
Magnificat			2	f.6v
Magnificat/Benedictus Dominus Deus			2	f.6v
Benedictus Dominus Deus			3	f.6r
Benedicamus Domino			2	f.7r
Iste Confessor	Hymn	Common of one Confessor	7	f.7r
Jesu Redemptor ominum	Hymn	Common of one Confessor	7	f.7r
Ave maris stella	Hymn	Immaculate Conception of Virgin Mary	1	f.7r
O Gloriosa Virginum	Hymn	Common Chants for Mary	8	f.7v
Veni Creator Spiritus	Hymn	Pentecost	8	f.7v
Spiritus Domini replevit	Responsory	1st Sunday after Pentecost	Responsory	f.8r
Christe fili Dei vivi	Responsory		Responsory	f.8r
Haec est Virgo sapiens et una	Antiphon	Common of Several Virgins	1	f.8v
Haec est virgo sapiens, quam Dominus	Antiphon	Common of Several Virgins	1	f.8v
Haec est quae nescivit	Antiphon	Purification of Mary/ Common of Several Virgins/Assumption of Mary	3	f.8v
Veni electa mea	Antiphon	Common of Several Virgins	1	f.8v
Ista est speciosa	Antiphon	Common of Several Virgins	3	f.9r
Sacerdos in eternum	Antiphon	Corpus Christi	1	f.9r
Miserator Dominus	Antiphon	Corpus Christi	2	f.9r
Caclicem salutaris	Antiphon	Corpus Christi	3	f.9v
Sicut novella olivarum	Antiphon	Corpus Christi	4	f.9v
Qui pacem point fines	Antiphon	Corpus Christi	5	f.9v

O quam suavis est	Antiphon	Corpus Christi	6	f.10r
Pange lingua gloriosi	Hymn	Corpus Christi	Mozarbic	f.10v
O sacrum convivium	Antiphon	Corpus Christi	5	f.10v
Sacris solemniis	Hymn	Corpus Christi	5	f.11r
Panem de caelo	Versicle	Corpus Christi		f.11r
Te Deum laudamus			4	f.11v
Posuit signum	Antiphon	Saint Agnes Virgin Martyr	7	f.14v
Amo Christum in cuius thalamum	Responsory	Saint Agnes Virgin Martyr	7	f.14v
Annulo suo subarravit me et immensis	Antiphon	Saint Agnes Virgin Martyr	7	f.15r
Ipsi sum desponsata	Antiphon	Saint Agnes Virgin Martyr	7	f.15v
Annulo suo subarravit me Dominus	Antiphon	Saint Agnes Virgin Martyr	7	f.15v
Induit me Dominus	Antiphon	Saint Agnes Virgin Martyr	7	f.15v
Nunc dimittis with minor doxology	Antiphon	Purification of Mary	7	f.16r
Adorna thalamum tuum	Antiphon	Purification of Mary	6	f.16v
Responsum accepit Simeon	Antiphon	Purification of Mary	6	f.17v
Cum inducerent purem Iesum	Verse	Purification of Mary	1	f.18r
Obtulerun pro eo Domino with minor doxology	Responsory	Purification of Mary	2	f.18r
Subvenite, Sancti Dei	Responsory	Requiem Mass		f.19r
Kyrie	Kyrie	Mass	7	f.20r
Memento mei Deus	Responsory	Job	2	f.20r
Lumen ad	Antiphon	Purification of Mary	7	f.20v

Rodríguez Mata, Excerpt of *Asperges me*, mm. 16–24, Encarnación Convent Choirbook 2, folios 115v–118r

Art Gardens in Convent Manuscripts

1.2a.1 Francisco Guerrero, *Missa Saeculorum Amen*, a4, Agnus Dei (tiple part), Decorated A Initial, Encarnación Choirbooks, vol. 1, fol. 74v

1.2a.2 Juan de Lienas, *Salve Regina*, a4, Snake in Tree (before tiple part), Encarnación Choirbooks, vol. 1, fol. 78v

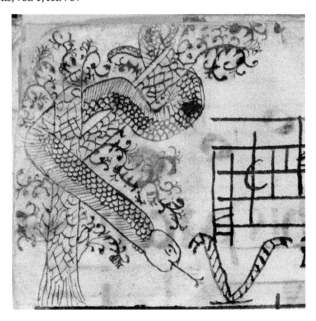

1.2a.3 Juan de Lienas, *Salve Regina*, a4, Bird (before alto part), Encarnación Choirbooks, vol. 1, fol. 79r

1.2a.4 Juan de Lienas, *Salve Regina*, a4, Snakes in Vines (before second tiple part), Encarnación Choirbooks, vol. 1, fol. 79v

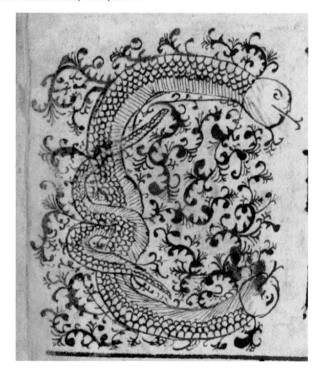

Nicolás de Texada Guzmán, Immaculate Conception, Jesús María Convent Profession Book, ca. 1584

In the outer frame the Virgin is surrounded by the seven virtues, from top left going clockwise: Faith, Charity, Hope, Fortitude, Temperance, Prudence, and Justice. The inner square has her surrounded by God the Father at the top, and a scroll beneath that reads words from the Song of Songs, "You are all beautiful, my love, and the stain of original sin is not in you." Continuing clockwise from below God's orb are the items and their allegorical titles affiliated with the Immaculate Conception's purity: beautiful like the moon, spotless mirror, tower of David, exalted like a Palm tree in Cades, lily of the valley, exalted like a cypress on Mt. Sion, sealed fountain, city of God, enclosed garden, plane tree exalted, well of water, fair olive tree, thornless rose, flower of the field, gate of heaven, chosen as the sun, star of the sea.

Anonymous, Immaculate Conception, Jesús María Convent Profession Book, ca. 1774

As the iconography of the Immaculate Conception gets established later in the seventeenth century, many of the attributes get reduced, often leaving (clockwise from bottom left) the tower of David, a well of water, the gate of heaven, a spotless mirror, a sealed fountain, and an enclosed garden. It is not even necessary to label the images anymore. Meanwhile, the "amica" (my love) from the Song of Songs text is now completely replaced with "María" in the text below the image.

Music references in Archbishop Payo Enríquez's Visits to Mexico City Convents, 1672–1675. Based on Leticia Pérez Puente, Gabriela Oropeza Tena, and Marcela Saldaña Solis, eds., *Autos de las visitas del arzobispo fray Payo Enríquez a los conventos de monjas de la ciudad de México, 1672–1675* (Mexico City: CESU-UNAM, 2005)

Purísima Concepción

AGN, Bienes Nacionales, Vol. 101, Exp. 4, folio 4r, September 5, 1672

Dressed in pontificals with mitre and crosier, his illustrious lordship arrived at the high altar, in which one of the chaplains opened the tabernacle of the said convent, and he incensed and adored the Blessed Sacrament that was in it, and he took it in his hands, and showed it to the people to adore, as the nuns sang what is called for. [Note that in all convents visited the bishop performed the adoration, and it is described with the exact same rubric for every location.]

Vestido su señoría ilustrísima de pontifical con mitra y báculo, y llegó al altar mayor donde abriendo el sagrario por uno de los capellanes de dicho convento y incensó y adoró el santísimo sacramento que estaba en él y lo cogió en las manos y enseñó al pueblo para que lo adorasen, cantando las religiosas lo que se observa.

AGN, Bienes Nacionales, Vol. 101, Exp. 4, folio 16r, September 15, 1672

In addition, may the chaplains of said convent be compelled to sing the passions in Holy Week but, if they do not possess either the appropriate voices or the decent intelligence for it, may they find someone to sing them and may they defray the cost out of their wages for the latter will supply what is supposed to be the obligation of the said chaplains. Said convent and administrator will help the chaplains by giving twenty pesos each year for that purpose. In addition, said administrator will give twenty-four pesos to the mother singers for Holy Week so that they might enjoy of a compensation for the work they have during those days.

Ítem, sean obligados los capellanes de dicho convento a cantar las pasiones en la semana santa, y no teniendo voces ni la inteligencia decente que conviene, busquen quien las cante pagándoles de sus salarios, pues han de suplir los que sirvieren en dicho ministerio lo que es de la obligación de dichos capellanes, a quienes ayudará el dicho convento y mayordomo, en su nombre, con veinte pesos cada año para dicho efecto. Ítem, dará dicho mayordomo a las madres cantoras, la Semana Santa, veinte y cuatro pesos para que gocen de algún alivio en el trabajo que tienen dichos días

AGN, Bienes Nacionales, Vol. 101, Exp. 4, folio 23v, February 6, 1675

As an aid in singing the passions, twenty pesos will be given to the mother singers in payment for the work of Holy Week; twenty-four pesos per year.

Para ayuda de cantar las pasiones, veinte pesos a las madres cantoras por el trabajo de la semana santa, veinte y cuatro pesos al año.

Regina Coeli

AGN, Bienes Nacionales, Vol. 101, Exp. 5, folios 16v, October 14, 1672

Expense for the *maestro* of music; likewise, thirty-five pesos will be given each year to the mother vicar of the choir for the *maestro* who writes the *villancicos* and the music for the choir; thirty-five pesos for the entire year.

Gasto del maestro de música, asimismo, se le dan a la madre vicaria de coro treinta y cinco pesos cada año para el maestro que hace los villancicos y música para el coro todo el año 35 pesos.

AGN, Bienes Nacionales, Vol. 101, Exp. 5, folios 17r, October 14, 1672

That which is given to them who sing the passions and the blessing of the serge: in addition, forty-two pesos will be given to them who sing the passions in Holy Week and to whom blesses the serge, that is, six pesos for each passion, for the two that are sung, and six pesos for the blessing of the serge. Attention, 20 pesos. That is enough.

Lo que se da a los que cantan las pasiones y bendición el sirio Ítem se dan a los que cantan las pasiones las semanas santas y al que hace la bendición del sirio, cuarenta y dos pesos a seis pesos cada pasión, de dos que se cantan, y seis pesos por la bendición del sirio. Ojo 20 pesos. Bastan

AGN, Bienes Nacionales, Vol. 101, Exp. 5, folios 20r, October 8, 1672

And likewise, the expense of forty-two pesos given to them who sing the passions of Holy Week and the rest that is included in paragraph sixteen of said memory has been changed for it falls under the obligations of the chaplains of said convent. And, in case they do not possess voices or aptitude to perform such task, may they appoint people who might do it in their stead; and the said convent will help them to defray the costs with twenty pesos and no more.

Y asimismo, reformaba y reformó el gasto de cuarenta y dos pesos que se han dado a los que cantan la pasión las semanas santas, y lo demás que se contiene, en el párrafo diez y seis de dicha memoria por ser del cargo de los capellanes de dicho convento; y en caso que no tengan voces y suficiencia para lo referido, pongan personas por su cuenta que suplan por los susodichos en dicho ministerio, y para la costa les ayude el dicho convento con veinte pesos y no más.

Jesús María

AGN, Bienes Nacionales, Vol. 101, Exp. 3, folios 23v, November 28, 1672

During the time of said day and octave, thirty-one pesos from the alms of the priest and the ministers who sing the Masses that have been requested by different people, as can be gleaned from the judgment of the mother Abbess.

En el tiempo de dicho día y octava, treinta y un pesos de la limosna del preste y ministros que cantan las misas que están dotadas por diferentes personas, como parece de la memoria que dio la madre abadesa.

AGN, Bienes Nacionales, Vol. 101, Exp. 3, folios 25r–25v, November 28, 1672

And because it is a logical custom to give the choir vicar eight pesos yearly for strings and paper, we order that [this tradition] be followed and continue.

Y por cuanto ha sido costumbre justa que se dan a la madre vicaria de coro para cuerdas y papel ocho pesos cada año, mandamos se observe y continúe.

Similarly, give twelve pesos a year to the teacher of music and another twelve pesos to the nuns who sing for Christmas eve [and] Christmas Vespers, or the equivalent in compensation for their work during the Christmas Masses.

Asimismo, se den doce pesos cada año por la música al maestro de ella y otros doce pesos a las religiosas cantoras la noche buena, víspera de pascua de navidad, por igual a como les cupiere para alivio del trabajo que han tenido en las misas de aguinaldo.

In addition, *petates* will be purchased twice a year for the choir and lofts. To this effect, eight pesos will be given by the administrator to the mother vicar of the choir every six months, which add to sixteen pesos per year and, likewise, said mother vicar will take care that the bells have ropes and she will warn the administrator in case any rope is missing.

Ítem, se comprarán dos veces al año petates para el choro y tribunas y para este efecto se entregarán por mano de el mayordomo a la madre vicaria de choro ocho pesos cada seis meses, que hacen al año diez y seis pesos, y asimismo, cuidará la dicha madre vicaria de que haya sogas en las campanas y de avisar al mayordomo quando falten.

San Jerónimo

AGN, Bienes Nacionales, Vol. 259, Exp. 27, folios 20r–20v, January 18, 1673

In addition, [they] ordered and commanded that the chaplains of said convent be in charge of singing the passions. In case they do not possess the skills required for the performance of such music, they ought to find someone to replace them in said task and they ought to pay the performers with their own money, although the convent will contribute with twenty pesos and no more than that amount.

Ítem, ordenó y mandó que el cantar las paciones sea a cargo de los capellanes de dicho convento, y si por razón de no tener la habilidad que conviene en la música para dicho efecto, busquen quien supla su falta a su costa, ayudando para ello el dicho convento con veinte pesos y no más.

In addition, the choir vicar is given twenty years every year, as is customary, for the compensation for the *maestro* who composes the music, six pesos for strings and reeds, and ten pesos for the *petates* for the high and low choirs.

Ítem ordena se den a la madre vicaria de coro cada año veinte pesos como a sido costumbre para el regalo del maestro que compone la música, y seis pesos para cuerdas y cañuelas, y diez pesos para petates para los coros alto y bajo.

And the choir vicar is given twenty pesos yearly, as is customary, for the gift to the teacher who composes the music, and six pesos for strings and reeds.

Ítem, se ordena a la madre vicaria de coro cada año veinte pesos como ha sido costumbre para el regalo del maestro que compone la música, y seis pesos para cuerdas y cañuelas.

Encarnación

AGN, Bienes Nacionales, Vol. 259, Exp. 26, folio 21r, February 11, 1673

And [the archbishop] orders and commands that the choir vicar be given forty pesos yearly, twenty for strings and other things that pertain to music and its instruments, and the other twenty to be disbursed equally among the convent singers on Christmas Eve to compensate them for their work during the celebration of the Christmas Masses. And we completely prohibit the spending that has taken place up to now on villancicos, since the old ones that they have can be repeated, and because it is believed that there is no shortage of pious poets whose charity can fulfill the need [for villancicos] of this convent.

Ítem, ordena y manda que a la madre vicaria de coro se le den en cada un año cuarenta pesos, los veinte para cuerdas y demás cosas que pertenecen a la música y sus instrumentos, y los otros veinte para que la víspera de navidad se repartan entre las religiosas músicas de dicho convento con igualdad, para alivio del especial trabajo que han tenido en la celebración de las misas de aguinaldo. Y, totalmente, prohibimos el gasto que se ha hecho hasta aquí en la paga de villancicos, pues, además que se podrán repetir los más antiguos con que se hallaren, se debe creer que nunca les faltarán poetas piadosos que por caridad se ejerciten en este ministerio constándoles la necesidad de este convento.

AGN, Bienes Nacionales, Vol. 259, Exp. 26, folio 28v, February 6, 1675

Forty pesos be given to the mother vicar for strings and another twenty [pesos] for the music for Christmas Vespers.

A la madre vicaria, cuarenta pesos los veinte para cuerdas y los otros veinte para que la víspera de navidad se repartan en las músicas.

Twenty pesos be given to the mother vicar for the choir *petates* and for the bells for the bells.

A la madre vicaria para petates de los choros y cordeles de las campanas, veinte pesos al año.

Santa Inés

AGN, Bienes Nacionales, Vol. 259, Exp. 31, folio 16r, March 20, 1673

Likewise, up to sixteen pesos will be handed over for instrument strings and reeds and for *patates* for the high choir. Thus, the expense sums up to six thousand one hundred and twenty-five pesos and five *tomines* according to the registries.

Asimismo, se entregan todos los años hasta diez y seis pesos para cuerdas y cañuelas de los instrumentos y para petates para el choro alto, con que monta el gasto seis mil ciento y veinte y cinco pesos y cinco tomines según consta de las partidas que se refieren 6 mil 125 pesos 5 tomines

San José de Gracia

AGN, Bienes Nacionales, Vol. 259, Exp. 30, folios 18v–19v, April 17, 1673

In addition, it is ordered that the current custom of saying every year fifty recited Masses and fourteen sung Masses for the soul of don Fernando de Villegas be maintained. [Fernando de Villegas] was a patron of the convent, according to what has been stipulated in said foundation, whose alms amount to thirty-nine pesos; twenty-five for the recited [Masses] and fourteen for the sung [Masses].

Ítem, se ordena que se continúe la costumbre que hasta hoy se ha tenido de que se digan cada año cincuenta misas rezadas y catorce cantadas por el ánima de don Fernando de Villegas, patrón que fue de dicho convento, en conformidad de lo capitulado en dicha fundación, cuya limosna importa treinta y nueve pesos, los veinte y cinco de las rezadas y los catorce de las cantadas.

In addition, it is ordered that thirteen sung Masses be said together with a deacon and subdeacon for the patrons of the convent's church. That is, for Juan Navarro and his wife. [Nine sung Masses] be said for the nine festivities of Our Lady, another one for the anniversary of the aforementioned, another one for the Vespers of St Andrew, another Mass for the King our lord, another Mass for the Day of the Dead, and another Mass for Ash Wednesday. [It is also ordered that] one peso in alms be given to the priest and four reales to the deacon and subdeacon, which sums up to twenty-six pesos in accordance to what is stipulated by the writs of said institution.

Ítem, se ordena y manda se digan trece misas cantadas con diácono y subdiácono por los patrones de la iglesia de dicho convento, Juan Navarro y su mujer, las nueve a las nueve festividades de nuestra señora, otra de aniversario por los susodichos, otra víspera de San Andrés por el rey nuestro señor, otra el día de difuntos y otra el miércoles de ceniza, y se dé de limosna al preste un peso y al diácono y subdiácono a cuatro reales, que hacen veinte y seis pesos en conformidad de lo capitulado en las escrituras de dicha fundación.

In addition, the administrator will give six pesos to the choir vicar each year for *petates* and ornaments for the high and low choirs. Similarly, [give] another six pesos [to the choir vicar] for the strings and reeds for the instruments in her care.

Ítem, dará el dicho mayordomo seis pesos cada año a la madre vicaria de coro para petates y aseo de dichos coros: alto y bajo. Asimismo, otros seis pesos para cuerdas y cañuelas de los instrumentos de su cargo.

And it is ordered that they continue the custom of giving eight pesos to the said [choir] vicar on the feast of Christmas and Easter to be distributed equally among the musician nuns who served on said solemnities.

Ítem se ordena se guarde la costumbre que se ha tenido de que se den ocho pesos la pascua de navidad y otros ocho la de resurrección a dicha madre vicaria para que los reparta entre las religiosas músicas que hubieren servido en dichas dos solemnidades a quienes les dará lo que les tocaré por iguales partes.

In addition, it is ordered that they continue the ongoing custom of saying ten sung Masses for each one of the nuns at the time of their death and that they spend the thirty-five pesos for the Masses. They have been informed that such interments are necessary.

Ítem, ordenó y mandó se continúe y guarde la costumbre que hasta hoy se ha tenido de decir diez misas cantadas por cada una de las religiosas al tiempo de su fallecimiento y que se gasten los treinta y cinco pesos que en lo referido y en los demás de dicho entierro se le ha informado ser necesarios como hasta hoy se ha hecho.

San Bernardo

AGN, Bienes Nacionales, Vol. 259, Exp. 28, folios 20 r–20v, August 1, 1673

In addition, as has been the custom, the administrator will give six pesos to the singers of said convent for the day of the Ascension.

Ítem, dé el dicho mayordomo, como a sido costumbre, seis pesos el día de la Ascensión para las religiosas cantoras de dicho convento.

In addition, as has been the custom, the butler will give out six pesos every year for strings and musical instruments.

Ítem, de dicho mayordomo seis pesos cada, año como a sido costumbre, para cuerdas y demás instrumentos músicos.

In addition, the custom be upheld that nine sung Masses be said for a nun who passes away and that eighteen pesos be spent [for these Masses].

Ítem, se guarde la costumbre de que se le digan a la religiosa que muriere nueve misas cantadas en que se gasten diez y ocho pesos.

Franciscan Coro Gestures, Excerpt from Manuel Aromir y Bustamante, *Reglas generales para dentro y fuera del coro*, ca. 1825

Entering Choir

When entering the choir, the nuns must adore the Blessed Sacrament, prostrating between the lectern ("fascistol") and the choir grate, until her lips touch the floor. If the liturgy has begun, she does the same veneration and goes directly to her place, bows her head toward the altar, then toward the choir [of nuns across from her], then she kneels with her face toward the altar until the superior signals her to get up. Of the two cantors, the oldest will be the leader ("hebdomada") of eight cantors on first class feasts and six on second class feasts. They all wear surplices. There are also acolytes for the candles and sensor, especially of the service is sung, not least Vespers. The leader ("hebdomadaria") and choir of eight wear capes. Not wearing them would be a lapse in uniformity, which is the most beautiful display in public acts ("gala más hermosa que tanto se procura en los actos públicos").

Order in the Choir

The nuns will be organized in the choir by age. The Office is prayed with a slow pause in the middle of the verse on double [feasts] and not so slow on semi double [feasts] and ferial days.

Sign of the Cross

At the start of every Office liturgy by the leader at the verse *Deus in adjutorium* at Prime with right hand open touching forehead with three fingers at *Deus*, lowering at *in adjutorium* to touch below the breast, touching the left shoulder at the word *meum* and the right shoulder at *intende*. Do not make a cross with your thumb and index finger and kiss them. She also does the sign of the cross at *Indulgentiam*.

Leader makes a sign of the cross with thumb only on lips and chest during *Domine labia mea* and *converte nos Deus* at Compline.

The entire community makes sign at Prime during *Dominus nos benedicat*.

The entire community makes sign at Compline during the words *patris, et filii, et spiritus sancti*.

Head nod: incline the head, keep body straight

During the Office when the following names are said: Jesus (deep head nod), Mary (medium head nod), St. Francis, other saints, and pope (minimal head nod).

For the Holy Innocents during the hymn *Salvate flores martyrum*

At *Gloriosa Domina* during *Benedicta.*

When *Salve Regina* is sung, at the words *Salve Regina* and *Spes nostra, salve.*

At the stations of the Cross during the words *quam crucem adoramus.*

At Mass, during the *Gloria* at the words *adoramus te,* and *suscipe deprecationem nostram.*

At Mass, during the *Credo* at the words *Credo in unum Deum* and *simul adoratur.*

When intoning psalm or antiphon, right after the intonation.

When crossing the middle of the choir, toward the altar (deep nod).

When acknowledging each other (minimal nod).

Profound bow: when you bend your torso with arms out and palm of hands are parallel to the knees

At the start of Our Father, *Ave Maria, Gloria Patri,* at Confession, at the end of every hymn that mentions the Trinity at Matins.

At Vespers, during *Confitebor tibi* (Psalm 110), at the phrase *Sanctum et terribile nomen ejus.*

At Vespers, during *Laudate pueri* (Psalm 112), at the phrase *sit nomen Domini benedictum.*

At the *Magnificat* during the phrase *sanctum nomen ejus.*

During the hymn *Tantum ergo* when the Blessed Sacrament is not exposed.

At Compline preces, *Benedicamus Patrem* until the phrase *qui tecum.*

At Matins, nod toward the leader at *Jube Domine benedicere.*

At Matins, nod at *Sit nomen ejus benedictum in saecula* during *Deus Judcium Tuum* (Psalm 71).

At Matins, nod at *Benedictum nomen majestatis ejus* during *Benedic, anima mea* (Psalm 102).

At Matins, nod at *Confiteantur nomini tuo magno, quoniam terribile et sanctum est* during *Dominus regnavit* (Psalm 98).

At Lauds, nod at *Benedicat nos Deus* during *Deus miseratur nostri* (Psalm 66).

At Lauds, nod at *Benedicamus Patrem* during canticle *Benedicite.*

At Prime, during the phrase *Dominum nos benedicat* until the phrase *Perducat aeternam.*

At the Salve Mass, nod during *Sancta parens*.

Note, most of these during the office are not performed by the leader so that she can recite/sing the words.

Genuflexion: right knee touches the floor

When passing the center of the choir, toward the Blessed Sacrament if it is exposed.

During the hymn *Tantum ergo* when the Blessed Sacrament is exposed.

During the phrase *Venite, adoremus, et procidamus* in *Venite exultemus Domino* (Psalm 94).

During the *Te Deum* at verse *Te ergo quaesumus*.

At the start of the hymn *Ave maris stella*.

At the start of the hymn *Veni creator*.

At the start of the hymn *Vexila Regis* through the phrase *O Crux ave*.

At the start of the Nativity hymn *Et nos, beata quos sacri*.

At the Office of Our Lady during the eighth blessing.

Cross arms across chest during genuflection at the start of *Veni creator* hymn and at *te ergo* of *te Deum*.

Genuflections happen while the words [indicated] are recited, not before or after. The singers should take care to go off pitch, and should genuflect after intoning the song if the opening phase is long.

Kneeling: both knees on the floor.

At the final antiphons of the Office of Our Lady except in Paschal time.

Kneel if a mistake is made, until [the superior] makes the signal [to get up].

At Compline, kneel during Our Father, *Ave Maria*, and *Credo*, except in Paschal time or Sundays when a profound bow will suffice.

Kneel when to pick up something you dropped.

At the Epistle on Good Friday when phrase *in Nomine Jesu* until the word *infernorum*.

When *Veni Creator* is sung.

During the Gospels when the following is said: *Verbum caro*, *Procidentes adoraverunt*, and *Incarnatus*.

To receive ashes, palms, and candles, kissing the candle and palm, and then the priest's hand.

To adore the cross before Good Friday.

On Holy Saturday during *Lumen Christi.*

Whenever speaking to the superior in the choir; everyone stand when she enters the choir, unless the Blessed Sacrament is exposed [then everyone remains kneeling].

Prostration: this is a sign of humility

At the Christmas Kalenda at the words *in Bethlehem Judæ* through the words *secundum carnem.*

During the Passions at the words *emisit Spiritum* and kiss the floor for the length of an Our Father.

At the final adoration of the cross on Good Friday, and one also kisses the cross without opening the eyes and says silently *adoramus te Christe.*

Dominican Coro Gestures, *De las inclinaciones*, Excerpt from Francisco Guerra, *Regla y constituciones para las religiosas recoletas dominicas*, 1789

Entering Choir

When the sisters come to the choir [they] bow profoundly toward the altar; and when they kneel ("pongan de rodillas") and get back up again, they do the profound bow again; and sit when they arrive at their spot; when the presider (like "hebdomadaria"?) signals, on knees, prostrated, or in profound bow, say Our Father, Ave Maria, and Creed: this way the hour (office) begins devoutly; when the presider makes the sign, they straighten up, turn toward the altar and make the sign of the cross; bow at *Gloria patri* until *sicut erat* in both choirs facing each other at the same time; at the *Gloria Patri of the Venite exultemus* (Psalm 95; 94 in Greek) invitatory that opens up Matins, one choir stands while the other across sits for first psalm. And they switch sitting and standing for every psalm from then on until the *Laudate Dominum de coelis* (final psalm 148 of Lauds) when everyone stays standing; this alternation between chois during psalms is done in all the other hours; **this also indicates that Matins and Lauds were sung together.

Head nod: incline the head, keep body straight

Whenever the names of Jesus, Mary, and St. Dominic are heard/invoked.

When they receive a garment, book, etc.

At *Sit nomen Domini benedictum* (blessing after Vespers or Lauds, or benediction).

Whenever the "prelada" asks her to do something.

When intoning psalm or antiphon, right after the intonation.

When passing in front of "prelada" or other nuns.

When they are sprinkled with holy water at the moment the water touches their head or when they are insenced ("turiboladas").

During Mass *Credo* at *Qui cum Patre, et Filio, etc.*

When the precious blood of Christ is mentioned.

When they are in refectory and pass through the center, they bow toward the image above the prioress's seat.

When the Invitatory is sung or said, when the verse *Quoniam ipsius* is said bow toward the altar.

During Lent, bow during the prayer *Super populum*.

Usque ad genua bow: bow crossing arms under the scapular, until head is parallel with knees

This bow is always done at the *Gloria Patri* during all the Office hours.

On final verse of hymns and penultimate verse of *Benedicte*.

During Mass at *Gloria in excelsis Deo* at the verses *Gratias agimus tibi* and *Suscipe deprecationem* and *Altissimus Jesu-Christe*.

During Mass at preface *Gratias agamus*, and when Jesus and Mary's names are mentioned, as well as in prayers, collects, and the *Salve* service.

At the blessing before lessons in choir or refectory.

At the Santa Maria prayer during the "Preciosa sangre"; Passion devotion; maybe station of the cross).

During prayers at the mention of St. Dominic's name.

At the blessing after Compline.

At the refectory at the prayers after eating; no prostrations or profound bows there.

Profound bow: bow crossing arms under the scapular, with an inward tuck so that knees can touch the elbows

Upon entering and exiting the Coro, with the addition of a genuflection.

When crossing from one choir to the other. . . . when crossing, thus toward Blessed Sacrament at altar.

At the Our Father before Lessons and after "Gracias" and at the prayer *Retribuere*, before and after the hours, in the Preces, and at Vespers and Matins for the Dead.

The nuns who say the Lessons at Matins, between the space that exists between the "coro" grate and the music stand ("facistol"), except at the Lessons for the Dead.

Also, at the first *Gloria Patri* of every hour and at the first prayer in both Mass and Office.

Whenever prostrations are omitted.

At the prayer at Mass after communion ("despues de la comunicada").

Genuflection: right knee touches the floor

In "coro" at *Salve Sancta parens* (Salve Service).

Intonation of *Salve* at Compline through *Regina;* stand up at *Mater*; again at *Eia ergo* through *O clemens.*

At *Veni Creator at* Terce during the Octave of Pentecost; and for the entire first strophe of the hymn at the taking of the habit and professions.

At Passion hymn, during *O Crux ave* through the end of the strophe.

At Trinity hymn, during *Adsumus* until the end of the strophe (*Adsumus et nos cernui*).

For hymn *Ave maris stella.*

At Mass during *Veni sancte spiritus* until *reple.*

During *Salve Regina* or Antiphon said after the hours.

During the *Te Deum* at verse *Te ergo quaesumus.*

At the Gospel on Epiphany during the words *Et procidentes*

At sung Mass of the cross ("Misa de la Cruz"), and Palm Sunday during the words *Omne genuflectatur* during the Epistle.

At the *Credo* during *Incarnatus* through *Crucifixus.*

During the final Gospel at *Verbum caro.*

At the antiphon *Sub tuum praesidium.*

At the responsory *O spem miram* said every day for St. Dominic.

During the psalm *Venite exultemus* at the verse *Venite adoremus.*

During Palm Sunday Procession when one sings *Ave rex* through *Redemptor mundi.*

When one kisses the bishop's hand.

At the end of nuns' burials at the antiphon *Clementissime Domine* during the words *Domine miserere* until the words *Super peccatores.*

Prostration: kneel and bow until elbows touch the knees

During ferial days, except in Pascal time, at first Our father and Hail Mary before the start of the Office hours and at first *Gloria Patri.*

At the precis of every Office and at the prayer after the preces.

Within Ferial Office at every Our Father, *Ave Maria*, and *Credo*, except at the Our Father before the lessons at Matins and during the "Preciosa."

At Our Father during Gracias after the *Fidelum* if prostration at Nones (Outside of Lent) or prostration at Vespers.

After *Tu autem Domine* between "fascistol" and "coro" grill by the one who reads the lessons at Matins.

At all ferial Masses, including Requiems, after *Dominus vobiscum* of first and last prayer.

At ferial Masses between *Sanctus and Agnus.*

Non-ferial Masses from elevation to Our Father.

At ferial offices during Our Father after the *Magnificat* Antiphon.

During the entire Psalm *Lauda anima mea*, *Prece* and Prayer, and after *Requiescat in pace*; the same at Lauds.

During Litanies after Compline, again only if ferial, not on saint day feast.

During disciplines and all other times *Confiteor Deo* to its completion (except non-ferial Compline and Prime).

During Matins of Holy Week throughout *Miserere* psalm, Prayer, and Our Father.

At the adoration of the cross on Good Friday, when priest says *Ecce lignum* until *Crucis*; then stand for the first antiphon and prostrate at the next antiphon through *Lignum cedrorum.*

**Seems like only during penitential times, since no prostration on last seven days of Advent (when O antiphons are sung). No prostrations throughout Pascal time through Corpus Christi, even if ferial time.

Venia: entire body stretched out on the floor leaning up on right side

During vigil of Annunciation at the singing of *Annuntiatio* during the Kalenda.

During vigil of Christmas at the singing of *Factus homo* during the Kalenda.

During chapter faults ("capitulo") when making accusation before superior ("prelada").

When being reprimanded by superior.

When causing an offence to another sister until the offended tells the offender to stand.

When a mistake is made singing, praying . . . in the choir until superior signals to get up.

APPENDIX 4.1

4.1 Decorated Initials of María Teresa de San Francisco, Name on Alto of part of Second Choir, Vidales, *Al aire que se llena de luces* (CSG.283)

Riva, *Cisne, no halagues*

Estribillo
Cisnes, no halagues,
a tu muerte, rigores
con suavidades.

Swan, do not flatter
rigors with melodiousness
when you die.

Coplas
1. Dulce cisne, que muriendo
de tu llanto entre raudales,
si das los ojos al agua
fías las voces al aire.

Sweet swan, dying
among the torrents of your weeping,
if you turn your eyes to the water,
you entrust your song to the air.

2. Gime y no cantes tu pena,
que saben mal ajustarse
destemplanzas del dolor
a consonancias del arte.

Moan, and do not sing your sorrow,
for the tunelessness of pain
knows how to conform
to the consonances of the skill.

3. Con cantar no se acreditan
tus sentimientos de grandes,
pues a cláusulas se ciñen
y se miden a compases.

Your feelings do not prove
to be great by singing,
for they are confined to cadences
and they are measured by measures.

4. La música del gemido
puntos al dolor no vague,
que el aliño de la queja
es el tormento desaire.

May the music of your moaning not
lead the notes astray to sorrow,
for the ornament of grievance
is torment's disdain.

5. A tu voz no se suspendan
de tus ojos los cristales,
que de la pena es el llanto
la armonía más suave.

May the crystals of your eyes
not hang from your voice,
for crying is the sweetest
harmony of sorrow.

6. Aprende esa palabra
que, de silencio, en disfraces
muere de amor mudo, cisne,
sí, nevado fénix, arde.

Learn that word,
for love dies mute, swan,
in guises of silence,
yes, snow-covered phoenix, burn.

Cáseda, *Pajarito que en el aire elevado*

Estribillo
Pajarito, en el aire elevado,
con dulces motetes,
festeja tu amor.
A cantar, con gran primor,
a este Dios sacramentado,
llega a comerle, no temas,
a este divino bocado.
No te engañe el corazón,
come contrito y llorando.
Pajarito, en el aire elevado.

Little bird, high in the air,
your love celebrates
with sweet motets.
Sing, with great skill,
to this sacramental God,
come to eat him, do not fear
this divine morsel.
May your heart not deceive you,
eat contritely and weeping.
Little bird, high in the air.

Coplas
1. Dulce armonía de plumas,
que, con sonora atención,
hoy rindes tantos gorjeos
a solo un trino que es Dios.

Sweet harmony of feathers,
that with sonorous attention
you yield today so many chirps
to one trinity that is God.

2. No cantes, porque te importa
para rendirle a tu amor,
más la firmeza en el pecho
que la mudanza en la voz.

Do not sing merely
to perform for your love,
firmness of faith in the heart
is greater than the flux of the voice.

3. Si el dolor de amante gimes,
no cantes sonoro,
mira que la destemplanza
hace armonía al dolor.

If you sigh because of a lover's grief,
do not sing sonorously,
notice that tunelessness
harmonizes with the pain.

4. Llora, pues, con los ojos,
retórico el corazón,
que está, en lo mudo del llanto,
lo elocuente del amor.

Cry, then, with your eyes,
with a rhetorical heart
that is mute from weeping,
the eloquence of love.

5. Mas, si quieres, con dulzura,
de esa forma cantar hoy,
forma bien tu voz los puntos,
porque está en los puntos Dios.

Yet, if you want to sing
in such a sweet way today,
let your voice form the notes well,
since God is in the notes.

6. Tu pesar no se suspenda
de esa dulce elevación,
ni tu dolor haga pausas,
aunque haga pausas tu voz.

May your grief not fall
from this sweet elevation,
nor your pain take rests,
even though your voice takes rests.

Riva, *Que enigma tan bello*

Estribillo
¿Qué cosa es aquella?
Que es más linda y bella,
con cuerpo y sin cara.
Que es hostia [ ]
Que cosa tan rara
que en una partícula
de [ ]
y es que Dios la ampara,
para ser más bella
cuando está sin cara.
Pues, sea en hora buena
sin cara más bella.
Vaya, vaya, vaya,
sea bella sin cara.

Coplas
1. Entre cándidos celajes,
todo un Dios está escondido,
que es todo pan a los ojos
y es todo Dios a los oídos.

2. La vista, el gusto y el tacto
no perciben lo divino,
no a los sentidos se da
por no dejarnos sentidos.

3. El al [ ] goza
este manjar peregrino,
y aun gozando su substancia,
no tiene fin su individuo.

4. Él es un pan animado
que es muerte para el indigno,
el alma y vida al dispuesto
y, en fin, es un pan de juicio.

What is that thing?
It is prettier and more beautiful,
with a body but without a face.
It is the Host [...]
It is such an extraordinary thing,
that in one particle
of [...]
and it is that God safeguards it,
to be more beautiful
when it has no face.
Be it always
more beautiful without a face.
Well, well, well,
be it beautiful without a face.

An entire God hides
between the candid clouds,
which is wholly bread to the eyes
and wholly God to the ears.

The sight, the taste, and the tact
do not perceive the divine,
he does not give himself to the senses
so as not to offend us.

The [soul] enjoys
this wandering delicacy,
and even by enjoying its substance,
his presence has no end.

He is an ensouled bread
that means death to the unworthy,
the soul and life to the willing,
and, in fact, he is a bread of judgment.

Instancia presentada por la abadesa y religiosas del Convento de la Purísima Concepción de Nuestra Señora la Virgen María, AGN/ Instituciones Coloniales/ Indiferente Virreinal/ Caja 0565/ Expediente 023

Blessed Father

The abbess and nuns of the royal and oldest Convent (throughout this Kingdom of New Spain in the West Indies) of the Immaculate Conception of Our Lady the Virgin Mary, of the Order of St. Francis, as far as the law is concerned, find ourselves prostrate with all veneration from afar before the greatness of Your Holiness and say: That it is true, as documented and known through word of mouth, that Br. Joaquín Niño de Cordova, priest of this Archdiocese of Mexico, since before becoming our convent chaplain, had brought to light, and founded a pious devotion and celebration in honor of Our Holy Jesus the Redeemer in the church of the Jesús María convent of this court: making reparation to His Majesty [Jesus Christ] with devotion and adoration over that cruel offense, and dark insult with which Herod disrespected, mocked, and tried [Our Lord] like a <u>lunatic</u>: dressing him in a white robe before and together with his court.

We know that on Holy Wednesday morning, this feast and devotion is celebrated with a solemn Mass and sermon, the use of a sumptuous altar of costly silver on which is placed an image of the said Jesus Christ, that is venerated in the Jesús María convent church, that it is well attended by secular and regular priests, and by people of both sexes, that with all devotion, humility, and reverence attend this tender pious devotion and celebration.

We are aware that Br. Joaquín Niño de Cordova has written (as we have seen) an Office and Mass, particularly for this celebration and devotion, with the effective desire . . . to spread this devotion, thus we know that the Procurators of the Jesuits of New Spain, have been charged, so that with all veneration, [this petition] may be placed in the giving and pious hands of Your Holiness, seeking approval and concession for all this New World of the West Indies, with other graces, and Indulgences as requested.

And from these remote lands with strong humble prayers and supplications rendered, we ask Your Holiness to hear us if only because we are religious women, your daughters, although unworthy, and grant that all this Kingdom of New Spain in the West Indies may pray as a double rite of the second class the said Office and Mass of the Scorn and Derision of the Redeemer dressed in white like a <u>lunatic</u>: in the third Friday of Lent, or the fourth when the third is prevented by the celebration of a greater feast . . . or any other unimpeded day in Lent, as this is a Passion Office.

Deign to grant to all clergy, secular and regular of both sexes—who are obliged to pray the canonic hours, that exist and are given—a plenary indulgence for praying diligently this proper Office of our Lord Jesus Christ Redeemer, despised, and mocked, dressed in white garments like a <u>lunatic</u>: and those who cannot pray it completely, because of legitimate impediments, can pray as much as they can to receive the plenary indulgence. For example, only Lauds, or the [little] hours [Terce, Sext, None], or Vespers with Compline.

Deign to grant a plenary indulgence as a jubilee indulgence for the day of the feast and devotion, as already described, the third Friday of Lent (or it can be transferred to any other if this one is unavailable) lasting from first Vespers until sunset of the indicated day, with permission to expose the Most Divine Sacrament of the Eucharist, or lasting from the First Vespers until sunset of another day, or just that same day of the feast: or only at the time of the sung Mass, depending on the availability of the churches, so that through the customary confession and communion and prayers all the faithful of both sexes may receive this indulgence by way of jubilee in hopes that this new feast and tender devotion will become a day of celebration throughout all of America.

Similarly, may the piety, zeal, and charity of Your Holiness grant all this for each and every one of the churches of this Kingdom of the West Indies for relief and repose of the souls of the faithful departed in purgatory, that these indulgences apply on this feast day (on the very day or if it is transferred [to another day]), establishing privileged altars[1] within all the churches in North America for all priests, secular and regular, that celebrate the Mass of this devotion to Our Lord Jesus Redeemer presented and mocked as a <u>lunatic</u> by Herod.

May all these graces and indulgences and privileges be perpetual and universal across this empire of North America so the poor little Indians, living in their remote villages, can participate and enjoy them [as well], since they lack year-around jubilees, and lack the joy of frequent exposition of the Sacramental Redeemer for public adoration.

To Your Holiness we ask and beg that you attend to our pious prayers and supplications, having repeated them many times, that you give your apostolic permission, granting what we ask in honor and glory of God, Our Lord and of the Passion of his son Jesus Christ, whose memory and remembrance we want, through this medium, to remain always among the faithful children of his and Your Holiness, so that our desires will come to fruition in their hearts.

Marina de San Francisco, Abbess
María Gertrudis de San José, Vicar
María Gertrudis de Guadalupe, Head of Council
Juana Estefanía del Señor San José, Council Member
María Hipólita de San José, Council Member
María Lucía del Señor San José, Council Member

Original text

Beatísimo Padre

La abadesa, y religiosas, del real y más antiguo Convento (en todo este Reino de la Nueva España, en las Indias Occidentales) de la Purísima Concepción de Nuestra Señora la Virgen María, del Orden de San Francisco, como mejor halla lugar por derecho, parecemos postradas con toda veneración desde aquí ante la grandeza de Vuestra Santidad y decimos: Que es cierto y nos consta por relación, y por la publica voz que el Br. Don Joaquín Niño de Córdova, presbítero de este Arzobispado de México, nuestro capellán, o párroco claustral: desde antes que fuese señalado por la sagrada mitra para nuestro tal capellán ya había sacado a luz, y fundado una piadosa devoción, y fiesta en honra de Nuestro Santo Jesús Redentor en la iglesia del monasterio, también real, de religiosas de Jesús María de esta corte: desagraviando a su Majestad con cultos de adoración y reverencia, de aquel cruel agravio, y negro improperio con que Herodes lo despreció, lo burló, y trató como loco:[2] vistiéndolo de una vestidura blanca delante de toda su corte, y con ella juntamente.

Sabemos que el miércoles santo por la mañana, se celebra esta fiesta, y devoción, con Misa solemne, y sermón que se dispone un suntuoso altar de costosa plata en que se coloca, una imagen del mismo Jesucristo Redentor Nuestro que se venera en dicha iglesia de religiosas de Jesús María, que ay mucha asistencia de eclesiásticos, seculares y regulares, y de pueblo de uno y otro sexo: que, con toda devoción, humildad, y reverencia, asisten a tan tierna como piadosa devoción, y fiesta.

Nos consta también que dicho Br. Don Joaquín Niño de Córdova ha compuesto (como lo hemos visto) un Oficio y Misa, propios de esta fiesta y devoción, con el deseo eficaz, y santo fin de que esta devoción se extienda, para lo cual sabemos que por medio de los reverendísimos padres procuradores de la Compañía de Jesús de esta Provincia de Nueva España, lo despacha, para que con toda veneración, sea puesto en las liberales y piadosas manos de Vuestra Santidad, pretendiendo su aprobación, y concesión para todo este nuevo mundo de las Indias Occidentales, con otras gracias, e Indulgencias que se pide.

Y nosotras desde estas remotas tierras con humildes ruegos fuertes, y rendidas suplicas, pedimos a Vuestra Santidad nos oiga siquiera porque somos mujeres religiosas sus hijas, aunque indignas, y nos conceda que en todo este Reino de la Nueva España en las Indias Occidentales, se rece bajo el rito doble de segunda clase, el citado oficio, y Misa del desprecio y burla del Redentor vestido de blanco como loco: en viernes tercero de Cuaresma, o en el de la semana siguiente que es el cuarto, cuando el tercero estuviere impedido con fiesta de mayor rito, o de igual a este, pero, intransferible por de precepto de oír Misa, o en otro cualquier día de la cuaresma no impedido, por ser este oficio de Pasión.

Que se digne conceder indulgencia plenaria a todos eclesiásticos, seculares y regulares, de uno y otro sexo, que obligados a rezar las horas canónicas las que haya y consigan, solo con la diligencia de rezar este propio oficio de Nuestro Señor Jesús Redentor despreciado y burlado vestido de una vestidura blanca como loco: y los que no pudieren por legitimo impedimento rezarlo todo, como recen la parte que pudieren. Por ejemplo, los Laudes solos, o solo las horas, o las Vísperas con Completes, también que hallan y consignan dicha indulgencia plenaria.

Que se digne conceder: indulgencia plenaria por modo de jubileo para el día de esta fiesta, y devoción, que es como dicho es el viernes tercero de cuaresma (y otro a que se traslade cuando este, o el siguiente cuarto estuvieren impedidos) desde las primeras Vísperas hasta puesto el sol de este señalado día, con facultad así mismo de exponer a la adoración publica de los fieles el Divinísimo Sacramento de la Eucaristía, o desde las primeras Vísperas hasta puesto el sol de otro día, o solo este día mismo de la fiesta: o solo al tiempo de la Misa cantada, según la posibilidad de las iglesias: en que confesando y comulgando y habiendo la oración que se acostumbra y se señala: todos los fieles de recepto de uno y otro sexo hallan y consignan dicha indulgencia por modo de jubileo, de suerte señor que se haga celebre este día de esta fiesta nueva y tierna devoción en toda esta América.

Que así mismo se digne la piedad, celo y caridad de Vuestra Santidad de conceder todo lo dicho para todas y cada una de las iglesias de este Reino de las Indias Occidentales con mas que pedimos para el alivio y descanso de las almas de los fieles difuntos del purgatorio, y es que estas indulgencias se les puedan aplicar por modo de sufragio y que en este día esta fiesta (ahora sea en él; ahora para en el que se traslade) todos los altares de todas y cada una de las iglesias de esta América septentrional, sean de privilegio de alma para todos los sacerdotes, seculares y regulares que celebrasen la propia Misa de esta devoción a Nuestro Señor Jesús Redentor presentado y burlado como loco por Herodes.

Que todas estas gracias e indulgencias y privilegios sean perpetuos, y universal a todo este imperio de la América septentrional para que los pobrecitos indios que viven en sus remotos pueblos participen y gocen también de ellos ya que carecen de jubileo circular, y de gozar a menudo la presencia de Jesús Redentor Sacramentado expuesto a la adoración pública.

Por tanto: a Vuestra Santidad pedimos y suplicamos postradas con toda humildad y reverencia ante Sus SS. PP. se sirva decir nuestros piadosos ruegos y atender a nuestras rendidas suplicas teniéndolas por repetidas una y muchas veces para el fin de despachar y dar sus apostólicas letras concediendo en ellas cuanto le pedimos a honra y gloria de Dios Nuestro Señor y de la Pasión de su hijo Jesucristo, cuya memoria y recuerdo queremos que por este medio permanezca siempre entre todos los fieles hijos suyos y de Vuestra Santidad para que en sus corazones haga el fruto que deseamos.

Marina de San Francisco, Abadesa
María Gertrudis de San José, Vicaria
María Gertrudis de Guadalupe, Maestre de Consejo
Juana Estefanía del Señor San José, Definidora
María Hipólita de San José, Definidora
María Lucía del Señor San José, Definidora

Diego de Oviedo, Hymns, *Manual de ejercicios para los desagravios de Cristo*, 1705

Buscando voy cuidadosa	I am carefully looking for
un instrumento sonoro,	a sweet-sounding instrument,
en que cantaros mi pena,	on which to sing my sorrow to you,
soberano dueño hermoso.	oh, beautiful sovereign Lord.
Mas mirándoos, vida mía,	But after looking at you
en este monte tan solo,	so lonely in this hill, oh, life of mine,
aceptó mi amor herido,	my wounded love acquiesced
pulsar las cuerdas que noto.	to pluck the strings that I notice.
Harpado dueño del alma,	Lacerated[1] Lord of the soul,
a quien los juncos más broncos,	whom the roughest reeds
y a quien los clavos crueles	and whom the cruel nails
enclavijaron al tronco.	interlocked[2] to the log.
A cuyas tirantes cuerdas,	To whose taut strings
comience un eco sonoro,	may a sweet-sounding echo[3] begin,
que resonando en los cielos	that, resounding in heaven,
el sol se eclipsó devoto.	may a devout sun be eclipsed.
Cantó Dimas, humillado,	Humiliated, Dimas sung
aquel verso lastimoso:	that pitiful verse:
Domine, memento mei,	*Domine, memento mei,*[4]
a quien sigo yo lloroso.	to whom I tearfully follow.
domine, memento mei,	*Domine, memento mei,*
amable, dueño piadoso,	gentle, compassionate Lord,
en ti, cantando, y a ti	I kneel at the foot of the cross,
al pie de la cruz me postro.	singing in you and to you.
Con vuestra licencia, Señor,	With your permission, Lord,
purificando mis labios,	I praise you in atonement
os alabo en desagravios,	purifying my lips
de agravios del pecador.	from the wrongs of the sinner.
Oíd mis voces, Señor,	Listen to my calls,[5] Lord,
lleguen hasta vos los ecos.	may the echoes[6] reach to you.
En el huerto está Jesús	Jesus is in the orchard
pegado su rostro al suelo,	with his face close to the ground,
sudando arroyos de sangre,	sweating streams of blood,
Cercado de desconsuelos.	surrounded by despair.
Alma, acompaña a tu Dios,	Soul, accompany your God,
lastímate del cordero,	and show pity for the lamb,
que porque vivas padece	for he suffers unspeakable torments
tan indecibles tormentos.	so that you may live.

Han culpado al inocente,
alma vil, por tus delitos,
no así le dejes matar,
Vuelve, alma, por tu Cristo.
Jueces, oídme, yo soy
el que peco, no mi Cristo:
dejadle libre, matadme,
míos son esos delitos.

They have blamed the innocent,
vile soul, because of your offenses;
do not let them kill him like that,
come back, soul, for your Christ.
Judges, listen to me, I am
the one who sins, not my Christ:
let him go free, kill me,
these trespasses are mine.

Rompe, esposo de mi vida,
los lazos del alma, rompe,
pues el amor no nos une,
a aquesse [sic] mármol informe.
¿Quien te despoja, mi Dios?
y para que a ti te azoten,
te amarran a una columna
aquellos crueles sayones.

Husband of my life, break
the bonds of the soul, break [them],
for love does not unite us
to that shapeless marble.
Who has stripped you, my God?
and those cruel executioners
tie you to a column
so that you may be beaten.

Rosa es ya Dios entre espinas,
que de espinas coronado,
es doctor de los dolores,
a fuer del sangriento grado.
Los juncos por más agudos,
sus dos sienes taladrando,
el víctor le dieron todos,
tanta ciencia laureando.

God is a rose among thorns,
for he is a doctor of sorrows
crowned by thorns
out of the bloody step[7].
The reeds, being sharper,
boring both his temples,
everyone cheered him,
celebrating so much wisdom.

Ángeles del cielo,
cantad con regocijo;
bendito sea Dios,
sea Dios bendito.

Angels of heaven,
sing with joy;
blessed be God,
God be blessed.

Sentenciado a muerte va,
alma, tu amante Jesús
con el peso de la cruz,
con ella no puede ya.
Por el suelo ensangrentado,
le puedes, alma, seguir,
también oirás su gemir
lastimoso, y ya cansado.

Your lover Jesus sentenced to death walks
carrying the weight
of the cross, oh soul,
and he can no longer stand it.
Soul, you can follow him
through the bloody ground,
and you will also hear
his pitiful and weary groaning.

Tremolando las banderas,
clarines roncos rompiendo
el aire, al aire levantan
el venturoso madero.
Corazón, si tienes alas,
las alas bate, rompiendo
el pecho donde asistieres,
a la vista de este objeto
el sol se cubre de luto,
la luna, y el firmamento:
tocan a pena los montes,
sus peñascos deshaciendo.

Waving the flags,
gruff bugles breaking
the air hoist the fortunate
piece of wood up in the air.
Heart, if you have wings,
flap those wings, breaking
the breast where you may dwell.
In the view of this object,
the sun is mourning
the moon and the firmament:
they move the mountains to pity
by undoing their rocks.

Ya tu Dios está en el campo,	Now your God is in the field
sus enemigos venciendo,	defeating his enemies,
acompáñale, criatura,	go to him, creature,
armada de sentimiento.	clad in feeling.
Parad potencias, parad,	Stop, nations[8], stop,
que ya es tiempo de sosiego,	for it is now time for peace,
pues que ya vuestro hacedor	because your maker
está clavado en el leño.	is nailed to the wood.
Muerto le miro, y me admire,	I looked at him dead, and I was amazed
de que con él no me muero,	to find that I do not die together with him,
más si gusta de que pene,	though if it pleases him that I repent,
quiero darle gusto en ello.	I want to please him in that.
A la sombra del árbol,	In the shadow of the tree,
donde mi dueño	where my lord
por mi bien reposa,	rests for my well-being,
guardaré su sueño.	I will watch his sleep.
¡Ay vida muerta!	Oh, dead life!
¡Ay mi Dios! ¿que es esto?	Oh, my God! What is this?
En los brazos de su madre,	In the arms of his mother
hallarás, alma, a tu esposo,	you will find your husband, oh soul,
o poco sientes su muerte,	oh you suffer little by his death,
o tu amor es tibio, y poco	oh your love is lukewarm and little.
si allí la vida no pierdes,	If you do not lose your life there,
no correspondes piadoso,	you are not corresponding piously,
más si quiera compasivo,	but you want to be compassionate,
a su madre di lloroso:	weeping, tell to his mother:
Madre, la más afligida,	Mother, the most sorrowful,
aquí os ofrezco mi vida,	here I offer my life to you,
para padecer con vos,	to suffer with you,
Madre, muramos los dos.	Mother, let us both die.
¡Ay, María soberana!	Oh, sovereign Mary!
¿Quien os ha robado el alma?	Who has stolen your soul?
Sálvete Dios, reyna, y madre	May God hail you, queen and mother
de misericordia, y vida,	of mercy and life,
y dulzura conocida,	and known sweetness,
esperanza firme nuestra.	our steadfast hope.
Dios te salve, fiel maestra	May God hail you, faithful master
de gracias, a ti llamamos	of grace, to you do we cry,
los desterrados, que estamos	poor banished that we are,
hijos de Eva en este valle	in this valley of tears,
de lágrimas, sin que halle	we the children of Eve, with a soul
el alma consuelo en él:	that cannot take comfort in him:
ea, pues, Señora, fiel	Then, oh Lady, faithful
abogada nuestra, y madre,	advocate of us, and mother,
hija del eterno padre,	daughter of the eternal Father,
vuelve a nosotros, Señora,	oh Lady, turn your eyes toward us,
tus ojos, que el cielo adora	that heaven so piously adores:
tan piadosos: y despúes	and then, after
de este valle, donde es	this valley, where all

todo gemir, y llorar,
danos el rico collar
de precio, y valor infinito,
fruto adorado, y bendito
de tu vientre: ¡O clemente!
Piadosa Judith, valiente,
dulce, misericordiosa,
siempre virgen, y hermosa
más que el cielo, muéstranos
a Jesús, madre de Dios
para que seamos dignos
de los dones peregrinos,
de las promesas que el bien nos han de
alcanzar.
Amén.

is sighing and weeping,
give to us the rich necklace
of infinite price and worth,
the beloved and blessed fruit
of your womb: Oh clement!
Pious Judith, brave,
sweet, merciful,
always virgin,
and more beautiful than heaven,
show Jesus to us, mother of God,
so that we may be made worthy
of the rare gifts,
of the promises that the good may
bring to us.
Amen.

Notes

Preface

* Ana Louise Keating defines Gloria Anzaldúa's *autohistoria-teoría* as a "theory developed by Anzaldúa to describe a relational form of autobiographical writing that includes both life story and self-reflection on this storytelling process. Writers of autohistoria-teoría blend their cultural and personal biographies with memoir, history, storytelling, myth, and/or other forms of theorizing. By doing so, they create interwoven individual and collective identities. Personal experiences—revised and in other ways redrawn—become a lens with which to reread and rewrite existing cultural stories. Through this lens, Anzaldúa and other autohistoria-teorístas expose the limitations in the existing paradigms and create new stories of healing, self-growth, cultural critique, and individual/collective transformation." In *The Gloria Anzaldúa Reader*, 319.

1. Sacramental learning consists of the formal and informal religious instruction offered by the Catholic Church. Since the Second Vatican Council, formal Roman Catholic religious instruction has typically consisted of serving in various unpaid roles for the liturgies, such as assisting in the distribution of communion or performing the readings at Mass, regular confession, and attending catechism classes offered to youth in preparation for the sacraments of Penance, Eucharist, and Confirmation. Similarly, couples attend pre-matrimonial and pre-baptismal lessons before they receive the sacrament of Matrimony and present their children for Baptism, respectively. Informal learning takes place in social settings, with clergy and nuns often the guests of honor around dinner and coffee tables. Here, I am extending Jessica L. Delgado's concept of sacramental learning, through which she addresses the experiences of early modern New Spanish laywomen with the sacraments of Penance and the Eucharist, and in laywomen's social interactions and negotiations with male clergy. See Delgado, *Laywomen and the Making of Colonial Catholicism*, 33–72. Kathleen Ann Myers refers specifically to confession as part of a "sacramental process" in *Neither Saints nor Sinners*, 11. See also Lavrin, *Brides of Christ*, 7.

Introduction

1. Vallarta, *Luz que guía al camino*, folio 164r.
2. Delgado, *Laywomen*, 33–72. The seven sacraments are Baptism, Communion, Penance (confession), Confirmation, Matrimony, Extreme Unction, and Holy Orders. See Carranza de la Miranda, *Comentarios del reverendísimo*, 341. On sacramental learning specifically targeted toward indoctrinating children to avoid lewdness in the

early modern Hispanic Church, see Lavrin, "The Erotic as Lewdness," 36. For more on the Church's sacraments and their development, see Rubin, "Sacramental Life."

3. Wobeser, *Sor Juana ante la muerte*, 50–54.

4. Lundberg, *Mission and Ecstasy*, 91 and 100–105; Wobeser, *Sor Juana ante la muerte*, 54.

5. Lundberg, *Mission and Ecstasy*, 120–126.

6. While discerning her calling to the convent life, María de San José (1656–1719), who eventually became an Augustinian nun in Puebla's Santa Mónica convent, tells of similar conversations with a convent abbess and with her sister, who was a professed nun in the San Jerónimo convent. See Myers and Powell, *Wild Country Out in the Garden*, 40–45.

7. Lavrin, *Brides of Christ*, 5.

8. Waisman, *Una historia de la música colonial hispanoamericana*, 45.

9. Vallarta, *Luz que guía al camino*, folio 164r.

10. Santos Morales and Arroyo González, *Las monjas dominicas*, 370.

11. The imitation of Christ has its roots in the martyrdom of the early saints. See Kieckhefer, "Imitators of Christ," 11–12.

12. By "early modern," I refer to the period roughly dating from 1500 to 1800. See Owens and Mangan, *Women of the Iberian Atlantic*, 1; Filippi and Noone, *Listening to Early Modern Catholicism*, 1–3. In addition to Filippi and Noone's volume, other works attending to the sounds of the post-Tridentine world (i.e., the Catholic Church's affairs after the Council of Trent), particularly sacred sounds in cities, include Baker and Knighton, *Music and Urban Society*; Dell'Antonio, *Listening as Spiritual Practice*; Fisher, *Music, Piety, and Propaganda*; Kendrick, *The Sounds of Milan*; Knighton and Mazuela-Anguita, *Hearing the City in Early Modern Europe*; Monson, "The Council of Trent Revisited." There is a lacuna in scholarship on the history of early modern women's music making more broadly, not just in Latin America, owing to the dearth of sources from non-church settings. See Muriel and Llédias, *Musica en las instituciones femeninas novohispanas*, 33–36.

13. The scarcity of convent sources stems from the effects of the nineteenth-century Mexican War of Reform (1857–1861), which annihilated many New Spanish convent music manuscripts and displaced others. Tovar, *La Ciudad de México*, 70; Schleifer, "The Mexican Choirbooks," 17. See also Waisman, *Una historia de la música colonial hispanoamericana*, 15.

14. Mexico City, the capital of New Spain, alone had twenty-two convents, all established before 1811. See Lavrin, *Brides of Christ*, 1, 377.

15. For Guadalajara, see Rivera y San Román, *Noticias históricas*, 1–37; Swain, "One Thousand Sisters," 269. For Querétaro, see Gunnarsdóttir, *Mexican Karismata*, 36. For San Miguel el Grande, see Chowning, *Rebellious Nuns*, 172–173.

16. The quote is from Lavrin, *Brides of Christ*, 4–5. See also Waisman, *Una historia de la música colonial hispanoamericana*, 45.

17. On the Encarnación's choirbooks, including transcriptions of some of the works, see Schleifer, "The Mexican Choirbooks." For the Santa Inés repertory, see Bal y Gay, *El códice del Convento del Carmen*. On the Concepción profession book, see Loreto López, *Tota pulchra*, 87–138; there is brief mention of this convent's choirbook with

chant for the Office (it is an antiphoner) at 133–134. Some transcriptions of the Santísima Trinidad repertory can be found in Stevenson, *Christmas Music From Baroque Mexico* and in Muriel and Lledías, *Música en las instituciones femeninas novohispanas*. Various publications on individual aspects of the Santísima Trinidad repertory have culminated in the recent cataloguing efforts by several CENIDIM researchers and their incorporation of sources attesting to the collection's origins and context: Tello, Hurtado, Morales, and Pérez, *Colección Sánchez Garza*, 217–262. It conveniently summarizes some of the initial work on the collection pioneered by Robert Stevenson and E. Thomas Stanford. See also Morales Abril, "Tres siglos de música litúrgica en la Colección Sánchez Garza"; Morales Abril, "*Serenísima una noche*," 18–21; Pérez Ruiz, "La Colección Sánchez Garza"; Tello, "La capilla musical del Convento de la Santísima Trinidad"; Tello, "Músicos ruiseñores." On Regina Coeli, see Johnson, *Cuaderno de tonos*.

18. The catalog and study by Tello et al. is the closest to a microhistorical account of the Santísima Trinidad convent's musical practices, which coincide with other Spanish and New Spanish trends, most notably the influence of Italian music by the eighteenth century. See Tello et al., *Colección Sánchez Garza*, 59. On the broader phenomenon of the Italianization of musical practices in eighteenth-century New Spain, see Davies, "The Italianized Frontier"; Ramos-Kittrell, *Playing in the Cathedral*, chapter 4. There were precedents for Italian influence on Spanish music in previous centuries as well. See Carreras and Fenlon, *Polychoralities*.

19. For instance, much of the contents in historian Rosalva Loreto López's monograph *Tota pulchra*, on the history of Puebla's Concepción convent, derive from materials held by the nuns currently living in that cloister, who only share their archival material with Loreto López. Their personal ceremonial book, not known about before Loreto López's book, contains notated chant for convent professions. Loreto López, *Tota pulchra*, 87–138. I am very grateful to Loreto López for providing me with pictures of the ceremonial.

20. Mónica Díaz (*Indigenous Writings*, 187) has described the zealous guardianship the contemporary nuns at the Corpus Christi convent have exhibited over their archival materials. Puebla's cathedral archive has remained closed to scholars for over a decade now. Even the Mexico City cathedral archive, now considered one of the most accessible archives to historians and musicologists, was hardly accessible to scholars before 1995. See Krutitskaya, *Los villancicos que se cantaron en la catedral*, 7–8.

21. See, for example, the circumstance regarding four villancicos described by Marín López and Zambrano in "¡*Ay, qué dolor!* (1701) de Antonio de Salazar," 573.

22. On the Santísima Trinidad repertory, see Tello et al., *Colección Sánchez Garza*, 18. The Encarnación choirbooks were acquired by American collectors at the end of the nineteenth century. See Schleifer, "The Mexican Choirbooks," 2–3. It is tempting to envision such purchases of material culture as being in line with the overall Mexican divestment of its land and labor force, among other things, to American and other foreign investors during the regime of President Porfirio Díaz. See the introduction to Lytle, *Bad Mexicans*. The tradition of Mexican book and manuscript sales to foreign collectors, however, predates the Porfiriato by a few decades, as Hubert Howe Bancroft rhapsodized in "From Bibliopolist to Bibliophile," 19 and 27.

23. In the context of eighteenth-century opera seria, Martha Feldman refers to aria scores as templates for a convention that had more flexibility than the written notes suggest; *Opera and Sovereignty*, 42–43. Given that we know so little about performance practice in the convents from where the music manuscripts came, I find the term "template" useful to avoid making any assumptions about how the music was executed, especially regarding the performance of villancicos and polyphony. Drew Davies suggests the need to do more research on villancico performance practice; "Introduction," xv. Regarding the scarcity of notated music from convents, see also Waisman, *Una historia de la música colonial hispanoamericana*, 307. The lack of surviving sources of notated music performed by nuns or lay women is not unique to New Spain and should not dissuade scholars from attempting to recover women's musical expressions from the past, as Stras would suggest in *Women and Music*, 36.

24. Kirk, *Convent Life in Colonial Mexico*, 1–7; Lavrin, *Brides of Christ*, 5; Myers, *Wild Country Out in the Garden*, xix; Waisman, 45. There is no doubt that research in South American archives, although outside the scope of this project, will also prove fruitful for expanding the discourse on women's contributions to Latin American music history, as demonstrated by a recent chapter on convent music from colonial Córdoba, Argentina. See Restiffo, "Ilustración, polifonía e identidad en Santa Catalina de Siena." See also Waisman, 44–46, 160–167, 307–311.

25. On the continuation of earlier colonial customs in nineteenth-century New Spain and independent Mexico, see Marín López, "El universo musical mexicano," 28; Waisman, 14. They echo Daniele Filippi's call for a *longue durée* approach when attending to the soundscape of early modern Catholicism, in "Catechismum modulans docebat," 144–147. Initial studies on late eighteenth-century and early nineteenth-century music pedagogy from Mexico City's Colegio de Belem and Colegio de San Ignacio de Loyola (schools for young women) have begun to expand the discourse on women's music in exciting directions while bridging the temporal gap between early modernity and modernity, coinciding with the end of Spanish colonial rule in New Spain. These studies will more fully inform our understanding of the region's diverse sonorities and of New Spanish music education. For a preliminary investigation into both convent and colegio music in Mexico, see Muriel and Lledías, *Música en las instituciones femeninas novohispanas*; Waisman, 45–46. Through the lens of villancico analysis, see Swadley, "The Villancico in New Spain 1650–1750," 266–305; see also Swadley, "Educating the American Girls." Faith Lanam's dissertation is the first full-length critical examination of the robust conservatory-like curriculum that young women encountered in the colegios; Lanam, "El Colegio de San Miguel de Belem." El Colegio de la Caridad in Mexico City also provided music training for young women; see Delgado, *Laywomen*, 153–155. On the repertory for the Colegio de Santa Rosa de Valladolid (present-day Morelia), see Bernal Jiménez, *El archivo musical del Colegio de Santa Rosa*. It is not clear whether any of the music from this colegio's collection was left by the Dominican nuns who formerly inhabited the building and transferred to a new cloister elsewhere in the city in 1738. On the transfer of the nuns, see Lavrin, *Brides of Christ*, 102–103. I echo Jesús Ramos-Kittrell's call for more research on

New Spanish music education; *Playing in the Cathedral*, 47. From the perspective of convents in Spain, Soterraña Aguirre Rincón (*Un manuscrito para un convento*, 103) attests to nuns' music education being obtained as a learn-by-doing process in the choir led by the choir mistresses, rather than in formal classroom instruction. This type of acquisition of musical skill likely included the memorization of texts before learning the notes (*solfas*).

26. Calderón de la Barca, *Life in Mexico*, 208. Even Catholics as early as the mid-eighteenth century were critical of the lifestyle in some New Spanish convents. See Chowning, *Rebellious Nuns*, 8. On unmodern places and their seeming inferiority, see Tanaka, *History Without Chronology*, 30.

27. Calderón de la Barca's journaling is consistent with other nineteenth-century histories claiming that the devotions and customs of nuns' convents lasted hundreds of years. See Ramírez Aparicio, *Los conventos suprimidos en México*, 417. See also Gunnarsdottir, "Una monja barroca en el México ilustrado," 373–374. Very recent studies on textual sources for New Spanish convent celebrations spanning the seventeenth through the nineteenth centuries share a common epistemological thread that Lavrín and Loreto López have denoted "teatralidad/ theatricality," in *El universo de la teatralidad conventual*, 15.

28. Tanaka, *History Without Chronology*, 3. On women's time, see Kristeva, "Women's Time."

29. Tanaka draws from Michel de Certeau's analysis of early modern mystical experience to support the decentering of chronological time, which itself debased mysticism during the Enlightenment. See *History Without Chronology*, 10–18.

30. Myers, *Word from New Spain*, 20–21; Ross, *The Baroque Narrative*, 163–165.

31. See Jaffary, *False Mystics*, 38–40.

32. Tanaka, *History Without Chronology*, 8.

33. Ramos-Kittrell succinctly summarizes the undertakings of New Spanish music scholarship from the first half of the twentieth century to the present, while also contributing to the scholarship on cathedrals, in *Playing in the Cathedral*, chapter 1 in particular. For more on cathedrals, see Davies, "The Italianized Frontier"; Enríquez Rubio et al., *Catálogo de obras de música*; Enríquez Rubio, *De música y cultura*; Kelsey and Kelsey, *Inventario*; Lehmann Goldman, "The Matins Responsory"; Marín López, "Música y músicos entre dos mundos"; Marín López, "Música local e internacional"; Morales Abril, "La música en la catedral de Puebla"; Tello, *Archivo musical de la Catedral de Oaxaca*; Turrent, *Autoridad, solemnidad y actores musicales*; Vilar-Payá, "Lo histórico y lo cotidiano." See also Marín López, *Músicas colonials a debate*, chapters 1–3, 5–6, 12, and 20. On mission music, see Bermúdez, "Sounds from Fortresses of Faith"; Candelaria, "Music and Pageantry"; "Bernardino de Sahagún's *Psalmodia*"; Dutcher Mann, *The Power of Song and Dance*; Latour, "Musical Encounters in Tenochtitlàn"; Ros-Fábregas, "'Imagine All the People'"; Russell, *From Serra to Sancho*. See also Baker, *Imposing Harmony*; Baker and Knighton, *Music and Urban Society*; Cashner, "Faith, Hearing, and the Power of Music"; Chávez Bárcenas, "Singing in the City of the Angels"; Illari, "Polychoral Culture"; Irving, *Colonial Counterpoint*; Vera, *The Sweet Penance of Music*, chapter 1.

34. Aguirre Rincón, *Un manuscrito para un convento*; Baade, "Music and Music-Making in Female Monasteries"; Chaves de Tobar, "La vida musical en los conventos femeninos de Alba de Tormes"; Fiore, "Musica nelle istituzioni religiose"; Gémbero Ustárroz, "*De rosas cercada*"; Glixon, *Mirrors of Heaven*; Hathaway, "Cloister, Court and City"; Hathaway, 'Music Charms the Senses"; Hills, *Invisible City*; "Veiling the Voice"; Kendrick, *Celestial Sirens*; Mazuela-Anguita, "La vida musical"; "Música conventual"; Monson, *Disembodied Voices*; Reardon, *Holy Concord*; Stras, *Women and Music*. For convent music in Vienna, see Page, *Convent Music and Politics*. On Bavarian convents, see Fisher, *Music, Piety, and Propaganda*, 63–74, 133–140.

35. The phenomenon of music circulation—not just the works of individual composers, but also music volumes pertaining to institutions (cathedral choirbooks, for example)—has generated scholarship emphasizing transfer and exchange across the early modern and nineteenth-century Hispanic and Lusophone world. See Marín López, *Músicas coloniales a debate*.

36. Tello et al., *Colección Sánchez Garza*, 269. Marín-López and Zambrano, for example, call the career trajectory of Antonio de Salazar (ca. 1650–1715) a type of *cursus honorum*, in which he ended up in the prestigious role of Mexico City cathedral chapel master after preceding posts in Puebla Cathedral and the Jesús Nazareno parish. See Marín-López and Zambrano, "¡*Ay, qué dolor*! (1701) de Antonio de Salazar," 571–572. In Cuzco, it was musicians from the local seminary who assisted convents with obtaining music and musical training. See Baker, *Imposing Harmony*, 120.

37. Through *obvenciones*, cathedral musicians received honorariums for performing in convents and other churches around Mexico City. See Ramos-Kittrell, *Playing in the Cathedral*, 45, 185.

38. Ramos-Kittrell (160–161) refers to the cathedral musicians' affiliations with the Capuchin convent/nuns in the mid-eighteenth century, which suggests it was the San Felipe de Jesús convent, since this was the only Capuchin convent in the city at the time. It is not clear what musical resources, if any, the San Felipe nuns had. See also Lavrin, *Brides of Christ*, 359–361; Salmeron, *Vida de la venerable Madre Isabel*, 117r; Tello et al., *Colección Sánchez Garza*, 266–267. Diana Swain draws on the chronicle of Sister María de las Llagas de Cristo Rivera y San Román, a nun whose life straddled the nineteenth and twentieth centuries and who survived the exclaustration during the 1860s, to reveal numerous musical continuities taking place in Guadalajara's Santa María de Gracia convent, not least the participation of cathedral musicians in nuns' professions. See Swain, "One Thousand Sisters," 269; Rivera y San Román, *Noticias históricas*, 1–37. The founding of new convents also called for cathedral musicians, as did major convent feast days. See Gómez de la Parra, *Fundación y primero siglo*, 56, 150; Mariana de la Encarnación, *Relación de la fundación*, 56. On the commissioning of musicians for special feasts across churches and convents in seventeenth-century Madrid, see Hathaway, "Cloister, Court and City," 212. For a study on this phenomenon across the broader region of Castille, see Baade, "Music and Music-Making in Female Monasteries," 111–112. See also Aguirre Rincón, *Un manuscrito para un convento*, 105–106.

39. Zavaleta, *Copia de la carta*, 23, 37.

40. Tello et al., *Colección Sánchez Garza*, 267; Waisman, *Una historia de la música colonial hispanoamericana*, 45–46, 308–309.

41. Centro de Estudios de Historia de México, Fundación Carlos Slim (CEHM), Documento 254, foja 1, rollo 4, fol. 1.
42. Tello et al., 268–271; Favila, "The Sound of Profession Ceremonies," 144–153.
43. On the benefits of convent dowry waivers for musicians in Cuzco, see Baker, *Imposing Harmony*, 121–123.
44. "Se ha dedicado con tesón al aprovechamiento de las niñas pobres que desean entrarse religiosas a título de músicas." In Archivo del Cabildo Catedralicio de la Ciudad de México (ACCMM), Correspondencia, Caja 24, Expediente 2. Transcribed in Marín López, "Música y músicos entre dos mundos," vol. 3, 143–145. Aguila does not appear to have been promoted. On the career path for musicians in the cathedral, see Ramos-Kittrell, *Playing in the Cathedral*, 63–64.
45. Like David McCreery, I consider the activities of cloistered nuns as contributing to the broader history of work and labor in Latin America. See McCreery, *The Sweat of Their Brow*, 95–96. Alejandro Vera has also discussed the labor involved in nuns' liturgical music making in Santiago de Chile; *The Sweet Penance of Music*, 2.
46. Burns, *Colonial Habits*, 4. I agree with Ramos-Kittrell (*Playing in the Cathedral*, 165) in referring to the musical activities of the *música religiosa* (musician nun) as work. The greatest impact that nuns had on the New Spanish economy, however, derives from much of the city property owned and rented out by the convents. See Lavrin, "Role of the Nunneries," 371–393. More broadly, Lavrin refers to convents as melting pots for the "everyday and spiritual" (lo cotidiano y lo espiritual), in "Cotidianidad y espiritualidad en la vida conventual," 240.
47. These relationships between male musicians and nun musicians have driven scholarship on convent music from broader colonial Latin America, primarily in the form of book chapters and articles. See, for example, Baker, *Imposing Harmony*, chapter 3; "Music in the Convents and Monasteries of Colonial Cuzco"; Cadenas García, "La música en la micro-sociedad 'espiritual' de mujeres mantuanas"; "Música, fiestas y ceremonias en el Convento de la Inmaculada Concepción de Caracas"; Cadenas, "Formación, adiestramiento y funcionalidad musical en Caracas"; Campos Olivares, "La práctica musical en el Convento de San José"; Estenssoro, "Música y fiestas en los monasterios de monjas limeños. Siglos XVII y XVIII"; *Música y sociedad coloniales*, chapter 1; Favila, "The Sound of Profession Ceremonies"; Lange, "Convento de San Lorenzo de Nuestra Señora de La Merced"; Morales Abril, "Tres siglos de música litúrgica"; "*Serenísima una noche*"; Muriel and Lledías, *La música en las instituciones femeninas*, chapter 5; Pérez Ruiz, "La Colección Sánchez Garza"; Restiffo, "Ilustración, polifonía e identidad en Santa Catalina de Siena"; Salazar Simarro, "Música y coro en el convento de Jesús María de México"; Swadley, "Educating the American Girls"; Tello, "La capilla musical del Convento de la Santísima Trinidad"; "Monjas y música"; "Músicos ruiseñores"; Tello et.al., *Colección Sánchez Garza*, chapters 2 and 3; Toquica and Restrepo, "Las canciones del coro alto"; Torres Vega, "Música en los espacios conventuales femeninos"; Vera, *The Sweet Penance of Music*, chapter 2; "Transcending the Walls of the Churches." Some relevant dissertations include Favila, "Music and Devotion"; Pedrotti, "La música religiosa en Córdoba del Tucumán"; Schleifer, "The Mexican Choirbooks"; Swadley, "The Villancico in New Spain," especially chapter 8.

48. Jaffary, *False Mystics*, 6–7.

49. Martínez, *Genealogical Fictions*, 20. See also Ramos-Kittrell, *Playing in the Cathedral*, 61–67.

50. O'Hara, *A Flock Divided*, 4.

51. O'Hara, 4.

52. Martínez, *Genealogical Fictions*, 20–21, 176; O'Hara, *A Flock Divided*, 3–4; Jaffary, *False Mystics*, 6–7.

53. Martínez, chapter 8; Cope, *The Limits of Racial Domination*, 20–21. This demographic of mixed-race people grew throughout the seventeenth century and represented some 25 percent of New Spain's population by the eighteenth century. See Seed, *To Love, Honor, and Obey*, 25; Jaffary, *False Mystics*, 49–52.

54. Jesus Ramos-Kittrell has probed cathedral musicians' attempts to distance themselves from racialized categories through illusive claims to "Spanishness," which resulted in certain men being given access to local designations of decency and quality, on account of fulfilling their musical aspirations. See Ramos-Kittrell, *Playing in the Cathedral*, 64, 167–170.

55. See, for example, Genovesi, *Carta*, 5. See also Lavrin, *Brides of Christ*, 21–23, 70, 209. On the social status of virginity, see Lavrin, *Sexuality and Marriage in Colonial Latin America*, 10–12.

56. Myers, *A Wild Country*, 270.

57. Delgado, *Laywomen*, 141.

58. Delgado, *Laywomen*, 141. See also Lavrin, *Brides of Christ*, 20–21; Muriel, *Cultura femenina novohispana*, 433–434; Myers, *Neither Saints nor Sinners*, 11.

59. There was also a hierarchy among the convent servant class. See Lavrin, *Brides of Christ*, 160–170; Van Deusen, *The Souls of Purgatory*, 27–31.

60. Noble indigenous women were thought to be more intellectually capable of becoming nuns than their lower-class counterparts, according to Church leaders. In addition, limiting admission to noble women was for practical purposes: there were many indigenous women who wanted to become nuns, and space was limited in the convents. See Díaz, *Indigenous Writings*, 7–8. See also Holler, *Escogidas Plantas*, 5–7; Lavrin, *Brides of Christ*, 20, 244–274. In Peru, the circumstances were much different, allowing noble indigenous women to profess as nuns and mestizas to profess as white-veil nuns since the sixteenth century, much sooner than in New Spain. See Burns, *Colonial Habits*, chapter 1.

61. Lavrin, *Brides of Christ*, 21; Jaffary, *False Mystics*, 39.

62. Jean Franco has identified a similar liminality, arguing that white women in New Spain were "at once privileged and devalued"; *Plotting Women*, xiii–xiv. Díaz considers the elite indigenous nuns of the Corpus Christi convent subalterns in the Spivakian sense; *Indigenous Writings*, 1–2. Alicia Gaspar de Alba refers to all women in New Spain, including white, Spanish *criollas*, as subaltern. Drawing on Alan Trueblood's work, Gaspar de Alba claims, "Like the land and the indigenous people, women were taken, claimed, owned, exchanged, pillaged, conquered, silenced, dispossessed of their own destinies"; *[Un]framing the "Bad Woman"*, 50. On applying the label of subaltern to the music of colonial Latin American composers because of their exclusion from the

Western European canon, see Waisman, "Subalternidad en musicas novohispanas." These recent studies clearly point to a hierarchy within subalternity, beyond the scope of this book, that should be examined more thoroughly.

63. Irving, *Colonial Counterpoint*, 3–7.

64. Bohlman, "Where They Came From," 173.

65. Franco, *Plotting Women*, 5–7. Sor Juana Inés de la Cruz's position between privilege and subjugation, and also between Mexican and peninsular writer, is referred to as "a paradoxical existence" in Gaspar de Alba, *[Un]Framing the "Bad Woman"*, 52.

66. Franco, *Plotting Women*, 23.

67. Gaspar de Alba, *[Un]Framing the "Bad Woman"*, 50. Finley (*Hearing Voices*, 157) and Webb (*The Divine Voice*, 69) have considered the broader history of women's oppression through silencing.

68. The conflicts that scholars of New Spanish convent culture attend to most frequently are attributed to the eighteenth-century Bourbon reforms, which aimed at bringing calced convents in line with the common lifestyle ("vida común") of the discalced orders. To my knowledge, the common lifestyle, enforced haphazardly throughout New Spanish convents, did not affect convent liturgical music. See Chowning, *Rebellious Nuns*; Kirk, *Convent Life in Colonial Mexico*, chapter 4; Lavrin, *Brides of Christ*, chapter 9. On other convent conflicts, see Chowning, "Talking Back"; Myers, *A Wild Country*, 274–276. For conflicts in Italian convents, see Monson, *Nuns Behaving Badly* and *Divas in the Convent*; Glixon, *Mirrors of Heaven*.

69. Gaspar de Alba, *[Un]Framing the "Bad Woman"*, 10. Gisela von Wobeser characterizes Sor Juana as obsessed with salvation, a product of her time, in *Sor Juana ante la muerte*, 44–55.

70. Quoted in Gaspar de Alba, *[Un]Framing the "Bad Woman"*, 60.

71. At the June 2019 "Atlantic Crossings" conference, hosted by Boston University's Center for Early Music Studies, scholars of various marginalized musics and musicians highlighted the critical need to diversify the sources and archives for (ethno)musicological inquiry into early modern soundscapes. The conference considered "early music" as broadly as possible to include music from the time of the first arrival of Europeans on the American continent through the times in which chattel slavery prevailed, specified by the call for papers on topics dating from 1492 through the long eighteenth century. For a review of the conference, see Vera, "Atlantic Crossings," 151–154. From the perspective of women's history, Perry, Chaudhuri, and Katz similarly stress the range of sources and "creativity" needed to investigate "hard-to-research subjects"; *Contesting Archives*, xv.

72. Vallarta, *Luz que guía al camino*, folio 135v.

73. See also Jaffary, *False Mystics*, 28–29.

74. On discourses of music in Victorian literature, see Solie, *Music in Other Words*, 45.

75. Taylor, *The Archive and the Repertoire*, 18–20.

76. Music manuscripts can hold "artifactual traces of dynamic phenomena in lived time," according to Feldman, in *Opera and Sovereignty*, 42.

77. In *Music and Urban Society in Colonial Latin America*, Geoffrey Baker notes the gap in Latin American music history resulting from the scholarly omission of women's

contributions to the study of urban soundscapes. Since women's convents were primarily located in cities, *Immaculate Sounds* begins to fill that void, which historians have long sought to integrate in their work on urban class, gender, race, mobility, and professionalism, this latter item I take to mean work. The topic of women's music in colonial Latin America—from the perspective of nuns' convents—is touched on briefly within studies of the broader musical activities of Lima and Santiago de Chile within Baker and Knighton's monumental volume, *Music and Urban Society*. See Knighton, "Music and Ritual in Urban Spaces"; Vera, "Transcending the Walls of the Church." See also Baker, *Imposing Harmony*, chapter 3. Convent music forms part of the broader "polychoral culture" of La Plata, as discussed in Illari, "Polychoral Culture," 27–29, 255, 304, 378, 390, 397. Baker, "The Resounding City," 20. Elsewhere, Baker notes that women's convents have been on the margins of Spanish and English musicological discourse, echoing Burns' remarks on the place of convents in colonial historiography. See Baker, *Imposing Harmony*, 260; Burns, *Colonial Habits*, 1.

78. Full records of music-related situations from a convent needing legal adjudication with the aid of a notary are often missing folios and follow-up correspondences. The majority of these extant records come from Mexico City's Archivo General de la Nación, where many convent sources were deposited after the exclaustration in the 1860s, if they were not completely destroyed by the Wars of Reform. Teresa de Tovar notes that paper records were often used to make explosives, as kindling, or even to wrap food. Books were often destroyed for such purposes as well. See Tovar, *La Ciudad de México*, 70; Lavrin, *Brides of Christ*, 5; Ross, *The Baroque Narrative*, 7–8. In commenting on the limited sources for notated music in Spanish convents, Aguirre Rincón notes that in addition to loss attributed to destruction, in some cases where convents cultivated oral traditions, they would simply request music from the composers for one-time use or memorization, then return it. They also improvised. See Aguirre-Rincón, *Un manuscrito para un convento*, 108–111.

79. Arenal and Schlau, *Untold Sisters*, 1–2. The literature is too extensive to list exhaustively here, but on Teresa of Ávila see, for example, Pérez-Romero, *Subversion and Liberation*; Weber, *Teresa of Avila and the Rhetoric of Femininity*. On María de Ágreda see Colahan, *The Visions of Sor María de Ágreda*; Fedewa, *María of Ágreda*. On Sor Juana Inés see Finley, *Hearing Voices*; Gaspar de Alba, *[Un]framing the "Bad Woman"*; Kirk, *Convent Life in Colonial Mexico*, chapter 5; *Sor Juana Inés de la Cruz*; Lavrin, "Unlike Sor Juana?"; Luciani, *Literary Self-fashioning in Sor Juana Inés De La Cruz*; Merrim, *Feminist Perspectives on Sor Juana Inés de la Cruz*; Poot-Herrera, *Sor Juana y su mundo*; Tenorio, *Los villancicos de Sor Juana*; Thomas, *Women and Gender*.

80. As Jorge Cañizares-Esguerra contends, "Late nineteenth-century liberal, anticlerical narratives transformed this woman into a Mexican female version of Galileo," with further propagation of these sentiments by Octavio Paz in the twentieth century; quoted in Gómez Herrero, "Radical Transformation." On the currency, see Favila, "On the Money."

81. The libretto is based on Alicia Gaspar de Alba's novel *Sor Juana's Second Dream*. The opera received its first performance with Opera UCLA in November 2019. On Sor Juana's lesbianism, see Gaspar de Alba, *[Un]framing the "Bad Woman"*, 44–49.

82. Gaspar de Alba, *[Un]framing the "Bad Woman"*, 33–34. She was "not a typical nun," as Asunción Lavrin puts it; "Values and Meaning of Monastic Life," 384.

83. Gaspar de Alba, *[Un]framing the "Bad Woman"*, 9.

84. Jennifer Eich clearly had the same agenda, as signaled by her extension of the common moniker for Sor Juana, "the tenth muse," to María Anna Águeda de San Ignacio in her book *The Other Mexican Muse*. See also Lavrin, *Brides of Christ*, 16.

85. See Palafox y Mendoza, *Regla y constituciones*; Pardo, *Vida y virtudes heroicas de la Madre María de Jesús Tomelín* (1676); Lemus, *Vida, virtudes, trabajos, favores y milagros de la Ven. M. Sor María de Jesús* (1683); Jesús María, *Vida, virtudes y dones sobrenaturales de la venerable sierva de Dios* (1756). On Isabel, see Salmeron, *Vida de la venerable Madre Isabel* (1675).

86. On Bárbara, see Torres, *Vida ejemplar y muerte preciosa de la Madre Bárbara* (1675). On Santa Catalina de Siena, see Franco, *Segunda Parte de la Historia de la provincial de Santiago de Mexico* (1645). By far the most comprehensive volumes on convent culture and history that have incorporated some of these sources' contents about everyday events in the convents and nuns' writing have been Asunción Lavrin's *Brides of Christ* and Josefina Muriel's *Conventos de monjas*. Sigüenza y Góngora's history of the Jesús María convent has received in-depth analysis in Glantz, "Un paraíso occidental"; Peña, "Prólogo"; Ross, *The Baroque Narrative*; Vera Tudela, *Colonial Angels*, 14–34. The three biographies of María de Jesús have also garnered attention with regard to her cause for beatification, considerably delayed until the nineteenth century. See Drago, *Sor María de Jesús Tomelín*; Loreto López, "Las pruebas del milagro"; Rubial García, "Los santos milagreros y malogrados de la Nueva España," 71–82. Aspects of her life are also peppered into Ibsen, *Women's Spiritual Autobiography*; Jaffary, *False Mystics*; Myers, *Neither Saints nor Sinners*. Alonso Franco is cited in Muriel, *Cultura femenina novohispana*, 44–120.

87. Ibsen, *Women's Spiritual Autobiography*, 11.

88. Ibsen, 12; Lavrin, *Brides of Christ*, 324; Loreto López, "Escrito por ella misma," 25; Myers, *Neither Saints nor Sinners*, 6; Vera Tudela, *Colonial Angels*, 35–54.

89. Taylor, *The Archive and the Repertoire*, 18–20. Indeed, I am contesting the traditional archive here, as is often required in contributing to women's history. See Perry, Chaudhuri, and Katz, *Contesting Archives*, xiv.

90. Franco, *Plotting Women*, 11–13.

91. Myers, *Wild Country Out in the Garden*, xix.

92. Arenal and Schlau, *Untold Sisters*, 14. On the further benefits of writing for women, see Ibsen, *Women's Spiritual Autobiography*, 65. Jodi Bilinkoff's study on the relationships between Spanish nuns and their confessors provides more specific context for the writings of women mystics; *Related Lives*, 9. Sarah E. Owens suggests that writing provided the world-traveling nun Sor Ana de Cristo (1565–1636) a form of agency, in *Nuns Navigating the Spanish Empire*, 1–5. On the agency accorded to mystic writers, because of their ability to directly communicate with God, see Myers, *Word from New Spain*, 33. See also Díaz, *Indigenous Writings*, 85–88; Franco, *Plotting Women*, 3.

93. Franco, 11–12.

94. Myers, *Neither Saints nor Sinners*, 4–15; *Wild Country Out in the Garden*, xxvii–xxviii. One reason why it was thought that nuns' biographies were popular to read among lay people was because novels were prohibited, but this prohibition did not mean that people did not read such fiction writing illicitly; see Franco, xiv–xv. Reading and writing in the convents were often assigned by male superiors or convent abbesses; see Bilinkoff, *Related Lives*, 9; Monteros, *En religiosos incendios*, 9. On the early modern practice of reading aloud, see Salmeron, *Vida*, folio 94v; Bouza, *Communication, Knowledge, and Memory in Early Modern Spain*, 51; Eissa-Barroso, "News, Censorship and Propaganda," 102–103.

95. Jaffary, *False Mystics*, 40; Rhodes, "Mysticism in History," 50–55. Ibsen refers to this as a "bricolage of hagiographic discourse," noting that a woman's character was more valuable to readers than her individuality, in *Women's Spiritual Autobiography*, 66. On the circulation of nuns' biographies, see Myers, *Neither Saints nor Sinners*, 4–5. See also Lavrin, "La vida femenina," 27–51.

96. Díaz, *Indigenous Writings*, 94. For a preliminary study of Mexico City's Franciscan Corpus Christi convent sources, see Muriel, *Las indias caciques de Corpus Christi*. Kristine Ibsen notes that the youthful virtue, typically from birth, that women experienced distinguishes their biographies from those of holy men, "emphasizing a progressive movement toward sanctity revealed at an early age rather than a single conversion experience"; *Women's Spiritual Autobiography*, 64–65.

97. Díaz, 94.

98. Díaz, 94. See also Franco, 13.

99. On confession, see Lavrin, "The Erotic as Lewdness," 50; Myers, *Neither Saints nor Sinners*, 12–15.

100. de Boer, *The Conquest of the Soul*, 43. See also Myers, *Neither Saints nor Sinners*, 6–8; Franco, 6.

101. Historian Julia Tuñon Pablos might be suspicious of the constructed narratives in nuns' biographies, because they mythologize select individuals, thus detracting from women's ordinary experiences. She highlights Sor Juana as one such mythic figure from the colonial period, as well as the Virgin of Guadalupe, the immaculist Marian apparition that manifested to the now-sainted Nahua man Juan Diego (d. 1548) close to Mexico City. See Tuñon Pablos, xv. Our Lady of Guadalupe has become a major Mexican devotion with buildup of her cult since the seventeenth century. See Davies, "Villancicos from Mexico City for the Virgin of Guadalupe," 229–231.

102. Díaz, *Indigenous Writings*, 101; Franco, *Plotting Women*, 13.

103. Arenal and Schlau comment on the quotidian exhibits in New Spanish nuns' biographies as a lineage of twelfth-century nuns' biographical writing, with origins reaching as far back as St. Augustine's *Confessions*; *Untold Sisters*, 15. See also Franco, 14. See also Vera Tudela, *Colonial Angels*, 7; Rubial García, "Los santos milagreros y malogrados de la Nueva España," 76–77.

104. Myers refers to orality as "the spoken" and to aurality as "the heard—including the hearing of texts read aloud." I would add sung texts as well. Furthermore, she implicates orality and aurality as important components of learning to write; *Wild*

Country Out in the Garden, xxv. Indeed, Sarah Finley describes aurality in the written works of Sor Juana Inés de la Cruz as "references to sound and music," in *Hearing Voices*, 1.

105. Myers, xxii.

106. It is a situation of "music in other words," as Ruth Solie has discussed in other contexts of women's music making and Andrew Dell'Antonio has observed in the writings of early modern Roman intellectuals. See Solie, *Music in Other Words*, chapter 3; Dell'Antonio, *Listening as Spiritual Practice*, 6–7.

107. I find linguistic anthropologist William Hanks' examination of discourse in indigenous and Spanish writings useful for reflecting on music's value and purpose within nuns' biographies: "The organization of a work is in some degree independent of both the world it purports to represent and the ideological perspective from which it does so. Even would-be realist description is at best selective, a refraction of what it claims to portray. This refraction is effected primarily in the thematic and stylistic construction of the work, which embodies ideological values rooted in the broader social context. No element can enter into the work purely on the basis of its form, without importing its value coefficients with it. Actors take these values for granted, as a familiar background." Hanks, *Intertexts*, 136; Díaz, *Indigenous Writings*, 86.

108. Myers, *Neither Saints nor Sinners*, 5; Lavrin, *Brides of Christ*, 196. Myers characterizes the religious material written in seventeenth- and eighteenth-century New Spain as vital and valuable within the worldview that produced it, in *Wild Country Out in the Garden*, xxi. On the host of other devotional literature that circulated in New Spanish households, including printed sermons, moral theology manuals, novenas, and pious poetry, see Traslosheros, "Utopía Inmaculada en la primavera mexicana," 96–97.

109. Rama, *The Lettered City*, 29–30; see also Taylor, *The Archive and the Repertoire*, 17.

110. Ochoa Gautier incorporates nature and voice into "the worlding of sound" in her aural epistemology of nineteenth-century Colombia; *Aurality*, 3–4.

111. On the lettered/resounding city, see Baker, "The Resounding City," 1–20; Ochoa Gautier, *Aurality*, 4. See also Seijas, *Asian Slaves in Colonial Mexico*.

112. Calderón de la Barca, *Life in Mexico*, 154.

113. See, for example, Fisher, *Music, Piety, and Propaganda*, 193; Knighton, *Hearing the City*, 413; Smith, *The Acoustic World*, chapter 3.

114. Sigüenza y Góngora, *Paraíso occidental*, fol. 176r; Chowning, *Rebellious Nuns*, 102; Lavrin, *Brides of Christ*, 141 and 168; Loreto López, *Tota pulchra*, 167–190; Mariana de la Encarnación, *Relación de la fundación*, 47; Toelle, "*Todas las naciones han de oyrla*," 437–450.

115. See Franco, *Plotting Women*, 13; Lavrin, *Brides of Christ*, 15. Stephanie Kirk also discusses the disjuncture between male-authored devotional texts and nuns' experiences, in *Convent Life in Colonial Mexico*.

116. Díaz, *Indigenous Writings*, 96. On the vihuela, see Griffiths, "Hidalgo, mercader, sacerdote o poeta."

117. Díaz, 96.

118. Inés de la Cruz, *Fundación del convento*; Mariana de la Encarnación, *Relación de la fundación*. See also Lavrin, "De su puño y letra." For an examination of the Jesús

María convent soundscape that draws on seventeenth-century music-philosophical concerns raised in Mariana de la Encarnación's and Inés de la Cruz's writings, as well as in Sigüenza y Góngora's *Paraíso occidental*, see Finley, "Más allá de la sonoridad."

119. Mariana de la Encarnación, *Relación de la fundación*, 30. Likewise, Margaret Chowning discusses how exhausting the work was for the musician nuns of La Purísima convent in San Miguel; *Rebellious Nuns*, 172–173.

120. See Mariana de la Encarnación, *Relación de la fundación*, 35; Lavrin, *Brides of Christ*, 147; Myers, *A Wild Country*, 270.

121. Mazuela-Anguita, "Música conventual," 9–10.

122. Calderón de la Barca, *Life in Mexico*, 208.

123. This was also the case in Iberian convents. See Aguirre Rincón, *Un manuscrito para un convento*, 102; Hathaway, "Cloister, Court and City," 211–212. Baker (*Imposing Harmony*, 117) tells of loas and comic villancicos performed to impress a high-ranking Franciscan friar who visited the Santa Clara convent in 1737 Cuzco.

124. Illari, "Polychoral Culture," 19. The polychoral style was especially suitable for Mass settings, psalms, the first Lamentation of Holy Week, and some villancicos, especially those for Christmas, but there were also exceptions to these rules that can probably be attributed to local custom. See López-Calo, *Historia de la música española*, 30–31. On the employment of polyphony to embellish feasts in Spanish convents, see Aguirre Rincón, *Un manuscrito para un convento*, 91, 103. The taste for polyphonic works by renowned sixteenth-century Spanish composers, such as Francisco Guerrero, Cristóbal de Morales, and Tomás Luis de Victoria, seems to have continued well into the eighteenth century, as indicated by eighteenth-century copies of their music in the Encarnación repertory. See Schleifer, "The Mexican Choirbooks," 15, 55–56. On the prestige of polyphony in Italian convents, see Kendrick, *Celestial Sirens*, 415. Polyphony also had symbolic meanings when performed for the profession rituals, particularly in Sienese convents. See Reardon, *Holy Concord*, 55.

125. Pérez Puente, *Autos de las visitas del Arzobispo*, 110.

126. Lehmann Goldman, "The Matins Responsory," 24.

127. On villancicos, see Davies, "Introduction," ix–x; Krutitskaya, *Villancicos que se cantaron en la catedral*; Laird, *Towards a History of the Spanish Villancico*; Knighton and Torrente, *Devotional Music in the Iberian World*; Tenorio, *Los villancicos de Sor Juana*, 39–52.

128. On the villancico as a musical sermon, see Hathaway, " 'Music Charms the Senses,' " 228–229.

129. Asunción Lavrin notes that women's convents maintained "an aura of respect and mystery that was lacking in male convents, inasmuch as monks were part of the world, and their own visibility in the streets made them familiar and accessible"; *Brides of Christ*, 2. Contributors to the volume *The Crannied Wall* aimed to investigate "women's relationship to religion, literature, the visual arts, and music" in early modern Europe, though mostly in Italy; Monson, *The Crannied Wall*, 1–2. A slice of the New Spanish convent devotional soundscape has been studied in Sarah Finley's monograph on the famous writings of Sor Juana Inés de la Cruz, including various theatrical works and villancicos. In *Hearing Voices: Aurality and*

New Spanish Sound Culture in Sor Juana Inés de la Cruz, Finley discusses the influence of early modern thinkers like Athanasius Kircher on Juana's rhetorically disguised critiques of the patriarchal structures that kept women out of the upper echelons of Church and political leadership, universities, and music composition. See also Díaz, "The Establishment of Feminine Paradigms," 58–59.

130. On the ideology of history, see Tanaka, 15 and 55.

131. Schiffman, *The Birth of the Past*, 4.

132. Lavrin, *Brides of Christ*, 197–198; Lavrin, "The Erotic as Lewdness," 55.

133. Helen Hills has drawn on Adriana Cavarero's philosophy of voice to re-embody the voices of cloistered nuns in early modern Naples, harking back to two foundational studies, Craig Monson's *Disembodied Voices* and Robert Kendrick's *Celestial Sirens*, which emphasize the invisibility of nuns' liturgical singing from within carefully crafted convent church spaces. Hills, "Veiling the Voice," 128; See also Cavarero, *For More Than One Voice*, 4; Monson, 40, 52; Kendrick, 47–48. This double veiling was also the topic of profession sermons; see Lavrin, *Brides of Christ*, 83.

134. On Pythagoras and the acousmatic, see Eidsheim, *The Race of Sound*, 1–2; Kane, *Sound Unseen*, 24.

135. Hills, 130; Monson, 40; Kendrick, 161–163; Reardon, *Holy Concord*, 97; Vallarta, *Luz que guía al camino*, folio 135v.

136. On the social construction of virginity in New Spain, see Jaffary, *Reproduction and Its Discontents*, 20–35; Lavrin, "Introduction," 10–11; Seed, *To Love, Honor, and Obey in Colonial Mexico*, 97.

137. This is in line with the teachings of Augustine and Thomas Aquinas, which were consistently re-articulated throughout the early modern period. See Hills, *Invisible City*, 49–50. The late eighteenth-century confessor Benito Díaz Gamarra notes how important it is for nuns to inflict pain on themselves to keep a virginal state of mind; see Lavrin, *Brides of Christ*, 193. Franco (*Plotting Women*, 5) calls this an "ideological purity."

138. Cavarero, *For More Than One Voice*, 6–11. As Lydia Goehr notes, music for religious devotion throughout the eighteenth century and beyond remained "regulated by the function of words"; *The Imaginary Museum of Musical Works*, 139.

139. Once more, Sor Juana Inés de la Cruz is the exception. A deep probing of her extensive oeuvre reveals her sexual agency and colonial feminism from Gaspar de Alba's Chicana feminist perspective in *[Un]Framing the "Bad Woman"*, chapter 1 (see especially pp. 46–50); and from a sound-studies perspective, we learn of Juana's female auralities, feminine intellect, and transgressions and feminine revoicings—the subtitles to chapters 3–5, respectively, in Finley, *Hearing Voices*.

140. Moral theologians of the early modern Hispanic Church preached against sins of both the body and mind. See Lavrin, "The Erotic as Lewdness," 39.

141. Salmeron, *Vida*, fol. 72r.

142. LaBelle, *Lexicon of the Mouth*, 130.

143. Rhodes, "Mysticism in History," 52–53.

144. As Rhodes (55) explains, this process was articulated through the writings of St. Teresa of Ávila, but also inspired by the works of Fray Luis de Granada and St. John of the Cross.

145. Dolar draws on Socratic, Rousseauian, and Kantian moral philosophy for his ethics of the voice; *A Voice and Nothing More*, 83–89.
146. Cavarero, *For More Than one Voice*, 6.
147. Finley, *Hearing Voices*, 127.
148. On Marian harmonies, see Finley, 100–106.
149. Webb, *The Divine Voice*, 204.
150. Monastic culture in fact shaped early modern political and economic power hierarchies that developed from the idealization of molding human bodies into disciplined soldiers. See Foucault, *Discipline and Punish*, 135–141.
151. Eidsheim, *The Race of Sound*, 1–38.
152. Auditory imagination allows us to speak with the dead, as the Franciscan Martín del Castillo Suggested in 1673. See Lavrin, "Los senderos interiores de los conventos de monjas," 6.
153. Burns, *Into the Archive*, 67. See also Dean, "Beyond Prescription," 295–296. Vera, also concerned with discipline in its penitential sense, describes archival sources as having an administrative character, out of which he draws out the personalities responsible for colonial Santiago's soundscape; *The Sweet Penance of Music*, 5.
154. Franco, *Plotting Women*, 5.
155. Voice studies attend primarily to issues about voice in modernity. The scant literature on sacred voice has primarily dealt with non-Christian or non–Roman Catholic faith traditions. See, for example, Eidsheim and Meizel, *The Oxford Handbook of Voice Studies*; Feldman and Zeitlin, *The Voice as Something More*; Ochoa Gautier, *Aurality*; Varwig, "Early Modern Voice." On the sacred, see Johnson, *Mormons, Musical Theater, and Belonging in America*; Schmidt, *Hearing Things*; Hirschkind, *The Ethical Soundscape*; Ingalls, *Singing the Congregation*, chapter 3; Jarjour, *Sense and Sadness*, chapter 2; Jones, *Flaming*; Webb, *The Divine Voice*; Weiner, *Religion Out Loud*. Sarah Finley's aforementioned monograph, *Hearing Voices*, is the first critical take on the gendered nuances of Sor Juana Inés de la Cruz's sacred and secular writings through the framework of sound and voice.

Chapter 1

1. Archivo General de la Nación, Mexico City (AGN), Indiferente Virreinal/Caja 2524/Expediente 16, folio 2r.
2. AGN/Indiferente Virreinal/Caja 2524/Expediente 16, folio 2v. Mata did not say "compose" (componer/compuestas), which could refer to composing poetry; see Chávez Bárcenas, "Singing in the City of Angels," 227–228. Mata was well known for composing chanzonetas and villancicos. See Schleifer, "The Mexican Choirbooks," 71; Stevenson, "Mexican Colonial Music Manuscripts Abroad," 207. The labeling of *chanzoneta* would be consistent with Leonardo Waisman's claim that in the earlier decades of the seventeenth century, this was the preferred term to refer to vernacular-texted sacred music; *Una historia de la música colonial hispanoamericana*, 173.

3. Responsories are Latin-texted musical selections that alternate with and respond to the Matins lessons in either plainchant or polyphony. See Goldman, "The Matins Responsory," 16–42. See also Enríquez Rubio, "¿Dónde están los responsorios?," 612. On the villancico's liturgical and paraliturgical placement, see, for example, Knighton and Torrente, *Devotional Music*, 1, 23, 108, 203.

4. Enríquez Rubio, "¿Dónde están los responsorios?," 617.

5. The account is preserved in AGN/Indiferente Virreinal/Caja 2524/Expediente 16, folios 1–2. The document also places Antonio Rodríguez de Mata in Mexico City sooner than 1614, as originally thought, unless there were two individuals with the same name. See Marín López, "Música y músicos entre dos mundos," vol. 1, 425.

6. Pérez Puente, *Autos de las visitas del Arzobispo Fray Payo Enríquez*, 110.

7. Mark Brill, "Rodriguez Mata, Antonio," Grove Music Online, accessed July 30, 2021, http://www.oxfordmusiconline.com/subscriber/article/grove/music/41458.

8. The Passion is located in *Mexican Choirbooks*, vol. 2, folios 115v–118r, and copied in vol. 5, folios 122v–125r. See also Rodríguez Mata, *Passions*, ed. Grey Brothers. Mata's *Asperges me* is polychoral, so each choir part is in a separate volume, and these were copied again as late as the middle of the eighteenth century in vols. 5 and 6. See *Mexican Choirbooks*, vol. 2, folios 42v–44r (second choir); vol. 3, folios 47v–49r (first choir); vol. 5, folios 60v–62r (second choir); vol. 6, folios 43v–45r (first choir). On the dating of the Encarnación choirbooks, see Schleifer, "The Mexican Choirbooks," 10–14.

9. Núñez, *Distribución de las obras ordinarias, y extraordinarias del día*, 36.

10. "En ninguna cosa pueden agradar más a su esposo que en alabarle con su canto que le agrada." In Fernández Cejudo, *Llave de oro*. While multiple copies of this rule exist, the version preserved at the Bancroft Library at the University of California, Berkeley is in a booklet with blank pages following the rule. Some fifty pages without folio numbers contain a written record of the archbishop's visit to the Encarnación, where this quote and other findings and areas for improvement within the convent are summarized. The source's call number is tF1207.F39x.

11. Monson, "The Council of Trent Revisited," 19–22. For a closer look into the Hispanic context, see Aguirre Rincón, *Un manuscrito para un convento*, 99–103; Ortiz, "Euterpe en los conventos," 240–241.

12. Burns, *Into the Archive*, 83–84.

13. See, for example, Salmeron, *Vida de la venerable Madre Isabel de la Encarnación, Carmelita descalza*, folio 86v.

14. Even after the Immaculate Conception was declared a formal dogma of the Catholic Church in 1854, there remained skeptics. See, for example, Hanstein, *The Immaculate Conception*, 9.

15. Following previous models of Marian devotional writing in her villancico texts, Sor Juana Inés de la Cruz exhibits a proto-feminism in her affinity to the Virgin Mary. See Merrim, "*Mores Geometricae*," 117–118; Tenorio, *Los villancicos de Sor Juana*, 93–94.

16. Lavrin, "The Erotic as Lewdness," 51.

17. Webb, *The Divine Voice*, 201–206. Similarly, Gary Tomlinson draws on Derrida to highlight that "writing has been considered an indirect representation of a presence

found embodied in speech. It has been seen as a sign of a sign of presence"; *The Singing of the New World*, 11.

18. Muriel, *Conventos de monjas*, 16.

19. Muriel, 16. Morose quips abound stemming from this sacrifice. Consider, for example, "Buried Alive in the New World Cloister," in Kirk, *Convent Life in Colonial Mexico*, chapter 17; "Neither alive nor dead did she return to the world" ("Ni viva ni muerta volvía al mundo"), in de la Maza, *Arquitectura de los coros de monjas*, 11.

20. Fernández de Mesa, *La fundadora de la santa concepción*, 161.

21. Manso y Zuñiga, *Regla y ordenaciones de las religiosas de la Limpia e Inmaculada Concepción*, folios 7v–8r.

22. Manso y Zuñiga, folio 8r.

23. Snakes and dragons were both synonymous with sin in medieval Mariology. See Robertson, "The Savior, the Woman, and the Head of the Dragon," 546–547.

24. Rubin, *Mother of God*, 35–37.

25. Rubin, 37; Steinberg, *Renaissance and Baroque Art*, 76–77; Webb, *The Divine Voice*, 16, 69.

26. Bellido, *Vida de la V.M.R.M. María Anna Águeda de San Ignacio*, 224.

27. Anzaldúa, "now let us shift," 543, 576.

28. Steinberg, *Renaissance and Baroque Art*, 76.

29. Steinberg, 77.

30. Steinberg (77) recalls the lexical difference in Greek *rhema*, "what is merely spoken and heard," versus *logos*, the Word of God.

31. Schmidt, *Hearing Things*, 56.

32. Rubin, *Mother of God*, 160.

33. The Immaculate Conception's history has been documented in studies from several pertinent disciplines. In late-medieval music history, see Robertson, "The Savior, the Woman, and the Head of the Dragon," 557–564. In New Spanish conventual history, see Loreto López, *Tota pulchra*, 211–225; Owens, *Nuns Navigating the Spanish Empire*, 26–28; and Ramos Medina, *Voto y juramento de la Inmaculada Concepción*, 9–22. In (New) Spanish art history, see Díaz and Stratton-Pruitt, *Painting the Divine*, 48–65; Monroy Ponce, Guadarrama Guevara, and Franco Velasco, *Un privilegio sagrado*; and Stratton, *The Immaculate Conception in Spanish Art*.

34. Stratton, *The Immaculate Conception in Spanish Art*, 21.

35. Stratton, 38–39; Alastruey, *Tratado de la Virgen Santísima*, 25.

36. Stratton, 103.

37. Philip IV descended from a long line of immaculist-supporting Habsburg royalty. See Ramos, *Identity, Ritual, and Power*, 26.

38. Translated in Pomplun, "Baroque Catholic Theologies of Christ and Mary," 109.

39. Devotion to the Immaculate Conception was a key element of Habsburg piety under Ferdinand II and Ferdinand III, for example. See Saunders, *Cross, Sword, and Lyre*; Weaver, "Music in the Service of Counter-Reformation Politics."

40. On *fax/hacha*, see the 1611 edition of Covarrubias, *Tesoro de la lengua castellana*, 460.

41. Sariñana, *Llanto del occidente*, folios 49v–50r.

42. See Arbeau, *Orchesographie*, folio 26v. I am grateful to Mary Channen Caldwell for informing me of this source.

43. See Lichtenwalter, *David: Dancing Like a King*, 13.

44. Sariñana, *Llanto del occidente*, folios 49r–50v. After the 1661 papal bull, the topic of the Virgin Mary's immaculacy or maculacy would no longer feature in university debates, in which Dominican scholars often cited St. Thomas Aquinas to contradict immaculists. See, for example, Gage, *Travels in the New World*, 106–107.

45. For other examples of "the 'musical iconography' of Mary Immaculate," see Foster, *Music and Power in Early Modern Spain*, chapter 6.

46. Graña Cid, *Mujeres, espiritualidad franciscana y feminismo en la Castilla renacentista*, 21.

47. Matesanz del Barrio, "El breviario de la Inmaculada Concepción y Ambrosio Montesino," 273.

48. *Breviarium secundum ordinem Sancte atque Inmaculate Concepcionis Beatissime Virginis Marie* (1551), folio 146.

49. Manso y Zuñiga, *Regla y ordenaciones de las religiosas de la Limpia e Inmaculada Concepción*, folios 11r–13r.

50. A volume containing the rules for all branches of the Franciscan order includes the Conceptionists. See *Constituciones generales para todas las monjas y religiosas, sujetas à la obediencia de la orden de nuestro Padre San Francisco* (1642). See also Loreto López, *Tota pulchra*, 19–20.

51. Vetancurt, *Teatro mexicano*, 344.

52. Ávila, *Colección de noticias de muchas de las indulgencias plenarias*, 7.

53. Aguilar, *Sermón del seráfico padre San Francisco*, v–vi.

54. Zumárraga is most remembered for having received the miraculous image of the Virgin of Guadalupe, an Immaculist icon, from the garment of an indigenous peasant Juan Diego. See Davies, "Villancicos from Mexico City," 230. The influence of the Franciscans on the spirituality of New Spain cannot be overstated. See Cohen, *The Franciscans in Colonial Mexico*; Myers, *A Wild Country*, 280.

55. Lavrin, *Brides of Christ*, 22.

56. Muriel, *Conventos de monjas*, 47–48, 137–138, 211–212, 305, 314, 352, 356. On the Sántisimo Rosario's transformation into the Santa Catalina convent, see Amerlinck de Corsi and Ramos Medina, *Conventos de monjas*, 265–268.

57. Muriel, 47.

58. Muriel, 438

59. *Relación histórica de la fundación de este Convento de Nuestra Señora del Pilar*, 1–13.

60. *Relación histórica*, 1–5.

61. *Relación histórica*, 10–11.

62. *Relación histórica*, 14–15.

63. *Relación histórica*, 17–19.

64. *Relación histórica*, 13. For more on Sister María Ignacia, see Lavrín and Loreto López, *El universo de la teatralidad conventual*, 52–102.

65. Amerlinck de Corsi, "Los albores del convento de la Purísima Concepción de México," 29.

66. Ramos Medina, *Voto y juramento de la Inmaculada Concepción*, 16; Mazín Gómez, *El cabildo catedral*, 191.

67. Ramos Medina, 13–19; Lavrin, *Brides of Christ*, 246–248.

68. Amerlinck de Corsi, "Los albores del convento de la Purísima Concepción de México," 14; Lavrin, *Brides of Christ*, 247. On beatas, see Socolow, *The Women of Colonial Latin America*, 107.

69. Lavrin, *Brides of Christ*, 20–21, 247.

70. Gonzalbo Aizpuru, *La educación de los criollos y la vida urbana*, 339.

71. Foz y Foz, *La revolución pedagógica en Nueva España*.

72. Monson, *The Crannied Wall*, 2. See also Amerlinck de Corsi, "Los albores del convento de la Purísima Concepción de México," 16; Loreto López, *Tota pulchra*, 18–21. On theology of containment, see Delgado, *Laywomen*, 141; Monson, *Nuns Behaving Badly*, 8. The post-Tridentine era, which coincided with the development of women's convents in New Spain, saw the intensification of nuns' enclosure. See Kirk, *Convent Life in Colonial Mexico*, 3–6

73. Christian, *Local Religion in Sixteenth-Century Spain*, 132; Graziano, *Wounds of Love*, 134; Mazuela-Anguita, "Una celestial armonía," 5.

74. Muriel, *Cultura femenina novohispana*, 433–434; Delgado, *Laywomen*, 4; Lavrin, *Brides of Christ*, 5.

75. Amerlinck de Corsi and Ramos Medina, *Conventos de monjas*, 33.

76. Muriel, *La sociedad novohispana*, 42. On La Purísima in San Miguel, see Chowning, *Rebellious Nuns*.

77. Sigüenza y Góngora, *Parayso occidental*, folio 18r–18v. See also Lavrin, *Brides of Christ*, 25; Ross, *The Baroque Narrative*, 87–88.

78. Muriel, *La sociedad novohispana*, 36.

79. Muriel, 48.

80. Balbuena, *Siglo de oro en las selvas de Erífile*, 76. In 1604, Balbuena claims that there were some eight hundred nuns in Mexico City. See the Luis Íñigo-Madrigal edition of Balbuena, *Grandeza mexicana*, 115.

81. "Distinguíanse las hijas de este convento sobre todo en la música . . ." Ramírez Aparicio, *Los conventos suprimidos en México*, 398.

82. Gordon, *Monteverdi's Unruly Women*, 24. In the nineteenth century, singing instructors began to locate the voice deeper in the chest. See Davies, *Romantic Anatomies of Performance*, 127–132. I am grateful to Jessica Peritz for signaling these sources to me. On further correlation between the throat and voice, see Cavarero, *For More Than One Voice*, 11; LaBelle, *Lexicon of the Mouth*, 4.

83. Córdova, *The Art of Professing*, 72–74.

84. On convents as metaphorical gardens, see Lavrin, *Brides of Christ*, 89, 271, 336; Kendrick, *Celestial Sirens*, 160–161; Myers and Powell, *Wild Country Out in the Garden*; Ross, *The Baroque Narrative*, 46–47. On Balbuena's influence on Góngora, see Ross, 62–63.

85. Muriel, *Conventos de monjas*, 356–360.

86. "¡Dichosa ciudad, donde las oraciones de vírgenes prudentes y esposas de Jesús repartidas en conventos son ejércitos de ángeles bien ordenados de coros terribles para el infierno y hermosos para el cielo, que en los conventos de monjas ha puesto Dios sus presidios y en ellos forma ejércitos que se oponen a los rigores de Dios, aplacan con sus ruegos y rinden a la divina justicia con sus oraciones, obligándole a repartir misericordias; son afrenta a los enemigos infernales e ignominia de sus astucias, porque es donaire del valor divino vencer con azucenas y triunfar con rosas, sujetando a elefantes demonios con mujeres palomas! No hay palabras con que ponderar la majestad con que en ellos se celebra el divino culto, la música, los olores, la grandeza de sus templos, limpieza de altares y asistencia en sus coros." Vetancurt, *Teatro mexicano*, 342. For another translation, see Córdova, *The Art of Professing in Bourbon Mexico*, 189–190.

87. The antiphon is also used at the start of some orders' professions. See Favila, "The Sound of Profession Ceremonies," 156.

88. Merrim, *The Spectacular City*, 150–152. The classics on *criollismo* are Bernal, *Mestizaje y criollismo* and O'Gorman, *Meditaciones sobre el criollismo*.

89. Chowning, 5.

90. "Jardín del señor." In Biblioteca Nacional de Mexico, Fondo Franciscano, vol. 105, folio 93r.

91. Flores Enríquez, "Jardines místicos," 51.

92. Amerlinck de Corsi and Ramos Medina, *Conventos de monjas*, 66.

93. Calderón de la Barca, *Life in Mexico*, 206.

94. Pérez Puente, *Autos de las visitas del Arzobispo*, 110.

95. These visits fulfilled the Council of Trent's orders that convents be monitored periodically. The records of the archbishop's visits are preserved at the Archivo General de la Nación and transcribed in Pérez Puente, *Autos de las visitas del Arzobispo*.

96. Pérez Puente, 3.

97. The pioneering study on this portraiture that also attends to its relationship with funerary portraits of deceased nuns is Montero Alarcón, *Monjas coronadas*.

98. Córdova, *The Art of Professing in Bourbon Mexico*, 48.

99. Córdova, 48, 86; Hamburger and Marti, *Crown and Veil*, 13.

100. Córdova, 78–79. See also, Rothenberg, *The Flower of Paradise*, 10.

101. Ruiz Gomar, *Catálogo comentado del acervo del Museo Nacional de Arte*, 113.

102. "Posuit signum in faciem meam, ut nullum praeter eum amatorem admittam." "Amo Christum in cujus thalamum introivi cujus mater virgo est cujus pater feminam nescit cujus mihi organa modulatis vocibus cantant: quem cum amavero casta sum cum tetigero munda sum cum accepero virgo sum." "Annulo suo subarrhavit me, et immensis monilibus ornavit me." "Induit me dominus ciclade auro testa, et immensis monilibus ornavit me." *Libro de Coro del Convento de Santa Inés de Montepulciano*, folios 15v–16r. These antiphons and responses were used for the ancient ritual of consecration of virgins, which became incorporated into professions. See Glixon, *Mirrors of Heaven*, 106–115; Kendrick, *Celestial Sirens*, 402; Monson, *Disembodied Voices*, chapter 10; Reardon, *Holy Concord*, 58–63.

103. *Regla y constituciones para las religiosas recoletas dominicas*, 169–171.

104. "Si es viuda se cantan las siguientes en lugar de esta. . . . Para las viudas." "Ipsi sum desponsata, cui Angeli serviunt, cujus pulchritudeinem Sol & Luna mirantur." "Annulo suo subarrhavit me dominus meus Jesus Christus et tamquam sponsam decoravit me corona." In *Libro de Coro del Convento de Santa Inés de Montepulciano*, folios 16r–16v.

105. *Regla y constituciones para las religiosas recoletas dominicas*, 145–165. While the chants for the feast of St. Agnes are only sung in the initiation rituals of some orders, *Veni sponsa Christi* for the Common of Virgins is sung in all orders. The rule books and/or ceremonials consulted are as follows. For Conceptionists and Hieronymites, see *Orden que se ha de guardar con la que entra en religión*, folios 3r–3v; *Ceremonial para las religiosas geronimas de México*; for Dominicans, *Regla y constituciones para las religiosas recoletas dominicas*, 145–165; *Ceremonial Dominicano*, 193r–195v. On the Carmelites, see *Manual o procesionario, de las religiosas Carmelitas*, 216–227; for the Company of Mary, see *Ceremonial para la admisión y dar el hábito a las religiosas, del Órden de la Compañía* (1811), 9–14; *Ceremonial para la profesión de las religiosas, del Órden de la Compañía*, 6–10; for Franciscans, see *Regla de la gloriosa Santa Clara*, 75–97; *Ordo ad induendum novitiam Monialem* in Loreto López, *Tota pulchra*, 123–132.

106. Myers and Powell, *Wild Country Out in the Garden*, xxv; Finley, *Hearing Voices*, 1.

107. *Orden que se ha de guardar*, folios 3r–3v.

108. See Hiley, *Western Plainchant*, 89; "Veni electa mea," in Lacoste, *Cantus*, https://cantus.uwaterloo.ca/search?t=veni+electa+mea (accessed October 2, 2021). See also Lavrin, *Brides of Christ*, 75–76.

109. For the Purísima Concepción manuscript, see facsimile of *Ordo ad induendum* in Loreto López, *Tota pulchra*, 123–132.

110. The male religious ceremonial books consulted, and some of their idiosyncrasies, are as follows. The Augustinians did not allow men to profess if they had been married less than two months at the time they wished to join a monastery; see *Regla de N.P. S. Augustin, Obispo, y doctor de la iglesia*, 137–149. Carmelites did not allow eunuchs or previously married men to profess without express permission of the prior general; see *Regla primitiva, y constituciones de los religiosos descalzos de la orden de la bienaventurada Virgen María del Monte Carmelo*, 158–167. On Dominicans: *Ceremonial Dominicano*, 189v–193r; the Franciscans specifically mention that previously married men are allowed to profess, in *Estatutos, y ordenaciones de la Santa Provincia de San Gregorio*, 2; on Jesuits: *Reglas de la Compañía de Jesús*, 362–371. All orders prohibited former criminals of any sort from joining their ranks. Thus, the specification of eunuchs in the Carmelite ceremonial could derive from the fact that castration was sometimes a punishment for various sexual crimes, not least for sodomy, bestiality, and rape of virgins. See Tortorici, *Sins against Nature*, 72, 125–127; Crawford, *Eunuchs and Castrati*, 51–52.

111. Salmerón, *Vida de la venerable Madre Isabel de la Encarnación*, folio 103v. The dedication page to the Brescian Introits also draws on this scene from the Book of Revelation. See Kendrick, *Celestial Sirens*, 11–12.

112. "¡O válgame Dios, lo que se han perdido por no ser vírgenes! O quien pudiese dar a entender al mundo la dignidad que pierden las que no lo son. . . . Dichosas las religiosas Carmelitas que guardaren su profesión con puntualidad, hasta que estén en la otra vida, no han de conocer la gran merced que Dios les hizo en su vocación." In Salmerón, folios 103v–104r.

113. Lavrin, *Brides of Christ*, chapter 7.

114. "No entraba en la música del cordero por haber sido casada." In Gómez de la Parra, *Fundación y primero siglo*, 252.

115. Myers, *Neither Saints nor Sinners*, 4–6.

116. Gordon, *Monteverdi's Unruly Women*, 39–41.

117. Jaffary, *Reproduction and Its Discontents*, 20–21.

118. "La soverana dignidad del sacratísimo vientre de María." In Franciscanos, *Instrucción, y doctrina*, 259.

119. Marian music often amplified the soundscape of local politics. See, for example, Baker, "The 'Ethnic Villancico,'" 404–408; Bartel, "Portal of the Skies," chapters 2–4; Cichy, "Changing Their Tune," 175–178; Davies, "Villancicos from Mexico City for the Virgin of Guadalupe;" Fisher, *Music, Piety, and Propaganda*, 24–26; Frandsen, *Crossing Confessional Boundaries*, 167–171; Rodríguez, "The Villancico as Music of State," 190; Wiesenfeldt, "'Majestas Mariae' als musikgeschichtliches Phänomen."

120. *Ritual Concepcionista*, Archivo de la Casa Madre Concepcionista, folio Vr.

121. Foucault, *Discipline and Punish*, 136.

122. Jaffary, *Reproduction and Its Discontents*, 24.

123. Ávila, *Pureza emblemática discurrida en la profesión de la M. Mariana de San Francisco*, 3v–4r.

124. Robertson, "The Savior, the Woman," 600. On paintings of the Woman of the Apocalypse, see Díaz and Stratton-Pruitt, *Painting the Divine*, 46. The warrior subject also made its way into Immaculate Conception villancicos performed at the Mexico City cathedral. See Krutitskaya, "Los villancicos cantados en la catedral de México," 121.

125. Ávila, *Pureza emblemática*, 4r.

126. Ávila, 3v–4r; translated in Lavrin, *Brides of Christ*, 79. Lavrin notes that references to such "ancient paintings" are common in sermons. For this image, Ávila cites Pierio Valeriano's 1556 study, *Hieroglyphica, sive, De sacris Aegyptiorvm literis commentarii*. That virginity could have a vocal component seems but a moment of contradiction of the ages-old maxim that chastity required silence. See Kirk, *Convent Life*, 101–102.

127. On the origins of the *Magnificat* from Hannah's prayer in the Book of Samuel, see Haupt, "The Prototype of the Magnificat," 617–632.

128. On the rosary, see Lavrin, *Brides of Christ*, 60.

129. "Verdaderamente, que desfallece la alma aqui, considerando esto." In Franciscanos, *Instrucción, y doctrina*, 260. St. Philip Neri, known for fainting before a painting of the Visitation, comes to mind as one of those mystics. His cult was quickly disseminated in New Spain after his 1622 canonization. See Barbieri, "To Be in Heaven," 206–208; Castañeda García, "Ilustración y educación."

130. Ávila, *Pureza emblemática discurrida en la profesión de la M. Mariana de San Francisco*, 3v–4r.

131. Kendrick, *Celestial Sirens*, 244–245.
132. Santoro, *Mary in Our Life*, 528.
133. Eguiarte Bendímez, "El púlpito y el convento," 311.
134. "Acordes cultos con que las Religiosas Músicas del Convento de N. Señora de Balvanera clausruaron la octava de la Natividad de N. Señora." In Eguiarte Bendímez, 311–328.
135. Eguiarte Bendímez, 332. The feast was on September 8, and so the octave would fall on September 15.
136. "La destreza de la música esta en subir y bajar, porque en bajar y subir consisten las especies de tonos y la elegancia de la composición. Ningún buen músico se baja, que no sea para levantar, ni levanta, que no sea para bajar." Quoted in Eguiarte Bendímez, 329.
137. Eguiarte Bendímez, 332–333.
138. "Todo lo cantado es del nacimiento de María." Quoted in Eguiarte Bendímez, 330.
139. Tello et al., *Colección Sánchez Garza*, 525–526.
140. Tello et al., 466–469; Pepe, "Testamento de Fabián Pérez Ximeno," 141–143.
141. Sabau García, *México en el mundo de las colecciones de arte*, 105.
142. Reiss, "Pious Phalluses and Holy Vulvas," 169–170. Pearls can also symbolize the baby Jesus' tears. See Krutitskaya, "Los villancicos cantados en la catedral de México," 67.
143. On the modality, see Waisman, *Una historia de la música colonial hispanoamericana*, 226; Nassarre, *Escuela música*, 78–79.
144. LaBelle, *Lexicon of the Mouth*, 116.
145. "¡O estado altísimo, en las esposas del señor, justamente comparado con los ángeles del cielo! ¡O estado altísimo! Que no solo se compara con los ángeles, sino en cierta manera les excede. Conservar pureza en aquella espiritual naturaleza es menos que conservar en la humana." Palafox y Mendoza, *Regla y constituciones*, 5r–5v.
146. On O exclamations, see Smith, *The Acoustic World*, 14–15.
147. On divine resonators, see Webb, *The Divine Voice*, 204.
148. *Regla, y constituciones que han de guardar las religiosas del convento del glorioso padre San Geronymo*, 46–47. Auditory imagination applies to Palafox, because keeping his memory alive through such reprints contributed to his cause for beatification, which began in 1696. See Fernández Gracia, *La buena memoria del Obispo Palafox*, 11; Seijas, *Asian Slaves in Colonial Mexico*, 22.
149. "Los diestros músicos llaman a un 'canto de fantasía,' y es aquel, cuando no contento el maestro con las leyes, o reglas de la música, que esto es cantar por lo común, busca en su idea, otro modo singular, que con distintas voces, quiebros, tonos o instrumentos, sin faltar a las reglas de la música, y sin arreglarse a ellas, saca el tono, que deleita y hasta a los diestros admira; viendo, que ni las reglas falta, ni se mide por las reglas. Esto hizo el Eterno Padre al cantar a María en el choro [*sic*] alto de la gloria." In Jaramillo, *Sermón en la anual, solemne fiesta, que a la Concepción Purísima de María, con título del choro alto*, folio 10r.
150. Jaramillo, folios 5v–9r.
151. "En el choro [*sic*] alto de esta iglesia, es la Madre María de la Trinidad, la que la voz levanta, 'Extollens vocem quaedam mullier;' en el choro alto de la gloria, es a la

Madre María, porque a María, como madre, entona la Trinidad." In Jaramillo, folio 1r. Sarah Finley traces the seventeenth- and eighteenth-century concern for sympathetic resonances between earthly and celestial harmonies based on the works of the Jesuit Athanasius Kircher and their dissemination and reception in New Spain. Finley then turns to the Marian harmonies evinced in Sor Juana Inés de la Cruz's villancicos for the Assumption, which resonate with the divine portrayal of the Virgin Mary that Jaramillo presents for the Immaculate Conception. Jaramillo was likely familiar with Kircher. See Finley, *Hearing Voices*, chapters 2–3.

152. For another interpretation of this biblical quote, see Navarro, *Voces del cielo repetidas en la tierra*, folio 2r.
153. The passage alludes to sound's imbrication with female intuition, knowledge, and intellectual development. See Finley, "Sounding the Feminine."
154. LaBelle, *Lexicon of the Mouth*, 4.

Chapter 2

1. Schleifer, "The Mexican Choirbooks," 13–14.
2. Cope, *The Limits of Racial Domination*, 58–59.
3. Stevenson, "Mexican Colonial Music Manuscripts Abroad," 213–214; Schleifer, "The Mexican Choirbooks," 5, 111. For Stevenson, the importance of the Encarnación manuscripts lies in their exemplary evidence that music of the Spanish Renaissance composers was being copied and performed in New Spanish cathedrals and convents well into the eighteenth century: the choirbooks contain the music of Guerrero, Morales, and Victoria, for example. Schleifer reveals concordances in European sources. Sotteraña Aguirre Rincón notes that nuns in Spain would request music without low voice parts, which might suggest that the Encarnación books were copied from male sources with the omission of text underlay. See Aguirre Rincón, *Un manuscrito para un convento*, 108.
4. Judith Etzion, "Romero, Mateo," Grove Music Online, accessed June 12, 2020, https://doi.org/10.1093/gmo/9781561592630.article.23769.
5. Illari, "Polychoral Culture," 19; Schleifer, "The Mexican Choirbooks," 13; Carver, *Cori Spezzati*, 128.
6. Schleifer, "The Mexican Choirbooks," 111–112.
7. Reconstructed from Biblioteca de Cataluña M788bis, no. 23, folios 99–124.
8. Tello, "Músicos ruiseñores," 29–30.
9. On musician nuns' anonymity, see Hills, "Veiling the Voice," 125; Kendrick, *Celestial Sirens*, 165.
10. See also Etzion, "Latin Polyphony in the Early Spanish Baroque," 79.
11. Judith Etzion (79) suggests the high solo voice is a possible influence from villancico compositional traditions of the early seventeenth century.
12. O'Regan, "The Church Triumphant," 302. On the lavish origins of the polychoral style, see Carver, *Cori Spezzati*, 3–5.
13. LaBelle, *Lexicon of the Mouth*, 104.

14. Kirk, *Sor Juana Inés*, 201.

15. Myers and Powell, *Wild Country Out in the Garden*, 270.

16. "Cantaba unas letras tán espirituales . . ." See Gómez de la Parra, *Fundación y primero siglo*, 327; Lavrin, *Brides of Christ*, 159.

17. Loreto López, *Tota pulchra*, 175.

18. Loreto López, 175. Loreto López also refers to such open sonorities as polyphonic, because their musicality combined voices and instruments. On the "interior-exterior" ("dentro-fuera") musical sonorities of early modern Barcelona convents, see Mazuela-Anguita, "Música conventual."

19. "Benedic, Dómine, dona tua, quae de tua largitate sumus sumpturi. Per Christum Dóminum nostrum. Amén." In *Regla y constituciones para las religiosas recoletas dominicas del sagrado monasterio de la gloriosa y esclarecida virgen Santa Rosa*, 30–32.

20. See *Regla, y constituciones que han de guardar las religiosas del convento del glorioso padre San Geronymo de la civdad de los Angeles*, 87–89.

21. "Los oídos tengan hambre de la palabra de Dios." In *Regla de N.G.P. San Agustín y constituciones de las religiosas*, 3.

22. De la Maza, *Arquitectura de los coros de monjas en México*, 10.

23. De la Maza, 13–18.

24. Favila, "The Sound of Profession Ceremonies," 154–157.

25. The Purísima Concepción convent in Mexico City also had its organ in the coro alto. See Ramírez Aparicio, *Los conventos suprimidos en México*, 428.

26. Salas Contreras, *Arqueología del ex convento de la Encarnación*, 29–36.

27. Hills, "Veiling the Voice," 121. See also Foucault, *Discipline and Punish*, 195–228. Jean Franco considers the panoptic situation of the confessional, in which mystic nuns told their visions to their confessors, ever attentive to the orthodoxy of nuns' raptures; *Plotting Women*, 6.

28. See Voelker, "Charles Borromeo's 'Instructiones Fabricae Et Supellectilis Ecclesiasticae." Helen Hills notes that some Neapolitan convents had as many as three choirs located in different parts of the church. The *chiesa interiore* (inner church), as the choir was called in Bolognese and Milanese convents, was often behind the high altar. For a helpful schematic, see Reardon, *Holy Concord Within Sacred Walls*, 7. On Bolognese convents, see Monson, *Divas in the Convent*, 251. Regarding convent churches in Milan, see Kendrick, *Celestial Sirens*, 29. A handful of Capuchin, Carmelite, and Company of Mary convents in New Spain had a lower choir flanking the high altar as well. See De la Maza, *Arquitectura de los coros de monjas en México*, 18–19; Loreto López, *Los conventos femeninos*, part 1; Amerlinck de Corsi and Ramos Medina, *Conventos de monjas*, 139.

29. Aribol, *Exemplar de religiosas*, 169–175.

30. Vicente Delgado, "Cantadas y cédulas de profesión de las monjas de Santa Ana de Ávila."

31. Davies, "The Italianized Frontier," 104–108.

32. "De manera que puedan estar en lo alto las mestizas y en lo bajo las niñas hijas de los naturales . . ." Quoted in Amerlinck de Corsi, "Los albores del convento de la Purísima Concepción de México," 14.

33. Martínez, *Genealogical Fictions*, 168.

34. Ramírez Montes, *Niñas, doncellas, vírgenes eternas*, 158. In seventeenth-century Lima, white-veil nuns, novices, and servants were placed in the coro bajo, and the black-veil nuns were in the coro alto, according to Nancy Van Deusen, but it is not clear for which liturgies. It was presumably for the Mass, since all members of the convent were required to attend Mass. See Van Deusen, *The Souls of Purgatory*, 22.

35. Archivo General de la Nación, Mexico City (AGN), Bienes Nacionales/Caja 130/ 30431/Expediente 6. For another example of a novice learning organ during the novitiate while also serving as a singer and harpist in the San Jerónimo convent in Mexico City, see Ortiz, "Euterpe en los conventos," 244.

36. "Coro de Maytines [sic] de verano." In Aribol, *Exemplar de religiosas*, 169–175.

37. Vera, *The Sweet Penance of Music*, 106. This is the opposite configuration from the eighteenth-century arrangement in the women's music school in Mexico City, the Colegio de Belem, in which, according to Josefina Muriel and Luis Lledías, the plainchant choir sang upstairs and the polyphony choir accompanied by instruments sang downstairs, within an architectural structure that appears to look like the convent coros. Unfortunately, this proposed configuration lacks primary-source evidence. See Muriel and Lledías, *La música en las instituciones femeninas novohispanas*, 115.

38. "Y se advierte que fuera de ser conveniencia manifiesta para lo sonoro de la música que se cante en el coro alto, es punto de gravedad y religión hacerse así porque no es justo que lo que es reprehensible y no parece bien en otros conventos como es cantar en coro bajo y con pública manifestación se permite.," from Archivo del Convento de las Gordillas, Libro de caja (Becerro) 1656, folios 33v–43v, quoted in Baade, "Music and Music-Making," 210.

39. Jimarez Caro, *Tipología de los templos conventuales*, 99.

40. Lamentably, De la Maza (*Arquitectura*, 13) did not cite any primary sources corroborating this arrangement, nor does Loreto López (*Los conventos femeninos*, part 1). Salas Contreras switches the direction, claiming that the coro bajo is where the office took place. Combined with the lack of sources from historians, the archeologist's claim suggests that it was difficult to pinpoint what was going on in each coro. See Salas Contreras, *Arqueología del ex convento de la Encarnación*, 62, 165. Frequent flooding would seem to have prevented the nuns at the Jesús María convent in Mexico City from using their coro bajo. See Salazar Simarro, "Música y coro en el convento de Jesús María de México," 30–33.

41. The organ was considered the most appropriate instrument for accompanying the liturgies, as stipulated in the first provincial church council in New Spain (1555), which aimed at unifying church practices in dioceses from as far south as contemporary Nicaragua to Durango in the north under the leadership of the archdiocese of Mexico City, some ten years independent from suffragan status under the archdiocese of Seville. See Martínez López-Cano, *Concilios provinciales mexicanos*, vol. 1, 1–2, 78–79.

42. Pardo, *Vida y virtudes heroicas de la Madre María de Jesús Tomelín*, 169r; Lemus, *Vida, virtudes, trabajos, favores y milagros de la Ven. M. Sor María de Jesús*, 321; Torres, *Vida ejemplar y muerte preciosa de la Madre Bárbara*, 169.

43. Palafox y Mendoza, *Regla y constituciones que han de guardar las religiosas*, 26v–27r.

44. "Acabado de tañir [*sic*] a prima (que dura más de media hora) bajaba a comulgar. Acabado, me subía a el coro, hasta las doce de el día." In Valdes, *Vida admirable, y penitente de la V.M. Sor Sebastiana*, 365. On her convent's coro alto and bajo, see De la Maza, *Arquitectura*, 48–50.

45. *Regla de la gloriosa Santa Clara*, 164.

46. *Regla dada por n. padre San Agustin a sus monjas*, 29–30; *Regla y constituciones para las religiosas recoletas dominicas*, 133–144.

47. Ramírez Aparicio, *Los conventos suprimidos en México*, 416–417.

48. *Regla, y constituciones, que han de guardar las religiosas . . . del glorioso padre San Geronymo*, 73–74. In the nineteenth century, Fanny Calderón de la Barca attended Christmas midnight Mass at the Santa Clara convent in Mexico City and noticed that the nuns took communion after Mass in their own separate communion session. Calderón de la Barca, *Life in Mexico*, 524.

49. Pérez Puente, *Autos de las visitas del Arzobispo Fray Payo Enríquez*, 76.

50. Viana Cadenas notes that an eighteenth-century inventory lists an organ and clavichord in the coro alto of the Inmaculada Concepción in Caracas. See Cadenas García, "Música, Fiestas y Ceremonias," 38.

51. This affixing of the archbishop's notifications to the coro alto entrance took place at the Purísima Concepción, Regina Coeli, San Jerónimo, Encarnación, San José de Gracia, and San Bernardo. See Pérez Puente, 17, 36, 84, 105, 147, 174.

52. "Como es costumbre." In Pérez Puente, 106.

53. Pérez Puente, 106.

54. Calderón de la Barca, *Life in Mexico*, 207–208. The organ she played was likely the instrument built by Gregorio Casela in 1747. See Suárez, *La caja de órgano en Nueva España*, 119. On the location of the organ in the coro alto of Guadalajara's Santa María de Gracia convent, see Swain, *One Thousand Sisters*, 51.

55. The Hieronymite convent rule prohibited polyphony all together. See Pérez Puente, 78.

56. Arenas Frutos, "Mecenazgo femenino," 32–33; *Regla de la gloriosa Santa Clara con las Constituciones de las Monjas Capuchinas*, 307–308.

57. Manso y Zuñiga, *Regla y ordenaciones de las religiosas de la Límpia e Inmaculada Concepción*, 40.

58. Manso y Zuñiga, 40.

59. On the political nature of abbess elections, and other convent ceremonies including professions and nuns' funerals, in early modern Barcelona, see Mazuela-Anguita, "Música conventual."

60. Loreto López, *Tota pulchra*, 178–179.

61. Palafox y Mendoza, *Regla y constituciones que se han de guardar*, folio 29v; *Regla de la gloriosa Santa Clara con las constituciones de las monjas Capuchinas*, 292.

62. *Regla, y constituciones, que por autoridad apostólica deben observar las religiosas del orden del máximo doctor S. Jerónimo*, folio 25v.

63. Chowning, *Rebellious Nuns*, 30–31; Lavrin, *Brides of Christ*, 35, 52, 62, 117, 374, 160–170; Muriel, *Conventos de monjas*, 320–321, 439–440.

64. Lavrin, *Brides of Christ*, 122, 160–170; Van Deusen, *The Souls of Purgatory*, 29.

65. Palafox, *Regla y constituciones que se han de guardar*, folio 29v.

66. "Las religiosas legas, por ser recibidas para oficios corporales, y para que con el sudor de su rostro coman el pan, no están obligadas al oficio divino como las del coro, sino que les basta oír misa rezada, y en lugar de las horas canónicas decir las oraciones del Padre Nuestro y Ave María, que acostumbran." In *Regla y constituciones para las religiosas recoletas dominicas*, 5–6.

67. *Regla de la gloriosa Santa Clara con las constituciones de las monjas Capuchinas*, 151–152.

68. *Regla de la Orden*, Biblioteca Nacional (BN), Madrid, Ms. 1111, folios 29–31.

69. *Regla de la Orden*, folios 29–31.

70. "Porque no haya defectos, ni yerros, principalmente, la que hace el Oficio, y los que han de decir, o cantar las lecciones, ásenlas [sic] antes de ir al coro." Palafox y Mendoza, *Regla y constituciones que han de guardar*, folio 28v.

71. "El Oficio Divino siempre se diga en tono con la pausa debida, que está señalada en medio de cada verso, salvo en las fiestas principales, que se dirá cantado, escusando [*sic*] toda vanidad, y multiplicidad de puntos en el canto. . . . Y porque no haya defectos en la pronunciación, y acentos, principalmente, en la que hace el Oficio, prevenga antes de entrar en el coro las antífonas, capitulas, lecciones, y oraciones, que ha de decir o cantar. Lo mismo hagan las cantoras . . ."; Manso Zuñiga, *Regla y ordenaciones de las religiosas*, 38–39.

72. *Regla de la gloriosa Santa Clara con las constituciones de las monjas Capuchinas*, 145. On calidad, see Ramos-Kittrell, *Playing in the Cathedral*, 64, 167–170.

73. Foucault, *Discipline and Punish*, 140–141.

74. Foucault, 143.

75. Foucault, 143.

76. "Paren mientes las monjas con gran cuidado, que sobre todas las cosas deben desear, de haber el espíritu del Señor y su santa obra, con pureza del corazón y con oración devota limpiando sus consciencias de los deseos terrenales y vanidades de este siglo y hacerse un espíritu con su esposo Jesucristo, por vínculo de amor, por el cual se alcanza el deseo entrañal de las virtudes, y perpetua enemistad con los vicios que contaminan las animas y nos apartan del Señor. Esta oración es la que nos hace amar a los enemigos, y orar por los que nos persiguen, y calumnian como lo dice el Señor. Y por esta tan excelente margarita se convierten en grande y suave dulzor el encerramiento trabajos y asperezas de la Religión. Pues porque esta obra tan necesaria para salvarnos, mejor se ejercita en esta santa orden, las que fueren del coro digan el oficio divino, cuanto a las fiestas solemnes, y fiestas de guardar, y sus octavas y dominicas primo ponendas, y dominicas forzadas, y ferias según el Breviario Romano . . ."; *Regla de la orden de la Concepción*, folio 7.

77. Manso y Zuñiga, *Regla y ordenaciones de las religiosas de la Limpia e Inmaculada Concepción*, folio 15r.

78. On nuns' gestures, see also Van Deusen, *The Souls of Purgatory*, 24.

79. Roach, *Cities of the Dead: Circum-Atlantic Performance*, 26.

80. "Las genuflexiones ni se hacen antes de las palabras que las piden ni después, sino al mismo tiempo de proferirlas. Y toda la comunidad aún las cantoras, especialmente si la cláusula es breve, y que en canto no quiebren la voz desafinándola. Pues siendo

larga la cláusula hay peligro de impedir la voz quebrantándola. Entonces, siendo solas las cantoras las que con canto dicen las cláusulas, la genuflexión se hace al fin de las palabras." In Aromir, *Reglas generales para dentro y fuera del coro*, 23–24.

81. "Así de qué servía el órgano?" In *Libro de Coro del Convento de Santa Inés de Montepulciano*, folio 87r. Trillanes also authored a substantial volume on how to accomplish all of the ceremonies in the Puebla cathedral choir in 1728. See Trillanes, *Directorio, que para las ceremonias*.

82. "Se toca tantito ínterin se hincan las que cantaron . . ."; in Tello et al., *Colección Sánchez Garza*, 174.

83. *Regla y constituciones para las religiosas recoletas dominicas*, 23–24.

84. "Y entre todos los oficios, sea siempre en todo el primero el divino oficio . . . no lo reces fuera del coro te ruego. . . . el coro ha de ser tu centro." In Vallarta, *Luz que guía al camino de la verdad y dirección de religiosas*, folio 168r.

85. "Fue de tan virginal encogimiento y modesta compostura, que nunca cantó sola, sino en comunidad." In Franco, *Segunda parte de la historia de la Provincia de Santiago*, 460. Such behavior aligns with the "corporativist and formalist" nature of early modern Catholicism. See Wobeser, *Sor Juana ante la muerte*, 48.

86. "Siempre que se expone el Santísimo Sacramento, es el coro de las divinas alabanzas como una celestial colmena, donde las ingeniosas, y laboriosas abejas racionales entran, y salen; y sucesivamente todo el día asisten fervorosas . . ."; Aribol, *Ejemplar de religiosas*, 333–334. The population density of some convents is what gave them the nickname of beehives, and it would seem that the coro was their epicenter. See Lundberg, *Mission and Ecstasy*, 9. For a musical precedent that uses bees allegorically, also attributed to Franciscan sources, see Loewen, *Music in Early Franciscan Thought*, 204–205.

87. "Aunque por la indisposición de salud que he tenido, estaba mi cuerpo un poco fatigado, en llegando a estar con mi Señor en el coro, descansaba. Empezaron Maitines, y yo con el cuidado de no perder al Señor de vista persevere, quitando alguna imaginación impertinente, que se cruzaba para embarazarme. Acabé de recogerme de modo, que parece toda me iba al corazón, y a la atención en mi Señor. Los oídos sentía se quedaban para oír, y la boca también para poder decir; pero hasta la vista corporal se inclinaba hacia el interior. Los afectos se aumentaban con el órgano, deshaciéndose mi alma en las divinas alabanzas. . . . Cuando me fui al coro, me sentía con el cuerpo aligerado, con gran quietud, que me estaría muchas horas sin cansarme. El Señor hace toda la costa. Cuando empezaron el Oficio Divino, ya me sentía con los deseos grandes de amar a mi Señor. Y estando en esta disposición, me quedaba algunas veces tan absorta con los afectos que sentía a mi Señor, que ni oía cantar, ni sabía dónde estaba, y ni de mí misma me acordaba; sino que las ansias que tenía, me tenían toda ocupada. Duraba poco este olvido, porque volvía en mí, y cantaba con las Religiosas, pero sin saber cómo, me volvía a quedar." In Aribol, 336–338. This passage also draws out links between spiritual and physical health that seem to persist in New Spanish devotional contexts. See, for example, Finley, "Exemplary sound and hearing," 210–213.

88. Graziano, *Wounds of Love*, 27.

89. Van Wyhe, "After Teresa," 92.

90. "Y quisiera tañer aquel instrumento, para alabar a mi señor con el corazón, labios, potencias, sentidos, y con todos los miembros de mi cuerpo. Esto me sucede, cuándo estoy en el coro con el corazón movido. Como que con cualquiera cosa, que sea de órgano, o alabanza del señor, se me aumentan los afectos." In Aribol, 339.

91. The Sienese lute-playing nun Suor Vannini went into ecstasy when she performed her instrument—the opposite of what Sister Jacinta's biography reports, since this time it is the performer herself who becomes ecstatic and not her listeners. See Reardon, *Holy Concord*, 106–107.

92. "Llamaba a la campana, 'la voz de Dios,' y no le parecía, que oía el sonido de un metal inanimado; sino que eran palabras del mismo Dios, que la llamavan a su obligación . . ."; Lemus, *Vida, virtudes, trabajos, favores y milagros de la Ven. M. Sor María de Jesús*, 69.

93. Lemus, 245.

94. Lemus, 70.

95. "Que el entrar en el coro antes de que viniesen las de más veía nacido, de que al primer golpe de la campana, que se tocaba para aquel efecto: veía que entraba en el la Reyna de los Ángeles María Santísima, acompañada de espíritus celestiales: y que por aquel motivo, y ejemplo, se anticipaba a ir al coro por esperar allí a su Señora." Lemus, 70.

96. Lemus, 407.

97. Myers, "A Transatlantic Perspective," 151.

98. Other examples of artwork depicting mystic experiences show the mystic staring away from, rather than looking directly at, the divine revelation, sometimes with the saintly apparition painted in the periphery of a canvas, as with the example of María de Jesús. A good example is Reni's *Saint Philip in Ecstasy contemplating the Virgin*, in Barbieri, "To Be in Heaven," 224.

99. "Asistía la venerable Madre un día del Ángel de la guarda, a las vísperas, y estándolas cantando las religiosas, sentadas por su orden en lugar que les tocaba: vio que entre cada dos religiosas estaba un ángel con un pimpollo verde, y hermoso en las manos. Descubrió también a la emperatriz de los cielos que presidia a uno, y otro coro celestial, y monástico. En esta forma se fueron prosiguiendo las vísperas, y en el espacio que duraron noto que aquellos verdes pimpollos . . . avían ya coronadose de vistosas, y fragrantes flores, y que al acabarse, recogían los Ángeles los fervores, y afectos de las religiosas, y los ofrecían como suaves aromas al Señor. Advirtió también la sierva del Señor que al tiempo que las religiosas entonaban el 'Gloria Patri et Filio et Spiritui Sancto' y se ponian en pie, inclinando las cabezas, también se levantaban los Ángeles, y hacían la misma humilde veneración: digna correspondencia de las naturalezas Angelica, y humana . . ."; in Lemus, 410–411.

100. Flowers' color, beauty, and sweet redolence made them the perfect allegory through which to describe all that was natural, colorful, and good: the consecrated host could be as white as a jasmine; the precious blood of Christ could be as red as a carnation; Mary was the purest lily, etc. On the presence, use, and meaning of flowers in New Spanish convents, see especially Manrique et al., *Monjas coronadas*, 134–151. As the title of Carlos de Sigüenza y Góngora's history on the Conceptionist Jesús María

convent suggests, it was a paradise, a true Eden where God cultivated the most perfect flowers, the nuns. See Sigüenza y Góngora, *Parayso occidental*. For a critical commentary on *Parayso occidental*, see Kathleen Ross, *The Baroque Narrative of Carlos de Sigüenza y Góngora: A New World Paradise* (Cambridge University Press, 1993). Robert Kendrick traces Milanese convent motet texts that deal with flowers to the Song of Songs in *Celestial Sirens*, 255.

101. Pardo, *Vida y virtudes heroycas de la Madre María de Jesús*, 168v–169v.

102. "Subiera esta esposa de Cristo, por sus méritos, desde el coro bajo, que es de los Ángeles en el cielo, al coro alto de los querubines, que con más cercanía gozan de Dios en la gloria." In Pardo, 169v.

103. Myers, *Neither Saints nor Sinners*, 41.

104. Genovesi, *Carta de el P. José Maria Genovesi, religioso profeso de la Compañía de Jesús*, 11.

105. Genovesi, 6.

106. Genovesi, 34.

107. Genovesi, 35.

108. Genovesi, 17.

109. Ross, *The Baroque Narrative*, 165–167. Similarly, in her autobiography the Puebla Augustinian María de San José (1656–1719) cites numerous saints' feast days to recall particular events that took place on those holy days. In addition, her divine visions were especially active after Matins. See Myers, *Wild Country Out in the Garden*, 50–51, 82–85.

110. Ross, 168.

111. Ross, 163–165; Kristeva, "Women's Time."

112. *Breviarium Romanum*, vol. 2 (1733), 555.

113. Rouget, *Music and Trance*, 128; Fink, *Repeating Ourselves*, 76–77.

114. Bynum, *Holy Feast and Holy Fast*, 194–207; Graziano, *Wounds of Love*, 15–27.

115. Hills, "Veiling the Voice," 121.

116. "Hija esa música no es a mi; no te alegres tanto … llora a las ofensas, que se me hacen; pues vienen los seglares a divertirse, con las músicas; y tus hermanas los hacen por divertirlos sin reverencia de mi cuerpo santísimo en el sacramento." In Torres, *Vida ejemplar y muerte preciosa de la Madre Bárbara*, 193. This example, and another similar occurrence of chastisement, in which the Virgin Mary comes to life and talks to a nun from a painting, can also be found in Lavrín and Loreto López, *El universo de la teatralidad conventual*, 16.

117. Torres, 193.

118. Torres, 194.

119. Torres, 193–194.

120. Torres, 195.

121. "En ninguna fiesta, ni ocasión, se hagan bailes, ni danzas en ambos coros, ni coloquios, y en las chanzonetas, y lo demás que se cantare, no haya cosa profana, que desdiga, de la compostura, y modestia religiosa. Por lo cual prohibimos guitarras, sonajas, tambores, y adufes, y otros instrumentos, que desdicen de la modestia y gravedad del culto divino y profesión religiosa." In Palafox y Mendoza, *Regla y*

constituciones que han de guardar las religiosas de los conventos de Nuestra Señora de la Concepción, folios 27r–27v. Thomas Gage, who traveled in New Spain throughout 1625–1637, critiqued nuns' convents for similar performative practices in the coros, in *Travels in the New World*, 72. More broadly, Palafox y Mendoza is well known for his opposition to theater in Puebla. See Palafox y Mendoza, *Discurso en favor de cierto religioso de vida ejemplar*. On theatricality in the convents, see Lavrín and Loreto López, *El universo de la teatralidad conventual*.

122. Soterraña Aguirre Rincón discusses how Spanish nuns turned secular poems from Lope de Vega, for example, into sacred poetry, in *Un manuscrito para un convento*, 111–112. In Archbishop Manso y Zuñiga's original Conceptionist Rule of 1635, reprinted verbatim in 1758, he said just as much, prohibiting profane songs during the Office and specifically in the presence of the Blessed Sacrament. See Manso y Zuñiga, *Regla y ordenaciones de las religiosas de la Limpia e Inmaculada Concepción*, folio 22r. For bans on villancicos altogether in eighteenth-century Peruvian convents, see Baker, *Imposing Harmony*, 114.

123. Torres, *Vida ejemplar y muerte preciosa de la Madre Bárbara*, 320–321.

124. Torres, 321.

125. Tello et al., *Colección Sánchez Garza*, 106.

126. Nims, *The Poems of St. John of the Cross*, vii–viii.

127. Rhodes, "Mysticism in History," 54.

128. The phrase "querer bien / to love genuinely" is even affiliated with the definition of "llano/easygoing" in the *Diccionario de autoridades*: "Todas le querian bien, por ser de condición llana y agradable. . . ./ All [women] love [him] genuinely because of his easygoing and agreeable demeanor. . . ." This language comes from poetry on courtly love. In addition, the notion of dividing up the Trinity is consistent with New Spanish gendered spirituality that took its rhetoric from traditional family dynamics and extended them to religious men and women, who left their nuclear families to form new ones in the Church. See Lavrin, "La familia en un contexto religioso," 148–149. For more on courtly love and eucharistic villancicos, see Chávez Bárcenas, "Poesía amatoria en la lírica devocional eucarística novohispana."

129. Nims, *The Poems of St. John of the Cross*, vii.

130. Águeda de San Ignacio, *Devociones varias*, 23–36.

131. *Regla de N.G.P. San Agustín y constituciones de las religiosas del sagrado orden de predicadores*, 22–23.

132. Jesús María, *Vida, virtudes y dones sobrenaturales*, 266–267.

133. Me puse a cantar, para que mi voz fuese oída del cielo más sonora, en el nombre de nuestra santa madre la iglesia: cuantas eran mis respiraciones, cuantas las letras, que pronunciaba, eran tantos actos de contrición, de humildad, de amor, y de agradecimiento, que yo ofrecía con mi corazón al soberano recién nacido; eran también tantos ruegos, con que le pedía abundancias de gracia para los fieles, la conversión de los pecadores, la reducción a nuestra santa fe de los herejes, y otras gracias, y favores en beneficio de personas particulares." Jesús María, 267.

134. "Señal de los afectos que insinúan nuestros labios y brota el corazón . . ."; in Parreño, *Novena*, 4.

Chapter 3

1. Córdova, *The Art of Professing*, 58–60.
2. Córdova, 59–60.
3. On the escudo, see Córdova, 60. On triangles in early modern art, see Zorach, *The Passionate Triangle*.
4. "Retrato de la M. María Anna Josefa de Sr. Sn. Ignacio: Religiosa Profesa en el Convento de Sr. Sn. José de Gracia: hija legitima de Dn. José Francisco Ventemilla, y de Dña. María García. Profesó el día 13 de octubre de 179[0s] de 16 años, 13 días de edad. Josephus ab Alzibar [sic] pinxt. a 179[0s]." It is unusual that the artist José de Alcíbar signed the portrait, as most profession portraits are anonymous. He in fact was a student of Miguel Cabrera, whose "Virgin of the Apocalypse" we observed in Chapter 1 in connection with the Immaculate Conception's iconography. Recall that the Conceptionist habit of white with a blue cape imitates the dress of Mary in her representations as immaculately conceived, depicted in this portrait's escudo. See Córdova, 49.
5. Córdova, 49; Cruz González, "Beyond the Brides of Christ," 105; Alcíbar, "Votive Portrait of Sor M. María Anna Josefa de San Ignacio," Museum of Fine Arts, Budapest (accessed October 26, 2021), https://www.mfab.hu/artworks/votive-portrait-of-sor-m-maria-anna-josefa-de-san-ignacio. In an exhibit on nuns' badges, the Denver Art Museum also has a small picture of this portrait dated 1793.
6. Music dowry waiver protocols date to at least the early sixteenth century and are well documented in Italian convents. See Kendrick, *Celestial Sirens*, 34; Monson, *Disembodied Voices*, 2; Stras, *Women and Music in Sixteenth-Century Ferrara*, 17.
7. "Excelentísimo e Ilustrísimo Señor, La abadesa vicaria y definidoras de este convento de nuestro padre santo San José de Gracia de la obediencia y filiación de vuestra excelencia ilustrísima puestas a sus pies en la más debida forma que haya lugar decimos que habiendo cumplido el año de su aprobación y noviciado Sor Mariana de San Ignacio, pide ser admitida a la solemne profesión y religiosa de coro y velo negro a título de música por organista y voz, para cuyo efecto, rendidamente suplicamos a vuestra excelencia provea lo necesario para las diligencias acostumbradas. Quedando en todo a la obediencia de vuestra excelencia ilustrísima con el afecto de humildes y atentas súbditas, que le veneran [al] ilustrísimo señor padre reverendísimo. María Rosa del Niño Jesús, Abadesa, María Micaela del Corazón de Jesús, Vicaria, Ana Ignacia de S. San José, Definidora, Juana de la Santísima Trinidad, Definidora, Clara de Jesús, Definidora, María Dolores de Jesús, Definidora." In Archivo General de la Nación, Mexico City (AGN), Instituciones Coloniales, Bienes Nacionales, Caja 313(3), 30655/21, Expediente 20, folio 2r. Definidoras were members of a council of older nuns in the convent who served as advisors to the abbess. See Lavrin, *Brides of Christ*, 132.
8. "Y siéndolo por su nombre y apellido de la religión, calidad, filiación, naturaleza, estado, y edad, dijo: llamarse como va expresado Sor Mariana de San Ignacio ser Española doncella natural de México, hija legítima de D[on] José Ventemilla, y D[oña] María Loreto García, de edad de diez y seis años cumplidos." Folio 2v.

9. It should be noted that the portrait spells the sitter's name as María Anna while the AGN documents label her Mariana or Marianna. All three are the same name: spelling anomalies like this are typical when dealing with such records because the details of personal names, locations, and so on, were dictated. See Burns, *Into the Archive*, 89–93.

10. Ramos-Kittrell, *Playing in the Cathedral*, 183.

11. Martínez, *Genealogical Fictions*, 356. See also Gharala, *Taxing Blackness*, 2–3.

12. Ochoa Gautier, *Aurality*, 3.

13. Córdova, 68.

14. Córdova, 68.

15. Burns, *Into the Archive*, 11, 68.

16. Lavrin, *Brides of Christ*, 51.

17. Catherine Bell teaches that strategy and repetition both shape ritualization, in *Ritual Theory, Ritual Practice*, 91.

18. On profession as spiritual marriage, see Lavrin, *Brides of Christ*, 416.

19. For another examination of the dowry-waiver process, see Ortiz, "Euterpe en los conventos," 243.

20. The notion of salvation economy is specifically attributed to the Christian disparaging of Jews, making enemies of them for their role in the Passion of Christ. I believe that it can aptly be applied to the circumstance of the Spanish blood-purity laws targeting and marginalizing not only Jews, but also Muslims and other groups. See Cohen, *Christ Killers*, 221. Profession villancicos, along with sermons, and other texts dedicated for profession celebrations form part of the wider theatricality of conventual life. See Lavrín and Loreto López, *El universo de la teatralidad conventual*, chapter 1.

21. "Votos y constituciones son las plumas con que vuela la religiosa hasta el cielo pero aunque son plumas pesan." In Vallarta, *Luz que guía al camino*, folio 129v.

22. On mode 5, see Nassarre, *Escuela música*, 78–79.

23. Tello et al., *Colección Sánchez Garza*, 269–270; Tello, "Musicos ruiseñores," 29–30.

24. *Albricias zagalas* (CSG.010), for one Paula, and Juan de Baeza's *Chansoneta a4 a la profesión de Theresica la chiquita* (CSG.134). See Favila, "The Sound of Profession Ceremonies," 155–160.

25. This information about nuns sponsoring various enhancements to the devotional life of their convents is found typically in convent expense books, such as those for the Mexico City Jesús María convent preserved at the Archivo Historico de la Secretaria de Salud (Fondo Jesús María). But see also, Jesús María, *Vida, virtudes y dones sobrenaturales de la venerable sierva de Dios*, 75–76.

26. Favila, "The Sound of Profession Ceremonies," 159.

27. Bombi, " 'The Third Villancico Was a Motet,' " 181–182.

28. Ortiz, "Euterpe en los conventos," 244.

29. "Para efecto de examinarse en la música y con asistencia de la madre priora y otras religiosas músicas de dicho convento que estaban en el coro bajo, y Antonio de Salazar Mro. de capilla de la dicha santa iglesia catedral, Br. José de Loaysa Agurto, y José de Espinosa bajonero de dicha capilla a quienes su merced nombró para dicho examen y habiendo sacado dichos maestros algunos papeles de música y las religiosas otros

los cantó y acompañó y así mismo tocando violón y vihuela, de lo cual quedaron muy contentas las religiosas." In AGN, Bienes Nacionales (014), Vol. 130 Ex. 6, folio 3v–4r.

30. Torrente, "Function and Liturgical Context," 102.

31. Marín López, "Música y músicos entre dos mundos," vol. 1, 198–199. Tello refers to the villancicos in the Santísima Trinidad convent repertory as extant in "papeles de música," in *Colección Sánchez Garza*, 17.

32. See Lavrin, "The Role of the Nunneries," 371–372.

33. Mazuela-Anguita, "Una celestial armonía," 5.

34. Calderón, *Life in Mexico*, 205–206.

35. Favila, "The Sound of Profession Ceremonies," 148–149.

36. Calderón, *Life in Mexico*, 208. On the regressive nature of repetition with respect to linear chronology see Tanaka, *History Without Chronology*, 39–40.

37. AGN, Bienes Nacionales (014), Vol. 85 Ex. 5, folio 1r. This source is also discussed in Ortiz, "Euterpe en los conventos," 246–247.

38. "Para suplir con el los bajos." Folio 1r.

39. "Y para tenerlo por necesario para el coro la madre vicaria de coro y las músicas en que acompaño, a satisfacción de dichas madres para lo que he pagado y pago ocho pesos cada mes a un maestro . . ."; folio 1r.

40. See, for example, the 3,000-peso dowry contract of one Sister María Andrea de San Isidro Diaz y Sariñana to profess in the Encarnación convent in 1707. AGN, Bienes Nacionales (014), Vol. 310 Ex. 34, folio 3r. Documents from the Encarnación from the mid-eighteenth century onward have the dowry listed at 4,000 pesos. See, for example, AGN, Bienes Nacionales (014), Vol. 1063 Ex. 11, folio 2r. For other examples, see Lavrin, *Brides of Christ*, 22, 370.

41. "Se ofrece con tantos afectos, que a veces nos edifica y enternece ver la puntualidad con que acude a todo aun sin tener la obligación . . ."; in AGN, Bienes Nacionales (014), Vol. 482 Ex. 29, folio 3r.

42. In the case of obligations, Foucault refers to disciplinary punishment as "isomorphic with obligation itself" by drawing on Jean-Baptiste de La Salle's 1706 pedagogy for Christian schools, *Conduite des écoles chrétiennes*; *Discipline and Punish*, 179–180, 210.

43. "Autos hechos sobre el hábito de bendición que pretende recibir para la religiosa de coro y velo negro en el convento de la Concepción Mariana de San José y Machuca a título de música." AGN, Bienes Nacionales (014), Vol. 130 Ex. 36.

44. Those listed in non-Spanish baptismal records typically had to pay tribute to the government. See Gharala, *Taxing Blackness*, 6–7.

45. Carrera, *Imagining Identity in New Spain*, 1–2. Further dispensation would be required for an "hija natural" to profess as a nun, but it was possible. See Lavrin, *Brides of Christ*, 21–22.

46. "Por cuanto nos hallamos sumamente faltas de cantoras por haberse muerto algunas que eran el todo del coro y fomento del culto divino por su mucha destreza y asistencia necesitamos de recibir otras en su lugar por ser pocos los que han quedado para este ministerio y que al presente se nos ofrece una música muy diestra que la hemos oído ya que canta en voz muy buena con tanta destreza y desembarazo que puede desde

luego entrar ejerciéndolo sin que sea necesario el adiestrarla. . . . [Es] hija legítima del contador Agustín Fernández Machuca difunto ya y de doña Isabel de Salazar su legítima mujer tan sumamente pobre que se sustenta de limosna y para conseguir el estado de religiosa a que se inclina por su mucha virtud le han enseñado la música . . ."; in AGN, Bienes Nacionales (014), Vol. 130 Ex. 36, folio 3r.

47. Ochoa Gautier, *Aurality*, 4–5.

48. Fisher and O'Hara, *Imperial Subjects*, 2. Sarah Owens and Jane Mangan place Spanish nuns at the center of that "sliding scale" too, in *Women of the Iberian Atlantic*, 10.

49. "No se puede hacer entre rejas." In AGN, Indiferente Virreinal, Vol. 1116 Ex. 2, folio 1r. The request was for the audition of an organist novice named María Francisca de la Santísima Trinidad. Given that, as we established in the previous chapter, the organ was likely to be located in the upstairs coro alto, it would make sense that the chapel masters would need to enter the cloister to observe her, as this would not be possible from the ground level.

50. "Pareció una mujer española que dijo llamarse Mariana de San José y ser la contenida en estos autos el dicho maestro de capilla sacó diferentes papeles y las músicas religiosas de dicho convento otros que los cantó y acompañó con dichos músicos, y así mismo por sola cantó diferentes letras tocando la arpa todo con mucha destreza y la voz es muy sonora." In AGN, Bienes Nacionales (014), Vol. 130 Ex. 36, folio 4r.

51. Carrera, *Imagining Identity in New Spain*, 31.

52. One convent source from the Franciscan Santa Clara convent in Atlixco colloquially calls titled musicians *música de balde*, literally "of the bucket," meaning free of charge. See Biblioteca Nacional de Mexico, Fondo Franciscano, Vol. 105, folios 91r–91v.

53. On the misleading nature of Spanish appearance, see Gharala, *Taxing Blackness*, 1. With regard to Spanish appearance's unreliability with respect to the calidad necessary to become a cathedral musician, see Ramos-Kittrell, *Playing in the Cathedral*, 68.

54. "Y es muy útil y necesario para que celebren los oficios divinos en dicho convento y que también la dicha Mariana de San José Machuca toca el arpa con que podrá ayudar a las demás compañeras que han quedado en el coro." In AGN, Bienes Nacionales (014), Vol. 130 Ex. 36, folio 5r.

55. Marín López, "Música y músicos entre dos mundos," vol. 1, 58.

56. "Parece puede servir muy bien, si no deja olvidar lo que sabe, y teniendo la precaución de prepararse con la debida anticipación, a imponerse en lo que haya de tocar." In AGN, Bienes Nacionales (014), Vol. 1116 Ex. 12, folio 12r.

57. AGN, Bienes Nacionales (014), Vol. 310 Ex. 35, folio 4r. Of all the dowry waiver protocols, Felipa's documents list the highest number of instruments in which one musician was competent.

58. Likewise at the San José de Gracia convent, the nuns requested in 1708 to admit one Nicolasa Benitez with a dowry waiver for her skills on bajón, as she could replace the singer Isabel de San Bernardo, who had died. See AGN, Bienes Nacionales (014), Vol. 482 Ex. 40, folio 3r.

59. "Está el coro con mucha necesidad para el culto divino y que la que actualmente lo puede hacer no le es posible por haberme encargado los médicos la conciencia de que expone a riesgo su vida." AGN, Bienes Nacionales (014), Vol. 310 Ex. 35, folio 3r.

60. Folio 5r.

61. "Tiene por cierto que será servicio de Dios ntro. Señor se le de el hábito de bendición. Porque tiene noticia [este declarante] que en el coro de dicho convento falta voz [e] instrumentos como ella lo[s] tiene." Folio 5r. Alejandro Vera reports a similar procedure for examining musician nuns in Chilean convents; "Transcending the Walls of the Churches," 177.

62. "Lo que mejor se pareció fue la voz de contralto que cantó con toda destreza." In AGN, Bienes Nacionales (014), Vol. 310 Ex. 35, folio 5r.

63. "Diestra en canto llano y canto de órgano." In AGN, Bienes Nacionales (014), Vol. 933 Ex. 54, folio 2v.

64. "Cantándolo a oído sin saber la música." Folio 2v.

65. "Está la una ciega con cataratas;" "La organista casi ciega." Folio 2v. On the conflicts that might arise from such disabilities, see Myers, *A Wild Country*, 274.

66. "Falta de voces." Folio 2v.

67. "Cargo de cuidar la música y canto llano en el coro y que no descaezca el culto divino y observancia regular." Folio 4r.

68. "Cargadas de Misas cantadas de capellanías y otras obligatorias de nuestro patrón fuera de las precisas funciones religiosas de entierros, maitines, y otras que vuestra ilustrísima no ignora son indispensables." Folio 4r.

69. The chaplaincy "was a mortgage which provided funds for the support of a chaplain (monk or priest) who cared for the spiritual needs of the nuns, officiated at the service of the convent church, or said several masses for the soul of the patron"; Lavrin, "The Role of Nunneries," 378. For more on chaplaincies, see Martínez López-Cano, von Wobeser, and Muñoz Correa, *Cofradías, capellanías, y obras pías en América colonial*. On chaplaincies concerning the cathedral and its music program, see Ramos-Kittrell, *Playing in the Cathedral*, 183.

70. AGN, Bienes Nacionales (014), Vol. 259 Ex. 30, folios 18v–19v.

71. Folios 18v–19v.

72. Mazuela-Anguita, "La vida musical en el monasterio de Santa María de Jonqueres," 42.

73. "Representada al Señor Arzobispo dicha necesidad y la pretensión de una niña noble, virtuosa y diestra en el arte y ejercicio de la música la cual tiene voz de contralto muy apropósito para coro y para lo que en el nuestro se necesita justamente elegante en el acompañamiento del arpa, hija legítima y con todas las circunstancias necesarias para la religión como consta de la fe de su bautismo . . ."; in AGN, Bienes Nacionales (014), Vol. 933 Ex. 54, folio 4r.

74. "A la cual hice tocar varias obras y otras cosas necesarias para el servicio del coro, en el instrumento de arpa; y así mismo tocó y solfeó los papeles y obras de música figurada de diversos tonos, cuantos delante le puse, con destreza, desembarazo, aire, e inteligencia." Folios 4r–4v.

75. "Dulce y muy apropósito para ayudar en aquellas cosas en que no ejercitare el instrumento de arpa . . ."; folio 4v.

76. "Limando y perfeccionando . . ."; folio 4v.

77. "Le decía yo al Señor que primero me quitara la vida que ofenderle porque mi intención era solo amarle y nunca ofenderle, y como el demonio me ponía muchas ocasiones por ofender al Señor, me tenía yo mucho, y así deseaba el venirme a esta

ciudad, y meterme en un convento. Y viendo que no tenía dote para ser religiosa me puse a aprender música y en breve la aprendí porque me cogía con principios de canto llano y sabía tocar el arpa y aprendí la solfa en dos años, de calidad que ya acompañaba en el violón y en el arpa cualquiera papel de música, y con el deseo que tenía de ser religiosa trabajé mucho en aprenderla, así de día como de noche, y me servía de mucha diversión." In Pozo y Calderón, *Autobiography*, folio 281. I am grateful to Asunción Lavrin for providing me with this source.

78. "[Sus padres] procrearon a la suso dicha por su hija legitima y como tal la criaron alimentaron llamándole siempre de hija y ella a los suso dichos de padre y madre en una casa y compañía y que el dicho Agustín Fernández y Doña Isabel de Salazar son españoles Cristianos viejos limpios de toda mala raza de moros, judíos y de los penitenciados por el santo oficio de la inquisición ni por otro tribunal. . . . Mariana de San José es persona virtuosa de buena vida y costumbres y que no tiene impedimento que le estorbe a recibir el hábito de bendición que pretende en el convento . . . "; in AGN, Bienes Nacionales (014), Vol. 310 Ex. 35, folio 2v of second bundle.

79. "Son españoles sin ninguna mezcla, nobles de toda la calidad de cristianos viejos límpios de toda mala raza . . ."; AGN/Instituciones Coloniales/ Indiferente Virreinal/ Caja 4086/ 27 Expediente 27, folio 5r–5v.

80. Covarrubias, *Tesoro de la lengua castellana* (1674), folio 155v.

81. Martínez, *Genealogical Fictions*, 157–159.

82. Martínez, 161–164.

83. Singers at the Descalzas Reales convent in Madrid also had to prove their blood purity. See Hathaway, "Cloister, Court and City," 42–43.

84. These characteristics were expected of the cathedral choir boys as well. See Ramos-Kittrell, *Playing in the Cathedral*, 79.

85. It was originally a recogimiento, "(a place where women withdrew from society), it served as the home for women from a large variety of social backgrounds and cultural groups—women escaping domestic violence or prostitution, women without financial support, and women sent there as punishment for crime, to name a few." In Lanam, "El Colegio de San Miguel de Belem," 2.

86. Obras pías "were the deeds of citizens or nuns who wished to support the expenses of a religious feast in the church of their chosen convent or other expenses of the nunnery. The pious deed usually entailed an obligation on the part of the convent to celebrate a number of masses for the soul of the donor." In Lavrin, "The Role of the Nunneries," 378.

87. "Produzca a mi alma alguna clementísima compasión en la divina justicia." Archivo del Cabildo Catedralicio de la Ciudad de México (ACCMM), Correspondencia 1617–1742, Rollo: 1287–1288, Libro: 24 Caja: 0 Exp: 0 U: 9.2, folio 2.

88. "Excluyendo severísimamente toda otra cualquiera casta, raza, o mixtura." Folio 11. On San Miguel's exclusiveness, see Lanam, "El Colegio de San Miguel de Belem," 38.

89. ACCMM, Correspondencia 1617–1742, Rollo: 1287–1288, Libro: 24 Caja: 0 Exp: 0 U: 9.2, folio 13r.

90. Folio 17r. On the devotion to St. Peter in the cathedral, see Krutitskaya, *Villancicos que se cantaron en la catedral*, 303–305.

91. "Autos de averiguación en torno a la calidad de María Ana de la Cámara, quien salió en el sorteo de huérfanas de la iglesia del convento de religiosas de San José de Gracia, por sospecharse de su calidad de mulata." In AGN, Indiferente Virreinal, Vol. 5594 Ex. 19.

92. "De ser hija de una hermana de una negra mandadera del mismo convento." In AGN, Indiferente Virreinal, Vol. 5594 Ex. 19, folio 2v.

93. "Lo dicho es público y notorio en todo el barrio de San José de Gracia." Folio 2v.

94. "A quien entiende por mulata." Folio 3v. On mulatta/o, see Martínez, *Genealogical Fictions*, 142–145.

95. Martínez, 163–164.

96. "Soy, pobre, española doncella sin amparo, razones tan recomendadas por las leyes a la protección de vuestra santísima . . . "; in AGN, Indiferente Virreinal, Vol. 5594 Ex. 19, folio 5r.

97. On the tradition of convents offering "protection" to women, see Lavrin, *Brides of Christ*, 415.

98. "Especialmente se pregunte a los testigos para la calidad de mi madre, y de sus padres mis abuelos . . ."; in AGN, Indiferente Virreinal, Vol. 5594 Ex. 19, folio 5r.

99. Folios 5v–8r.

100. "Son españoles y no ha oído cosas en contrario." Folio 6v.

101. "No tiene noticia de que sea parienta." Folio 7v.

102. For instances in which phenotypical descriptions made their way into the blood purity confirmation process, see Martínez, *Genealogical Fictions*, 248–249.

103. "El defecto que se le suponía de ser su madre hermana de una mulata." Folio 9r.

104. Folio 9r. On villancicos for the Purification, see Tello et al., *Colección Sánchez Garza*, 545–546. It was a major feast for the cathedral, celebrated as a double second-class feast with "Vespers, salve, procession, Terce and Mass with instruments . . . "; Marín López, "Música y músicos entre dos mundos," vol. 1, 228.

105. Tello et al., *Colección Sánchez Garza*, 289.

106. Cashner, *Hearing Faith*, 19; Chávez Bárcenas, "Singing in the City of Angels," 72. Cashner classifies villancicos about music as "metamusical," in *Hearing Faith*, 6.

107. Bristol, *Christians, Blasphemers, and Witches*, 26.

108. Krutitskaya, *Villancicos que se cantaron en la catedral*, 237. Though in these villancicos shadow is a metaphor for sin, shadows throughout Christian history have had varied meaning. See Gill, "'Until Shadows Disperse,'" 258. Sor Juana's meditations for the novena to the Virgin of the Incarnation, inspired by the Ignatian meditations and María de Ágreda's *Mística ciudad de Dios*, also make use of the light and shadow metaphor. See Wobeser, *Sor Juana ante la muerte*, 48–49.

109. Jones, *Staging "Habla de Negros"*, 126.

110. We know that Nicólas Ximénez de Cisneros sat on various music auditions for the cathedral, which were presumably more involved and intense than those for nuns' convents. On Ximénez de Cisneros, see Tello et al., *Colección Sánchez Garza*, 544–546.

111. These quotes are taken from transcriptions in Gallagher, "The Family Background of the Nuns of Two Monasterios in Colonial Mexico," 282–283. On the methods put

in place by the Spanish colonial government to determine indigenous purity, see Martínez, *Genealogical Fictions*, 104–105.

112. Bristol, *Christians, Blasphemers, and Witches*, 55. For other rare cases of black nuns in the early modern Spanish-speaking realm, see Brewer-García, *Beyond Babel*, chapter 5; Houchins and Fra-Molinero, *Black Bride of Christ*; Van Deusen, *The Souls of Purgatory*; Rowe, *Black Saints*, chapter 6. For an example of a black beata from colonial Brazil, see Spaulding, "Covert Afro-Catholic Agency."

113. Nicholas Jones calls this episteme "African Baroque"; "Sor Juana's Black Atlantic," 278.

114. Bristol, 56.

115. Bristol, 55.

Chapter 4

1. Tello et al., *Colección Sánchez Garza*, 66.

2. The tenor part indicates that it is for violon.

3. I am grateful to Mark Lomano for his assistance with this text.

4. Muriel and Lledías, *La música en las instituciones femeninas*, 412.

5. "En manos del señor arzobispo, hicimos nuestra profesión reiterando los votos y prometiendo guardar la regla primitiva de nuestra Señora del Carmen. Con esto nos puso los velos negros y dio la comunión dando fin a este acto con las demás ceremonias de nuestra sagrada religión, y con muchos villancicos." In Mariana de la Encarnación, *Relación de la fundación del convento antiguo*, 64.

6. The idiom comes from the proverb "aún se come el pan de la boda/the wedding bread is still eaten," explained in a 1740 dictionary as follows: "That is, the wedding feast is scarce over, it is all love and mirth. The new married couple have not had time to find fault with one another, or to fall out, because the wedding joys are fresh, it is the honeymoon still." In Pineda, *Nuevo diccionario, español e ingles e ingles y español*, 338. See also *Diccionario de autoridades*.

7. See Baker, *Imposing Harmony*, 35–55; Bynum, *Holy Feast and Holy Fast*, 48–72; Chávez-Bárcenas, "Singing in the City of Angels," Chapters 5 and 6; Curcio-Nagy, *The Great Festivals of Colonial Mexico City*, 28–30; Dean, *Inka Bodies*, 1–22; Krutitskaya, *Villancicos que se cantaron en la catedral*, 223–229; Muir, *The Biblical Drama*, 22–28; Powell, "A Machine for Souls," 273; Ramos, *Identity, Ritual, and Power in Colonial Puebla*, 78–87; Rubin, *Corpus Christi*, 9, 176–181; Sigaut, "La fiesta de Corpus Christi," 19–40.

8. Owens, *Nuns Navigating the Spanish Empire*, 33. On the Corpus Christi procession in Mexico City, see Curcio-Nagy, 28–30. On processions in Puebla, see Ramos, 70–87.

9. Nuns' advocacy for eucharisitc devotion seems to have superceded enclosure rules that might yield their complete absence from the civic celebration of Corpus Christi. As Linda Curcio-Nagy observes, once when the Mexico City Corpus Christi procession stopped in front of the Santa Clara convent, the nuns dropped confetti over the crowds from their roofs; "Giants and Gypsies," 5. This is consistent with Miguel de

Torres's recollection that nuns were given permission to see street processions for major feast days from their convent rooftops, a treat that Sister Bárbara was too austere to take part in; *Vida ejemplar y muerte preciosa de la Madre Bárbara*, 160.

10. Rhodes, "Mysticism in History," 54; Arenal and Schlau, *Untold Sisters*, 11–13.

11. Ávila, *The Interior Castle*, 177.

12. Warner, *Alone of All Her Sex*, 129–131.

13. Warner, 129.

14. Manning Stevens, "Sacred Heart and Secular Brain," 270.

15. Sor Juana Inés de la Cruz was clearly aware of the effects of resonance. See Finley, *Hearing Voices*, 105–106.

16. Arenal and Schlau, *Untold Sisters*, 12.

17. Macedo, *Eva, y Ave, o María triunfante*, 247–248.

18. Drawing on the teachings of St. Paul, St. Augustine correlated the Old Testament as the shadow of the New Testament, of which Christ is the embodiment. See Gill, "'Until Shadows Disperse,'" 266.

19. Bellido, *Vida de la V.M.R.M. María Anna Águeda de San Ignacio*, 224. See also Warner, *Alone of All Her Sex*, 18.

20. Rubin, "Sacramental Life."

21. On the visual art affiliated with the fall of Adam and Eve and the Eucharist, see Powell, "A Machine for Souls," 288–291.

22. Rubin, *Corpus Christi*, 142.

23. Rubin, 142.

24. Rubin, 143–145.

25. Some tabernacles and monstrances were even built in the shape of statues of Mary. See Rubin, 145.

26. Riaño, *The Industrial Arts in Spain*, 25–26.

27. Garduño Pérez, "Un viril hecho un sol," 115.

28. "Allí cantaban dulcísimos cánticos, tomados de la sagrada escritura, a la sacratísima virgen, y al verbo humanado en su purísimo vientre. Tu vientre (cantarían) es como un montón de trigo cercado de azucenas; porque tiene en sí el pan del cielo, cercado de purezas virginales. Hermoso eres, Señor, sobre todos los hijos de los hombres, derramádose ha la gracia en tus labios, y también en los labios de tu santísima madre: especialmente después que con ellos dio su consentimiento para la encarnación, diciendo: 'he aquí la esclava del Señor.' ¡O, qué gozos tan soberanos causarían estos angélicos canticos en la alma de la soberana preñada!" In Franciscanos, *Instrucción, y doctrina de novicios*, 261. St. Francis himself had meditated on the Virgin pregnant with the Body of Christ disguised as bread, "awestruck before God 'come down' into a Virgin, 'hiding under the form of a little bread.'" Quoted in Bynum, *Holy Feast and Holy Fast*, 99.

29. The piece dates from around 1642. See Tello et al., *Colección Sánchez Garza*, 103.

30. Tello et al., 103.

31. Rojo de Costa, *Sermon en la profesión de la Madre María de S. Simón*, folio 10v–11r. On *hortus conclusus* (enclosed garden), see Ross, *Figuring the Feminine*, 111. Similar horticultural poetry is found in Hildegard von Bingen's writing that emphasized Mary's singing as a product of her artistically fruitful virginal womb, in which God

"planted in [her] innards all varieties of music in all its florid tones." Holsinger, "The Flesh of the Voice," 98–102. On the gendered political implications of the enclosed garden in early modern England, see Stallybrass, "Patriarchal Territories: The Body Enclosed," 129.

32. Bellido, *Vida de la V.M.R.M. María Anna Águeda de San Ignacio*, 202.

33. Kilroy-Ewbank, *Holy Organ or Unholy Idol*, 172; Ruiz Jiménez, "The 'Circular' Forty Hours Devotion in the Convent of La Trinidad (1765)"; Torrente, "Function and Liturgical Context of the Villancico," 194.

34. Bellido, *Vida de la V.M.R.M. María Anna Águeda de San Ignacio*, 202.

35. In early modern Spanish wedding traditions, the madrina took the veil from the groom's shoulder and placed it over the head of the bride, symbolizing their union. See Dehouve, "El matrimonio indio frente al matrimonio español," 78.

36. Salmerón, *Vida de la venerable Madre Isabel de la Encarnación*, folios 110v–111r.

37. Mystic nuns often described divine union as a feeling of burning. See Lavrin, *Brides of Christ*, 92.

38. Warner, *Alone of All Her Sex*, 81.

39. Warner, 82–89; Krutitskaya, *Villancicos que se cantaron en la catedral*, 263.

40. Krutitskaya, 261.

41. Krutitskaya, 269–270.

42. Krutitskaya, 264–265.

43. Finley, *Hearing Voices*, 95–96.

44. Similarly, we saw in Chapter 1 how Immaculate Conception devotion was peppered into Christmas villancicos.

45. "Cual sería la disposición de la gran reina para su última comunión." In Bellido, *Vida de la V.M.R.M. María Anna Águeda de San Ignacio*, 226–227.

46. "Habiendo recibido a el divino hijo, y quedando sumergida en estrechísima unión con la madre amabilísima." In Bellido, 226–227.

47. Rubin, *Mother of God*, 132.

48. Bellido, 225.

49. Núñez, *Distribución de las obras ordinarias*, 62.

50. Palafox, *Regla y constituciones, que han de guardar las religiosas*, folio 10r.

51. *Regla y constituciones para las religiosas recoletas dominicas*, 58–59

52. *Regla, y constituciones, que por autoridad apostólica deben observar las religiosas del orden del máximo doctor S. Jerónimo*, folio 16r.

53. *Regla y constituciones de las religiosas de Santa Brígida*, 16.

54. "Considera, que el amor de Cristo, no se contentó con habernos redimido a costa de su Pasión, y muerte, expendiendo por nuestro amor toda su substancia, sino que quiso, que este mismo beneficio se repitiese frecuentemente en el sacrificio del altar, porque aun después de redimidos, habíamos de ser pecadores, y supo que le habíamos de volver a ofender." In Lanciego y Eguilaz, *Carta pastoral*, folios 26v–27r.

55. On Palafox's departure to Spain, see Vilar-Payá, "Lo histórico y lo cotidiano."

56. "Recibir a su esposo con pureza y con frecuencia." In Palafox, *Puntos*, folios 15r–15v.

57. Palafox, *Puntos*, folios 15r–15v.

58. "Entra el fuego que consume nuestras culpas." In Palafox, *Puntos*, folio 15r.

59. "Se convierte en su Dios." In Palafox, *Puntos*, folio 15r.

60. "¡O unión celestial y eterna! en la cual se junta el cielo con la tierra para hacer la tierra Cielo. ¡O unión celestial y eterna! en la cual lo divino se toca con lo humano y hace a lo humano divino." In Palafox, *Puntos*, folio 15r. This transformation was also preached by St. Bonaventure in a sermon on the Song of Songs. See Rubin, *Corpus Christi*, 27.
61. Smith, *The Acoustic World*, 14–15.
62. For nuns' shortcomings that might lead to a potential assignment of spiritual communion, see Kirk, *Convent Life in Colonial Mexico*, chapter 3; Lavrin, *Brides of Christ*, chapter 7.
63. Rubin, *Corpus Christi*, 150.
64. Rubin, 150.
65. Torres, *Vida ejemplar y muerte preciosa de la Madre Bárbara*, 234.
66. Torres, 234.
67. "Si todas las enfermas . . . levantaran con vehementes deseos las alas del espíritu para volar a su esposo Sacramentado; yo les aseguro, que en premio de su devoción; os consiguieran la sanidad." Torres, 234–235.
68. Rubin, *Corpus Christi*, 169.
69. Covarrubias, *Tesoro de la lengua castellana* (1611), folio 286v.
70. Nassarre, *Escuela música*, 79–80.
71. Lavrin, *Brides of Christ*, 197. See also Ibsen, *Women's Spiritual Autobiography*, 37–40.
72. "Vino a la Madre María de Jesús el mismo Dios sacramentado a la boca, entrándosele por los labios su esposo, entonces más dulce, por más nuevamente comunicable, pues vino a introducirse en su pecho con accidentes de sacramento, y vuelos de enternecido. De esta suerte con un amor que despuntaba en prodigio, y una asistencia, que se declaraba en milagro, le dio a su virgen esposa, el esposo celestial en acuesta ocasión el regalo del pan de la boda, las arras de la eternidad de la vida, y la comunión de su cuerpo sacramentado, sin estorbarle la inhibición de la prelada, el gusto mayor de toda la gloria escondida, y todo el bien en los candores de una forma, comunicada a esta apacible paloma, que así gustaba el grano más puro del laurel más glorioso, en el círculo cándido del sacramento." In Pardo, *Vida y virtudes heroicas de la Madre María de Jesús*, folios 132v–133r. On the use of the term *forma* for the host, see Noone, *Music and Musicians in the Escorial*, 163.
73. Ables, *The Body of the Cross*, 15.
74. Precedents for flying hosts into the mouths of mystics can be seen in the life of St. Catherine of Siena and other late medieval women. See Debby, *The Cult of St. Clare*, 107; Rubin, *Corpus Christi*, 120.
75. Torres, *Vida ejemplar y muerte preciosa de la Madre Bárbara*, 294–295.
76. Torres, 295.
77. "Conocen los senos de las conciencias." In *Regla y constituciones de las religiosas recoletas dominicas*, 59.
78. "Juzgábase como esposa preparada ya para las espirituales nupcias, que habia de celebrar con la Majestad Suprema; y finalmente se hallaba ya, como desposada en la posesión gloriosa, y reciproca inmanencia, con que se gozaba en Cristo transformada toda su alma, y el Señor todo unido, y transformado en su esposa." In Torres, 296.

79. "Alégranos sumamente, ver el ejemplo, y espíritu con que por la misericordia divina, siguen las vírgenes de nuestro obispado, al Cordero de Dios, su esposo." In Palafox, *Regla y constituciones que han de guardar las religiosas*, folios 3v–4r.

80. Ossorio, *Exaltación del divino esposo Jesús*, 8.

81. "Le tenemos como redentor y en discurso de su Pasión santa se humilló entregándose a los tormentos como cordero mansísimo sin abrir para la queja los labios." In Ossorio, 8.

82. Ossorio, 9.

83. Torres, *Vida ejemplar y muerte preciosa de la Madre Bárbara*, 202.

84. "Para estas octavas solemnes componen las religiosas musas algunos sagrados poemas, que cantan al son de templados, y sonoros instrumentos en músicas harmoniosas, y al tiempo que estas se cantaban en el coro meditaba la Madre Bárbara el sentido de sus letras, y solía oírlas de las inteligencias soberanas; y porque entre las muchas, que se cantan tengan las buenas músicas, que lo son las almas devotas en metro harmonioso el rythma [*sic*], que el doctor angélico Santo Tomás compuso para tributar adoraciones a la sacramentada grandeza, que celebran con cantos los más encumbrados serafines; me pareció traducir al castellano, el mismo rythma, que Santo Tomás dejó escrito en el latino, así por ser tan devote, como porque fue de todo un Santo Tomás, glorioso estudio, y lo fue también de un rey tan soberano, como David no solamente cantar, sino bailar también a vista de todo el pueblo, delante de la arca santa en que iba el mana, figura del sacramento eucarístico, y en suma es la Eucharistia Cithara Iesu, en su rigoroso anagrama, y así pues, el dulce, y divinísimo Jesús es quien la toca mientras se come en la mesa, no será ofensa de la sobriedad religiosa, sino lisonja de la devoción tierna, cantarle a su majestad el siguiente rythma, que contiene las heroicas virtudes, y elevados pensamientos, que hallarán en él los que lo cantaren devotos." In Torres, 322. I am grateful to Javier Patiño Loira for assistance in deciphering this quote.

85. "La vista, el gusto, el tacto, si te tocan, en lo que más perciben, más se engañan. Y solo el oído seguro te confiesa, porque es testigo fiel de tu *palabra* [*sic*]." Torres, 322.

86. Henschenius et al., *Imago primi saeculi Societatis Iesu*, 463; Calderón, *El divino Orfeo*, 27.

87. Monson, *Disembodied Voices*, 109; Surtz, *The Guitar of God*.

88. For the date range for *Qué música divina*, see Tello et al., 116.

89. Skeris, *CHROMA THEOU*, 141. For a detailed music analysis of *Qué música divina*, see Cashner, *Hearing Faith*, 197–217. Cashner notes that the coplas come from Sánchez, *Lyra Poética*, 190–191. The same villancico has been examined from the perspective of gendered musical iconography, in Sacristán Ramírez, "Singing the Eucharist to the Kithara of Jesus," 145–150. My focus on the text here emphasizes Sister Bárbara's meditation on the "sentido de sus letras/meaning of the words," in Torres, *Vida ejemplar y muerte preciosa de la Madre Bárbara*, 322.

90. Lanciego y Eguilaz, *Carta pastoral*, folio 19r–19v.

91. Griffiths, "Hidalgo, mercader, sacerdote o poeta," 15–17.

92. Carranza de la Miranda, *Comentarios del reverendísimo*, 341; Griffiths, "The Vihuela," 169.

93. Carranza de la Miranda, 344.

94. Krutitskaya, *Los villancicos que se cantaron en la catedral*, 28.

Chapter 5

1. AGN/ Instituciones Coloniales/ Indiferente Virreinal/ Caja 0565/ Expediente 023, folio 2v.

2. Bysted, *The Crusade Indulgence*, 11.

3. Plank, "A Seventeenth-Century Franciscan Opera," 188. Favila, "Music and Devotion," 223. I concur with Nuria Salazar Simarro and Sarah E. Owens that Conceptionists are in fact not Franciscans; "Cloistered Women in Health Care," 141.

4. On privileged indulgences (or privileged altar), see Tingle, *Indulgences After Luther*, 83.

5. Sister María Anna Águeda de San Ignacio of Puebla's Santa Rosa convent explains in her Passion meditations that the white tunic "singled out the insane/señalaba a los fatuos" and was placed on Christ to humor Herod. Her meditation is steeped in vocality, suggesting that Christ remained silent when Herod asked him to perform a miracle to prove his innocence because his voice had already been silenced by Herod himself, who had ordered the execution of Christ's precursor and cousin John the Baptist. See Águeda de San Ignacio, *Devociones Varias*, 64–65.

6. Marina de San Francisco proposed that it be instilled across all of North America.

7. Lavrin, *Brides of Christ*, 351.

8. Parra, *De el bien, excelencias y obligaciones*, 729–730.

9. "Así como todos los misterios de la Misa son una viva representación de la Pasión de Cristo Nuestro Señor, así también todas las horas canónicas se instituyeron principalmente para memoria de ella." Parra, 729.

10. Núñez, *Distribución de las obras ordinarias*, 77.

11. See Zavaleta, *Copia de la carta*, 12.

12. Derbes, *Picturing the Passion*, 7–8; Graham and Kilroy-Ewbank, *Visualizing Sensuous Suffering and Affective Pain*, 167–266; Larkin, "Liturgy, Devotion, and Religious Reform," 495–498.

13. Johnson, "Franciscan Passions," 95–96; Burkhart, *Holy Wednesday*, 23–24.

14. "Debe darles tiempo para que lean libros de santa doctrina y gran devoción, y que aprendan a sentir la Pasión de nuestro Señor y amarla e imitarla, que este es el a. b. c. en que nuestro padre San Francisco y todos los santos aprendieron y principiaron; conviene a saber sentir la Pasión de nuestro redentor y animarse a imitarla por la suavidad de su amor, que él comunica a los que de veras estudian en su cruz y Pasión." *Regla de la orden de la Concepción*, folio 15.

15. Pardo, *Vida y virtudes heroicas de la Madre María de Jesús*, folios 192v–193r.

16. "Porque así se dispusiesen con más sentidas a la celebración de la Semana Santa, que se seguía, meditando con atenciones cotidianas los trabajos, congojas, dolores, y heridas de su crucificado esposo, y enamorado muerto: continuaron las convocadas vírgenes, el cuidado de decir este número [treinta y tres] de veces la oración del Credo, repitiéndola todos aquellos días, que corrieron hasta el viernes que llama de

Lázaro (y es el antecedente al viernes santo) y en el sobredicho penúltimo viernes de la Cuaresma, llevaron aquella escuadra de almas vírgenes (que conducía y acaudillaba la Madre María de Jesús) la imagen de un sagrado crucifico, que hoy se venera en el coro colocado en el comedio de uno de sus lienzos, le pusieron en un altar con mucha reverencia de adornos, y afectos. A este tiempo aquel simulacro mudo, o imagen muerta del crucifijo, teniendo siempre cerrados los párpados, abrió milagrosamente entonces los ojos, y los clavó aquel Señor clavado en la cruz, o los puso dulcemente en todas las religiosas, que habían frecuentado la devoción dicha, y permaneció mirando a las mismas esposas suyas, que en esta ocupación le habían servido. . . . [La] Madre María de Jesús: pidió a su soberano y muerto en la cruz esposo: que se dignase de también dar la bendición a las religiosas todas de aquella clausura." Pardo, 193r.

17. On divine infinity, see Kendrick, *Fruits of the Cross*, 60.
18. The moment of the "divine glance" from Peter's denial in Luke's Gospel was featured prominently in Lasso's motet "Vide homo, quae pro te patior" in his cycle *Lagrime di San Pietro*. The piece was composed during Lasso's service under the Duke of Bavaria, a Catholic region heavily influenced by early modern Spanish asceticism. See Fisher, "Per mia particolare devotione," 170–171.
19. Ross, *The Baroque Narrative*, 52, 85.
20. Manso y Zuñiga, *Regla y ordenaciones de las religiosas de la Limpia e Inmaculada Concepción*, 43–44.
21. No extant examples of music specific to convent mortification rituals exist from New Spain as they do from Italian convents, according to Craig Monson, "Le pene sofferte per Te son glorie" (presentation at the 2013 annual meeting of the American Musicological Society).
22. Lavrin notes that biographers found the mortification practices of nuns seeking to imitate Christ's suffering especially effective for the drama they sought in their narratives; *Brides of Christ*, 193–195.
23. Kendrick, *Celestial Sirens*, 46.
24. On the "challenge to chastity" in convents, see Lavrin, *Brides of Christ*, chapter 7.
25. Lavrin, *Brides of Christ*, 321. The strength of role model nuns would serve as an example to those nuns who inevitably succumbed to so-called weakness attributed to their sex. Especially considered a weakness was the practice of developing strong friendships, platonic or otherwise, within the convent walls. See Kirk, *Convent Life in Colonial Mexico*, 55–65; Lavrin, *Brides of Christ*, 241 and 251.
26. This would contradict the long-held belief, drawn from the teachings of Luis de Granada among others, that women were weak and lecherous, the cause of sin among the stronger (male) sex. See Lavrin, "The Erotic as Lewdness," 40. For precedents from the early Church fathers blaming Eve, and femininity by association, for the downfall of Adam/humanity, see Clifton, "Gender and Shame," 643–645. The "manly" strength of holy women also has its roots in the teachings of the Church fathers and later in Medieval theology. See Harness, "Chaste Warriors and Virgin Martyrs in Florentine Musical Spectacle," 80.
27. Torres, *Vida ejemplar y muerte preciosa de la Madre Bárbara*, 156. Sor Juana also promoted similar mortification practices. See Wobeser, *Sor Juana ante la muerte*, 61.
28. Torres, 155.

29. "Confortada con su varonil esfuerzo." Torres, 155. On the male attributes accorded to St. Teresa of Ávila, see Rowe, *Saint and Nation*, 112.

30. Parreño, *Novena*, 61.

31. Parreño, 61. Similarly, Gregory of Nyssa drew a comparison between the tambourine and virgin women. See Harness, "Chaste Warriors and Virgin Martyrs in Florentine Musical Spectacle," 79.

32. Cruz González, "Beyond the Bride of Christ," 102–107; see also Salazar Simarro, "El papel del cuerpo en un grabado del siglo XVIII."

33. On *Crux Fidelis*, see Szövérffy, "Crux Fidelis."

34. Cruz González, 112–123.

35. Cruz González, 123–125.

36. "Sean mis manos enclavadas con las vuestras, mi corazón traspasado con la lanza, que penetró el vuestro, mis pies penetrados, como los vuestros, de clavos: muero yo Jesús con vos en vuestra cruz, y muera de vuestro santo amor." Jesús María, *Vida, virtudes y dones sobrenaturales*, 111.

37. " 'Hija esta es la cruz de la religión: todas las que la llevan, y abrazan con gusto, tienen estos consuelos en ella misma. Llévala con mucho amor; y di a tus hermanas, que se resignen en ella, y vivirán con gusto en la vida, y tendrán mucho premio en la hora de la muerte.' Con tan divina enseñanza, quedó en su cruz crucificada Bárbara tan gozosa."; Torres, *Vida ejemplar y muerte preciosa de la Madre Bárbara*, 163.

38. Graziano, *Wounds of Love*, 28.

39. "Y como en la cruz del cielo le dio la mejor cítara a su amada el verdadero Apolo, luego que la pulsó con el espíritu, le infundió numen con que pudo cantar congratulándose Bárbara en su crucifixión estos versos." In Torres, *Vida ejemplar y muerte preciosa de la Madre Bárbara*, 164. Sister Juana de la Cruz, the sixteenth-century Franciscan mystic from Spain, experienced a similar ecstatic, musical crucifixion; see Surtz, *Guitar of God*, 68. We know that Bárbara's biographer, Torres, was familiar with Juana de la Cruz's life, as he mentions examples from it (301). The musical metaphor had a long tradition that passed through the writings of St. Bonaventure, Hildegard of Bingen, and Clement of Alexandria. See Monson, *Disembodied Voices*, 80–91.

40. Tenorio, *Los villancicos de Sor Juana*, 74.

41. Torres, *Vida ejemplar y muerte preciosa de la Madre Bárbara*, 359–360.

42. Roure, *El soberano cedro de María*, 3.

43. Salmerón, *Vida de la venerable madre Isabel de la Encarnación*, folios 110v–111r.

44. Such manuals had a longer history spanning over a century of use. See Burdette, "Reparations for Christ Our Lord: Devotional Literature, Penitential Rituals, and Sacred Imagery in Colonial Mexico City," 358.

45. On the centrality of the Virgin Mary's cult in Passion devotion, see Kendrick, *Fruits of the Cross*, 23; *Singing Jeremiah*, 21–22.

46. Bestul, *Texts of the Passion*, 113. The *Stabat Mater*, the famous sequence about the Virgin Mary's distress over Christ's Passion, for example, is attributed to the Franciscan Jacopo da Todi; see Warner, *Alone of All Her Sex*, 217. In seventeenth- and eighteenth-century New Spain, the Jesuits also promoted the Virgin of Sorrows in

their churches through visual art; see Bargellini, "Jesuit Devotions and *Retablos* in New Spain," 687–689.

47. "The seven sorrows of Mary are: the prophecy of Simeon; the flight into Egypt; having lost Christ in the Temple; meeting Jesus on his way to Calvary; standing at the foot of the cross; the deposition; the burial of Christ," as Drew Davies notes in his contextualization of the eighteenth-century Durango cathedral repertory for the Virgin of Sorrows; "The Italianized Frontier," 386–390. Willem Elders also notes that there have been any number of sorrows associated with the Virgin, from five to as many as twelve. As might be expected, earlier European composers drew on the symbolism of the number seven in music for the Virgin of Sorrows; *Symbolic Scores*, 151–156. Robert Kendrick notes that seventeenth-century Passion devotion music was generally open to numerological and scientific symbolism as well; *Fruits of the Cross*, 94–99. For more on the iconography of the Virgin of Sorrows, see Díaz and Stratton-Pruitt, *Painting the Divine*, 86–87.

48. Díaz and Stratton-Pruit, 18.

49. Parreño, *Novena*, 1–3.

50. Leyva Rendón, "Recupera INAH historia y esplendor de Nuestra Señora de las Aguas."

51. The Gospel of Nicodemus is also known as the Acts of Pilate (*Acta Pilati*). On this gospel as the source for Mary's fainting and weeping at the crucifixion, see Kendrick, *Fruits of the Cross*, 105.

52. Díaz and Stratton-Pruitt, *Painting the Divine*, 86.

53. Kristeva, "Stabat Mater," 142–145.

54. Kristeva, 144.

55. Kristeva, 144.

56. Kristeva, 141–145. On the primacy of Mary's maternal love in the doctrine of her intercessory power, see Warner, *Alone of All Her Sex*, 286.

57. Kristeva, 143.

58. Kristeva, 143.

59. Sarmiento, *Harmonicos dolores*, 5 de 16 contenido. The pagination of Sarmiento's sermon in these footnotes corresponds with the pagination of its digitized format found through the link in the bibliography. The feast was celebrated twice in the Spanish Church, including the Friday before Palm Sunday, according to the Roman calendar, and additionally on September 15 after 1735. See Davies, "The Italianized Frontier," 392.

60. "Cantar de fantasía, dicen los músicos, es salirse de las reglas del arte sin apartarse del sonoro compás." In Sarmiento, *Harmonicos dolores*, 22 de 24 preliminares. Fantasias were typically instrumental and not vocally extemporized. However, there are cases in which, of all instruments, the vihuela could accompany pieces known as fantasias, suggesting a broader definition that could employ voice. See Griffiths, "The Vihuela," 162–163.

61. Cohen, *Christ Killers*, 221.

62. Cohen, 20.

63. "¿Y no se templara este instrumento para que suene acorde la cítara? Sí. ¿Y quién lo ha de templar? El judío: que él es quien atormenta a Cristo crucificándole de tres clavos, devanándole sus sacratísimos nervios. Tirantes de tres clavijas. Pues tiemble el hebreo, si él solo sabe crucificar, para que cante María, pues ella sola sabe sentir, toma esa cítara judío, tire las cuerdas al tormento tu crueldad. Tira, tuerce las clavijas. ¡O blasfemo, y como aprieta! ¡Fuerte tormento! Pero con todo aprieta el tiemble tirano, que aún está bajo el tono de esa cítara, y desea padecer más ese inocente, que atormentas. Tira más judío. Bien tirante está este nervio." In Sarmiento, *Harmonicos dolores*, 3 de 16 contenido.

64. Kendrick, *Fruits of the Cross*, 6. See also HaCohen, *The Music Libel Against the Jews*; Marissen, *Lutheranism, Anti-Judaism, and Bach's St. John Passion*.

65. "Pulsemos ahora esta cuerda, oigamos como suena. ¡Válgame Dios, que bien suena! Ea hebreo, dale más tormento a esa cítara, no dejes de la mano las cuerdas, para que lo des, pasado de tu crueldad, levante a cueza divina cítara, más armonía, dulce la voz. Tira. Aprieta, tuerce los nervios. ¡Oye como levanta de punto el tormento! Toquemos ahora esta cuerda, veamos si está en buen tono. ¡Válgame Dios, y que dulzura! Prosigue israelita, aprieta más, tira más esas cuerdas, tiempla. ¡Oye que agrio está el tiro! Pulsemos ahora esta cuerda, veamos, si está en tono fijo. ¡Válgame Dios, y que suavidad! Ya basta hebreo, ya basta, no tires más; que ya está templada esa cítara, porque no hay ya tormento que darle as esas cuerdas, estando ya consumados los dolores todos, que han de padecer a questos sacratísimos nervios tirantes de tres clavijas: *Consummatum est*. . . . Ya habéis oído, que bien suenan. Que bien se dan la mano en la cruz con admirable armonía templados, lo dulce con lo agrio, el tormento con el gozo, el gemido con el canto. Y pues, ¿quién ha de discantar en lo armónico y bien templado de este plectro? ¿Quién ha de cantar en la dulzura de esta cítara? María, que está al pie de ese instrumento. . . . ¡O María co-redentora nuestra!" In Sarmiento, *Harmonicos dolores*, 3 de 16, 4 de 16 , 15 de 16 contenido.

66. Rubin, *Mother of God*, 159. On the conversos, see Martínez, *Genealogical Fictions*, 61. See also Curcio-Nagy, "Faith and Morals," 161–162.

67. Lavrin, *Brides of Christ*, 360.

68. "Es un coro de vírgenes hijas del gran Domingo ... que siguen a la cordera del cielo Inés ... aplaudiendo en sus metros las gloriosas penas de Jesús, cantando en la muerte de Cristo, los alegres dolores de María. . . . ¡Por cierto acertada música!" In Sarmiento, *Harmonicos dolores*, 2 de 16 contenido.

69. Sarmiento, *Harmonicos dolores*, 13 de 16 , 14 de 16 contenido.

70. Sarmiento, *Harmonicos dolores*, 12 de 16 contenido.

71. On Mary's co-passion, see Fulton, *From Judgment to Passion*, 202.

72. Davies, "The Italianized Frontier," 234–235.

73. Tello et al., *Colección Sánchez Garza*, 71.

74. Since the early seventeenth-century villancicos of Gaspar Fernández, even as far back as the music of Guerrero, it was typical to represent multiple characters with corresponding voice parts. See Waisman, *Una historia de la música colonial hispanoamericana*, 198.

75. Astell, *The Song of Songs*, 44.

76. Palafox y Mendoza, *Obras del ilustrísimo*, vol. 5, 468–469.

77. Palafox y Mendoza, 380–382.

78. On the use of flat keys in Virgin of Sorrows music, symbolizing Mary's sweetness, see Davies, "The Italianized Frontier," 398–399.

79. Nassarre, *Escuela música*, vol. 1, 76–77; Ortiz, "Mysticism and Early Modern Musical-Cosmological Paradigms," 247–249.

80. Vicente, "Successful Mystics and Failed Mystics," 136.

81. "Toda letra que tratare de cosas tristes o deprecaciones de juicio o de cosas espantosas será mayor acierto el componerla por este tono . . ."; Nassarre, 77.

82. Ardanaz was active in the cathedrals of Pamplona and Toledo. For more on Ardanaz, see Tello et al., *Colección Sánchez Garza*, 307.

83. Fischer, " 'Per mi particolare devotione,' " 209; Powers, "Tonal Types," 448–450.

84. Lorente, *El porque de la música*, 564–565.

85. "Los compositores que compusieren música en este tono sean todas aquellas letras que hablaren de cosas tristes, llorosas, y de engaño . . ."; in Nassarre, *Escuela música*, vol. 1, 79–80.

86. Stein, "Opera and the Spanish Political Agenda," 157. On the use of rhythm and meter for affective purposes in seventeenth-century villancicos, see Cashner, "Imitating Africans"; Chávez Bárcenas, "Singing in the City of Angels," 155–156, 190. See also Waisman, *Una historia de la música colonial hispanoamericana*, 192–193.

87. "Porque como Adán dio por disculpa que su compañera le había ayudado, y facilitado a el pecado, así su madre, como co-redentora le había acompañado a redimir el mundo, y por su medio le encargaba les fascilitase como madre el buen logro de la redención; y nosotros la obligásemos con nuestro amor, y nos valiésemos de su poderosa intercesión." In Bellido, *Vida de la V.M.R.M. María Anna Águeda de San Ignacio*, 224.

88. Lavrin, *Brides of Christ*, 45.

89. "Hija mira esta espina, que mi hijo santísimo tuvo en una cien de su sagrada cabeza: siempre la haz de traer en la tuya para alivio de tus tribulaciones." Torres, *Vida ejemplar y muerte preciosa de la Madre Bárbara*, 257.

90. Torres, 257.

91. "Postrada a los pies de un santo crucifico hacía oración a las dos sacratísimas llagas de sus pies, pidiendo la guiase por el camino de la humildad." Torres, 259.

92. Torres, 260. On the implications of mystic nuns drinking from Christ's side wound as reversal of menstruation and the erotic implications of this interaction as "a negation of phallocentrism," see Franco, *Plotting Women*, 18–19.

93. Torres, 260.

94. Torres, 263–274.

95. Torres, 272.

96. The *endecha* was a poetic form for expressing sadness. See Álvarez Sellers, *Literatura portuguesa y literatura española*, 354.

97. Torres, *Vida ejemplar y muerte preciosa de la Madre Bárbara*, 273–274. A similar prose veneration was written by Sister María Anna Águeda de San Ignacio of Puebla's Santa Rosa for meditations on Christ's dead body at the Passion. See Águeda de San Ignacio, *Devociones Varias*, 37–52.

98. Matter, "Lectio Divina," 151.

99. Kendrick, *Fruits of the Cross*, 21.
100. Kendrick, 21.
101. The palm is also a symbol for virginity, supporting further the notion that the vow of chastity was akin to martyrdom. See Kirk, *Sor Juana Inés de la Cruz and the Gender Politics*, 196.
102. This adds another layer to the argument that martyrdom was interpreted by Sor Juana as a form of female knowledge creation, in Kirk, *Sor Juana Inés de la Cruz*, 195–198. See also, Finley, "Sounding the Feminine," 29–30. On the doctrine of the Immaculate Conception and Mary's wisdom, see Bergman, "A Maternal Genealogy of Wisdom."

Epilogue

1. "Con encendidas ansias de amor." In Jesús María, *Vida, virtudes y dones sobrenaturales*, 320.
2. Jesús María, 323–330.
3. "Últimamente, llegó la hora de vísperas . . . resonando las campanas del convento con festivos repiques: entrando por las puertas de la iglesia una concertada danza a celebrar con un festín el día; rompiendo el aire sonoras chirimías, y trompetas, y entonando en el coro las religiosas con suavísimos cánticos las divinas alabanzas." In Lemus, *Vida, virtudes, trabajos*, 436.
4. Pardo, *Vida y virtudes heroicas*, folio 213r.
5. "Con ardentísimos deseos de ver, y gozar eternamente a su esposo." In Torres, *Vida ejemplar y muerte preciosa de la Madre Bárbara*, 503.
6. Torres, 93, 504.
7. "Pues Cristo Señor Nuestro les dio en la cruz el ejemplo para esta recomendación piadosa a todos los padres de familias." In Torres, 504.
8. Torres, 504–505.
9. Torres, 505–506.
10. "El fin de todas será la salvación, y perfección propia, y de el prójimo, siguiendo este instituto, a imitación de la gloriosa Virgen María." In *Instituto y constituciones*, 9.
11. Gaspar de Alba, *[Un]Framing the "Bad Woman"*, 9–19.
12. Gaspar de Alba, 19.
13. See Loreto López, *Tota pulchra*, regarding some of the Purísima Concepción convent's holdings. A recent article in *Relatos e historias en México* by Elena Díaz Miranda demonstrates how unknown works of art about/related to convent culture remain in private collections. The article depicts a painting in a *coleccion particular* of a supposed eighteenth-century Puebla convent coro (alto) with nuns busying about a central *fascistol* (lectern for music) before a large, gilded altar. My efforts to find out more about this rare painting, that to my knowledge has not been documented anywhere else, have been time consuming and fruitless so far. See Díaz Miranda, "¿Cuáles eran las tentaciones de la carne en las monjas novohispanas?"
14. Myers, *Neither Saints nor Sinners*, 6.

Appendix 5.1

1. A privileged altar is one in which an indulgence can be granted to a soul in purgatory by special permission from the Pope.
2. Emphasis underline in original document.

Appendix 5.2

1. Possibly also a play on the word for "harp," as in "being like a harp."
2. "enclavijado" also means "with pegs," as in a musical instrument.
3. Also, a musical term denoting the repetition of concluding syllables or words, sung softer by a different voice (or choir or musical instrument).
4. "Lord, remember me."
5. Also, a musical term denoting pitch, as in "pitches."
6. Same as in note three.
7. Also, a "degree," as a doctor's degree, and "quality."
8. "Potencias" may also mean the three faculties of the soul: memory, will, and understanding.

Select Bibliography

Primary Sources

Aguilar, Esteban de. *Sermón del seráfico padre San Francisco: en la fiesta que le celebra su ilustre, y devota cofradía fundada en el religioso convento de religiosas de Regina Coeli a cuyas expensas se imprime.* Mexico City: Viuda de Bernardo Calderón, 1668.

Arbeau, Thoinot. *Orchesographie. Et traicte en forme de dialogve, par leqvel tovtes personnes pevvent facilement apprendre & practiquer l'honneste exercice des dances.* Lengres: Imprimé par lehan des Preyz, 1589.

Aribol, Antonio. *Ejemplar de religiosas, en la penitente, virtuosa, y maravillosa vida de la venerable madre Sor Jacinta de Atondo, religiosa de nuestra seráfica madre Santa Clara, y abadesa que fue del Real Convento de Santa Catalina de Zaragoza.* Zaragoza: Herederos de Manuel Roman, 1716. Biblioteca Nacional de México Fondo Reservado, Mexico City, Monografías 922.246 ATO.ar. 1716.

Aromir y Bustamante, Fray Manuel. *Reglas generales para dentro y fuera del coro: arregladas a las ceremonias que usa la orden de ntro. Seráfico padre Sn. Francisco.* 1825. Mexico City: Centro de Estudios de Historia de México. Clasificación 271.372.(091) ARO. Libro No. 9,995.

Ávila, José de. *Colección de noticias de muchas de las indulgencias plenarias y perpetuas: que pueden ganar todos los fieles de Cristo, que con la debida disposición, visitaren en sus respectivos días las iglesias que se irán nombrando en ellos en esta corte de México.* Mexico City: Felipe de Zúñiga y Ontiveros, 1787.

Ávila, Juan de. *Pureza emblemática discurrida en la profesión de la M. Mariana de San Francisco, religiosa de Santa Clara.* Mexico City: Viuda de Juan de Ribera, 1686.

Bellido, José. *Vida de la V.M.R.M. María Anna Águeda de San Ignacio, primera priora del religiosísimo convento de dominicas recoletas de santa Rosa de la Puebla de Los Ángeles.* Mexico City: Imprenta de la Biblioteca Mexicana, 1758.

Breviarium romanum ex decreto S. Concilii Tridentini restitutum Pii V Pont. Max. jussu editum . . . . Plantinius, 1733.

Carranza de la Miranda, Bartolomé. *Comentarios del reverendísimo Señor Fray Bartolomé Carranza de Miranda, Arzobispo de Toledo, etc. sobre el catecismo.* Anvers: Martin Nucio, 1558.

Ceremonial de los religiosos de la orden calzados de la Santísima Trinidad. Madrid: D. Joachin Ibarra, 1780.

Ceremonial Dominicano en el cual se trata de las cosas que conducen al modo uniforme y orden de celebrar los oficios divinos con las ceremonias del orden de predicadores. Madrid: Por la viuda de D. Francisco Nieto, 1694.

Ceremonial para la admisión y dar el hábito a las religiosas, del Órden de la Compañía de María Santísima, llamadas de la Enseñanza. Mexico City: Oficina de Arizpe, 1811.

Ceremonial para la profesión de las religiosas, del Órden de la Compañía de María Santísima, llamadas de la Enseñanza. Mexico City: Oficina de Arizpe, 1812.

Ceremonial para las religiosas geronimas de México. Mexico City, ca. 17th century. The Hispanic Society of America, B2911.

Choirbook from the Convento de Santa Inés. Newberry Library Microfilm 1314.

Covarrubias, Sebastián de. *Tesoro de la lengua castellana, o española.* Madrid: Luis Sanchez, 1611.

Estatutos, y ordenaciones de la Santa Provincia de San Gregorio de religiosos descalzos de la regular, y más estrecha observancia de N.S.P.S. Francisco. Manila: Convento de Nuestra Señora de Loreto, 1753.

Fernández Cejudo, Juan. *Llave de oro, para abrir las puertas del cielo. la regla y ordenaciones de las monjas de la Inmaculada Concepción de Nuestra Señor, la Madre de Dios.* Reprinted in Mexico City: Imprenta de María Fernández y Jáuregui, 1815.

Franciscanos. *Instrucción, y doctrina de novicios: sacada de la de San Buenaventura, con que se crian los novicios de la santa provincia de San Diego de México, de la mas estrecha observancia regular de Nro. S. P. Francisco.* Mexico City: José Bernardo de Hogal, 1738.

Franco, Alonso. *Segunda parte de la historia de la Provincia de Santiago de Mexico, Orden de Predicadores en la Nueva España.* Mexico City: Imprenta del Mueso Nacional, [1645] 1900.

Genovesi, José María. *Carta de el P. José María Genovesi, religioso profeso de la Compañía de Jesús á la muy R.M. abadesa del religiosísimo Convento de la Encarnación de la ciudad de México, en que le dá noticia de las virtudes de la M. María Josepha de la Encarnación, religiosa del mismo convento, que murió á 13. de septiembre de 1752.* Mexico City, 1753.

Gómez de la Parra, José. *Fundación y primero siglo: crónica del muy religioso convento de Sr. Sn. José de Religiosas Carmelitas Descalzas de la ciudad de Puebla de los Ángeles.* Puebla: Viuda de Miguel Ortega, 1732.

Hanstein, J. F. *The Immaculate Conception: The History of a Roman Catholic Dogma, or How Heresy Becomes a Tenet of Faith.* London: William Stevens, 1857.

Henschenius, Godefridus, Johannes Bolland, Sidronius de Hossche, Jacques van de Walle, and Jean de Tollenaere. *Imago primi saeculi Societatis Iesu a Provincia Flandro-Belgica eiusdem Societatis repraesentata.* Antwerp: Balthasar Moretus, 1640.

Instituto y constituciones de la orden de la Compañía de María, nuestra señora. Zaragoza: Imprenta de Francisco Moreno, 1745.

Jaramillo, Marcos. *Sermon en la annual, solemne fiesta, que a la Concepción Purísima de María, con título del choro alto.* Mexico City: Herederos de la Viuda de Francisco Rodriguez Lupercio, 1713.

Jesús María, Félix de. *Vida, virtudes y dones sobrenaturales de la venerable sierva de Dios Sor María de Jesús religiosa profesa en el V. Monasterio de la Inmaculada Concepción de la Puebla de los Ángeles en las Indias Occidentales.* Rome: Imprenta de Joseph y Phelippe de Rossi, 1756.

Lanciego y Eguilaz, Miguel de. *Carta pastoral, que el ilustrísimo Señor Maestro D. Fray Joseph de Lanciego, y Eguilaz, Arzobispo de México . . . Escribe a sus amadas hijas las religiosas de toda su filiación.* Mexico City: Miguel de Rivera Calderón, 1716.

Lemus, Diego de. *Vida, virtudes, trabajos, favores y milagros de la Ven. M. Sor María de Jesús religiosa en el insigne Convento de la Limpia Concepción de la ciudad de los Ángeles en la Nueva España y natural de ella.* León: Acosta de Anssion y Posuel, 1683.

Libro de aniversarios y dotaciones y obligaciones. Archivo Histórico de la Secretaría de Salud, Mexico City, Fondo Jesús María, MS129.

Libro de Coro del Convento de Santa Inés de Montepulciano. Biblioteca Nacional de Antropología e Historia, Mexico City. 1705. Colección Antigua Vol. 968.

Lorente, Andrés. *El Porqué de la música, en que se contiene los quatro artes de ella, canto llano, canto de organo, contrapunto, y composición.* Alcalá de Henares: Imprenta de Nicolás de Xamarés, 1672.

Macedo, Antonio de Sousa de. *Eva, y Ave, o María triunfante. Theatrode la erudición, y philosofía Cristiana: en que se representan los dos estados del mundo: caido en Eva, y levantado en Ave.* Madrid: Imprenta de la Viuda de Francisco del Hierro, 1731.

Manso y Zuñiga, Francisco de. *Regla y ordenaciones de las religiosas de la Limpia e Inmaculada Concepción.* Mexico City: Imprenta del Nuevo Rezado de los Herederos de Doña María de Rivera, 1758. Biblioteca Nacional de Antropología e Historia, Mexico City, Colección General, XXIV, 2, 26 and VI, 2, 30.

Manual o procesionario, de las religiosas Carmelitas. Madrid: Imprenta de Joseph Doblado, 1775.

Mexican Choir Books. 6 vols. 1600–1799. Newberry Library Special Collections. VAULT oversize Case MS 5148.

Nassarre, Pablo. *Escuela música según la práctica moderna.* 2 vols. Zaragoza: Herederos de Diego de Larumbre, 1724.

Navarro, Francisco. *Voces del cielo repetidas en la tierra en obsequio de la Purísima Concepción de María.* Mexico City: Miguel de Rivera Calderón, 1703.

Núñez de Miranda, Antonio. *Distribución de las obras ordinarias, y extraordinarias del día, para hacerlas perfectamente, conforme al estado de las señoras religiosas. instruidas con doce máximas substanciales, para la vida regular, y espiritual, que deben seguir. sale a luz a solicitud, y expensas de las señoras religiosas del Convento Real de Jesús María, quienes la dedican a Cristo Señor Nro. Sacramentado.* Mexico City: Viuda de Miguel de Ribera Calderón, 1712.

Orden que se ha de guardar con la que entra en religión y modo con que se ha de vestir de hábito a las religiosas de la regla de la Purísima Concepción de Nuestra Señora, y de San Jerónimo, sujetas al ordinario de este Arzobispado de México. Reprint. Mexico City: En la imprenta nueva de la Biblioteca Mexicana, 1756.

Ossorio, Diego. *Exaltación del divino esposo Jesús con el sacrificio de un corazón amante, sermón que en la solemne profesión hizo de religiosa de coro y velo negro, Sor Josepha María de S. Antonio, en el Convento de Señoras Religiosas de la Purísima Concepción de esta corte, el día 20 de julio de este año de 1760.* Mexico City: En la Imprenta de la Biblioteca Mexicana, 1760.

Palafox y Mendoza, Juan de. *Discurso en favor de cierto religioso de vida ejemplar, a quien castigó rigurosamente un prelado superior, porque subió a predicar al púlpito de cierto convento de religiosas, al tiempo y cuando se representaba en él una mal ordenada comedia, de que resultaron muchos daños. 1645. Epístola exhortatoria a los curas y beneficiados de la Puebla de los Ángeles,* edited by Efraín Castro Morales. Puebla: Museo Mexicano, 2003.

Palafox y Mendoza, Juan de. *Obras del ilustrísimo, excelentísimo, y venerable siervo de Dios, don Juan de Palafox y Mendoza, de los supremos consejos de Indias y Aragón, obispo de la Puebla de los Ángeles, y de Osma, arzobispo electo de México, virrey, y capitán general de Nueva España.* 15 vols. Madrid: Imprenta de don Gabriel Ramirez, 1762.

Palafox y Mendoza, Juan de. *Puntos que el Senor Obispo de la Puebla de los Angeles, Juan de Palafox y Mendoza deja encargados y encomendados a las almas a su cargo al tiempo de partirse de estas provincias a los reynos de Espana.* Puebla: Impreso por el Bachiller Juan Blanco de Alcazar, 1649.

Palafox y Mendoza, Juan de. *Regla y constituciones que han de guardar las religiosas de los conventos de Nuestra Señora de la Concepción y la Santísima Trinidad de la ciudad de los Ángeles.* Biblioteca Nacional de México Fondo Reservado, Mexico City. 1641. RSM 1641 M4CON.

Pardo, Francisco. *Vida y virtudes heroicas de la Madre María de Jesús Tomelín, religiosa profesa en el Convento de la Limpia Concepción de la Virgen María N. Señora de la ciudad de los Ángeles.* Mexico City: Viuda de Bernardo Calderón en la Calle de San Agustín, 1676.

Parra, Juan Martínez de la. *Luz de verdades católicas y explicación de la doctrina cristiana.* Madrid: Francisco de Hierro, 1722.

Parra, Juan Sebastián de la. *De el bien, excelencias y obligaciones, de el estado clerical y sacerdotal.* Sevilla: Matias Clavijo, 1615.

Parreño, José Julián. *Novena en honra de Nuestra Señora de los Dolores, que con el renombre de las Aguas, venera el religiosísimo Convento Real de Jesus Maria de esta ciudad de México.* Mexico City: Herederos de Don Felipe de Zúñiga y Ontiveros, 1794.

Pineda, Pedro. *Nuevo diccionario, español e ingles e ingles y español: que contiene la etimología, de la propia, y metafórica significación de las palabras, términos de artes y ciencias.* F. Gyles, 1740.

Pozo y Calderón, María Casilda del. *Autobiography and Other Papers Relating to the Venerable María Casilda del Pozo: Mexico: ms., 1682–1730.* Bancroft Library, BAN MSS M-M 201–204 FILM.

Regla dada por nuestro padre San Agustín a sus monjas: Con las constituciones para la nueva recolección de ellas. Madrid: Diego Díaz de la Carrera, 1648.

Regla de la gloriosa Santa Clara con las Constituciones de las Monjas Capuchinas. Madrid: Luis Sánchez, 1647.

Regla de la Orden de la Concepción de Nuestra Señora de la ciudad de Toledo, dada por Julio II. ca. XVI–XVII. Biblioteca Nacional de España, MS 1111. http://catalogo.bne.es/uht bin/cgisirsi/?ps=bmFLm1g2Vw/BNMADRID/7611583/9.

Regla de N.G.P. San Agustín y constituciones de las religiosas del sagrado orden de predicadores. Mexico City: Imprenta de D. María de Rivera, 1691.

Regla primitiva, y constituciones de los religiosos descalzos de la orden de la bienaventurada Virgen María del Monte Carmelo. Puebla: Imprenta de la viuda de Miguel de Ortega y Bonilla, 1756.

Regla y constituciones de las religiosas de Santa Brigida. Mexico City: Viuda de D. José Bernardo de Hogal, 1744.

Regla y constituciones para las religiosas recoletas dominicas del sagrado monasterio de la gloriosa y esclarecida virgen Santa Rosa de Santa Maria, fundadora de la ciudad de la Puebla de los Angeles ...: lleva al fin el modo de dar el hábito y hacer la profesion conforme á la observancia de sus estatutos. Puebla: Real Seminario Palafoxiano, 1789.

Regla, y constituciones, que han de guardar las religiosas del convento del glorioso padre San Geronymo de la civdad de los Angeles. Puebla: Seminario Palafoxiano, 1773.

Regla, y constituciones, que por autoridad apostólica deben observar las religiosas del orden del máximo doctor S. Jerónimo, en esta ciudad de México. Mexico City: Herederos de la Viuda de Bernardo Caderón, 1702.

Reglas de la Compañía de Jesús, y la carta de la obediencia d nuestro glorioso padre S. Ignacio. 1749. British Library, General Reference Collection 4092.a.5.

Relación histórica de la fundación de este Convento de Nuestra Señora del Pilar, Compañía de María, llamada vulgarmente la Enseñanza, en esta ciudad de México, y compendio de la vida y virtudes de N.M.R.M. María Ignacia Azlor y Echeverz, su fundadora y patrona. Mexico City: Felipe de Zúñiga y Ontiveros, 1793.

Ritual Concepcionista. Archivo de la Casa Madre Concepcionista.

Rojo de Costa, Juan. *Sermon en la profesión de la Madre María de S. Simon en el convent de religiosas de San Jerónimo de la ciudad de México*. Mexico City: Viuda de Bernardo Calderón, 1668.

Roure, Nicolas. *El soberano cedro de María, en el excelso Líbano de su pureza*. Barcelona: Rafael Figuero, 1697.

Salmerón, Pedro. *Vida de la venerable Madre Isabel de la Encarnación, Carmelita descalça, natural de la ciudad de los Ángeles*. Mexico City: Francisco Rodriguez Lupercio, 1675.

Sánchez, Vicente. *Lyra Poética*. Zaragoza: Manuel Roman, 1688.

Sarmiento, José. *Harmonicos dolores, música dulce de María Ssma. al pie de la cruz.* Puebla: Herederos del Capitán Juan de Villa-Real, 1697. http://catarina.udlap.mx/ xmLibris/projects/biblioteca_franciscana/xml/myBook.jsp?key=book_e383ea. xml&id=libro_antiguo_sace&objects=/ximg&db=/db/xmlibris/system/metadata/

Sariñana, Ysidro. *Llanto del occidente en el ocaso del mas claro sol de las Españas. fúnebres demostraciones . . . en las exequias del rey Felipe IIII. . . . en la iglesia metropolitana de México*. Mexico City: Viuda de Bernardo Calderón, 1666.

Sigüenza y Góngora, Carlos de. *Paraíso occidental: plantado y cultivado por la liberal benéfica mano de los muy católicos y poderosos Reyes de España, nuestros señores, en su magnifico Real Convento de Jesús María de México: facsímile de la primera Edición (México, 1684)*. Mexico City: Facultad de Filosofía y Letras, Universidad Nacional Autónoma de México: Centro de Estudios de Historia de México Condumex, 1995.

Torres, Miguel de. *Vida ejemplar y muerte preciosa de la Madre Bárbara Josepha de San Francisco, religiosa de velo, y coro del Convento de La Santísima Trinidad, de la Puebla de los Ángeles*. Mexico City: Por los Herederos de la Viuda de Francisco Rodríguez Lupercio, 1725.

Trillanes, Isidro Martínez de. *Directorio, que para las ceremonias de el altar, y de el choro en todos los días de el año, deve observarse en esta Santa Iglesia Catedral, de la ciudad de los Ángeles*. Puebla: Viuda de Miguel de Ortega, 1728.

Valdes, José Eugenio. *Vida admirable, y penitente de la V.M. Sor Sebastiana Josefa de la Santísima Trinidad, Religiosa de coro y velo negro en el religiosísimo convento de señoraas religiosas Clarisas de San Juan de la Penitencia*. Mexico City: Imprenta de la Biblioteca Mexicana, 1765.

Valeriano, Pierio. *Hieroglyphica, sive, De sacris Aegyptiorvm literis commentarii*. Basel: Michael Isengrin, 1556.

Vallarta, Martin de. *Luz que guía al camino de la verdad y dirección de religiosas: para que muera la monja contenta y sosegada en su retiro y tenga por paraíso a su convento. Por un confesor de las comunidades de las señoras religiosas sujetas al ordinario de la ciudad de los Ángeles*. 1728. Biblioteca Nacional de México Fondo Reservado, Mexico City, Archivos y Manuscritos, MM MS.622.

Zavaleta, Joaquina María. *Copia de la carta que la M.R.M. Joaquina María de Zavaleta, abbadesa del Monasterio de San Phelipe de Jesus y pobres Capuchinas de esta imperial ciudad de México, escribe a las M. RR. MM. preladas de los demas monasterios, dandoles noticia de las heroycas virtudes y dichosa muerte de la M.R.M. Agustina Nicolasa Maria de los Dolores Muñoz y Sandoval*. Mexico City: Imprenta nueva de la Bibliotheca Mexicana, 1755.

Secondary Sources

Ables, Travis E. *The Body of the Cross: Holy Victims and the Invention of the Atonement.* New York: Fordham University Press, 2021.

Águeda de San Ignacio, María Anna. *Devociones Varias.* Edited by Clara Ramírez and Claudia Llanos. Mexico City: UNAM, 2019.

Aguirre Rincón, Soterraña. *Un manuscrito para un convento: el libro de música, dedicado a Sor Luisa en 1633: Convento de Santa Clara de Carrión de los Condes.* Valladolid: Edades del Hombre, 1998.

Alastruey, Gregorio. *Tratado de la Virgen Santísima.* Madrid: Biblioteca de Autores Cristianos, 1956.

Álvarez Sellers, Rosa M. *Literatura portuguesa y literatura española: influencias y relaciones.* València: Universitat de València, 1999.

Amerlinck de Corsi, María Concepción. "Los albores del convento de la Purísima Concepción de México." *Boletín de Monumentos Históricos* 39 (2018): 11–29.

Amerlinck de Corsi, María Concepción, and Manuel Ramos Medina. *Conventos de monjas: fundaciones en el México virreinal.* Mexico City: CONDUMEX, 1995.

Anzaldúa, Gloria E. "Now Let Us Shift . . . the Path of Conocimiento . . . Inner Work, Public Acts." In *This Bridge We Call Home: Radical Visions for Transformation*, edited by Gloria E. Anzaldúa and AnaLouise Keating, 540–576. New York: Routledge, 2002.

Apel, Willi. *The History of Keyboard Music to 1700.* Translated by Hans Tischler. Bloomington: Indiana University Press, 1972.

Arenal, Electa. "Where Woman Is the Creator of the Wor(l)d; Or, Sor Juana's Discourses on Method." In *Feminist Perspectives on Sor Juana Inés de la Cruz*, edited by Stephanie Merrim, 124–141. Detroit: Wayne State University Press, 1991.

Arenal, Electa, and Stacey Schlau, eds. *Untold Sisters: Hispanic Nuns in Their Own Works.* Translated by Amanda Powell. Albuquerque: University of New Mexico Press, 2009.

Arenas Frutos, Isabel. "Mecenazgo femenino y desarrollado conventual en Puebla de los Ángeles." In *Manifestaciones religiosas en el mundo colonial Americano*, edited by Clara García Ayluardo and Manuel Ramos Medina, 29–40. Mexico City: Centro de Estudios de histora de México CONDUMEX, 1994.

Arias, Santa, and Raúl Marrero-Fente. "Negotiation between Religion and the Law." In *Coloniality, Religion, and the Law in the Early Iberian World*, edited by Santa Arias and Raúl Marrero-Fente, ix–xxiv. Nashville: Vanderbilt University Press, 2014.

Astell, Ann W. *The Song of Songs in the Middle Ages.* Ithaca, NY: Cornell University Press, 1990.

Ávila, Teresa of. *The Interior Castle.* Translated by Kieran Kavanaugh and Otilio Rodriguez. Mahwah, NJ: Paulist Press, 1979.

Baade, Colleen Ruth. "Music and Music-Making in Female Monasteries in Seventeenth-Century Castile." PhD dissertation, Duke University, 2001.

Baker, Geoffrey. "The 'Ethnic Villancico' and Racial Politics in 17th-century Mexico." In *Music and Urban Society in Colonial Latin America*, edited by Geoffrey Baker and Tess Knighton, 399–408. Cambridge: Cambridge University Press, 2011.

Baker, Geoffrey. *Imposing Harmony: Music and Society in Colonial Cuzco.* Durham, NC: Duke University Press, 2008.

Baker, Geoffrey. "Latin American Baroque: Performance as a Post-colonial Act?" *Early Music* 36, no. 3 (2008): 441–448.

Baker, Geoffrey. "Music in the Convents and Monasteries of Colonial Cuzco." *Latin American Music Review* 24, no. 1 (2003): 3–41.

Baker, Geoffrey. "The Resounding City." In *Music and Urban Society in Colonial Latin America*, edited by Geoffrey Baker and Tess Knighton, 1–20. Cambridge: Cambridge University Press, 2011.

Baker, Geoffrey, and Tess Knighton, eds. *Music and Urban Society in Colonial Latin America*. Cambridge: Cambridge University Press, 2011.

Bal y Gay, Jesús, ed. *El códice del Convento del Carmen*. Mexico City: Instituto Nacional de Bellas Artes, 1952.

Balbuena, Bernardo. *Siglo de oro en las selvas de Erífile*. Madrid: Por Ibarra, 1821.

Bancroft, Hubert Howe. "From Bibliopolist to Bibliophile." *Bancroftiana* 98 (March 1989): 5–32.

Barbieri, Constanza. "'To Be in Heaven': St. Philip Neri Between Aesthetic Emotion and Mystical Ecstasy." In *The Sensuous in the Counter-Reformation Church*, edited by Marcia B. Hall and Tracy E. Cooper, 206–229. Cambridge: Cambridge University Press, 2013.

Bargellini, Clara. "Jesuit Devotions and *Retablos* in New Spain." In *The Jesuits: Cultures, Sciences, and the Arts, 1540–1773*, vol. 1, edited by John W. O'Malley, S.J., Gauvin Alexander Bailey, Steven J. Harris, and T. Frank Kennedy, S.J., 680–698. Toronto: University of Toronto Press, 1999.

Bartel, Kate. "Portal of the Skies: Music as Devotional Act in Early Modern Europe." PhD dissertation, University of California, Los Angeles, 2006.

Bell, Catherine. *Ritual Theory, Ritual Practice*. Oxford: Oxford University Press, 2009.

Bermúdez, Egberto. "Sounds from Fortresses of Faith and Ideal Cities: Society, Politics, and Music in Missionary Activities in the Americas, 1525–1575." In *Listening to Early Modern Catholicism: Perspectives from Musicology*, edited by Daniele V. Filippi and Michael Noone, 301–326. Leiden: Brill, 2017.

Bernal Jiménez, Miguel. *Morelia colonial: el archivo musical del Colegio de Santa Rosa de Santa María de Valladolid*. Morelia: Sociedad Amigos de la Música, Ediciones de la Universidad Michoacana, 1939.

Bestul, Thomas H. *Texts of the Passion: Latin Devotional Literature and Medieval Society*. Philadelphia: University of Pennsylvania Press, 1996.

Bilinkoff, Jodi. *Related Lives: Confessors and their Female Penitents, 1450–1750*. Ithaca, NY: Cornell University Press, 2005.

Bohlman, Philip V. "Where They Came From: Reracializing Music in the Empire of Silence." In *Audible Empire: Music, Global Politics, Critique*, edited by Ronald Radano and Tejumola Olaniyan, 161–184. Durham, NC: Duke University Press, 2016.

Bombi, Andrea. "'The Third Villancico Was a Motet': The Villancico and Related Genres." In *Devotional Music in the Iberian World, 1450–1800: The Villancico and Related Genres*, edited by Tess Knighton and Álvaro Torrente, 149–188. Burlington, VT: Ashgate, 2007.

Bouza, Fernando. *Communication, Knowledge, and Memory in Early Modern Spain*. Philadelphia: University of Pennsylvania Press, 1999.

Brewer-García, Larissa. *Beyond Babel: Translations of Blackness in Colonial Peru and New Granada*. Cambridge: Cambridge University Press, 2020.

Briscoe, James T. *New Historical Anthology of Music by Women*. Bloomington: Indiana University Press, 2004.

Bristol, Joan Cameron. *Christians, Blasphemers, and Witches: Afro-Mexican Ritual Practice in the Seventeenth Century*. Albuquerque: University of New Mexico Press, 2007.

Brown, Meg Lota, and Kari Boyd McBride. *Women's Roles in the Renaissance*. Westport, CT: Greenwood Press, 2005.

Burkhart, Louise M. *Holy Wednesday: A Nahua Drama from Early Colonial Mexico*. Philadelphia: University of Pennsylvania Press, 1996.

Burns, Kathryn. *Colonial Habits: Convents and the Spiritual Economy of Cuzco, Peru*. Durham, NC: Duke University Press, 1999.

Burns, Kathryn. *Into the Archive: Writing and Power in Colonial Peru*. Durham, NC: Duke University Press, 2010.

Bynum, Caroline Walker. *Holy Feast and Holy Fast: The Religious Significance of Food to Medieval Women*. Berkeley: University of California Press, 1987.

Bysted, Ane. *The Crusade Indulgence: Spiritual Rewards and the Theology of the Crusades, C. 1095–1216*. Leiden: Brill, 2014.

Cadenas, Viana. "Formación, adiestramiento y funcionalidad musical en Caracas (s. XVII–XXIX): profesión y oficios musicales en el ámbito feminino." In *Música colonial iberoamericana: interpretaciones en torno a la práctica de ejecución y ejecución de la práctica*, edited by Victor Rondón, 71–82. Santa Cruz de la Sierra, Bolivia: Asociación Pro Arte y Cultura, 2004.

Cadenas García, Viana. "La música en la micro-sociedad 'espiritual' de mujeres mantuanas: Convento de la Inmaculada Concepción de Caracas (siglos XVII–XIX)." *Revista de la Sociedad Venezolana de Musicología* 5 (2005): 449–479.

Cadenas García, Viana. "Música, fiestas y ceremonias en el Convento de la Inmaculada Concepción de Caracas (Siglos XVII–XVIII)." In *Mujeres, negros, y niños en la música y sociedad cultural iberoamericana*, edited by Víctor Rondón, 19–38. Santa Cruz de la Sierra, Bolivia: Asociación Pro Arte y Cultura, 2002.

Calderón de la Barca, Frances. *Life in Mexico*. Berkeley: University of California Press, 1982.

Calderón de la Barca, Pedro. *El divino Orfeo*. Edited by J. E. Duarte. Pamplona: Universidad de Navarra, 1999.

Campos Olivares, Citlali. "La práctica musical en el Convento de San José o Santa Teresa la Antigua de la Ciudad de México." Thesis, Universidad Nacional Autónoma de México, 2006.

Candelaria, Lorenzo. "Bernardino de Sahagún's *Psalmodia Christiana*: A Catholic Songbook from Sixteenth-Century New Spain." *Journal of the American Musicological Society* 67, no. 3 (2014): 619–684.

Candelaria, Lorenzo. "Music and Pageantry in the Formation of Hispano-Christian Identity: The Feast of St. Hippolytus in Sixteenth-Century Mexico City." In *Music and Culture in the Middle Ages and Beyond: Liturgy, Sources, Symbolism*, edited by Benjamin Brand and David J. Rothenberg, 89–108. Cambridge: Cambridge University Press, 2016.

Carrera, Magali Marie. *Imagining Identity in New Spain: Race, Lineage, and the Colonial Body in Portraiture and Casta Paintings*. Austin: University of Texas Press, 2003.

Carreras, Juan José, and Iain Fenlon, eds. *Polychoralities: Music, Identity and Power in Italy, Spain and the New World*. Kassel: Edition Reichenberger, 2013.

Carver, Anthony F. *Cori Spezzati: The Development of Sacred Polychoral Music to the Time of Schutz*. Cambridge: Cambridge University Press, 1988.

Cashner, Andrew A. "Faith, Hearing, and the Power of Music in Hispanic Villancicos, 1600–1700." PhD dissertation, University of Chicago, 2015.

Cashner, Andrew A. *Hearing Faith: Music as Theology in the Spanish Empire*. Leiden: Brill, 2020.

Cashner, Andrew A. "Imitating Africans, Listening for Angels: A Slaveholder's Fantasy of Social Harmony in an 'Ethnic Villancico' from Colonial Puebla (1652)." *Journal of Musicology* 38, no. 2 (2021): 141–182.

Castañeda García, Rafael. "Ilustración y educación: La Congregación del Oratorio de San Felipe Neri en Nueva España (siglo XVIII)." *Historia Crítica* 59 (2016): 145–164.

Cavarero, Adriana. *For More Than Once Voice: Toward a Philosophy of Vocal Expression*. Translated by Paul A. Kottman. Stanford, CA: Stanford University Press, 2005.

Chaves de Tobar, Matilde del Tránsito. "La vida musical en los conventos femeninos de Alba de Tormes-Salamanca." PhD dissertation, University of Salamanca, 2009.

Chávez Bárcenas, Ireri E. "Poesía amatorial en la lírica devocional eucarística novohispana." *Bulletin of Spanish Studies*, doi: 10.1080/14753820.2023.2176675.

Chávez Bárcenas, Ireri Elizabeth. "Singing in the City of Angels: Race, Identity, and Devotion in Early Modern Puebla de los Ángeles." PhD dissertation, Princeton University, 2018.

Chowning, Margaret. *Rebellious Nuns: The Troubled History of a Mexican Convent, 1752–1863*. Oxford: Oxford University Press, 2006.

Chowning, Margaret. "Talking Back: Nuns, *Beatas*, and *Colegialas* Invoke Rights and Constitutional Principles in Late Colonial and Early Nineteenth-Century Mexico." *Colonial Latin American Review* 29, no. 1 (2020): 115–138.

Christian, William A. *Local Religion in Sixteenth-Century Spain*. Princeton, NJ: Princeton University Press, 1989.

Cichy, Andrew. "'Changing Their Tune': Sacred Music and the Recasting of English Post-Reformation Identity at St. Alban's College, Valladolid." In *Listening to Early Modern Catholicism*, edited by Daniele V. Filippi and Michael Noone, 173–186. Leiden: Brill, 2017.

Clifton, James. "Gender and Shame in Masaccio's *Expulsion from the Garden of Eden*." *Art History* 22, no. 5 (1999): 637–655.

Cohen, Jeremy. *Christ Killers: The Jews and the Passion from the Bible to the Big Screen*. Oxford: Oxford University Press, 2007.

Cohen, Thomas M., Jay T. Harrison, and David Rex Galindo, eds. *The Franciscans in Colonial Mexico*. Norman: University of Oklahoma Press, 2021.

Colahan, Clark A. *The Visions of Sor María de Ágreda: Writing Knowledge and Power*. Tucson: University of Arizona Press, 1994.

Cope, R. Douglas. *The Limits of Racial Domination: Plebeian Society in Colonial Mexico City, 1660–1720*. Madison: University of Wisconsin Press, 1994.

Córdova, James M. *The Art of Professing in Bourbon Mexico: Crowned-Nun Portraits and Reform in the Convent*. Austin: University of Texas Press, 2014.

Crawford, Katherine. *Eunuchs and Castrati: Disability and Normativity in Early Modern Europe*. New York: Routledge, 2018.

Cruz González, Cristina. "Beyond the Bride of Christ: The Crucified Abbess in Mexico and Spain." *The Art Bulletin* 99, no. 4 (2017): 102–132.

Curcio-Nagy, Linda A. "Faith and Morals in Colonial Mexico." In *The Oxford History of Mexico*, edited by William H. Beezley and Michael C. Meyer, 143–176. Oxford: Oxford University Press, 2010.

Curcio-Nagy, Linda A. "Giants and Gypsies: Corpus Christi in Colonial Mexico City." In *Rituals of Rule, Rituals of Resistance: Public Celebrations and Popular Culture in Mexico*, edited by William H. Beezley, Cheryl English Martin, and William E. French, 1–26. Wilmington, DE: Scholarly Resources Inc., 1994.

Curcio-Nagy, Linda A. *The Great Festivals of Colonial Mexico City: Performing Power and Identity*. Albuquerque: University of New Mexico Press, 2004.

Davies, Drew Edward. "Introduction." In *Manuel de Sumaya, Villancicos from Mexico City*, edited by Drew Edward Davies, ix–xliv. Middleton, WI: A–R Editions, 2019.

Davies, Drew Edward. "The Italianized Frontier: Music at Durango Cathedral, Español Culture, and the Aesthetics of Devotion in Eighteenth-Century New Spain." PhD dissertation, University of Chicago, 2006.

Davies, Drew Edward. "Villancicos from Mexico City for the Virgin of Guadalupe." *Early Music* 29, no. 2 (2011): 229–244.

Davies, James Q. *Romantic Anatomies of Performance*. Berkeley: University of California Press, 2014.

Dean, Carolyn. "Beyond Prescription: Notarial Doodles and Other Marks." *Word & Image: A Journal of Verbal/Visual Enquiry* 25, no. 3 (2009): 293–316.

Dean, Carolyn. *Inka Bodies and the Body of Christ: Corpus Christi in Colonial Cuzco, Peru*. Durham, NC: Duke University Press, 1999.

Debby, Nirit Ben-Aryeh. *The Cult of St. Clare of Assisi in Early Modern Italy*. Burlington, VT: Ashgate, 2014.

de Boer, Wietse. *The Conquest of the Soul: Confession, Discipline, and Public Order in Counter-Reformation Milan*. Leiden: Brill, 2001.

Dehouve, Danièle. "El matrimonio indio frente al matrimonio español (siglos xvi al xviii)." In *El matrimonio en Mesoamérica ayer y hoy: unas miradas antropológicas*, edited by David Robichaux, 75–94. Mexico City: Universidad Iberoamericana, 2003.

De la Maza, Francisco. *Arquitectura de los coros de monjas en México*. 3rd ed. Mexico City: Universidad Autónoma de México, 1983.

Delgado, Jessica L. *Laywomen and the Making of Colonial Catholicism in New Spain, 1630–1790*. Princeton, NJ: Princeton University Press, 2018.

Dell'Antonio, Andrew. *Listening as Spiritual Practice in Early Modern Italy*. Oxford: Oxford University Press, 2011.

Derbes, Anne. *Picturing the Passion in Late Medieval Italy Narrative Painting, Franciscan Ideologies, and the Levant*. Cambridge: Cambridge University Press, 1996.

Díaz, Josef, and Suzanne Stratton-Pruitt. *Painting the Divine: Images of Mary in the New World*. Albuquerque, NM: Fresco Books, 2014.

Díaz, Mónica. "The Establishment of Feminine Paradigms: Translators, Traitors, Nuns." In *The Cambridge History of Latin American Women's Literature*, edited by Ileana Rodríguez and Mónica Szurmuk, 52–65. Cambridge: Cambridge University Press, 2015.

Díaz, Mónica. *Indigenous Writings from the Convent: Negotiating Ethnic Autonomy in Colonial Mexico*. Tucson: University of Arizona Press, 2010.

Díaz, Mónica, and Rocío Quispe-Agnoli. "Introduction: Uncovering Women's Colonial Archive." In *Women's Negotiations and Textual Agency in Latin America, 1500–1799*, edited by Mónica Díaz and Rocío Quispe-Agnoli, 1–16. New York: Routledge, 2016.

Díaz Miranda, Elena. "¿Cuáles eran las tentaciones de la carne en las monjas novohispanas?" *Relatos e Historias en México* 105. Accessed February 4, 2022. https://relatosehistorias.mx/nuestras-historias/cuales-eran-las-tentaciones-de-la-carne-en-las-monjas-novohispanas.

Dolar, Mladen. *A Voice and Nothing More*. Cambridge, MA: The MIT Press, 2006.

Drago, Margarita. *Sor María de Jesús Tomelín (1579–1637), concepcionista poblana: la construcción fallida de una santa*. Madrid: Editorial Pliegos, 2018.

Dutcher Mann, Kristin. *The Power of Song and Dance in the Mission Communities of Northern New Spain*. Stanford, CA: Stanford University Press, 2010.

Eguiarte Bendímez, Enrique A. "El púlpito y el convento: dos sermones en los conventos novohispanos de Regina Coeli (1699) y Valvanera [sic] (1706)." *Mayéutica* 42 (2016): 263–344.

Eich, Jennifer. *The Other Mexican Muse: Sor María Anna Águeda de San Ignacio (1695–1756)*. New Orleans, LA: University Press of the South, 2004.

Eidsheim, Nina Sun. *The Race of Sound: Listening, Timbre and Vocality in African American Music*. Durham, NC: Duke University Press, 2019.

Eidsheim, Nina Sun, and Katherine Meizel, eds. *The Oxford Handbook of Voice Studies*. Oxford: Oxford University Press, 2019.

Eissa-Barroso, Francisco A. "News, Censorship and Propaganda in the *Gazeta de Mexico* during the Summer of 1808." In *The Configuration of the Spanish Public Sphere: From the Enlightenment to the Indignados*, edited by David Jiménez Torres and Leticia Villamediana González, 89–108. New York: Berghahn Books, 2019.

Enríquez Rubio, Lucero. "¿Dónde están los responsorios?" In *De Nueva España a México: el universo musical mexicano entre centenarios (1517–1917)*, edited by Javier Marín López, 609–625. Sevilla: Universidad Internacional de Andalucía, 2020.

Enríquez Rubio, Lucero, et al. *Catálogo de los papeles y libros de música del archivo del Cabildo Catedral Metropolitano de México Proyecto Musicat-ADABI*. http://www.musi cat.unam.mx/nuevo/adabi.html.

Enríquez Rubio, Lucero, ed. *De música y cultura en la Nueva España y el México independiente: Testimonios de innovación y pervivencia*. 2 vols. Mexico City: Instituto de Investigaciones Estéticas, UNAM, 2014.

Estenssoro, Juan Carlos. "Música y fiestas en los monasterios de monjas limeños: siglos XVII y XVIII." *Revista Musical de Venezuela* 16, no. 34 (1997): 127–135.

Estenssoro, Juan Carlos. *Música y sociedad coloniales: Lima 1680–1830*. Lima: Colmillo Blanco, 1989.

Etzion, Judith. "Latin Polyphony in the Early Spanish Baroque: Suggestions for Stylistic Criteria." *Anuario Musical* 56 (2001): 75–81.

Favila, Cesar D. "Music and Devotion in Novohispanic Convents, 1600–1800." PhD dissertation, University of Chicago, 2016.

Favila, Cesar D. "On the Money." In "Un mariachi de respuestas a la décima musa" (Dossier section, Alicia Gaspar de Alba). *Aztlán: A Journal of Chicano Studies* 44, no. 2 (2019): 203–206.

Favila, Cesar D. "The Sound of Profession Ceremonies in Novohispanic Convents." *Journal of the Society for American Music* 13, no. 2 (2019): 143–170.

Fedewa, Marilyn H. *María of Ágreda: Mystical Lady in Blue*. Albuquerque: University of New Mexico Press, 2011.

Feldman, Martha. *Opera and Sovereignty: Transforming Myths in Eighteenth-Century Italy*. Chicago: University of Chicago Press, 2007.

Feldman, Martha, and Judith T. Zeitlin, eds. *The Voice as Something More: Essays toward Materiality*. Chicago: University of Chicago Press, 2019.

Fernández de Mesa, Blas. *La fundadora de la santa concepción: comedia en dos partes*. New York: P. Lang, 1996.

Fernández Gracia, Ricardo. *La buena memoria del obispo Palafox y su obra en Puebla*. New York: IDEA, 2014.

Filippi, Daniele V. "'Catechismum modulans docebat': Teaching the Doctrine through Singing in Early Modern Catholicism." In *Listening to Early Modern Catholicism: Perspectives from Musicology*, edited by Daniele V. Filippi and Michael Noone, 129–148. Leiden: Brill, 2017.

Filippi, Daniele V., and Michael Noone, eds. *Listening to Early Modern Catholicism: Perspectives from Musicology*. Leiden: Brill, 2017.

Fink, Robert. *Repeating Ourselves: American Minimal Music as Cultural Practice*. Berkeley: University of California Press, 2005.

Finley, Sarah. "Exemplary Sound and Hearing in Sensory Treatises from the Early Modern Spanish-speaking World." *The Senses and Society* 13, no. 2 (2018): 203–218.

Finley, Sarah. *Hearing Voices: Aurality and New Spanish Sound Culture in Sor Juana Inés de la Cruz*. Lincoln: University of Nebraska Press, 2019.

Finley, Sarah. "Más allá de la sonoridad: huellas del pensamiento musical en el convento de Jesús María de México." *Boletín de monumentos históricos* 45, (January–April 2019): 68–81.

Finley, Sarah. "Sounding the Feminine in Sor Juana's Villancicos to St. Catherine of Alexandria (1691)." *Calíope: Journal of the Society for Renaissance and Baroque Hispanic Poetry* 25, no. 1 (2020): 24–43.

Fiore, Angela. "Musica nelle istituzioni religiose femminili a Napoli (1650–1750)." *Studi Pergolesiani* 10 (2015): 99–124.

Fisher, Alexander J. *Music, Piety, and Propaganda: The Soundscapes of Counter-Reformation Bavaria*. Oxford: Oxford University Press, 2014.

Fisher, Alexander J. "'Per mia particolare devotione': Orlando di Lasso's *Lagrime di San Pietro* and Catholic Spirituality in Counter-Reformation Munich." *Journal of the Royal Musical Association* 132, no. 2 (2007): 167–220.

Fisher, Andrew B., and Matthew D. O'Hara, eds. *Imperial Subjects: Race and Identity in Colonial Latin America*. Durham, NC: Duke University Press, 2009.

Flores Enríquez, Alejandra Mayela. "Jardines místicos carmelitanos y su representación en la pintura del siglo XVIII: Alegorías de la perfección monjil." MA thesis, Universidad Nacional Autónoma de México, 2014.

Foster, Timothy. *Music and Power in Early Modern Spain: Harmonic Spheres of Influence*. New York: Routledge, 2022.

Foucault, Michel. *Discipline and Punish: The Birth of the Prison*. Translated by Alan Sheridan. New York: Vintage Books, 1995.

Foz y Foz, Pilar. *La revolución pedagógica en Nueva España (1754–1820): María Ignacia de Azlor y Echevers y los colegios de la enseñanza*. 2 vols. Madrid: Instituto Gonzalo Fernández de Oviedo, 1982.

Franco, Jean. *Plotting Women: Gender and Representation in Mexico*. New York: Columbia University Press, 1989.

Frandsen, Mary E. *Crossing Confessional Boundaries: The Patronage of Italian Sacred Music in Seventeenth-Century Dresden*. Oxford: Oxford University Press, 2011.

Fulton, Rachel. *From Judgment to Passion: Devotion to Christ and the Virgin Mary, 800–1200*. New York: Columbia University Press, 2002.

Gage, Thomas. *Travels in the New World*. Edited by J. Eric S. Thompson. Norman: University of Oklahoma Press, 1958.

Gallagher, Sister Ann Miriam. "The Family Background of the Nuns of Two *Monasterios* in Colonial Mexico: Santa Clara, Querétaro; and Corpus Christi, Mexico City (1724–1822)." PhD dissertation, Catholic University of America, 1972.

Garduño Pérez, María Leticia. "Un viril hecho un sol: del simbolismo en la platería sacra." In *Lo sagrado y lo profano en la festividad de Corpus Christi*, edited by Montserrat Galí Boadella and Morelos Torres Aguilar, 111–126. Mexico City: Universidad Nacional Autónoma de México, 2008.

Gaspar de Alba, Alicia. *Sor Juana's Second Dream: A Novel*. Albuquerque: University of New Mexico Press, 1999.

Gaspar de Alba, Alicia. *[Un]framing the "Bad Woman": Sor Juana, Malinche, Coyolxauhqui, and Other Rebels with a Cause*. Austin: University of Texas Press, 2014.

Gembero Ustárroz, María. "*De rosas cercada*: Music by Francisco de la Huerta for the Nuns of Santa Ana de Ávila (1767–78). In *Devotional Music in the Iberian World, 1450–1800: The Villancico and Related Genres*, edited by Tess Knighton and Álvaro Torrente, 321–362. Burlington, VT: Ashgate, 2007.

Gharala, Norah L. A. *Taxing Blackness: Free Afromexican Tribute in Bourbon New Spain*. Tuscaloosa: University of Alabama Press, 2019.

Gill, Meredith J. "'Until Shadows Disperse': Augustine's Twilight." In *The Sensuous in the Counter-Reformation Church*, edited by Marcia B. Hall and Tracy E. Cooper, 252–272. Cambridge: Cambridge University Press, 2013.

Glantz, Margo. "Un paraíso occidental: el huerto cerrado de la virginidad." In *Parayso occidental, Carlos de Sigüenza y Góngora*, edited by Manuel Ramos, XVII–XLVI. Mexico City: UNAM, 1995.

Glixon, Jonathan. *Mirrors of Heaven or Worldly Theaters?: Venetian Nunneries and Their Music*. Oxford: Oxford University Press, 2017.

Goehr, Lydia. *The Imaginary Museum of Musical Works: An Essay in the Philosophy of Music*. Oxford: Oxford University Press, 1992.

Gómez Herrero, Fernando. "The Radical Transformations in the Spanish Empire Do Not Fit into Conventional Anglo Models and Liberal Narratives: Interview with Jorge Cañizares-Esguerra." December 14, 2020. https://www.fernandogherrero.com/single-post/radical-tranformations-in-the-spanish-empire-do-not-fit-into-conventional-anglo-models.

Gonzalbo Aizpuru, Pilar. *Historia de la educación en la época colonial: el mundo indígena*. Mexico City: El Colegio de México, 1990.

Gonzalbo Aizpuru, Pilar. *História de la educación en la época colonial: la educación de los criollos y la vida urbana*. Mexico City: El Colegio de México, 1990.

Goodliffe, Jonathan, ed. "Madre, la de los primores (Juana Inés de la Cruz)." *Choral Public Domain Library*, 2011. http://www1.cpdl.org/wiki/index.php/Madre,_la_de_los_pr imores_(Juana_In%C3%A9s_de_la_Cruz.

Gordon, Bonnie. *Monteverdi's Unruly Women: The Power of Song in Early Modern Italy*. Cambridge: Cambridge University Press, 2005.

Graham, Heather, and Lauren G. Kilroy-Ewbank, eds. *Visualizing Sensuous Suffering and Affective Pain in Early Modern Europe and the Spanish Americas*. Boston: Brill, 2018.

Graña Cid, María del Mar. *Mujeres, espiritualidad franciscana y feminismo en la Castilla renacentista*. Salamanca: Universidad Pontificia de Salamanca, 2003.

Graziano, Frank. *Wounds of Love: The Mystical Marriage of Saint Rose*. Oxford: Oxford University Press, 2004.

Griffiths, John. "Hidalgo, mercader, sacerdote o poeta: vihuelas y vihuelistas en la vida urbana." *Hispánica lyra: revista de la Sociedad de la Vihuela*, no. 9 (2009): 14–25.

Griffiths, John. "The Vihuela: Performance Practice, Style, and Context." In *Performance on Lute, Guitar, and Vihuela*, edited by Victor Anand Coelho, 158–179. Cambridge: Cambridge University Press, 2005.

Gunnarsdóttir, Ellen. *Mexican Karismata: The Baroque Vocation of Francisca de los Ángeles, 1674–1744*. Lincoln: University of Nebraska Press, 2004.

Gunnarsdóttir, Ellen. "Una monja barroca en el México ilustrado: María Ignacia del Niño Jesús en el convent de Santa Clara de Querétaro, 1801–1802." In *Diálogos espirituales: Manuscritos femeninos hispanoamericanos, siglos XVI–XIX*, edited by Asunción Lavrin and Rosalva Loreto López, 364–383. Puebla: UDLA, 2006.

HaCohen, Ruth. *The Music Libel Against the Jews*. New Haven, CT: Yale University Press, 2013.

Hamburger, Jeffrey F., and Susan Marti, eds. *Crown and Veil: Female Monasticism from the Fifth to the Fifteenth Centuries*. New York: Columbia University Press, 2008.

Hanks, William F. *Intertexts: Writings on Language, Utterance, and Context*. Lanham: MD, Rowman & Littlefield, 2000.

Hathaway, Janet. "Cloister, Court and City: Musical Activity of the Monasterio de las Descalzas Reales (Madrid), ca. 1620–1700." PhD dissertation, New York University, 2005.

Hathaway, Janet. "'Music Charms the Senses . . .': Devotional Music in the *Triunfos festivos* of San Ginés, Madrid, 1656." In *Devotional Music in the Iberian World, 1450–1800: The Villancico and Related Genres*, edited by Tess Knighton and Álvaro Torrente, 219–230. Burlington, VT: Ashgate, 2007.

Haupt, Paul. "The Prototype of the Magnificat." *Zeitschrift der Deutschen Morgenländischen Gesellschaft* 58, no. 3 (1904): 617–632.

Hiley, David. *Western Plainchant: A Handbook*. Oxford: Oxford University Press, 1993.

Hills, Helen. *Invisible City: The Architecture of Devotion in Seventeenth-Century Neapolitan Convents*. Oxford: Oxford University Press, 2004.

Hills, Helen. "Nuns and Relics: Spiritual Authority in Post-Tridentine Naples." In *Female Monasticism in Early Modern Europe*, edited by Cordula van Wyhe, 11–38. Burlington, VT: Ashgate, 2008.

Hills, Helen. "Veiling the Voice of Architecture." In *Hearing the City in Early Modern Europe*, edited by Tess Knighton and Ascensión Mazuela-Anguita, 117–131. Turnhout: Brepols, 2018.

Hirschkind, Charles. *The Ethical Soundscape: Cassette Sermons and Islamic Counterpublics*. New York: Columbia University Press, 2006.

Holler, Jacqueline. *Escogidas Plantas: Nun and Beatas in Mexico City, 1531–1601*. New York: Columbia University Press, 2001.

Holsinger, Bruce Wood. "The Flesh of the Voice: Embodiment and the Homoerotics of Devotion in the Music of Hildegard of Bingen (1098–1179)." *Signs* 19, no. 1 (1993): 92–125.

Houchins, Sue E., and Baltasar Fra-Molinero, trans. *Black Bride of Christ: Chicaba, an African Nun in Eighteenth-Century Spain*. Nashville, TN: Vanderbilt University Press, 2018.

Ibsen, Kristine. *Women's Spiritual Autobiography in Colonial Spanish America*. Gainesville: University of Florida Press, 1999.

Illari, Bernardo. "Polychoral Culture: Cathedral Music in La Plata (Bolivia), 1680–1730." PhD dissertation, University of Chicago, 2002.

Inés de la Cruz. *Fundación del convento de Santa Teresa la Antigua*. Edited by Clara Ramírez and Claudia Llanos. Mexico City: UNAM, 2014.

Ingalls, Monique M. *Singing the Congregation: How Contemporary Worship Music Forms Evangelical Community*. Oxford: Oxford University Press, 2018.

Irving, David. *Colonial Counterpoint: Music in Early Modern Manila*. Oxford: Oxford University Press, 2010.

Jackson, Barbara Garvey. *"Say Can You Deny Me": A Guide to Surviving Music by Women from the 16th through the 18th Centuries*. Fayetteville: University of Arkansas Press, 1994.

Jaffary, Nora E. *False Mystics: Deviant Orthodoxy in Colonial Mexico*. Lincoln: University of Nebraska Press, 2008.

Jaffary, Nora E. *Reproduction and Its Discontents in Mexico.* Chapel Hill: University of North Carolina Press, 2016.

Jarjour, Tala. *Sense and Sadness: Syriac Chant in Aleppo.* Oxford: Oxford University Press, 2018.

Jimarez Caro, Luz del Carmen. *Tipología de los templos conventuales poblanos: análisis arquitectónico comparativo.* Puebla: Benemérita Universidad Autónoma de Puebla, 2008.

Johnson, Calvert, ed. *Cuaderno de tonos de Maitines de Sor María Clara del Santísimo Sacramento.* Colfax, NC: Wayne Leupold Editions, 2005.

Johnson, Jake. *Mormons, Musical Theater, and Belonging in America.* Urbana: University of Illinois Press, 2019.

Johnson, Norman Scott. "Franciscan Passions: Missions to the Muslims, Desire for Martyrdom and Institutional Identity in the Later Middle Ages." PhD dissertation, University of Chicago, 2010.

Jones, Alisha Lola. *Flaming? The Peculiar Theopolitics of Fire and Desire in Black Male Gospel Performance.* Oxford: Oxford University Press, 2020.

Jones, Nicholas R. "Sor Juana's Black Atlantic: Colonial Blackness and the Poetic Subversions of *Habla de negros.*" *Hispanic Review* 86, no. 3 (2018): 265–285.

Kane, Brian. *Sound Unseen: Acousmatic Sound in Theory and Practice.* Oxford: Oxford University Press, 2014.

Keating, AnaLouise, ed. *The Gloria Anzaldúa Reader.* Durham, NC: Duke University Press, 2009.

Kelsey, Mary Ann, and Harry Kelsey. *Inventario de los libros de coro de la Catedral de Valladolid-Morelia.* Zamora: El Colegio de Michoacán, 2000.

Kendrick, Robert L. *Celestial Sirens: Nuns and Their Music in Early Modern Milan.* Oxford: Oxford University Press, 1996.

Kendrick, Robert L. *Fruits of the Cross: Passiontide Music Theater in Habsburg Vienna.* Oakland: University of California Press, 2018.

Kendrick, Robert L. *Singing Jeremiah: Music and Meaning in Holy Week.* Bloomington: Indiana University Press, 2014.

Kendrick, Robert L. *The Sounds of Milan, 1585–1650.* Oxford: Oxford University Press, 2002.

Kieckhefer, Richard. "Imitators of Christ: Sainthood in the Christian Tradition." In *Sainthood: Its Manifestations in World Religions*, edited by Richard Kieckhefer and George D. Bond, 1–42. Berkeley: University of California Press, 1998.

Kilroy-Ewbank, Lauren G. *Holy Organ or Unholy Idol? The Sacred Heart in the Art, Religion, and Politics of New Spain.* Leiden: Brill, 2019.

Kirk, Pamela. *Sor Juana Inés de la Cruz: Religion, Art, and Feminism.* New York: Continuum, 1998.

Kirk, Stephanie. *Convent Life in Colonial Mexico: A Tale of Two Communities.* Gainesville: University Press of Florida, 2007.

Kirk, Stephanie. *Sor Juana Inés de la Cruz and the Gender Politics of Knowledge in Colonial Mexico.* New York: Routledge, 2016.

Knighton, Tess. "Music and Ritual in Urban Spaces: The Case of Lima, c. 1600." In *Music and Urban Society in Colonial Latin America*, edited by Geoffrey Baker and Tess Knighton, 21–42. Cambridge: Cambridge University Press, 2011.

Knighton, Tess, and Asunción Mazuela-Anguita, eds. *Hearing the City in Early Modern Europe.* Turnhout: Brepols, 2018.

Knighton, Tess, and Álvaro Torrente, eds. *Devotional Music in the Iberian World, 1450–1800: The Villancico and Related Genres*. Burlington, VT: Ashgate, 2007.

Kristeva, Julia. "Stabat Mater." Translated by Arthur Goldhammer. *Poetics Today* 6, no. 1/2 (1985): 133–152.

Kristeva, Julia. "Women's Time." Translated by Alice Jardine and Harry Blake. *Signs* 7, no. 1 (1981): 13–35.

Krutitskaya, Anastasia. "Los villancicos cantados en la catedral de México (1690–1730): edición y estudio." PhD dissertation, Universidad Nacional Autónoma de México, 2011.

Krutitskaya, Anastasia. *Villancicos que se cantaron en la catedral de México (1693–1729)*. Mexico City: UNAM, 2018.

LaBelle, Brandon. *Lexicon of the Mouth: Poetics and Politics of Voice and the Oral Imaginary*. London: Bloomsbury Academic, 2014.

Laird, Paul R. *Towards a History of the Spanish Villancico*. Warren, MI: Harmonie Park, 1997.

Lanam, Faith S. "El Colegio de San Miguel de Belem: Mexico's First Female Music Conservatory." PhD dissertation, University of California, Santa Cruz, 2018.

Lange, Francisco Curt. "Convento de San Lorenzo de Nuestra Señora de la Merced, Córdoba, Argentina." *Latin American Music Review / Revista de Música Latinoamericana* 7, no. 2 (1986): 221–247.

Larkin, Brian R. "Liturgy, Devotion, and Religious Reform in Eighteenth-Century Mexico City." *The Americas* 60, no. 4 (2004): 493–518.

Latour, Melinda. "Musical Encounters in Tenochtitlàn / Mexico City." In *The Cambridge History of Sixteenth-Century Music*, edited by Iain Fenlon and Richard Wistreich, 161–169. Cambridge: Cambridge University Press, 2019.

Lavrin, Asunción. *Brides of Christ: Conventual Life in Colonial Mexico*. Stanford, CA: Stanford University Press, 2008.

Lavrin, Asunción. "De su puño y letra: epístolas conventuales." In *El monacato femenino en el imperio español: monasterios, beaterios, recogimientos y colegios. Homenaje a Josefina Muriel*, edited by Manuel Ramos Medina, 43–61. México: Centro de Estudios de Historia de México CONDUMEX, 1995.

Lavrin, Asunción. "The Erotic as Lewdness in Spanish and Mexican Religious Culture During the Sixteenth and Seventeenth Centuries." In *Eroticism in the Middle Ages and Renaissance: Magic, Marriage, and Midwifery*, edited by Ian Moulton, 35–57. Turnhout: Brepols, 2016.

Lavrin, Asunción. "Introduction: The Scenario, the Actors, and the Issues." In *Sexuality and Marriage in Colonial Latin America*, edited by Asunción Lavrin, 1–43. Lincoln: University of Nebraska Press, 1989.

Lavrin, Asunción. "La familia en un contexto religioso: el caso de Nueva España." In *Familias y redes sociales: cotidianidad y realidad del mundo iberoamericano y mediterráneo*, edited by Sandra Olivero Guidobono, Juan Jesús Bravo Caro, and Rosalva Loreto López, 125–160. Madrid: Iberoamericana Vervuert, 2021.

Lavrin, Asunción. "La vida femenina como experiencia religiosa: Biografía y hagiografía en hispanoamerica colonial." *Colonial Latin American Review* 2, no. 1–2 (1993): 27–51.

Lavrin, Asunción. "Los senderos interiores de los conventos de monjas." *Boletín de monumentos históricos, tercera época* 30 (January–April 2014): 6–21.

Lavrin, Asunción. "The Role of the Nunneries in the Economy of New Spain in the Eighteenth Century." *The Hispanic American Historical Review* 46, no. 4 (1966): 371–393.

Lavrín, Asunción. *Sexuality and Marriage in Colonial Latin America*. Lincoln: University of Nebraska Press, 1989.

Lavrín, Asunción. "Unlike Sor Juana? The Model Nun in the Religious Literature of Colonial Mexico." In *Feminist Perspectives on Sor Juana Inés de la Cruz*, edited by Stephanie Merrim, 61–85. Detroit: Wayne State University Press, 1991.

Lavrín, Asunción. "Values and Meaning of Monastic Life for Nuns in Colonial Mexico." *The Catholic Historical Review* 58, no. 3 (1972): 367–387.

Lavrín, Asunción. "Women and Religion in Spanish America." In *Women and Religion in America*. Vol. 2, *The Colonial and Revolutionary Periods*, edited by Rosemary Radford Ruether and Rosemary Skinner Keller, 42–78. New York: Harper & Row, 1981.

Lavrín, Asunción, and Rosalva Loreto López. *El universo de la teatralidad conventual en Nueva España, siglos xvii–xix*. San Antonio: Biblioteca Arte & Cultura UNAM San Antonio, 2022.

Lavrín, Asunción, and Rosalva Loreto López. *Monjas y beatas: la escritura femenina en la espiritualidad barroca novohispana siglos xvii y xviii*. Puebla: Universidad de las Américas, 2002.

Lehmann Goldman, Dianne. "The Matins Responsory at Mexico City Cathedral, 1575–1815." *Revista de Musicología* 38, no. 1 (2015): 319–326.

Leyva Rendón, Gabriel Ulises. "Recupera INAH historia y esplendor de Nuestra Señora de las Aguas, imagen 'milagrosa' del antiguo convento de Jesús María." *Boletín* 69 (March 20, 2019). https://www.inah.gob.mx/boletines/8008-recupera-inah-historia-y-esplendor-de-nuestra-senora-de-las-aguas-imagen-milagrosa-del-antiguo-conve nto-de-jesus-maria.

Lichtenwalter, Larry. *David: Dancing Like a King*. Hagerstown, MD: Review and Herald Publishing Association, 2005.

Loewen, Peter. *Music in Early Franciscan Thought*. Boston: Brill, 2013.

López-Calo, José. *Historia de la música española 3, Siglo XVII*. Madrid: Alianza Música, 1983.

Long, Pamela. *Sor Juana/Música: How the Décima Musa Composed, Practiced, and Imagined Music*. New York: Peter Lang, 2009.

Loreto López, Rosalva. "Escrito por ella misma: Vida de la madre Francisca de la Natividad." In *Monjas y beatas: La escritura femenina en la espiritualidad barroca novohispana, siglos xvii y xviii*, edited by Asunción Lavrín and Rosalva Loreto López, 24–39. Puebla: Universidad de las Américas, 2002.

Loreto López, Rosalva. "Las pruebas del milagro en el proceso de beatificación de la madre María de Jesús en los siglos XVIII y XIX." In *Memoria del I Coloquio Historia de la Iglesia en el Siglo XIX*, edited by Manuel Ramos Medina, 351–368. Mexico City: Centro de Estudios de Historia de México Condumex, 1998.

Loreto López, Rosalva. *Los conventos femeninos y el mundo urbano de la Puebla de los Ángeles del siglo XVIII*. Mexico City: El Colegio de México, 2000.

Loreto López, Rosalva. *Tota pulchra: Historia del monasterio de la Purísima Concepción de Puebla siglos xvi-xix*. Puebla: Benemerita Universidad Autónoma de Puebla, 2017.

Luciani, Frederick. *Literary Self-Fashioning in Sor Juana Inés de la Cruz*. Lewisburg, PA: Bucknell University Press, 2004.

Lundberg, Magnus. *Mission and Ecstasy: Contemplative Women and Salvation in Colonial Spanish America and the Philippines*. Uppsala: Swedish Institute of Mission Research, 2015.

Lytle Hernández, Kelly. *Bad Mexicans: Race, Empire and Revolution in the Borderlands.* New York: W.W. Norton, 2022.

Manrique, Jorge Alberto, et al. *Monjas coronadas: vida conventual femenina en Hispanoamérica.* Mexico City: Museo Nacional del Virreinato, 2003.

Matesanz del Barrio, María. "El Breviario de la Inmaculada Concepción y Ambrosio Montesino: Una noticia bibliográfica." *Revista de Filología Románica* 2, no. 14 (1997): 273–281.

Mariana de la Encarnación. *Relación de la fundación del convento antiguo de Santa Teresa.* Edited by Clara Ramírez and Claudia Llanos. Mexico City: UNAM, 2015.

Marín López, Javier. "El universo musical mexicano entre centenarios (1517–1917): una introducción." In *De Nueva España a México: el universo musical mexicano entre centenarios (1517–1917)*, edited by Javier Marín López, 25–34. Sevilla: Universidad Internacional de Andalucía, 2020.

Marín López, Javier. "Música local e internacional en una catedral novohispana de provincias: Valladolid de Michoacán (XVII–XVIII)." In *Música y catedral, nuevos enfoques, viejas temáticas*, edited by Jesús Alfaro Cruz and Raúl Torres Medina, 87–105. Mexico City: UACM, 2010.

Marín López, Javier. "Música y músicos entre dos mundos: la catedral de México y sus libros de polifonía." PhD dissertation, University of Granada, 2007.

Marín López, Javier, ed. *Músicas coloniales a debate: procesos de intercambio euroamericanos.* Madrid: Ediciones del Instituto Complutense de Ciencias Musicales, 2018.

Marín López, Javier, and Tess Knighton. "The Musical Inventory of Mexico Cathedral, 1589: A Lost Document Rediscovered." *Early Music* 36, no. 4 (2008): 575–596.

Marín López, Javier, and Raúl Zambrano. "¡*Ay, qué dolor!* (1701) de Antonio de Salazar: contextos para un villancico barroco transcrito por Manuel M. Ponce." In *De Nueva España a México: el universo musical mexicano entre centenarios (1517–1917)*, edited by Javier Marín López, 569–590. Sevilla: Universidad Internacional de Andalucía, 2020.

Marino, John A. "The Zodiac in the Streets: Inscribing 'Buon Governo' in Baroque Naples." In *Embodiments of Power: Building Baroque Cities in Europe*, edited by Gary B. Cohen and Franz A. J. Szabo, 203–229. New York: Berghahn Books, 2008.

Marissen, Michael. *Lutheranism, Anti-Judaism, and Bach's "St. John Passion."* Oxford: Oxford University Press, 1998.

Martínez López-Cano, María del Pilar. *Concilios provinciales mexicanos.* Mexico City: Universidad Nacional Autónoma de México, Instituto de Investigaciones Históricas, 2004.

Martínez López-Cano, María del Pilar, Gisela von Wobeser, and Juan Guillermo Muñoz Correa, eds. *Cofradías, capellanías y obras pías en la América colonial.* Mexico City: Universidad Nacional Autónoma de México, 1998.

Martínez, María Elena. *Genealogical Fictions: Limpieza de Sangre, Religion, and Gender in Colonial Mexico.* Stanford, CA: Stanford University Press, 2008.

Matter, Anne E. "Lectio Divina." In *The Cambridge Companion to Christian Mysticism*, edited by Amy Hollywood and Patricia Z. Beckman, 147–156. Cambridge: Cambridge University Press, 2012.

Mazín Gómez, Oscar. *El cabildo catedral de Valladolid de Michoacán.* Zamora: El Colegio de Michoacán, 1996.

Mazuela-Anguita, Ascención. "La vida musical en el monasterio de Santa María de Jonqueres en los siglos XVI y XVII: Agraïda y Eugènia Grimau." *Revista Catalana de Musicología* 8 (2015): 37–79.

Mazuela-Anguita, Ascención. "Música conventual para ceremonias urbanas del mundo hispánico a inicios de la Edad Moderna." *Hoquet: Revista del Conservatorio Superior de Música de Málaga* 20 (2022): 1–30.

McCreery, David. *The Sweat of Their Brow: A History of Work in Latin America*. New York: M. E. Sharpe, 2000.

Méndez Montoya, Angel F. *The Theology of Food: Eating and the Eucharist*. New York: John Wiley & Sons, 2009.

Merrim, Stephanie, ed. *Feminist Perspectives on Sor Juana Inés de la Cruz*. Detroit: Wayne State University Press, 1991.

Merrim, Stephanie. "*Mores Geometricae*: The 'Womanscript' in the Theater of Sor Juana Inés de la Cruz." In *Feminist Perspectives on Sor Juana Inés de la Cruz*, edited by Stephanie Merrim, 94–123. Detroit: Wayne State University Press, 1991.

Merrim, Stephanie. *The Spectacular City, Mexico, and Colonial Hispanic Literary Culture*. Austin: University of Texas Press, 2010.

Monroy Ponce, Diego, Jorge Guadarrama Guevara, and Rosa María Franco Velasco, eds. *Un privilegio sagrado: La Concepción de María Inmaculada. Celebración del dogma en México*. Mexico City: Museo de la Basílica de Guadalupe, 2005.

Monson, Craig A. "The Council of Trent Revisited." *Journal of the American Musicological Society* 55, no. 1 (2002): 1–37.

Monson, Craig A., ed. *The Crannied Wall: Women, Religion, and the Arts in Early Modern Europe*. Ann Arbor: University of Michigan Press, 1992.

Monson, Craig A. *Disembodied Voices: Music and Culture in an Early Modern Italian Convent*. Berkeley: University of California Press, 1995.

Monson, Craig A. *Divas in the Convent: Nuns, Music, and Defiance in Seventeenth-Century Italy*. Chicago: University of Chicago Press, 2012.

Monson, Craig A. "'Le pene sofferte per Te son glorie, vittorie d'un'Alma ch'ha fe': Bodily Mortification in Convent Choir Lofts." Paper presented at the Annual Meeting of the American Musicological Society, Pittsburgh, PA, November 2013.

Monson, Craig A. *Nuns Behaving Badly: Tales of Music, Magic, Art and Arson in the Convents of Italy*. Chicago: University of Chicago Press, 2012.

Montero Alarcón, Alma. *Monjas coronadas: profesión y muerte en hispanoamérica virreinal*. México: Museo Nacional del Virreinato, 2008.

Monteros, Sebastiana Villanueva Cervantes Espinosa de los. *En religiosos incendios*. Mexico City: Universidad Nacional Autónoma de México, 1995.

Morales Abril, Omar. "La música en la catedral de Puebla de los Ángeles (1546–1606)." *Heterofonía* 35, no. 129 (2003): 9–47.

Morales Abril, Omar. "*Serenísima una noche*, de Fray Jerónimo González: revisión crítica y apuntes para su interpretación." *Heterofonía* 41, no. 141 (2009): 9–29, 157–160.

Morales Abril, Omar. "Tres siglos de música litúrgica en la Colección Sánchez Garza: Aproximación panorámica a través de siete muestras." *Heterofonía* 40, no. 138–139 (2008): 67–105, 167–220.

Muir, Lynette R. *The Biblical Drama of Medieval Europe*. Cambridge: Cambridge University Press, 1995.

Muriel, Josefina. *Conventos de monjas en la Nueva España*. Mexico City: Santiago, 1946.

Muriel, Josefina. *Cultura femenina novohispana*. Mexico City: UNAM, 1994.

Muriel, Josefina. *La sociedad novohispana y sus colegios de niñas*. Mexico City: Universidad Nacional Autónoma de México, 2004.

Muriel, Josefina. *Las indias caciques de Corpus Christi*. Mexico City: Universidad Nacional Autónoma de México, 2001.

Muriel, Josefina, and Luís Lledías. *La música en las instituciones femeninas novohispanas*. Mexico City: Universidad Nacional Autónoma de México, 2009.

Myers, Kathleen Ann. *Neither Saints Nor Sinners: Writing the Lives of Women in Spanish America*. Oxford: Oxford University Press, 2003.

Myers, Kathleen Ann. "A Transatlantic Perspective: The Influence of Teresa's Model on New World Women." In *Approaches to Teaching Teresa of Ávila and the Spanish Mystics*, edited by Alison Weber, 148–156. New York: Modern Language Association of America, 2009.

Myers, Kathleen Ann, ed. *Word from New Spain: The Spiritual Autobiography of Madre María de San José (1656–1719)*. Liverpool: Liverpool University Press, 1993.

Myers, Kathleen Ann, and Amanda Powell, eds. *A Wild Country Out in the Garden: The Spiritual Journals of a Colonial Mexican Nun*. Bloomington: Indiana University Press, 1999.

Nims, John Frederick, trans. *The Poems of St. John of the Cross*. 3rd ed. Chicago: University of Chicago Press, 1979.

Noone, Michael. *Music and Musicians in the Escorial Liturgy Under the Habsburgs, 1563–1700*. Rochester, NY: University of Rochester Press, 1998.

Ochoa Gautier, Ana María. *Aurality: Listening and Knowledge in Nineteenth-Century Colombia*. Durham, NC: Duke University Press, 2014.

O'Hara, Matthew D. *A Flock Divided: Race, Religion, and Politics in Mexico, 1749–1857*. Durham, NC: Duke University Press, 2010.

O'Regan, Noel. "The Church Triumphant: Music in the Liturgy." In *The Cambridge History of Seventeenth-Century Music*, edited by Tim Carter and John Butt, 283–323. Cambridge: Cambridge University Press, 2005.

Ortiz, Mario A. "Euterpe en los conventos femeninos novohispanos." In *Aproximaciones a Sor Juana*, edited by Sandra Lorenzano, 239–252. Mexico City: Universidad del Claustro de Sor Juana, 2005.

Ortiz, Mario A. "Mysticism and Early Modern Musical-Cosmological Paradigms." In *Approaches to Teaching Teresa of Ávila and the Spanish Mystics*, edited by Alison Weber, 247–258. New York: Modern Language Association of America, 2009.

Owens, Sarah E. *Nuns Navigating the Spanish Empire*. Albuquerque: University of New Mexico Press, 2017.

Owens, Sarah E., and Jane E. Mangan, eds. *Women of the Iberian Atlantic*. Baton Rouge: Louisiana State University Press, 2012.

Page, Janet K. *Convent Music and Politics in Eighteenth-Century Vienna*. Cambridge: Cambridge University Press, 2014.

Pedrotti, Clarisa. "La música religiosa en Córdoba del Tucumán durant la época colonial (1699–1840)." PhD dissertation, Universidad National de Córdoba, 2013.

Peña, Margarita. "Prólogo." In Carlos de Sigüenza y Góngora, *Parayso occidental*, 13–32. Mexico City: Consejo Nacional para la Cultura y las Artes, 1995.

Pepe, Edward. "Testamento de Fabián Pérez Ximeno." *Heterofonía* 36, nos. 130–131 (2004): 141–144.

Pérez Puente, Leticia, ed. *Autos de las visitas del Arzobispo Fray Payo Enríquez a los conventos de monjas de la Ciudad de México (1672–1675)*. Mexico City: UNAM, 2005.

Pérez-Romero, Antonio. *Subversion and Liberation in the Writings of St. Teresa of Avila*. New York: Rodopi, 1996.

Pérez Ruiz, Bárbara. "La Colección Sánchez Garza: reflexiones en torno a sus vertientes de investigación y su proyección (1965–2015)." In *Cuarenta años de investigación musical en México a través del CENIDIM*, edited by Yael Bitrán Goren, Luis Antonio Gómez, and José Luis Navarro, 301–321. Mexico City: INBA, 2016.

Perry, Mary Elizabeth, Nupur Chaudhuri, and Sherry J. Katz, eds. *Contesting Archives: Finding Women in the Sources*. Champaign: University of Illinois Press, 2010.

Pierce, Donna. "Unknown Artist, Young Woman with a Harpsichord. Mexico, 1735–50." *Denver Art Museum Online Collections*. 2015. https://denverartmuseum.org/object/ 2014.209.

Pierce, Donna, Rogelio Ruiz Gomar, and Clara Bargellini. *Painting a New World: Mexican Art and Life, 1521–1821*. Austin: University of Texas Press, 2004.

Plank, Steven E. "A Seventeenth-Century Franciscan Opera: Music for a Chigi Princess." *Franciscan Studies* 42 (1982): 180–189.

Pomplun, Trent. "Baroque Catholic Theologies of Christ and Mary." In *The Oxford Handbook of Early Modern Theology, 1600–1800*, edited by Ulrich L. Lehner, Richard A. Muller, and A. G. Roeber, 104–118. Oxford: Oxford University Press, 2016.

Poot-Herrera, Sara, ed. *Sor Juana y su mundo: una mirada actual*. Mexico City: Fondo de Cultura Ecónomica, 1995.

Powell, Amy. "A Machine for Souls: Allegory Before and After Trent." In *The Sensuous in the Counter-Reformation Church*, edited by Marcia B. Hall and Tracy E. Cooper, 273–294. Cambridge: Cambridge University Press, 2013.

Powers, Harold. "Tonal Types and Modal Categories in Renaissance Polyphony." *Journal of the American Musicological Society* 34, no. 3 (Autumn 1981): 428–470.

Rama, Angel. *The Lettered City*. Translated by John Charles Chasteen. Durham, NC: Duke University Press, 1996.

Ramírez Aparicio, Manuel. *Los conventos suprimidos en México: estudios biográficos, históricos y arqueológicos*. Mexico City: J.M. Aguilar y Cia, 1861.

Ramírez Montes, Mina. *Niñas, doncellas, virgenes eternas: Santa Clara de Queretaro (1607–1864)*. Mexico City: Universidad Nacional Autonoma, Instituto de Investi-gaciones Estéticas, 2005.

Ramos, Frances L. *Identity, Ritual, and Power in Colonial Puebla*. Tucson: University of Arizona Press, 2012.

Ramos Kittrell, Jesús. "Dynamics of Rituals and Ceremony in the Metropolitan Cathedral of Mexico City 1700–1750." PhD dissertation, University of Texas at Austin, 2006.

Ramos Kittrell, Jesús. *Playing in the Cathedral: Music, Race, and Status in New Spain*. Oxford: Oxford University Press, 2016.

Ramos Medina, Manuel. *Imagen de santidad en mundo profano: historia de una fundación*. Mexico City: Universidad Iberoamericana, Departamento de Historia, 1990.

Ramos Medina, Manuel, ed. *Voto y juramento de la Inmaculada Concepción en el Convento de San Jerónimo de la Ciudad de México, siglos XVII al XIX*. Mexico City: Centro de Estudios de Historia de México, 2011.

Reardon, Colleen. *Holy Concord within Sacred Walls: Nuns and Music in Siena, 1575–1700*. Oxford: Oxford University Press, 2002.

Reiss, Ben. "Pious Phalluses and Holy Vulvas: The Religious Importance of Some Sexual Body-Part Badges in Late-Medieval Europe (1200–1550)." *Peregrinations: Journal of Medieval Art and Architecture* 6, no. 1 (2017): 151–176.

Restiffo, Marisa. "Ilustración, polifonía e identidad en Santa Catalina de Sena, Córdoba del Tucumán." In *Músicas coloniales a debate: procesos de intercambio euroamericanos*, edited by Javier Marín López, 243–258. Madrid: Ediciones del Instituto Complutense de Ciencias Musicales, 2018.

Rhodes, Elizabeth. "Mysticism in History: The Case of Spain's Golden Age." In *Approaches to Teaching Teresa of Ávila and the Spanish Mystics*, edited by Alison Weber, 47–56. New York: Modern Language Association of America, 2009.

Riaño, Juan F. *The Industrial Arts in Spain*. New York: Scribner and Welford, 1879.

Rivera y San Román, María de las Llagas de Cristo. *Noticias históricas de la fundación del convento de religiosas de Sta. María de Gracia de Guadalajara*. Guadalajara: Ancira, 1924.

Robertson, Anne Walters. "The Savior, the Woman, and the Head of the Dragon in the Caput Masses and Motet." *Journal of the American Musicological Society* 59, no. 3 (Fall 2006): 537–630.

Rodríguez, Pablo-L. "The Villancico as Music of State in 17th-Century Spain." In *Devotional Music in the Iberian World, 1450–1800: The Villancico and Related Genres*, edited by Tess Knighton and Álvaro Torrente, 189–198. Burlington, VT: Ashgate, 2007.

Rodríguez Mata, Antonio. *Passions*. Edited by Grey Brothers. Middleton, WI: A-R Editions, 2012.

Ros-Fábregas, Emilio. "'Imagine All the People . . .': Polyphonic Flowers in the Hands and Voices of Indians in 16th-century Mexico." *Early Music* 40, no. 2 (2012): 177–189.

Ross, Jill. *Figuring the Feminine: The Rhetoric of Female Embodiment in Medieval Hispanic Literature*. Toronto: University of Toronto Press, 2008.

Ross, Kathleen. *The Baroque Narrative of Carlos de Sigüenza y Góngora: A New World Paradise*. Cambridge: Cambridge University Press, 1993.

Rothenberg, David J. *The Flower of Paradise: Marian Devotion and Secular Song in Medieval and Renaissance Music*. Oxford: Oxford University Press, 2011.

Rouget, Gilbert. *Music and Trance: A Theory of the Relations between Music and Possession*. Chicago: University of Chicago Press, 1985.

Rowe, Erin Kathleen. *Black Saints in Early Modern Global Catholicism*. Cambridge: Cambridge University Press, 2019.

Rowe, Erin Kathleen. *Saint and Nation: Santiago, Teresa of Avila, and Plural Identities in Early Modern Spain*. University Park: Pennsylvania State University Press, 2011.

Rubial García, Antonio. "Los santos milagreros y malogrados de la Nueva España." In *Manifestaciones religiosas en el mundo colonial americano*, edited by Clara García Ayluardo and Manuel Ramos Medina, 51–88. Mexico City: INAH, CONDUMEX, Universidad Iberoamericana, 1997.

Rubin, Miri. *Corpus Christi: The Eucharist in Late Medieval Culture*. Cambridge: Cambridge University Press, 1991.

Rubin, Miri. *Mother of God: A History of the Virgin Mary*. New Haven, CT: Yale University Press, 2009.

Rubin, Miri. "Sacramental Life." In *The Cambridge History of Christianity: Christianity in Western Europe c. 1100–c. 1500*, edited by Miri Rubin and Walter Simons, 219–237. Cambridge: Cambridge University Press, 2009.

Ruiz Gomar, Rogelio. *Catálogo comentado del acervo del Museo Nacional de Arte, Nueva España*. Vol. 2. Mexico City: INBA, 2004.

Ruiz Jiménez, Juan. "The 'Circular' Forty Hours Devotion in the Convent of La Trinidad (1765)." *Paisajes Sonoros Históricos*, 2016. http://historicalsoundscapes.com/evento/566/granada/en.

Russell, Craig H. *From Serra to Sancho: Music and Pageantry in the California Missions*. Oxford: Oxford University Press, 2012.

Sabau García, María Luisa. *México en el mundo de las colecciones de arte.* Vol. 3. Mexico City: Gobierno de la República, 1994.

Sacristán Ramírez, Carolina. "Singing the Eucharist to the Kithara of Jesus: Women, Music, and Intellectual Devotion in Painting from New Spain." *Music in Art: International Journal for Music Iconography* 45, no. 1/2 (2020): 135–154.

Salas Contreras, Carlos. *Arqueología del ex convento de la Encarnación de la Ciudad de México: edificio sede de la Secretaría de Educación Pública.* Mexico City: Instituto Nacional de Antropología e Historia, 2006.

Salazar Simarro, Nuria. "El papel del cuerpo en un grabado del siglo XVIII." In *Cuerpo y religión en el México barroco*, edited by Antonio Rubial García and Bieñko de Peralta, 109–144. Mexico City: INAH, 2011.

Salazar Simarro, Nuria. "Música y coro en el convento de Jesús María de México." In *Keyboard Music in Female Monasteries and Convents of Spain, Portugal and the Americas*, edited by Luisa Morales, 29–48. Almería: Asociación Cultural LEAL, 2011.

Salazar Simarro, Nuria, and Sarah E. Owens. "Cloistered Women in Health Care: The Convent of Jesús María, Mexico City." In *Women of the Iberian Atlantic*, edited by Sarah E. Owens and Jane E. Mangan, 128–147. Baton Rouge: Louisiana State University Press, 2012.

Santoro, Nicholas J. *Mary in Our Life: Atlas of the Names and Titles of Mary, the Mother of Jesus, and their Place in Marian Devotion.* Bloomington, IN: iUniverse, 2011.

Santos Morales, María de Cristo, and Esteban Arroyo González. *Las monjas dominicas en la cultura novohispana.* Mexico City: Instituto Dominicano de Investigaciones Históricas de la Provincia de Santiago de México, 1992.

Saunders, Steven. *Cross, Sword, and Lyre: Sacred Music at the Imperial Court of Ferdinand II of Habsburg (1619–1637).* Oxford: Clarendon Press, 1995.

Schiffman, Zachary Sayre. *The Birth of the Past.* Baltimore: Johns Hopkins University Press, 2011.

Schleifer, Eliyahu. "The Mexican Choirbooks at the Newberry Library (Case Ms VM 2147 C36)." PhD dissertation, University of Chicago, 1979.

Schmidt, Leigh Eric. *Hearing Things: Religion, Illusion, and the American Enlightenment.* Cambridge, MA: Harvard University Press, 2002.

Schorsch, Jonathan. *Swimming the Christian Atlantic: Judeoconversos, Afroiberians and Amerindians in the Seventeenth Century.* Leiden: Brill, 2009.

Seed, Patricia. *To Love, Honor, and Obey in Colonial Mexico.* Stanford, CA: Stanford University Press, 1988.

Seijas, Tatiana. *Asian Slaves in Colonial Mexico: From Chinos to Indians.* Cambridge: Cambridge University Press, 2014.

Sigaut, Nelly. "La fiesta de Corpus Christi." In *Lo sagrado y lo profano en la festividad de Corpus Christi*, edited by Montserrat Galí Boadella and Morelos Torres Aguilar, 19–40. Mexico City: Universidad Nacional Autónoma de México, Benemérita Universidad Autónoma de Puebla, Instituto de Ciencias Sociales y Humanidades "Alfonso Vélex Pliego," 2008.

Skeris, Robert A. *CHROMA THEOU: On the Origins and Theological Interpretation of the Musical Imagery Used by the Ecclesiastical Writers of the First Three Centuries, with Special Reference to the Image of Orpheus.* Altötting: Verlag Alfred Coppenrath, 1976.

Smith, Bruce R. *The Acoustic World of Early Modern England: Attending to the O-Factor.* Chicago: University of Chicago Press, 1999.

Socolow, Susan Migden. *The Women of Colonial Latin America*. Cambridge: Cambridge University Press, 2000.

Solie, Ruth. *Music in Other Words: Victorian Conversations*. Berkeley: University of California Press, 2004.

Spaulding, Rachel. "Covert Afro-Catholic Agency in the Mystical Visions of Early Modern Brazil's Rosa Maria Egipçíaca." In *Women's Negotiations and Textual Agency in Latin America, 1500–1799*, edited by Mónica Díaz and Rocío Quispe-Agnoli, 38–61. New York: Routledge, 2016.

Steinberg, Leo. *Renaissance and Baroque Art: Selected Essays*. Chicago: University of Chicago Press, 2020.

Stevenson, Robert M. "Mexican Colonial Music Manuscripts Abroad." *Notes, Quarterly Journal of the Music Library Association* 29, no. 2 (1972): 203–214.

Stras, Laurie. *Women and Music in Sixteenth-Century Ferrara*. Cambridge: Cambridge University Press, 2018.

Stratton, Suzanne L. *The Immaculate Conception in Spanish Art*. Cambridge: Cambridge University Press, 1994.

Suárez, María Teresa. *La caja de órgano en Nueva España durante el barroco*. Mexico City: CENIDIM, 1991.

Surtz, Ronald E. *The Guitar of God: Gender, Power, and Authority in the Visionary World of Mother Juana de la Cruz (1481–1534)*. Philadephia: University of Pennsylvania Press, 1990.

Swadley, John. "Educating the American Girls: The *maestros* José Gavino Leal and Ricardo de la Main in Mexico, 1718–1747." In *Músicas coloniales a debate: procesos de intercambio euroamericanos*, edited by Javier Marín López, 259–266. Madrid: Ediciones del Instituto Complutense de Ciencias Musicales, 2018.

Swadley, John. "The Villancico in New Spain 1650–1750: Morphology, Significance and Development." PhD dissertation, Canterbury Christ Church University, 2014.

Swain, Diana Romero. "One Thousand Sisters: Religious Sensibility and Motivation in a Spanish American Convent, Santa María de Gracia, 1588–1863." PhD dissertation, University of California, San Diego, 1993.

Szövérffy, Joseph. "'Crux Fidelis . . .': Prolegomena to a History of the Holy Cross Hymns." *Traditio* 22 (1966): 1–41.

Tanaka, Stefan. *History Without Chronology*. Amherst: Lever Press, 2019.

Taylor, Diana. *The Archive and the Repertoire: Performing Cultural Memory in the Americas*. Durham, NC: Duke University Press, 2003.

Tello, Aurelio. *Archivo musical de la catedral de Oaxaca*. Mexico City: CENIDIM, 1990.

Tello, Aurelio. "La capilla musical del Convento de la Santísima Trinidad de Puebla en los siglos XVII y XVIII." In *Mujeres, negros, y niños en la música y sociedad cultural iberoamericana*, edited by Víctor Rondón, 52–61. Santa Cruz de la Sierra, Bolivia: Asociación Pro Arte y Cultura, 2002.

Tello, Aurelio. "Monjas y música o de cómo las esposas de Dios volcaban su devoción en acordes y métricas armonías." In *Cuaderno de tonos de maitines de Sor María Clara del Santísimo Sacramento*, edited by Calvert Johnson, vi–xx. Colfax, NC: Wayne Leupold Editions, 2005.

Tello, Aurelio. "Músicos ruiseñores, vicisitudes de un villancico de supuesta autoría, fallida transcripción y arbitraria interpretación." *Heterofonía* 36, nos. 130–131 (2004): 27–40.

Tello, Aurelio. "Sor Juana Inés de la Cruz y los maestros de capilla catedralicios o de los ecos concertados y las acordes músicas con que sus villancicos fueron puestos en métrica armonía." *Data: Revista del Instituto de Estudios Andinos y Amazónicos* 7 (1997): 7–32.

Tello, Aurelio, Nelson Hurtado, Omar Morales, and Bárbara Pérez. *Colección Sánchez Garza: estudio documental y catálogo de un acervo musical novohispano*. Mexico City: INBA, 2018.

Tenorio, Martha Lilia. *Los villancicos de Sor Juana*. Mexico City: El Colegio de México, 1999.

Thomas, George Antony. *Women and Gender in the Early Modern World: Politics and Poetics of Sor Juana Inés de La Cruz*. Burlington, VT: Ashgate Publishing, 2012.

Tingle, Elizabeth C. *Indulgences After Luther: Pardons in Counter-Reformation France, 1520–1720*. New York: Routledge, 2015.

Traslosheros H., Jorge E. "Utopía Inmaculada en la primavera Mexicana: *Los sigueros de la virgen sin original pegado*, primera novela novohispana, 1620." *Estudios de Historia Novohispana* 30 (2004): 93–116.

Toelle, Jutta. "*Todas las naciones han de oyrla*: Bells in the Jesuit *reducciones* of Early Modern Paraguay." *Journal of Jesuit Studies* 3 (2016): 437–450.

Tomlinson, Gary. *The Singing of the New World: Indigenous Voice in the Era of European Contact*. Cambridge: Cambridge University Press, 2007.

Toquica, Constanza, and Luis Fernando Restrepo. "Las canciones del coro alto de la iglesia del Convento de Santa Clara." *Cuadernos de Literatura* 6, no. 12 (2001): 90–117.

Torrente, Álvaro. "Function and Liturgical Context of the Villancico in Salamanca Cathedral." In *Devotional Music in the Iberian World, 1450–1800: The Villancico and Related Genres*, edited by Tess Knighton and Álvaro Torrente, 99–148. Burlington, VT: Ashgate, 2007.

Torres Vega, José Martín. "Música en los espacios conventuales femeninos." In *Histoiras de la arquitectura en Michoacán, una mirada desde las fuentes*, edited by Catherine R. Ettinger, Eugenio Mercado López, and José Martín Torres Vega, 165–177. Morelia: Universidad Michoacana de San Nicolás de Hidalgo, 2020.

Tortorici, Zeb. *Sins against Nature: Sex and Archives in Colonial New Spain*. Durham, NC: Duke University Press, 2018.

Tovar, Teresa de. *La Ciudad de México y la utopía en el siglo XVI*. Mexico City: Seguros de México, 1987.

Tuñón Pablos, Julia. *Women in Mexico: A Past Unveiled*. Translated by Alan Hynds. Austin: University of Texas Press, 1999.

Turrent, Lourdes. *Autoridad, solemnidad y actores musicales en la Catedral de México (1692–1860)*. Mexico City: Centro de Investigaciones y Estudios Superiores en Antropología Social (CIESAS), 2013.

Van Deusen, Nancy E. *The Souls of Purgatory: The Spiritual Diary of a Seventeenth-Century Afro-Peruvian Mystic, Ursula de Jesús*. Albuquerque, NM: University of New Mexico Press, 2004.

Van Wyhe, Cordula. "After Teresa: Mysticism in Seventeenth-Century Europe." In *Approaches to Teaching Teresa of Ávila and the Spanish Mystics*, edited by Alison Weber, 83–94. New York: Modern Language Association of America, 2009.

Vera, Alejandro. Review of "Atlantic Crossings: Music from 1492 through the Long 18th Century." *Eighteenth-Century Music* 17, no. 1 (2020): 151–154.

Vera, Alejandro. *The Sweet Penance of Music: Musical Life in Colonial Santiago de Chile*. Oxford: Oxford University Press, 2020.

Vera, Alejandro. "Transcending the Walls of the Churches: The Circulation of Music and Musicians of Religious Institutions in Colonial Santiago de Chile." In *Devotional Music in the Iberian World, 1450–1800: The Villancico and Related Genres*, edited by Tess Knighton and Álvaro Torrente, 171–185. Burlington, VT: Ashgate, 2007.

Vera Tudela, Elisa Sampson. *Colonial Angels: Narratives of Gender and Spirituality in Mexico, 1580–1750*. Austin: University of Texas Press, 2000.

Vetancurt, Augustín de. *Teatro mexicano: descripción breve de los sucesos ejemplares, históricos, políticos, militares y religiosos del nuevo mundo occidental de las indias, 1698*. 4 vols. Mexico City: Impr. de I. Escalante, 1871.

Vicente, Marta V. "Successful Mystics and Failed Mystics: Teaching Teresa of Ávila in the Women's Studies Classroom." In *Approaches to Teaching Teresa of Ávila and the Spanish Mystics*, edited by Alison Weber, 134–147. New York: Modern Language Association of America, 2009.

Vicente Delgado, Alfonso de. "Cantadas y cédulas de profesión de las monjas de Santa Ana de Ávila." *Paisajes Sonoros Históricos*, 2019. http://www.historicalsoundscapes. com/evento/1016/avila/es.

Vilar-Payá, Luisa. "Lo historico y lo cotidiano: un juego de libretes de coro para la consagración de la Catedral de Puebla y la despedida del Obispo Palafox (1649)." *Revista de Musicología* 40, no. 1 (2017): 135–176.

Vilar-Payá, Luisa. "Música, política y ceremonia en el día de la consagración de la catedral de Puebla." *Historia Mexicana* 70, no. 4 (2021): 1869–1916.

Voelker, Evelyn Carole. "Charles Borromeo's 'Instructiones Fabricae Et Supellectilis Ecclesiasticae,' 1577. A Translation with Commentary and Analysis." PhD dissertation, Syracuse University, 1977.

Waisman, Leonardo J. "Subalternidad en músicas novohispanas: dos fragmentos." In *De Nueva España a México: el universo musical mexicano entre centenarios (1517–1917)*, edited by Javier Marín López, 591–608. Sevilla: Universidad Internacional de Andalucía, 2020.

Waisman, Leonardo J. *Una historia de la música colonial hispanoamericana*. Buenos Aires: Gourmet Musical Ediciones, 2019.

Warner, Marina. *Alone of All Her Sex: The Myth and the Cult of the Virgin Mary*. Oxford: Oxford University Press, 2013.

Weaver, Andrew H. "Music in the Service of Counter-Reformation Politics: The Immaculate Conception at the Habsburg Court of Ferdinand III (1637–1657)." *Music & Letters* 87, no. 3 (2006): 361–378.

Weaver, Mary Jo. *Cloister and Community: Life within a Carmelite Monastery*. Bloomington: Indiana University Press, 2002.

Webb, Stephen H. *The Divine Voice: Christian Proclamation and the Theology of Sound*. Eugene, OR: Wipf & Stock, 2004.

Weber, Alison. *Teresa of Avila and the Rhetoric of Femininity*. Princeton, NJ: Princeton University Press, 1996.

Weiner, Isaac. *Religion Out Loud: Religious Sound, Public Space, and American Pluralism*. New York: NYU Press, 2013.

Wiesenfeldt, Christiane. "'Majestas Mariae' als musikgeschichtliches Phänomen? Einflüsse der Marienverehrung auf die Messe des 16. Jahrhunderts." *Archiv für Musikwissenschaft* 65, no. 2 (2008): 103–120.

Wobeser, Gisela von. *Sor Juana ante la muerte*. Mexico City: UNAM, 2021.

Zorach, Rebecca. *The Passionate Triangle*. Chicago: University of Chicago Press, 2011.

Index